Power versus Law in Modern China

POWER VERSUS LAW IN MODERN CHINA

CITIES, COURTS,
AND THE
COMMUNIST PARTY

QIANG FANG
AND
XIAOBING LI

UNIVERSITY PRESS OF KENTUCKY

Scholarly publisher for the Commonwealth,
serving Bellarmine University, Berea College, Centre College of Kentucky,
Eastern Kentucky University, The Filson Historical Society, Georgetown College,
Kentucky Historical Society, Kentucky State University, Morehead State
University, Murray State University, Northern Kentucky University,
Transylvania University, University of Kentucky, University of Louisville,
and Western Kentucky University.

Editorial and Sales Offices: The University Press of Kentucky
663 South Limestone Street, Lexington, Kentucky 40508-4008
www.kentuckypress.com

Library of Congress Cataloging-in-Publication Data

Names: Fang, Qiang, 1968- author. | Li, Xiaobing, 1954- author.
Title: Power versus law in modern China : cities, courts, and the Communist
    Party / Qiang Fang and Xiaobing Li.
Other titles: Power vs. law in modern China
Description: Lexington, Kentuckey : The University Press of Kentucky, [2017]
    | Series: Asia in the new millennium | Includes bibliographical references
    and index.
Identifiers: LCCN 2017036486| ISBN 9780813173931 (hardcover : alk. paper) |
    ISBN 9780813173948 (pdf) | ISBN 9780813173955 (epub)
Subjects: LCSH: Abuse of administrative power—China. | Abuse of
    rights—China. | Political corruption—China. | Courts—China. | Civil
    rights—China. | Rule of law—China. | Law enforcement—China. | Zhongguo
    gong chan dang.
Classification: LCC KNQ2760 .F38 2017 | DDC 342.5108/8—dc23
LC record available at https://lccn.loc.gov/2017036486

Member of the Association of
American University Presses

Contents

Note on Transliteration

The *Hanyu pinyin* romanization system is applied to Chinese names of persons and places and Chinese terms. A person's name is given in the Chinese way, surname first, such as Jiang Zemin. Some popular names have traditional Wade-Giles spellings appearing in parentheses after the first use of the *Hanyu pinyin* in the entry, such as Mao Zedong (Mao Tse-tung), as do popular names of places like the Yangzi (Yangtze) River. Exceptions are made for a few figures, whose names are widely known in reverse order, such as Sun Yat-sen (Sun Zhongshan or Sun Yixian) and Chiang Kai-shek (Jiang Jieshi), and a few place and institutional names, such as Tibet (Xizang) and Peking (Beijing) University. Names of Chinese Americans are written in the American English way, the first name followed by the last, such as Qiang Fang and Xiaobing Li.

Abbreviations

ACFTU	All-China Federation of Trade Unions
ACWA	All-China Women's Association
CASS	China Academy of Social Science
CCDI	Central Commission for Discipline Inspection
CCP	Chinese Communist Party
CCTV	China Central Television
CCYL	Chinese Communist Youth League
CMC	Central Military Commission
CPG	Central People's Government
CPPCC	Chinese People's Political Consultative Conference
GAPP	General Administration of Press and Publications
GMD	Guomindang (Chinese Nationalist Party, or Kuomintang, KMT)
GNP	gross national product
HPRS	Household production responsibility system
IMAR	Inner Mongolia Autonomous Region
IMPP	Inner Mongolian People's Party
KMT	Kuomintang (Chinese Nationalist Party, or Guomindang, GMD)
MFN	most-favored nation
MPS	Ministry of Public Security
NGO	nongovernment organization
NPC	National People's Congress
PAP	People's Armed Police
PLA	People's Liberation Army
PRC	People's Republic of China
RFA	Radio Free Asia
RMB	*Renminbi* (Chinese currency)
ROC	Republic of China
SWAT	Special Weapons and Tactics
TAR	Tibet Autonomous Region
UN	United Nations
WTO	World Trade Organization
XUAR	Xinjiang Uyghur Autonomous Region

Introduction

Power versus Law
in Chinese History

Until the morning of June 12, 2008, Zhang Qilong never shed tears in front of his young son. The forty-five-year-old computer engineer, educated in New Zealand and working for an information-technology company in Shanghai, began weeping as he poured gasoline over himself, his wife, Pan Rong, and five-year-old Xiaolong. The three of them cried together as Zhang struck the lighter and the small family burst into flames.

"Can you show us a court order?" Pan Rong had desperately asked at 9:00 A.M. as, outside the home, she faced the wrecking crew, which included policemen, city officials, and a removal crew equipped with heavy vehicles. It soon became obvious that there was no court order, and shortly after 9:30[1] the wrecking crew began its work. Pan and Zhang helplessly watched the machines breaking through their locked door, smashing their furniture and belongings. In the living room, young Xiaolong was frightened and began crying loudly as the whole building shook and the ceiling began to fall. Then, as they had planned, Zhang lit his wife, his young son, and himself on fire to protest the violation of their property rights.[2]

The fate of this family is not unique. In 2008–2009, there were reports of more than a dozen self-immolation suicides in Chinese cities.[3] Even more residents were either shot by police or buried alive by removal crews during the urban construction movement.

China became urbanized in the first decade of the twenty-first century. In 2002, 223 million Chinese lived in cities, a figure that rose to 695 million by 2014 and stood at close to 800 million in 2016. Shanghai is now China's largest city with 23 million residents. While the urban movement has seen 100 million rural laborers successfully transferred to the cities to work in industries that desperately demand free and cheap labor, serious problems, such as overcrowding and substandard housing, have arisen as a result of this unprecedented large-scale development. In addition, because of a lack of transportation, health services, and fire protection, organized crime has reached crisis stage. Among other concerns, housing-related issues have become the focus of an anguished national conversation about the future of the country.

As illustrated by citizens such as the Zhang family in Shanghai, battles are being fought over legal protection, political transparency, the abuse of power, corruption, and even the legitimacy of the CCP, which remains the state's dominant political party and continues to control the mass media.

Westerners—and in particular college students—often raise critical questions: Why does the Chinese legal system assist the party-controlled government rather than its urban residents? How does the CCP manipulate the court to serve its political agenda? What would happen if individuals sued the government? Why do newly developed, highly commercialized cities continue to support the Party rather than fight against it?

This book intends to answer these vital questions by examining certain major legal cases from 1995 to 2013 in four large cities: Wuhan, Xuzhou, Shanghai, and Chongqing. It will highlight cases of administrative litigation and details of petitions sparked by urban removal and housing construction and demonstrate how some metropolitan officials and city dwellers themselves have become victims of China's urbanization. Our conclusions may contradict popular statements that the rapid urbanization of the PRC has benefited cities at the cost of the countryside, where peasants lost land, numbers, and political power to the urban-centered economic reforms.[4]

We argue that the Party created its new political power bases in the cities during urbanization from the mid-1990s to the 2010s. The recently established urban power/interest groups consist of the second generation of revolutionary veterans, pro-CCP entrepreneurs, returning intellectuals sent by the government to obtain degrees and training overseas, and bureaucrats, who are typically CCP members. With political support and special treatment, privileges, and protection, this group has assumed control of city governments and taken advantage of urbanization to generate considerable capital. In return, the urban power/interest groups support the CCP and carry out its policies through the legal system by controlling the "knife hilt" (daobazi) while ignoring the interests and rights of professionals, middle-class families, and private business owners. The court works for the Party as well as the government. Therefore, most of the metropolitan governments are Party governments, and today's China remains a Party state. Meanwhile, urban residents and new migrants not only struggle to survive but also attempt to be heard through the legal process and to avoid victimization. Whenever citizens sue the city government, the powerful always prevail.

This work examines the political survival of the CCP and its transformation as a result of China's urbanization—moving from a party that during the period 1949–1989 claimed to represent the people to a party that since 1995 has represented power/interest groups. Our interdisciplinary analysis explores political science, civil law, history, and mass media sources, ultimately revealing that China's urbanization has unique characteristics that have transformed the country and the CCP.

The CCP successfully adapted to the changing economic and social environment and controlled the growing cities through power sharing and balancing power among competing political, technocratic, and business interest groups. Such sharing and balancing of power demands a more dynamic and localized political organization, one that gives some urban interest groups a part in the decision-making process but excludes the middle classes, who have demanded a representative government, a civil society, and democracy in China.

The "Knife Hilt"

More than two thousand years ago, Han Feizi, one of the greatest legalists in the Warring States Era (ca. 475–221 BCE), discussed a famous Chinese fable: A man from the state of Chu wanted to sell both spears and shields on the street. He first bragged that his shields were so hard that nothing could pierce them. Then he boasted about the sharpness of his spears, able to penetrate all shields. A bystander asked him what would happen if he used his spear to pierce his shield, and he had no answer.[5] The title of this fable is *Maodun* (Contradiction).

This fable can be applied to the recent interpretation of the relationship between law and power by the Chinese government. On February 24, 2013, Xi Jinping, China's president, emphasized the importance of the rule of law in China: "Any organization or individual must act within the range of the constitution and the laws. Any citizen, social organization, and state organs must use the constitution and laws as their behavior principles, exert their rights and power, and fulfill their duties and obligations in accordance with the constitution and the laws."[6]

In early 2014, however, Xi made seemingly contradictory remarks about relations between the CCP and the law while speaking at a top executive conference of politicians and members of the judiciary. Invoking former president Jiang Zemin's talk at the CCP's Fifteenth National Congress in 1997, he noted that both CCP policies and state laws mirrored the fundamental interests of the people and, thus, that there was no difference between them. "The Party leads the people to enact and enforce the constitution and laws," he said. "[The CCP] must lead the legislation, guarantee the law enforcement, and become the leader in conforming to the law." Here, he seemed to stress the rule of law again. But he then shifted his topic to the Party's leadership of the judiciary. He told political and legal officials (i.e., judges, procurators, and the police) that they must adhere to the Party's leadership: "The leadership of the Party is in tune with the leadership of the people."[7]

On the following day, the principal mouthpiece of the CCP, the *People's Daily*, published an editorial that went further than Xi had in explaining the relationship between law and the Party: "As the national power mechanism of the people's dictatorship, the political and legal organs are the knife hilt (*daobazi*) of the Party and the people. Therefore, they must be under the absolute control of the Party. To correctly deal with relations among Party policies and state laws, stick to the Party's leadership, and make sure that the judiciary fulfill their duties independently and justly, [we] must not only steadfastly hold on but also strengthen and improve the Party's leadership of politics and law."[8]

The central issue of two of Xi's talks in less than a year was the relationship between law and the CCP. Because the CCP has always been the ruling power in the PRC, the relationship between law and the CCP is actually that between law and power. In his earlier speech, Xi supposedly advocated the supremacy of the law over the CCP. However, his later talk insisted that the judiciary had to be the knife hilt of the CCP, which is similar to what Pitman Potter terms *legal instrumentalism.*[9] However, the term *knife hilt* was not an invention of the *People's Daily* or Xi. It first appeared in the public media in 1957, the year the CCP launched the Anti-Rightists movement against intellectuals who had strongly called for democracy and the rule of law.[10] On December 20, 1957, the *People's Daily* noted that the political and legal departments were the knife hilts of the CCP, meaning that the judiciary and the police were tools of the Party and should not be independent.[11] The revival of the term *knife hilt* quickly drew criticism from some observers. In one article, Zhong Shu, a critic of the CCP, argued that the revival of the term was meant to save the Party and stab the people and that Xi Jinping wanted to make certain that the knife hilt would be in his hands and not those of Zhou Yongkang, the former head of the powerful political and legal commission and a political foe of Xi.[12] Yu Jianrong, a researcher at the CASS, stated that so long as the judiciary was still a knife hilt of a certain organization (i.e., the CCP), there would be no social justice.[13]

By claiming to make the law above everything and in the meantime requiring the judiciary to be its knife hilt, the CCP was surely facing a contradiction of its own making. As in the classic fable of Han Feizi, if someone were to ask President Xi Jinping: How could the CCP be both above the law and below the law? What will happen if the CCP violates the law? Would the judiciary, the knife hilt of the CCP, be able to bring the Party to justice? Xi would likely not have good answers. Many scholars refer to the current relationship between law and power in the PRC as the rule *by* law.[14]

The rule by law, however, is just one aspect of the relationship between law and power in China. In fact, the relationship between law and power is quite complicated. On the one hand, law and power are different and in many respects contradict each other; on the other, they often work closely and harmoniously together. According to Sinkwan Cheng, there are two kinds of law: law in books and law in action. The first kind is "often associated with justice," while the second "reveals the operation" of power. Law and justice are often said to be inseparable—in theory at least.[15]

The scope of law discussed in this book primarily refers to state and local laws. The power is the ruling power or political power. When we discuss law and power, it is inevitable to usher in another important term: *justice.* In *De re publica,* Cicero pointed out that law was actually justice because it reflected "the one reason that differentiated humans from animals and made them resemble gods."[16]

In medieval Europe, law was clearly regarded as "supreme" and the "expression of justice."[17] Neither justice nor law can be disconnected from power. As Dorwin Cartwright argues: "[Power] reveals both the oppressive and benevolent faces of the law. Only through power can law act as an oppressive and benevolent apparatus." Likewise, the French philosopher Blaise Pascal noticed the close relationship between justice/law and power/force: "Justice without force is impotent [and] force without justice is tyrannical."[18]

POWER VERSUS LAW IN IMPERIAL CHINA

Like many other polities, China has strong links to its past, and any understanding of its paradoxical legal system and perspectives on leadership must begin with a study of its history. Such a study helps us find answers to the following questions: What has been the relationship between power and law in Chinese history? Has power always been above the law throughout Chinese history? Have any previous rulers attempted to elevate the law above power? If so, how long has a ruler followed the law? To what extent has the CCP in urbanized China inherited legal asymmetry from past Chinese rulers?

Aside from the aforementioned rule by law, there are two additional major forms of relations between law and power: the rule *of* law and rule *without* law.[19] Both, like the rule by law, have been practiced in China's long history. In contrast to the rule by law, the rule of law means that "government in all its actions is bound by rules fixed and announced beforehand."[20] Although many scholars have argued that China had only the rule by law and not the rule of law in the imperial periods,[21] recent studies have shown that, if the sine qua non of the rule of law is that "government power [is] limited not by opposing force but by legal rules,"[22] many rulers in most periods of imperial China did consciously respect the law and subject their policies to it.[23] The rule without law is an extreme form of the relationship between law and power in which power is unbridled and not bound by any law. The ruler or ruling party has absolute discretionary power, and the utterances of the ruler or ruling party are tantamount to law. The rule without law took place during only a handful of relatively short periods, such as the reigns of Sui Wendi (r. 581–604) and Wu Zetian (r. 690–705) and the Cultural Revolution (1966–1976).

While the bulk of this book will be devoted to the relations between law and power in China's contemporary urbanization movement, it is highly useful and even necessary to look into the relations between law and power in imperial China. An overview of law versus power in the past will help us better understand the complexity of the present relations between law and power. Moreover, a brief historical account allows us to obtain a clearer understanding of the historical heritage and potential impact on the PRC in the foreseeable future. In offering such an account, we postulate answers to the following questions regarding law and power in China's recent urbanization movement: Has the CCP fulfilled its promises of constructing the rule of law after 1978? How does the PRC continue to ignore the law, including the Constitution? Why does the PRC ruling power refuse to act within the law? To what extent does the CCP—the ruling party—differ from rulers in the historical dynasties and republics?

From the very beginning of Chinese history, some rulers acknowledged the importance of the law as well as its enforcement. More importantly, these rulers knew to respect the independence of the judiciary. For example, Gao Yao, the first known judge in Chinese history, served as a law enforcement officer under both semilegendary kings Yao and Shun. According to *Shangshu* (The ancient book), Gao told King Yao that the law was bestowed by heaven and not by the king. This is probably the first time in Chinese history that a judge linked the law to heaven, purposely warning the ruler that law was supreme, holy, and independent.[24] Gao not only stressed the importance of an independent judiciary but also strictly enforced the law. When a disciple asked Mencius, a prominent Confucian scholar second only to Confucius, what Gao would do if King Shun's father, Gu Sou, murdered someone, Mencius replied that he would arrest him and bring him to justice and that not even Shun could "meddle in the judicial affair."[25] Here, Mencius seemed to understand that King Shun would respect the independence of the judiciary led by Gao. In the Eastern Zhou (770–221 BCE), legalists such as Guan Zhong, Lord Shang Yang (390–338 BCE), and Han Feizi (ca. 280–233 BCE) had all not only demonstrated the "fundamental premises of the rule of law" but also championed the supremacy of the law and equality before the law.[26]

Chinese emperors were to some degree constrained by law, but only to the extent of their acceptance of moral expectations, ancestor laws, family ritual, and customary law.[27] In early Chinese history, Han Wendi (r. 180–157 BCE) and Tang Taizong (r. 626–649) were rulers who best respected the supremacy of law over power. To cite only one case, in 177 BCE, after Wendi's carriage horses were startled by a man, Wendi immediately had the man detained and sent to Zhang Shizhi, the highest-ranking judicial official. Zhang later told Wendi that the man should be fined in accordance with the Han law and reminded Wendi that rulers and commoners alike should abide by the law. Despite his original wish to execute the man, Wendi accepted Zhang's rationale and his verdict. But, in his memorial to Wendi, Zhang also noted that the Han law allowed the emperor to execute a person without notifying the judiciary. The seeming quandary of the relations between law and power existed not only in the Han but also in subsequent periods, including today's PRC. The guarantee of the rule of law came from the ruler. As a ruler in the Han, Wendi had the power to appoint and dismiss Zhang Shizhi. If Wendi had no intention of complying with the law, he could have rejected Zhang's rationale and insisted on executing the man. Yet, unlike many other emperors of the Han dynasty, he refrained from doing so because he understood the significance of the connection between the law and the fate of his family empire.[28]

In terms of esteeming law's supremacy, Tang Taizong, the second emperor of the Tang dynasty (618–907), whose reign was hailed as one of China's best periods, was no inferior to Han Wendi. In 642, when a capable and meritorious general was accused of corruption and should have been executed in accordance with the Tang code, Taizong felt sympathy for the old man and was loath to kill him. But he also understood that padoning him was akin to violating the law. He decided to beg the ministers for mercy. Had Taizong been like many other rulers in the Tang and later periods, including that of the PRC, who put their power above the law, he would not have had to make such an embarrassing plea to his ministers. He could easily have pardoned the general with an edict. The reason he begged the ministers was that he believed that law came from heaven and could not be infringed.[29] If the law was divine, then any secular power should be subject to it. As Geoffrey MacCormack observes: "The [Chinese] emperors themselves, despite the occasional abuse of power, did not regard themselves as being in a position to act according to their own desires."[30]

In imperial China, rulers' deference to the law largely relied on their self-consciousness rather than on an institutional mechanism. The pardon of the general was just one of the cases where Taizong had broken the law. Tang Taizong had admitted that he could not make all decisions in accordance with the law.[31] If he, a talented and able ruler, had infringed the law many times, other less competent rulers stood no chance.

For many scholars, China's authoritarianism reached its peak in the Ming and Qing dynasties. Consequently, the spirit of the rule of law, however inconsistently practiced in the Han and Tang eras, vanished completely in the Ming. In the words of the famous historian Wu Han, who was denounced and killed during the Cultural Revolution, Zhu Yuanzhang (1368–1398), the founder of the Ming, abandoned the imperial tradition of consciously respecting written and customary laws. While it is true that many Ming and Qing rulers frequently neglected the law and even broke it (a judgment based on our readings of the Ming and Qing histories), the superiority of the law in the minds of many rulers was not very different from the situation in previous periods. Many Ming and Qing rulers, like their predecessors in the Han and Tang, recognized the significance of legal justice and at times consciously upheld the law against power. After China lost the Opium Wars in the nineteenth century, the Qing rulers were forced to sign a series of unequal treaties (*bupingdeng tiaoyue*). But mainstream Chinese scholarly bureaucrats insisted that Chinese culture was more civilized than that of the West and refused to change. It was not until the Sino-Japanese War in 1894–1895, and especially the invasion of the Eight Powers Alliance in 1900–1901, that most officials, including the throne, finally realized the urgent need to conduct comprehensive reform. Although the proposal to establish an administrative court was, like the civil law and the criminal law, not formally adopted in the late Qing, most of it was restored in the early republic.

After an outline of the complex relations between law and power in imperial China, we arrive at a possible conclusion. In theory, Chinese emperors controlled the judiciary and had the power to appoint judicial officials. If an emperor refused to follow the law, no official was able to stop him. Despite the lack of a mechanism that could limit their absolute power, many Chinese rulers chose not to break the law because of their consciousness of the supremacy of the law over their power. From the Han through the Qing, both capable and less adept rulers consistently believed that the law should be fair, that they must share the law with the people, and that they had no legal prerogative. Second, the law in imperial China contained not just state laws but also family and customary laws that were either ancestral or Confucian. In the case of Ming Shenzong, the customary law that the son of a concubine could not be heir apparent forced Shenzong to back down in the face of opposition from court officials. Third, some rulers such as Zhu Yuanzhang and Nerhaci ascribed the fall of the Yuan and Ming to the laxity of law enforcement. Each thus took substantial measures to emphasize the law and to strengthen its implementation. Finally, the insistence of upright and brave officials such as Zhang Shizhi in the Han and Zhao Pu in the Song could sometimes effectively forestall emperors' power and force them to obey the law.

New Problems: The Republic and the People's Republic

China emerged as the first republic in Asia following the demise of the Qing dynasty in 1911.Former emperors abruptly became presidents, and subjects became citizens. In early 1912, Sun Yat-sen, the interim president of the republic, enthusiastically pronounced that all Chinese people would be emperors in the republic.[32] The founders of the ROC began with the intention of achieving the ideal of judicial independence. In late 1912, the new justice minister, Xu Shiying, stated that judicial independence was both the main element of a constitutional state and the principal spirit of a rule-of-law state (*fazhiguo*).[33] In early 1913, after the liberal prime minister Song Jiaoren was assassinated in Shanghai, President Yuan Shikai (who reportedly was behind the killing) proposed the formation of a special court to investigate the case so that he could control the process. Xu Shiying, however, insisted that the case be judged by a regular (criminal) court.[34]

In 1914, the administrative court proposed in the late Qing was finally created, and its prime aim was to protect citizens' rights from government power. Because many republican judges had formerly studied in the West or Japan, the court possessed a firm faith in judicial independence and dared to challenge republican leaders. In January 1917, Prime Minister Duan Qirui ordered that the court accept only lawsuits against unlawful government action and that punishments be made in accordance with the Administrative Litigation Law. Cases brought to and accepted by other government organs would, pursuant to presidential orders, be out of the court's jurisdiction. The court disputed the order in a report to the president, saying that the prime minister's order would limit the people's constitutional right to petition. "Under the guise of this order," the court argued, "all the decisions made by various government bodies would automatically [risk] becoming the decisions of the president." The court was concerned that other government bodies might take advantage of this order to prevent complaints about illegal government decisions. The rationale was that, once a government body's request was endorsed by the president, it would be difficult for people to file a lawsuit in response. "If this happened," the court cautioned, "it would extremely restrict [*jiduan xianzhi*] people's constitutional rights to appeal."[35]

The superiority of the law faced new challenges in the later republic (1927–1949) when the GMD, led by Generalissimo Chiang Kai-shek (Jiang Jieshi), dominated China. The GMD had made significant progress in its laws. For example, it implemented a new civil law whose central theme was the concept of rights. Under it, women, minors (under age eighteen), and daughters would not be treated differently than men, seniors, and sons, which was a far cry from the so-called Confucianized law in the dynasties. A widow would have equal rights to share her husband's inheritance with their sons and daughters. Marriages would be based on an agreement between a man and a woman of their own accord.[36]

Nevertheless, in the GMD period judicial power was generally inferior to political power. The practice of the rule of law in the early republic failed to persist in the later republic. The most serious abuse of power came from the top of the GMD. Hence, under GMD rule, the good but short-lived tradition of respecting the law and of judicial independence in the early republic was reduced to a partial tool of the GMD. During the internecine battles between the GMD and the CCP, the judiciary had largely left unchallenged the extralegal or unlawful prosecutions the GMD brought against its enemies, allowing the political power or the GMD to become superior to the law. What was left of judicial independence and the consensus regarding legal supremacy among judges and political leaders was further eroded under CCP rule of the PRC.

The CCP was founded in 1921 with the assistance of the Russian Bolsheviks. In nearly three decades, the once-small party took advantage of Soviet support, the Japanese invasion, and able leadership and, defeating the GMD, its one-time ally, established the PRC in 1949.

From its inception, the PRC quickly adopted the principles laid out by Karl Marx and Vladimir Lenin in reforming its legal system. As early as 1871, the aftermath of the Paris Commune prompted Marx to make one of his most important arguments, that "the working class cannot simply lay hold of the ready-made state machinery, and wield it for its own purposes."[37] In agreement with Marx, ,the prolific Bolshevik theorist and revolutionary Lenin wrote: "The proletariat cannot simply win state power in the sense that the old state apparatus passes into new hands, but must smash this apparatus, must break it and replace it by a new one."[38]

As the longtime archenemy of the GMD, the CCP had determined to repeal all its laws and dismantle its legal institutions even before it took over mainland China. The Party also made clear that the judiciary would be a tool that the ruling class would wield against its enemies. In February 1949, seven months prior to the founding of the PRC, an order approved by CCP leader Mao Zedong was issued openly announcing that the new people's republic would repeal all six laws (*liufa*) of the GMD and replace them with fresh "people's laws."[39]

Despite abolishing the old laws, the CCP had to retain most GMD-appointed judges for the time being, owing to their legal training and ability to write professional verdicts. For example, it was former GMD judges who in late 1949 helped the Shanghai People's Court draft the Guidelines for Dealing with Cases, which were not dissimilar from the GMD codes. Although the Supreme Court chastised some terms of the guidelines for being too lenient to class enemies, the old judges continued to use the guidelines to make judgments and to treat class enemies lawfully.[40]

The backdrop of the Cold War, and particularly the outbreak of the Korean War in June 1950, intensified the CCP's crackdown on counterrevolutionaries, including former GMD officials, spies, military officers, guerrillas, and local thugs, among others. On October 10, 1950, Mao and the central government issued a directive demanding the end of all lenient policies toward counterrevolutionaries and implemented the Party policy of combining leniency and suppression.[41] As a result, military commissions across China took over the main task of suppressing the counterrevolutionaries. In Shanghai, the Shanghai Military Control Commission (Shanghai junshi guanzhi weiyuanhui) and the Shanghai People's Court began summarily arresting alleged counterrevolutionaries and executing many of them without a trial.[42] The remnants of judicial independence and right to a relatively fair trial disappeared, and the people's court became a tool of the Party.

In 1952, the CCP launched a legal movement to purge old judicial personnel from the court owing to their "anti-Revolution and antipeople" thoughts. They were replaced by CCP cadres, veterans of the PLA, progressive workers and farmers, and young intellectuals who had little or no legal education.[43] Unfortunately, despite their political reliability, these new judicial personnel did more harm than good. Some people complained that the courts were very inefficient. They sarcastically mocked: "Under GMD rule, litigants had to pay more money; in the PRC, litigants need a long life." More serious problems caused by the new judges and police were the increasing use of torture and increased numbers of false arrests, judgments, and executions.[44]

The darkest era of the law in the PRC was the Cultural Revolution, a period similar to the rule without law.[45] Fearing that the CCP was being dominated by bourgeois ideology and thus "producing capitalist-type socioeconomic relationships in society at large," Mao launched the Great Proletariat Cultural Revolution in 1966 to revitalize socialism in China.[46] However, the political movement swiftly degenerated into an upheaval in which untold numbers of people suffered arbitrary detainment, torture, and execution.[47] In his study of mass killings in three provinces, Yang Su argues that this tragic period had two important features: violence and state sponsorship, both of which were rooted in the "Stalinist doctrine of unmasking hidden enemies."[48] According to the historian Maurice

Meisner, the repression of radicals reached its apogee in 1970 when General Xu Shiyou accused over 100,000 people of leftist heresies and many were executed, imprisoned, or exiled to labor reform camps.[49] Condemned as a capitalist system, the judiciary as a whole was temporarily terminated. The resulting legal vacuum created absolute power. Without legal protection, many people were killed simply because of their supposedly counterrevolutionary views.[50]

LAW VERSUS POWER IN URBANIZED CHINA

Mao's death in 1976 marked an abrupt end to the Cultural Revolution. Many new Party leaders like Deng Xiaoping had been attacked during the Cultural Revolution. Having a direct and personal experience of the lawless period, these new leaders launched a comprehensive legal reform aiming to overhaul the judicial system and construct the rule of law. As a result of the reform, thousands of new laws were promulgated—including crucial laws such as the Judge Law, the Lawyer Law, the Criminal Law, the Criminal Procedure Law, and the Administrative Litigation Law—that, if properly implemented, might effectively check the power of governments and officials. Recent Party leaders such as Jiang Zemin and Hu Jintao have both advocated the importance of law and promised to construct the rule of law in China. However, despite all the advancements made toward legal reform, the CCP still falls short of endorsing an independent judiciary, due process, and a potent mechanism to enforce the law, particularly constitutional law. Without these key elements of the rule of law maintaining checks on power, the Party would, like rulers in both imperial China and the later republic, find it impossible to resolve the inveterate problem of the relationship between law and power.

China today is a judicial regime with legal practices profoundly influenced by the lasting revolutionary spirit of Mao. Like many rulers in Chinese history, the CCP and the central government frequently intervene in court judgments, as evidenced by death sentences passed on corrupt officials. The role of the Central Committee for Disciplinary Inspection of the CCP is much more important than that of the court in a trial. Despite certain legal formalities, this is evident in the 2013 case of Bo Xilai, the powerful head of the city of Chongqing, and his wife, Gu Kailai, who were tried and sentenced for corruption and murder. Second, the type of political campaign developed during the crackdown on counterrevolutionaries continued in the "Strike Hard" campaign initiated in 1983, which executed twenty-four thousand people in just one year.[51] Toward the end of the first decade of the twenty-first century, another campaign aimed at "Cleaning Up the Mafia" meant to eliminate those who violated public order or were responsible for "economic crimes." This campaign was based on special regulations that made it possible to expedite legal procedures and increase the number of cases punishable by death. Given the sufficient examples of unlawful means adopted in this campaign spearhead by Bo Xilai in Chongqing between 2009 and 2010, including the absence of public trials, summary executions, the systematic use of torture, obstacles meant to block effective legal assistance, and incitement to public outrage, one can easily see the resemblance to extralegal practices during the Mao era.

This overview of Chinese history shows that relations between law and power are quite convoluted and inconsistent. Theoretically, many scholars, and especially the legalists, had championed a concept of the importance of law similar to the modern concept of the rule of law. In practice, many imperial rulers such as Han Wendi and Tang Taizong frequently respected the divinity and supremacy of the law and consequently constrained their power. Yet the overwhelming power of the ruler invariably compromised the law, and compliance with the law largely occurred owing to a legal consciousness of individual rulers. During the early republic, the government in Beijing, heavily influenced by the West, adopted the rule of law and judicial independence. The late republic under the GMD took the form of a Party state and particized the judiciary. The remnants of judicial independence were eliminated in the PRC, and the judiciary became a knife hilt of the CCP. Though the CCP kicked off a sweeping legal reform in 1978 and tried to restore the rule of law in the late 1990s, political power continues to subvert the law, and the nature of law as a Party tool remains unchanged.

Evolution of Power: Decaying or Resilient?

After the crackdown on the 1989 Tiananmen demonstrators, many Western scholars initially thought that the CCP would soon collapse. But, almost thirty years later, the PRC has not only experienced one of the highest economic growth rates in world history but also enjoyed a certain political stability. The CCP has accomplished this through co-opting political, economic, and academic elites, deepening legal reform, and widening its openness and communication with the West. In the early years of the twenty-first century, scholars in the United States debated whether the PRC was decaying or resilient. The political scientist Andrew Nathan argued that, although after the Tiananmen Massacre many observers predicted that Party rule would collapse, the CCP seemed to find a way to be resilient. He alarmed readers with the claim that the resilience of the Party may suggest "that authoritarianism is a viable regime form even under conditions of advanced modernization and integration with the global economy."[52] Similarly, Martin Jacques praised the current PRC political situation as the most stable since 1976. He also said that the CCP was endeavoring to establish a "civilization-state" based on Confucianism, which was superior to the declining Western nation-state.[53] However, Minxin Pei countered that, while it was true that the CCP had attained great success in maintaining power and co-opting elites, those accomplishments would strengthen the Party only temporarily. He asserted that, with the Party growing more corrupt, CCP control would begin to decay once the economy suffered a recession.[54]

The unprecedented historical transition of the PRC after 1989 has also drawn attention from legal scholars as well as political scientists. In 2000, Bruce Dickson offered "a useful framework for analyzing the CCP's policies of coopting new elites and forging links with non-party organizations, as well as understanding the problems that have arisen as a consequence."[55] In 2008, however, he concluded that, to share in the economic benefits, private entrepreneurs support the Party's agenda rather than promoting democratization in China.[56] In 2011, he predicted that, if the CCP succeeded, it might be able to "preempt or postpone" political and legal reforms.[57]

Unlike Dickson, some scholars have moved away from elite-level dynamics and instead study the political continuity at the local level by providing a bottom-up view. For example, in 2006, Kellee S. Tsai explained "the most populous non-transition case in the world" by contending that, "under certain circumstances, the etiology of formal institutional change lies in the informal coping strategies devised by local actors to evade the restrictions of formal institutions."[58] In 2007, she questioned the widely accepted modernization theory that capitalism can lead to democracy. She classified the "coping strategies" of business owners into four categories: "avoidant, grudgingly acceptant, loyally acceptant, and assertive": "Only those in the latter category hold the potential for making direct demands for democracy."[59] The legal scholar Randall Peerenboom considers this as China's path rather than a problem, "or at least that it is too early to tell."[60] He believes that "China is now following the path of other East Asian countries that have achieved sustained economic growth, established the rule of law, and developed constitutional or rights-based democracies, albeit not necessarily liberal rights-based democracies."[61]

Power versus Law in Modern China voices the complaints and resentments in the cities and interprets government policies and legal practices. The lawsuits to be examined in this work are all nationally well-known cases from the 1990s to the present. They show how the Party restructured its relationship to a changing society and reacted to political, economic, legal, and social issues such as urban construction, housing policies, and the rights of private citizens. Clearly, the Party does not want to lose control of the cities, and especially the support of the middle class, in the midst of the largest urbanization movement in Chinese history. Although the CCP had tried to adopt more conciliatory policies when dealing with the middle class, it, like many rulers in Chinese history, continued to use force to subdue law and disregarded legitimate requests. In so doing, it risks wasting the enormous efforts it has made in the past thirty years to propel China toward the rule of law. The middle class complainants in Wuhan and Xuzhou resorted to mostly lawful methods to protect their rights. The four urban cases discussed in this book will provide readers with an excellent microcosm of the asymmetrical relations between law and power in China today. These cases unveil the ingrained tradition in Chinese history that the ruling parties tend to abuse their power and neglect law in dealing with the people, no matter how legitimate their claims or how aggrieved the claimants. In that regard, the CCP, like its pre-decessors in both previous dynasties and previous republics, continues to treat law as merely a tool rather than a Damocles sword that poses a formidable and forceful threat to the Party.

In Wuhan, Xuzhou, Shanghai, and Chongqing, the purposeful and exces-sive use of coercion, harassment, fabricated charges, and torture by CCP offi-cials and law enforcement officers triggered immense resistance from the middle class. While the law-abiding middle-class complainants were eventually over-whelmed by government power, their unsatisfied grievances could in the future very likely turn to resentment of and enmity toward the Party. The exodus of rich and educated middle-class families to the West in recent years is just one sign of the middle class discontented with the CCP and reflects to some degree a "lack of confidence in their own domestic political and economic systems."[62] Middle-class families who have had similar experiences to those in Wuhan, Xuzhou, Shanghai, and Chongqing but have chosen to stay in China may oppose the Party during economic crisis or at least fold their arms and refuse to support it. Accordingly, from the viewpoint of the asymmetrical relationship between law and power, the CCP is all but secure. In addition, the CCP's tight control on power and its refusal to comply with the law echo the practices of the polities in China's past and sug-gest that it cannot continue as a viable regime, at least in the long run.

PRIMARY SOURCES AND CHAPTERS

Few areas of research in China studies pose more difficulties than the evolution of the CCP during urbanization, primarily because of the unique position of urban-ization in Chinese society and its relationship to the legitimacy of the Party's authority. Also, the metropolitan government papers and court documents are not readily available to Western researchers. We have discovered primary sources representing important lawsuits that encompass news reports and current litera-ture on these cases. This book opens up an unprecedented number of new official documents that will certainly stimulate intellectual dialogue and urge fresh con-sideration both in the academy and among a general readership in America and the West. In terms of primacy, our primary sources comprise personal interviews, privately collected material, court documents, and official papers.

We have conducted exclusive interviews with many individuals who were policy makers, key players, witnesses, and complainants as well as plaintiffs and their attorneys. Some were officials, advisory board members, or police officers behind numerous complaints and administrative lawsuits. It is crucially impor-tant to note that, during their tenure in office, the court decisions, policy imple-mentations, and law enforcements were subordinate to the political leadership and Party authorities in these four cities.

After the interviews, we explored archival materials at four tiers of the Chi-nese government. From the bottom up, the first level of the official sources is from the urban district governments (*qu zhengfu*), the second from the municipal governments (*shi zhengfu*), the third from provincial governments (*sheng zhengfu*), and the fourth from the central government in Beijing. These official documents ensure a viable cross section for analysis and allows us to interpret a series of fundamental issues and present a crucial understanding of the salient political challenges.

The third group of primary sources comprises court papers, police records, and legal documents from the cases we examine. Most cases involve district, municipal, county, provincial, and supreme courts, at all levels. These papers indicate that Party leaders strongly believed that the legal system should serve, rather than restrict, the power of the CCP. In many cases, the government was not able (or willing) to rectify itself through the existing legal system. In the meantime, during the trials, the mass media made an attempt to identify checks and balances.

The last group of sources includes urban news reports, newspaper articles, and journalistic investigations. Most of the cases we researched became hot topics that were covered both locally and nationally. It is clear that the Chinese mass media have a long way to go before freedom of speech and freedom of the press become a reality, but the value for our study of their coverage of events cannot be underestimated. These sources provide a balanced perspective on the lawsuits, make new contributions to ongoing debates concerning China's political and legal reforms, and introduce a fresh approach to the study of contemporary China.

This book covers Chinese politics and legal practices in four cities. It situates the legal system and landmark cases in the context of Chinese society while taking into account patterns, progress, and challenges. Chapter 1 looks into the lawsuit submitted by many Wuhan residents against their city government. Although the residents—most of whom were affluent homeowners—all had lawful certificates when they bought their new apartments along the Yangzi (Yangtze) River, the local government demanded in 2001 that they evacuate immediately. The fierce fight to preserve their homes would last for 130 days.

Chapter 2 shows that, believing in the legitimacy of their documents and their rights, the Wuhan homeowners organized committees and fought a tug-of-war with the local government over compensation. Local officials began taking illegal and forceful means to intimidate them, including secret arrests, detainments, and other forms of covert pressure. After repeated failures in persuading lawyers in both Wuhan and Beijing, the residents finally managed to find two audacious local lawyers to accept their case against the city government. The lawsuit filed collectively by over 100 Wuhan residents became the first administrative lawsuit in twenty-first-century China.

Chapter 3 continues the discussion of the case before the Supreme Court in 2002. Not surprisingly, the court swiftly dismissed the lawsuit. The chapter also looks at the many just and natural forms of resistance practiced by Waitan Garden residents to safeguard their homes. After all their efforts proved to be in vain, these staunch defenders finally realized that the CCP had gained full control of their city and that it was too powerful for the law to prevail.

Chapter 4 examines the lawsuit submitted by Wang Peirong, an associate professor at the China Mining University, against the city government of Xuzhou, Jiangsu Province. After Wang and thousands of other faculty and staff moved into their new university-built apartments in 1999, they found that the antitheft doors that had been installed were defective and virtually useless. As a result, many tenants lost personal property to thieves. When infuriated homeowners elected Wang to complain to the local government, local officials simply ignored the complaint.

Chapter 5 continues the coverage of the Wang case from 2005 to 2013, including Wang's eighteen-month incarceration. Wang was involved in a bloody fight against the head of the Neighborhood Committee of Fenghuayuan, Liu Yongxiu. Although Liu did not himself have much power, he had powerful backing from the local government. Responding to accusations that he had embezzled a large sum of public money belonging to all the residents, he launched a ferocious battle against Wang. After Wang began shifting the focus of his charges toward the powerful mayor, the situation turned unfavorable to Wang. In the local court, Liu sued Wang for slander, resulting in Wang's eighteen-month imprisonment. The fact is that the "legal asymmetry" built into Chinese law—under which officials often enjoy certain legal privileges or immunity and commoners, no matter how credible they are or how cogent their evidence might be—means that justice cannot be obtained in the face of formidable political power.

Chapter 6 considers urban power abuse from a different perspective by examining the violations of the law and the downfall of two powerful local Party chiefs: Chen Liangyu in Shanghai and Bo Xilai in Chongqing. Both had abused their power during their tenure in office. In 2003, Chen was behind the coerced relocation of hundreds of residents in order to assist his relatives and friends. When a brave lawyer tried to defend the aggrieved complainants, the Shanghai court sentenced him to three years in prison. Chen's ultimate fall in 2006 was the result of a power struggle and not his illegal activities. Bo Xilai was more prominent than Chen. Shortly after he was appointed as the head of Chongqing in 2007, he kicked off a radical but quite popular movement championing the Communist tradition and tackling organized crime. Yet he and his police lieutenant, Wang Lijun, adopted mainly illegal means, such as torture and perjured testimony, to extract confessions from the alleged criminals and punish lawyers who had dared challenge their policies. Like Chen, Bo's fall had nothing to do with his massive infringements of the law but was largely due to a power struggle that he lost. Despite the overwhelming evidence against them, what mattered in the end was, not the law, but power.

Understanding its political and legal systems and the new challenges its government faces is one of the most significant issues that China faces in the twenty-first century. Even as the new leadership under Xi Jinping works to maintain economic growth at home while seeking a growing role on the global political stage, China is not yet a country ruled by law. The well-known legal cases presented here will provide readers with a much closer and more comprehensive understanding of the convoluted and dynamic relations between power and law, commoners and local officials, the government and the CCP. While most Chinese, and especially the ruling Party, are celebrating the economic miracle, the adverse and ingrained relationship between power and law is and will remain a major obstacle to China's ongoing transformation from a conventional authoritarian agrarian society to a modern urbanized nation characterized by democracy and the rule of law.

1

Urban War at the Yangzi River

This book analyzes four cases that drew much attention from major public media and were once nationally recognized. All took place during the height of China's latest urbanization movement. Through several years of detailed interviews with insiders and careful documentation of original materials such as complaint letters, indictments, public meetings, posters, flyers, and pictures, the case studies reported in this book will vividly reconstruct the lawful resistance of the defenseless victims. These confrontations between law and power, to some extent tragic and stirring, offer readers a window onto the practice and function of law in contemporary China.

A "Freak"

To begin, we analyze the Waitan Garden residential community, arguably the first collective administrative litigation in twenty-first-century China. In early 2002, almost 130 Waitan Garden homeowners brought a collective lawsuit before the Supreme Court accusing the Wuhan municipal government of illegally approving the Waitan Garden project whose later demolition caused huge financial losses to the homeowners.

Waitan Garden was located at the east gate of the Hanyang District in Wuhan, Hubei Province's capital and largest city. Historically, Wuhan (including the districts of Hanyang, Hankou, and Wuchang) had been known as the "Thoroughfare of Nine Provinces" in central China, and its Hankou District was, in William Rowe's words, "the most important inland commercial city of the Ch'ing empire" and a city of "nearly unparalleled ethnic and occupational complexity."[1] The 1911 revolution overthrew the Qing dynasty and created the Republic of China, further raising the reputation of the city. Waitan Garden was the first and only residential complex built on the riverbed of the Yangzi River, the third longest river in the world. The gate of Waitan Garden was originally a sluice gate. The Waitan Garden project was designed in two phases. The first phase consisted of the construction of 140 apartments, for a total living space of twenty-one thousand square meters. All of them quickly sold out. The second phase resulted in forty-nine thousand square meters of living space, and shortly after completion 90 percent of the new apartments had been sold.[2] By the time the project was demolished, the overall direct investment of the developer, the Wuhan Hongya Industrial Company, had exceeded 160 million RMB (for comparison, the RMB/ US dollar conversion rate was eight to one). Add to this the cost of compensating the homeowners for decorating expenses, relocating the homeowners, demolishing Waitan Garden, and managing of the riverbed, and the final figure is easily in excess of 300 million RMB.[3]

To many people, and especially the Waitan Garden homeowners, the night of January 25, 2002, was miserable and unforgettable. That night, the local government ordered the demolition of the first unit of the Waitan Garden complex. Because the building housed the least number of people, its destruction proceeded relatively easily and smoothly. The remaining residential buildings were to be destroyed before April 1, 2002. The demolition, albeit only during its first phase, was promptly hailed by some major national media as a victory for law and the people. As one of the CCP's most important mouthpieces, the Xinhua News Agency (Xinhuashe, the New China News Agency) wasted no time throwing its support behind the demolition. On January 25, it published a report in which it claimed: "The broad masses [guangda qunzhong] believe that the demolition of a building that has infringed the Flood Control Law of the People's Republic of China [Zhonghua renmin gongheguo fanghongfa] and affected the overall situation of flood prevention [fangxun] is compatible with the fundamental interests of the broad masses and fully demonstrates the authority of the law."[4]

Xinhua's use of the term broad masses is rather surprising. While it was quite common among major state media before 1980, broad masses was not commonly used in 2002 (and is not commonly used today) because of the Chinese media's "commercial revolution" after Deng Xiaoping's 1992 call for deepening reform and accelerated economic development. However, Xinhua retained its status as one of the CCP's principal mouthpieces and did not then and does not now have to worry about the increasingly competitive media market and the diminishing government subsidies received by most state media, including the prominent and popular China Youth Daily (Zhongguo qingnianbao).[5] Its unique political and financial privileges allowed and continue to allow it to persist in the use of unscientific, inaccurate, obsolete, and propagandistic terms such as broad masses.

Indeed, as was the practice of most PRC state media in the past, Xinhua cited only a few Wuhan residents in its report—hardly enough to be representative of the "broad masses." Surely, few of the four hundred–plus Waitan Garden homeowners and their families would agree with the report.

As if a single report was not enough to scare future lawbreakers, Xinhua noted in another report published the same day that the local government's action to correct "its own improper [budang] administrative activity [allowing the construction of Waitan Garden]" had drawn positive comments from experts on both water resources and the law. "They all believe that the action [i.e., the demolition of Waitan Garden] has forcefully safeguarded the dignity of the law [falüde zunyan] and mirrored the progress of the time [shidaide jinbu]." One lawyer was quoted as saying: "The action of blowing up the building let people see the faith and hope of China's efforts to implement the rule of law."[6]

Like Xinhua, CCTV later praised the demolition of Waitan Garden, just in a more poetic way. "The first unit of Waitan Garden has lost its previous nobility and beauty," it said. "The headquarters of the National Flood Control have already issued an order to blow it up. The surrounding area is quiet, and people are waiting in the quietness . . . for the sound of explosion that embodies the authority of law and represents law's dignity!"[7]

Apart from the principal state media, other national and regional media also did not want to miss this historic moment. They went further than Xinhua and CCTV by calling for a serious investigation of those officials who had initially approved the Waitan Garden project and for the fair treatment of the homeowners. For example, on January 29, 2001, the *Workers' Daily* (*Gongren ribao*) invoked some local people's opinion that the government should seriously look into those officials who had initially approved the project and not let the country shoulder the cost of demolition. "Waitan Garden is a very typically illegal building," the report argued. "Its fate from birth, construction, and demolition should give rise to the serious rethinking of the government administrations. Such alarming negative teaching material should not end with an explosion."[8]

The *Southern Weekend* (*Nanfang zhoumo*) is a Guangzhou-based newspaper renowned for its boldness in exposing government corruption and unlawful policies. Unlike other national media, it called Waitan Garden a "freak [*guaitai*]" and expressed deep compassion for the homeowners. "Who is going to compensate the homeowners?" it asked. Some homeowners told reporters that they were innocent and that the local government should not shift the loss resulting from its illegal approval of Waitan Garden onto them. The newspaper also accused the local government of having violated the 2001 Regulations Regarding the Management of Urban Housing Demolition (Chengshi fangwu chaiqian guanli tiaoli) in dealing with the homeowners. "Many homeowners have said that the local government did not follow the law [in approving Waitan Garden] at the beginning," the reporters wrote, "and now the demolition should conform to the law. [The local government] should not repeat its mistakes." Finally, the *Southern Weekend* predicted that a fierce confrontation was inevitable because the local government had taken forcible action in relocating the homeowners and, in the meantime, the homeowners had sued the local government in the Hubei Provincial High Court.[9]

For most outsiders, the information provided by both Xinhua and CCTV was quite brief and sketchy. Many issues remained obscure and needed to be addressed. For instance, if the demolition of Waitan Garden was a victory for the law, why had construction been approved in the first place? What was behind the hasty demolition? Had those local officials who originally approved the project been punished? Would the government compensate the homeowners who had lawfully bought their apartments? If so, where would the money come from?

While both the *Workers' Daily* and the *Southern Weekend* called for further investigation of those accountable for the demolition and the dire fate of the homeowners, neither mentioned the tremendous psychological and economic impacts on most homeowners and their families. As public interest in the case died down in the following months, both newspapers lost interest in it as well. Also, neither was audacious enough to report the tug-of-war between the homeowners—whose defense of their homes was considered by some "rightful resistance" or "natural resistance"—and local officials.[10] Those unexplored questions will be addressed in detail in the following chapters.

The Legality of the Freak

The Waitan Garden project was initiated in 1994 when the pace of China's urbanization movement escalated to an unprecedented level. To make Wuhan a twenty-first-century international metropolis and enhance their "political accomplishments" (*zhengji*), both Hubei and Wuhan officials vowed to beautify their city and transform its backward image. The bund of the Hanyang District on the west side of the Yangzi River had long been covered with weeds, silt, and waste, a state that to the local officials was highly incongruous with a metropolitan Wuhan. Inspired by the Shanghai Bund, an internationally famous riverside tourist destination,[11] local leaders in Hubei planned to construct something similar in Wuhan. Thus, Waitan Garden, situated along the Hanyang riverside, became a part of the local efforts to build a more attractive Wuhan.

Waitan Garden served a second purpose—taming the Yangzi River floodwaters. Prior to the disastrous 1998 flood, the local government had spent enormous amounts of money and effort on flood control. Some local leaders proposed developing Waitan Garden as a way to kill two birds with one stone: it could attract a developer and thus funding, thereby reducing the heavy financial burden of flood control while beautifying the water's edge and the city.

On August 3 and 16, 1995, Li Daqiang, then the vice governor of Hubei, chaired two conferences on the initiation of Yangzi City Garden (Changjiang chengshi huayuan, later changed to Waitan Garden). The conference minutes were completed on September 15, which made Waitan Garden the first experimental project in the construction of a Shanghai-like bund in Wuhan. The minutes also demanded that the project fully guarantee the safety of Wuhan in times of flooding. Before the Flood Control Law became effective on January 1, 1998, there had been no state law that explicitly prohibited construction on the riverbed of the Yangzi River. However, in Hubei, a local law referred to as the Implementing Method of Managing Riverbeds (Hedao guanli shishi banfa) granted the local government the right to approve riverbed construction under "special circumstances." Although the term *special circumstances* was vague, it at least provided the Waitan Garden project with a certain legitimacy at the beginning.[12]

With the strong endorsement of the local government, the developer, Wuhan Hongya, easily obtained all the necessary legal certificates: the construction project planning permit (*jianshe gongcheng guihua xukezheng*), the building project construction permit (*jianzhu gongcheng shigong xukezheng*), the permit to sell commercial housing in Wuhan (*Wuhanshi shangpinfang xiaoshou xukezheng*), the investment permit (*touzi xukezheng*), the land use permit (*tudi shiyongquanzheng*), and the planning inspection permit (*guihua yanshou xukezheng*). Apart from the construction project planning permit, which was issued by the Ministry of Construction of the PRC (Zhonghua renmin gongheguo jianshebu), the other five permits were issued by the Wuhan municipal government. A completely legal permitting process was crucial if buyers were to be attracted to the project; it also laid a legitimate foundation for the Waitan homeowners' suit against the local government.[13]

The head of Wuhan Hongya, Xiao Xinfu, later said that it was the Flood Control Office (Fangxunban) of the Hanyang district that had "dragged" him into the Waitan Garden project because in 1995 no one dared to build residential apartments on the riverbed.[14] It seems that at first Xiao had no interest in the project. However, according to the *Southern Weekend,* he later changed his mind and began "busily" seeking any projects in Wuhan after suffering a big investment loss in Hainan Province. To demonstrate appreciation to the local government for offering him the project, Xiao donated millions to the flood-control units in Wuhan in the name of supporting local flood control.[15]

Contrary to the charges by state media that Waitan Garden posed a potential threat to flood control, the developer from the outset set flood control as a primary goal in designing and constructing the project. To protect against floodwater, the developer had taken the following measures:

1. A vacant level was built beneath each housing unit. The height of the vacant level was 31.4 meters, higher than the highest recorded flood stage in Wuhan history. This vacant level proved to be quite effective. During the 1998 flood, for example, the floodwater had reached only one-third of the height of the vacant level.
2. The height of the bund was not increased so that floodwaters would not be trapped.
3. To strengthen the levee, the developer had driven a total of fifteen hundred piles. Each pile was driven twenty-two to thirty-one meters deep, greatly enhancing the strength of the bund and the levee.
4. A wave-resistance levee ten meters wide and one thousand meters long was built, effectively preventing the waves and the undercurrents of the Yangze River from eroding the beach (*tan'an*).
5. Before Wuhan Hongya began construction, it signed an affidavit guaranteeing the safety of the levee. Therefore, it worked with the existing sluice rather than opening a new one.

As soon as the first stage of construction was finished—in October 1998—both the provincial and the city flood-control offices inspected the project and found that all technological targets had met standards. Hence, Waitan Garden was not only legal but also of high quality.[16]

Unaware to what extent Waitan Garden's location on the Yangzi riverbed was acceptable to potential local buyers, the developer at first kept a low profile and did only limited advertisement. Surprisingly, however, sales were extremely brisk, and before long all the first-stage apartments had been sold. Encouraged by the unexpectedly strong sales, the developer flooded the public media with advertisements once the second-stage construction had been completed in late 2000. Suddenly, seductive and tempting words romanticizing riverside life—for example, "I will give you the Yangzi River [woba changjiang songgeini]," "My home is right on the bank [wojia jiuzai anshangzhu]," and "Choose to live along the water [zeshui erju]"—flooded the major media in Wuhan.

While the first stage of the Waitan Garden project, which took place before the Flood Control Law was enacted, had a hint of legitimacy, some media and local government quickly questioned the validity of the second stage, which took place almost three years after the passage of the law. For example, in May 2000, when some leaders in the Hubei Province Water Resource Department (Hubeisheng shuiliting) had heard about the start of the second stage, they dispatched people to try to stop the construction. Furthermore, they issued "A Circular Regarding the Illegal Construction of the Hanyang Waitan Garden on the Upper Part of the Wuhan Hanyang Yangzi River Bridge" ("Guanyu Wuhanshi Hanyangqu changjiang daqiao shangshou hanyang waitan huayuan xiaoqu weizhang shigong detongbao") in the name of the Headquarters of Flood Control and Drought Resistance in Hubei Province (Hubeisheng fangxun kanghan zhihuibu). The circular made it clear that the Waitan Garden project had violated the law: "Although the Yangzi River Garden [Waitan Garden] project had gone through all the formalities of planning and flood control in 1996, it has not submitted an application following the procedures of constructing projects within the range of riverbed management [hedao guanli fanwei]. For that reason, the construction has broken the regulations . . . and must stop."[17]

One month later, however, the Hubei Province Water Resource Department issued another statement surprisingly reversing its previous decision that Waitan Garden was illegal. "Because the Wuhan Waitan Garden project has been approved by the provincial government as an experimental project of Wuhan planned use of the river beach," the new statement said, "[the department] in principle agrees to let the Wuhan Hongya Industrial Co. Ltd. continue the Waitan Garden's second-stage construction on the East-Gate Bund [dongmen waitan] of Hanyang."[18]

On December 23, 2000, the China Economic Times (Zhongguo jingji shibao) quoted Pan Rongzhou, the chief engineer of Wuhan Flood Control Headquarters, as saying that the Waitan Garden project had never undergone any scientific appraisal. The first stage would no doubt have an adverse impact on flood control of the Yangzi River, so "why did [the government] approve the second stage?" Pan asked. The report ended by posing a serious question to Wuhan residents: "People living in flood-controlled regions of the downstream absolutely have the right to ask: 'Is the [Waitan Garden project] not too bold and too clever?'"[19]

The fate of the *China Economic Times* report is no different than that of the Hubei Province Water Resource Department report mentioned earlier. In a follow-up report the following month, the *Times* made a conflicting announcement that the inspection of the Hubei and Wuhan Water Resource Departments showed that the Waitan Garden project had met all technological standards.[20] Once again, suspicions about the legality of Waitan Garden died down, and second-stage construction went ahead without further trouble.

When the second-stage construction was over in late 2000, Waitan Garden had a total of 450 commercial housing units that contained seven apartment units, eleven villas, and one office building. With complete legal documentation, high quality, and a beautiful location, it was very popular among the middle and upper middle classes in Wuhan and other parts of the country. Before its destruction in early 2002, 90 percent of the apartments had been sold, and hundreds of families had moved in.

Who were the buyers of the high-end Waitan Garden apartments? What were their occupations? To what extent did the buyers' social status have any impact during their future efforts to protect their rights? Most working-class people in Wuhan would balk at the high price of Waitan Garden. The Waitan Garden homeowners were largely government officials, businessmen, and wealthy specialists such as lawyers, doctors, singers, scholars, journalists, poets, and college presidents. It was said anonymously that one of the homeowners was one of China's ten richest persons.[21] As the *Jinghua Times* reported on January 26, 2002, the Wuhan officials seeking the demolition of Waitan Garden gained an additional legal headache from the eight lawyers living there.[22]

However, the relatively higher social status and power of the Waitan Garden homeowners turned out to be a double-edged sword in their subsequent efforts to defend their property rights. On the one hand, their higher social status and connections helped them reach powerful people, such as the bodyguard of President Jiang Zemin, CCTV anchors, and reporters for the influential Xinhua News Agency and many other Chinese and Hong Kong newspapers. Making such contacts would be inconceivable to people of most other social classes. On the other hand, their higher income and social status would conversely become their Achilles heel as they would be more likely than would the lower classes to bow to government pressure and make concessions. As we will discuss later, while several hundred Waitan Garden homeowners joined the rights protection movement initially, only around one hundred eventually decided to sue the local government.

In China, the late chairman Mao Zedong (Mao Tse-tung) had first accused the middle and upper middle classes of "weakness." As early as December 1925, his influential "An Analysis of China's Social Classes" argued that the middle class/national capitalists were two-faced: they could be both revolutionary and reactionary.[23] In another article published on December 27, 1935, Mao was more explicitly critical of the middle class/national capitalists. "One of the main characteristics of the politics and economy in a semicolonial society," he wrote, "is the weakness of the national capitalists." He also noted that it was the inherent "weakness" of the national capitalists that determined their revolutionary incompleteness and compromise.[24]

The Sudden Collapse of the Sky

On November 19, 2001, CCTV's *Focal Interview* (*Jiaodian fangtan*), famous for its unrelenting criticism of local officials, denounced Waitan Garden as an explicit violation of the 1998 Flood Control Law because it was built outside the flood-control dam of the Yangzi River: "Just two years after the great [Yangzi River] flood in 1998, a huge residential complex has been built on the riverbed of the narrowest section of the Yangzi River in Wuhan.... According to the 1998 Flood Control Law, article 22 clearly states that it is prohibited to build anything on the riverbed that may hamper the draw-off of floodwater.... However, [the local government] in Wuhan has unlawfully approved this commercial building project, resulting in tremendous threats to the draw off of floodwater and people's safety."[25]

In 2004, about three years after the Waitan Garden exposé, CCTV revealed the story behind its bold report. People following the development of the project assumed that the developer had extremely strong backers in the local government. When CCTV reporters went to Hubei to investigate, both Hubei and Wuhan officials declined to be interviewed and directed them to the water resource specialists in the province. The specialists denied that the project had violated the Flood Control Law, pointing to a local regulation that allowed construction on the riverbed on "special request" (*teshu xuyao*). The reporters found the explanation unsatisfactory and unconvincing as the specialists repeatedly failed to describe what the "special request" was.[26]

The *Focal Interview* report was shocking news to most local officials. According to a homeowner representative (*yezhu daibiao*), after Premier Zhu Rongji watched the it, he immediately called the leadership of Hubei province and expressed serious concerns with Waitan Garden. The next day, the cover page of the *Wuhan Morning Post* (*Wuhan chenbao*) ran a complete transcription of the report.[27]

The pressure on the local leaders in both Hubei (the provincial government) and Wuhan (the city government) was immense. As in other authoritarian states, in the PRC local officials derive their power and position from their superiors and not from the people. If the ordinary people are infuriated by their policies, local officials can still pay little attention and, in some extreme cases, even crack down on any protests. Yet few dared to ignore their superiors, let alone the leaders in the central government. In the words of Brigid Harrison and Thomas Dye: "The central attitudes of authoritarianism are dominance and submission—dominance over subordinates in any power hierarchy and submissiveness toward superiors."[28]

For officials in Hubei and Wuhan, CCTV and especially the CCP leaders behind CCTV were their superiors to whom they had to submit. They felt compelled to make a speedy decision on the fate of Waitan Garden: preserve it or demolish it? On November 21, 2001, two days after the CCTV report, more than sixty local officials met at Waitan Garden. Most of them continued to believe that the complex should not be destroyed because the original design had already fully taken flood control into account. The meeting lasted about three hours, and consensus was reached on five points:

1. Waitan Garden is a historical problem that does not affect flood control and flood confluence (*huihong*).
2. The specialists from the provincial water resource departments and especially from the Yangze River Water Resource Committee would review the Waitan Garden project again. Its conclusions would be respected.
3. A detailed report would be drafted so that the Party secretary and the governor of Hubei Province could bring it with them to Beijing for a central economic conference scheduled on November 27, 2001. They would give the detailed report in person to Premier Zhu Rongji.
4. No action should be taken regarding Waitan Garden for fear that it would have detrimental psychological impacts on the homeowners.
5. Because of the significance and complexity of this case, all media coverage must cease.

Obviously, the outcome demonstrated that the Hubei officials were unwilling to tear down Waitan Garden unless there was a clear order was issued by the central leaders. Unlike most other government meetings, this one was relatively open, and Zhang Lijun, the developer's project manager, was invited and allowed to stay for the duration.

In the meantime, however, the further bad news came to Hubei that Premier Zhu Rongji had specifically talked about Waitan Garden during a recent meeting in Beijing. In the middle of the meeting, he denounced the project for risking people's lives by moving them outside the levee. He angrily asked: "If such a project has been approved, has any corruption been involved?" On hearing this, the local officials in Hubei realized that there was no hope of saving Waitan Garden because no one would want to risk his or her political career for the sake of the neighborhood.[29] After all, the 300 million RMB cost of demolishing Waitan Garden would not come from the pockets of those officials. From then on, both the Hubei and the Wuhan officials determined to resort to whatever means, legal or illegal, to force the homeowners to give up their lawfully acquired homes.

While the CCTV report stunned most local leaders, it was tantamount to the sky falling for most Waitan Garden homeowners. In their eyes, they were innocent—if anyone had violated the law, it was the local officials or the developer. Before the homeowners bought their beautiful apartments, they had made sure that the project had proceeded legally. But suddenly, they were told that it was illegal and had to be demolished. While it was true that most Waitan Garden homeowners belonged to the middle class and had decent incomes or occupations, there were still around 60 percent who had assumed mortgages to buy their apartments. A few of them had even sold their former apartments or ancestral properties.[30]

Many Waitan Garden homeowners were furious at the sudden change of tone by some local officials. On the afternoon of November 19, leaders of the Yangzi River Water Resource Committee (Changjiang shuili weiyuanhui), the Hubei Provincial Water Resource Department, and the Flood Control Office had inspected Waitan Garden and agreed that it would not hinder flood-control efforts. Chen Min, an engineer working for the Yangzi River Water Resource Committee, also joined the group and agreed with its conclusion. But, when interviewed on that evening's *Focal Interview*, he reversed his position. "Why did he [Chen Min] make two opposite conclusions? Why did he come to Waitan Garden that afternoon? Did he support the official consensus or not?" one homeowner asked later.[31]

The residents of Waitan Garden had expended a great deal of time and energy searching out, purchasing, and furnishing their apartments and consequently had trouble believing that the complex really would be torn down. For example, Yan Fengjun and her husband, Tang Hanqing, were both doctors. Owing to her heroic and extraordinary role in organizing the Waitan Garden homeowners, Yan was later singled out as the principal target (*yihao mubiao*) by the local officials and the police. To buy an ideal place for their retirement, Yan and her husband sold their former apartment and bought a new one in Waitan Garden for 400,000 RMB. They liked their new home so much that they had spent 200,000 RMB more on decoration. Right after Yan heard about the CCTV report, she felt, as she put it, like she was "hit by a thunderbolt." However, like many other homeowners, she did not really believe that such a large residential complex would be destroyed and continued to buy furniture for her new home.[32]

Another Waitan Garden homeowner named Han Junru, a newspaper reporter, described how he bought his apartment in 2011. He and his wife were overjoyed by their new home, and they had spent the whole summer decorating it. "We had infinite enthusiasm [in our new home], which was like our second child," Han said. "Throughout that summer, I slept on the floor, pouring dark sweat [*heihan*], and I had not written a word [for his newspaper reporting job]. When the decoration was finished, the once vacant apartment seemed to be a living thing." To buy their new home, he and his wife had spent all their hard-earned savings and also assumed a large mortgage.[33]

In an extreme case, one twenty-year-old homeowner, Fu Yuanyuan, was exceptionally audacious and composed. She persistently defied the CCTV report and the government orders by continuing to decorate her apartment right up until Waitan Garden was demolished. When the local officials tried to stop the workers she hired from decorating, Fu told them to keep going since it was she who was paying them and not the local officials.[34]

Many Waitan Garden homeowners believed that the CCTV report was highly misleading, especially on three points. First, it said that the gate of the complex had breached the Yangzi River flood-control wall. The fact was that that gate had been the sluice door of the flood-control wall for decades. The sluice door could be opened when there was a flood and closed otherwise. Instead of damaging the flood-control wall, construction had actually strengthened the levee by preventing water penetration and thus protecting riverbanks and slopes.

Second, the CCTV report claimed that the levee was two to three meters higher than the first floor of the Waitan Garden apartment buildings. Indeed, if that were true, the levee would not be able to withstand approaching floodwaters and the first floor of the apartment buildings would be submerged and the levee damaged. But that was demonstrably not the case. The homeowners and the developer accused the CCTV reporters of losing their "professional ethics [zhiye daode]" and "deliberately neglect[ing] the truth." In fact, the first floor of the apartment buildings was built on three-meter-high stilts, the height of the stilts mimicking that of the original levee and allowing floodwater to flow unobstructed. If the stilts did not block the floodwater, then Waitan Garden could not be charged with adversely affecting flood control. There could be no better proof of this than the 1998 Yangzi River flooding, said to be the worst in the past hundred years.[35]

Finally, the CCTV report asserted that the main buildings of Waitan Garden had been initiated in 2000 and completed in 2001. Because of that, the project had infringed the 1998 Flood Control Law. However, as we have pointed out earlier, the local government approved construction in early 1995, and the first phase had been completed in 1997, clearly before the 1998 Flood Control Law. Most homeowners moved into Waitan Garden in 1997 and 1998. What the report claimed were the "main buildings" were simply products of the second stage of construction.

All the homeowners interviewed believed that it was CCTV's false report that misled leaders and flood-control officials, who accordingly decided to demolish the whole Waitan Garden complex.[36]

The homeowners' criticisms of the CCTV report, whether they are factually correct or not, have little chance of being publicized anywhere in China today. Since its establishment in 1949, the PRC has been an authoritarian Party-state with a firm grip on the public media.[37] As a result, almost all public media in the PRC are state owned. While there have been significant changes in the 1990s, such as cuts in state subsidies and the rise of the Internet, the CCP's control of public media remains tight. As one of the Party's principal mouthpieces, CCTV has long been distrusted and denounced as offering sheer propaganda.[38] But its political and dominant role in televised media has rendered CCTV an overwhelming and unchallengeable power in China. So long as it was CCTV that released those reports, it and other state media would not tolerate any contradicting reports or questions. In the case of the Waitan Garden report, no one dared to question its factual errors. If there were no public media willing to speak for them, the dissatisfied and powerless Waitan Garden homeowners would have no other choice than rightful (lawful) and even natural (unlawful) resistance.

Law versus Power: First Contest

Relations between the Waitan Garden homeowners and the local government had been generally cordial as the latter had championed the Waitan Garden project and the homeowners loved their cozy homes. The harmony was ruined overnight by the surprisingly critical November 19, 2001, CCTV report. Worse, that report quickly pitted the local government against the Waitan Garden homeowners. Shortly after the local officials realized that it was impossible to preserve Waitan Garden, they had to turn against the homeowners. The homeowners were equally stunned and baffled by the CCTV report and did not want to surrender without a fight. They were determined to protect their homes. Therefore, a contest inevitably emerged with the local officials on the one side and the homeowners on the other. Local officials, presumably enforcers of the law, had abused their power through unlawful means, such as coercion, wiretapping, interception, harassment, and violence to force people to abandon their Waitan Garden homes. Meanwhile, the powerless homeowners had resorted to mostly legal methods, such as petitions and administrative litigation, in their attempt to preserve their homes. In that regard, the contest between the local Hubei and Wuhan officials and the Waitan Garden homeowners is more aptly described as a contest between law and power.

The first contest between law and power began on November 25, 2001, six days after the CCTV report. Yan Fengjun, the chief female organizer and homeowner activist, was on her way to buy a sofa for her new apartment when she got a phone call from a friend working in the Real Estate Department of the Hanyang District who told her that she had received a notice from higher-level government officials that Waitan Garden would be demolished. She also warned her not to buy any furniture for her apartment. Stunned by the astonishing news, Yan immediately ran down to the Waitan Garden sales office (*shoulouchu*) to ask the developer whether her friend's information was correct. Both the assistant to the general manager and one of the vice general managers confirmed the information.

While Yan was talking with the developer's managers, many dejected homeowners had received the news and thronged the sales office. Yan asked the others what they wanted to do if their homes were going to be razed. After discussion, the twenty-plus homeowners arrived at the conclusion that the destruction of Waitan Garden would be impossible. A talented organizer, Yan asked the developer to give her the names and contact information for all the homeowners so that she could convene a meeting. The developer would not agree to share the information. Yan had to ask the homeowners to write down their names and contact information and urged them to inform other residents to meet that afternoon in the lobby of the sales office.[39]

Around fifty homeowners came to the afternoon meeting. Hu Yan, both a homeowner and a lawyer, quickly became the center of the meeting. Homeowners prodded him to compose a joint appeal. His "The Voices of Homeowners" ("Yezhu husheng") became the first appeal. It argued that, although the homeowners were not specialists in flood control, it was an indisputable fact that the first-stage Waitan Garden projects had not blocked the big floods in both 1997 and 1998. In addition, if Waitan Garden was an illegal project, the homeowners remained lawful owners of their properties because they had all the required government permits. The "Voices" finally offered a bold challenge to the local government: "Here, we solemnly express our heartfelt wishes to the government (and those reporters of CCTV's *Focal Interview* who are pleading to demolish Waitan Garden in the name of the people) that 'We will live and die with Waitan Garden.'"[40]

All the homeowners at the meeting signed their names. The next day, Yan distributed "The Voices of Homeowners" to over one hundred people. On November 27, more than two hundred agitated homeowners swarmed the lobby of the sales office. Yan presided over this formal meeting. The homeowners unanimously agreed to print "The Voices of Homeowners" on a huge banner and let all homeowners sign their names. In addition, they wanted to print some slogans and hang them in the square in front of the sales office. Both measures were meant to show the determination of all the homeowners to defend their properties.[41]

In contrast to such other social groups as workers, students, farmers, and small businessmen, most Waitan Garden homeowners had higher education levels, better careers, and more power and connections. For example, Jin Baoqiang was an affluent and intelligent company manager. When Yan Fengjun gave him a name tag—name tags were distributed so that all homeowners involved would know each other—Jin immediately suggested that each homeowner pay 50 RMB for the name tags, the money to be used to finance future activities. All the homeowners supported Jin's suggestion, and Jin himself soon emerged as one of the leaders of the rights protection movement.[42]

Finding a place to print "The Voices of Homeowners" proved to be the first headache for the homeowners. Most local Hanyang print shops refused the job because of its antigovernment content. Yan finally approached a friend in Hankou, one of the three main districts in Wuhan, who agreed to print it. To most homeowners, the day of November 28 was scary unforgettable—the day they experienced their first direct confrontation with the local police. In the morning, when Yan brought the printed materials to the Waitan Garden sales office, she spotted some new faces among the homeowners already gathered there. After a while, more homeowners came to the site, and several women began opening the huge cloth (twenty-four square meters in size) on which "The Voices of Homeowners" was printed. While everyone was concentrated on unfurling the banner, one strange man suddenly told Yan that he was the owner of unit 8 and that he wanted to get some information from her. He then took her out to a white car and asked whether the homeowners had an organization. She said that there was no homeowners' committee, much less a formal organization. He continued to ask whether the homeowners had a leader. She replied that all the activists were volunteers and there was no leader. He warned her that the actions of the homeowners were improper because they seemed to oppose the government. She flatly rejected that charge and told him that they simply wanted to express their views.

Suddenly, Yan saw many police officers rush out of the sales office with the printed "The Voices of Homeowners" and other handbills. Many female homeowners chased after them. At that moment, Yan and the other homeowners found the square outside the sales office filled with more policemen. Yan got out of the car and confronted the policemen, trying to take back the materials. But another policeman came up and grabbed her arm. The policeman holding her then shouted to the others: "She is obstructing the public affairs [fang'ai gongwu] and [we will] take her away." Yan shook off the policeman's hands and angrily questioned his legal right to take her away. Some policemen had already entered their vehicles parked outside Waitan Garden. Seeing more homeowners coming after him, the policeman who had grabbed Yan jumped into his vehicle and fled.[43]

The policeman who threatened to arrest Yan and those who had seized the printed materials clearly believed they had acted lawfully. Anyone who opposed the government or stopped the police from taking action was, in their view, breaking the law. Nevertheless, Article 35 of the PRC Constitution guarantees the freedom of speech, the freedom of the press, the freedom of assembly, and freedom of demonstration. The homeowners' assembly in the sales office and their written protest were both legal under the constitution. The police had no right to remove the printed materials. Furthermore, the policeman's intimidation of Yan was a brazen violation of Article 37 of the PRC Constitution, which states: "Citizens may not be arrested except with the approval or by decision of a people's procuratorate or by decision of a people's court, and arrests must be made by a public security organ. Unlawful deprivation or restriction of citizens' freedom of person by detention or other means is prohibited; and unlawful search of the person of citizens is prohibited."[44]

The article clearly notes that the police must first have approval from the people's procuratorate before they can arrest any citizen of the PRC. If the policeman had arrested Yan, her constitutional rights would have been violated. Why did the policeman threaten to arrest her? Was it not his duty to safeguard the constitution? This case reveals a weakness in the relationship between law enforcement and the constitution that extends more broadly and problematically. He Weifang, a law professor at Peking (Beijing) University, argues not only that China's constitution has an intrinsic defect in that it is tainted by political ideology but also that it was not well implemented. And, for that reason, he asserts, somewhat sardonically, that Chinese constitutional law teachers are the group of people "who are most troubled by their conscience because they teach untruthful things to their students."[45] In the case of Waitan Garden, we see that one of the reasons for the impotency of the PRC constitution is that law enforcement officials completely ignore the law themselves.

Three hundred years ago, the Enlightenment philosopher Montesquieu (1689–1755) was already warning people about the adverse consequences of a union between legislative power and judiciary power. As he put it: "When the legislative and executive powers are united in the same person, or in the same body of magistrates, there can be no liberty. . . . Again, there is no liberty, if the judiciary power is not separated from the legislative and executive. Were it joined with the legislative, the life and liberty of the subject would be exposed to arbitrary control; for the judge would be then the legislator. Were it joined to the executive power, the judge might behave with violence and oppression."[46] Owing to the dire prospect of united legislative, judiciary, and executive powers, Montesquieu upheld a separation of powers among the three main branches of government. Although Montesquieu was not the first person to advocate such a separation of powers,[47] his theory was more detailed and convincing and thus laid a foundation for the US Constitution in 1787.[48]

Montesquieu warned that the merging of any two of the three main government powers would result in arbitrary power and no liberty for the people, but the CCP in fact firmly controls all three. In other words, the CCP is not only the administrator of the state but also the legislator and the enforcer of the law. This can explain why the police had no fear in seizing the materials belonging to the Waitan Garden homeowners and why they could disregard Yan's constitutional rights and threaten to arrest her. In comparison with the omnipotent power of the government, the laws (including the PRC Constitution) are too weak to be heeded and respected.

No sooner had the police vehicles departed with the printed materials than a bus arrived carrying delegates of the Hanyang People's Congress. While the homeowners did not know why the delegates were there, they hoped that they would be willing to listen to their complaints. But the police on the square forcibly separated the homeowners from the delegates. When some homeowners insisted on talking to the delegates, one policeman yelled: "You are resisting the government, and it is against the law!" Yan stood in front of the policeman and argued with him vehemently. Not wanting to get involved in the quarrel, the delegates stopped their short inspection tour and left.[49]

Clearly, this is another example of police abuse of power. It was inappropriate for the police, as enforcers of the law, to say that the homeowners' attempt to talk to the delegates was an example of resisting the government and thus breaking the law. According to the PRC constitution and the 1995 petition law, the homeowners have the right to complain to the people's delegates about their grievances. As the people's representatives, the delegates are supposed to hear grievances and address them. If the people's representatives do not listen to petitions, what then are their responsibilities? And why would people elect them?

In the PRC, almost all so-called people's delegates are not actually elected by the people, whether they are representing the NPC, one of the provincial people's congresses, or that of the Hanyang District. Even if there were an election, people would be able to vote for only those candidates whose names have been hand-picked by the leaders of their work units.[50] Many Western journalists and scholars have long identified the Chinese people's congress as having no teeth and rubber-stamping directives from higher-level leaders. Russell L. Moses, a Beijing-based scholar, told a *New York Times* reporter that Chinese leaders saw the people's congresses as "an enormously useful administrative arm of the state, not a location for loyal opposition."[51] In the words of William C. Jones: "[Chinese people's] congresses are in fact rubber stamps that do as they are told by whoever is in power at their level. The meetings of a congress are ceremonial occasions."[52] Although recent studies have shown some positive signs in both national and local congresses,[53] the people's congresses in general remain largely ornamental. That they are fundamentally ineffectual at the central and local levels can be attributed to the paradox of the Chinese constitution. On the one hand, the constitution claims that the NPC is the highest power organ in China, responsible for and supervised by the people; on the other hand, it specifies that the CCP is more powerful than the NPC.[54] The constitution fails to explain what would happen should the people's congresses take actions that are not in the Party's interests. The congresses, whose members are not elected by the people, have largely been obedient to the Party and dare not challenge it. Consequently, had the homeowners had the opportunity to complain to the delegates of the Hanyang congress, the delegates either would not have listened to them carefully or would not have the power to satisfy their grievances through challenging the local government.

The homeowner Ye Shousheng was a retired middle school teacher. He asked the local police to return the materials they had seized, pointing out that the homeowners had the right to present their views inside Waitan Garden. But he was told that the materials had been turned over to higher-level government officials and thus could not be returned.

Still, many homeowners refused to accept failure and debated their next move. Rather than cooperate with other homeowners, a few of them decided to act alone. For example, on November 28, the same day that the police assaulted the homeowners, one anonymous article entitled "Please Do Not Waste the Taxpayers' Money (400m RMB)" was secretly posted on the Internet. It remarked that the developer of Waitan Garden had all the legal permits and that the project had been in development since 1994. It also asked: "From 1994 to 2001, had the local government fulfilled its obligations? Had all levels of inspectors functioned properly? If the problem stemmed from local government approval, it was the local government that should bear the responsibility and not the homeowners and taxpayers." It went on: "If a project that has been approved by the local government cannot be protected, who else dares to come [to Wuhan] and invest?" Finally, it begged the public media, the NPC, and the State Council to dispatch specialists in water resources to seriously review the impact of Waitan Garden on flood control and take reasonable measures to resolve this issue.[55]

On the morning of November 29, an even larger number of homeowners again assembled in the sales office. After a heated discussion about the fate of Waitan Garden, most suggested a modification of "The Voices of Homeowners." The biggest change was a direct accusation that local officials were violating the law. The argument was that the planned demolition of Waitan Garden was nothing but an effort by some local officials to escape investigation by higher-ups. The new "Voices" then promised the local government that the homeowners would not engage in any unlawful activities, such as demonstrating in the streets or blocking traffic on the Yangzi River Bridge. All the homeowners wanted was for the government to pay attention to their claims regarding the legality of their properties at Waitan Garden. They argued that, because the local government had granted illegal permits and approval, it should correct its own mistakes. The new "Voices" continued: "The cost of demolishing Waitan Garden is tremendous. The compensation alone is said to be 200–300 million RMB, which is hard-earned taxpayer money, and it further demonstrates the abuse of power of the government. In addition to its disrespect of taxpayers, the government also violates the interests of other taxpayers. The government's decision [to demolish Waitan Garden] is using a bigger mistake to correct a smaller one."

Like the previous one, the new "Voices of Homeowners" tried to remind the government that Waitan Garden had survived two of the biggest Yangzi River floods in history. More important, the homeowners complained that, owing to the time and energy devoted to their properties, they had a great emotional investment in them. "Why does the government not listen to the voices of the homeowners?" they asked. "One of President Jiang Zemin's 'Three Represents' [sange daibiao] is to represent the interests of the people.[56] Are our legitimate interests inferior to the official posts [wushamao]?" The new "Voices" ended with the same slogan as the old one: "We will live and die with Waitan Garden."[57]

The new "Voices" was applauded as more rational than the first because it charged the government with violating the law and abusing its power. It also sought to look into government responsibilities. While the homeowners reiterated that they were prepared to "live and die" with Waitan Garden, they also allowed that they would use only legal means, or, in Kevin O'Brien's terms, "right resistance" and not "natural resistance" such as "unlawful" or "extreme" means.[58]

Learning from previous experience, this time the homeowners printed the new "Voices" not on a banner but on paper and mailed copies to the provincial and city governments. It is worth noting that the letters sent by aggrieved people to government officials are called *petition letters* (*shangfangxin*), a system that had been formally legalized by the CCP in the 1995 Regulations Regarding Letters and Visits (*xinfang tiaoli*).[59] This built on a tradition of comparable forms of petition existing in China for over two thousand years. The CCP inherited the petition system from previous polities and made some modifications. Claiming that it was the representative of the commoners, the CCP gave people a broad right to petition and, as in the ROC but not in the post-Sui (581–607) dynasties, there had been no punishment for people who lodged skipping-level petitions (*yueji shangfang*) until 1995.[60]

On December 1, probably knowing that the government would not back off from demolishing Waitan Garden, the homeowners sent another letter entitled "The Government Needs to Fully Reconsider the Issue of Waitan Garden Before Taking Action" ("Waitan huayuan wenti qingzhengfu sansier houxing") to the local government. In it, they raised for the first time the issue of compensation for their losses, including the price of their apartments, decorating costs, and emotional and other indirect losses. Moreover, the letter reminded the government that China had joined the WTO and that therefore it should act in compliance with the law. If the law was unsatisfactory, it should be amended immediately. Because people's interests should be above everything, the homeowners asked the government not to take any hasty action regarding Waitan Garden. The letter concluded with a stunning and courageous warning of a potential lawsuit: "[If the government takes any wrong actions,] China, a new WTO member, will witness its first internationally known administrative litigation of commoners suing officials [*mingaoguan*] in Wuhan. We believe that the law will provide us with a satisfactory result. It is because the twenty-first century is a rule-of-law society!"[61]

Unlike previous petition letters in which they swore to die with their beloved homes, the homeowners now began preparing for the worst-case scenario and thinking about compensation. But they wanted to convey a message that they would take legal action if their requests were not satisfied.

The litigation threatened by the homeowners was not unprecedented. The Administrative Litigation Law was passed by the NPC in 1989 and became effective in 1990. The goal of the law was to protect people's legal rights against official violations. Article 2 of the law clearly states that, if a citizen or an organization "considers that his or its lawful rights and interests have been infringed upon by specific administrative conduct of an administrative organ or its personnel, the citizen or the organization shall have the right to bring a lawsuit" to the administrative court. To prevent an administration from utilizing its power to meddle in the court adjudication, Article 3 states that the people's courts "shall, in accordance with the law, exercise judicial power independently with respect to administrative cases, and shall not be subject to interference by an administrative organ."[62] The Waitan Garden homeowners hoped that the Administrative Litigation Law would, as it claimed, be a useful and effective weapon allowing them to force the local government to refrain from taking any irrational or outrageous action.

LAW VERSUS POWER: SECOND CONTEST

While the homeowners were busy organizing and sending their petition letters, the local government—at both the provincial and the municipal levels—was also working hard to strategize the next step in driving the homeowners out of Waitan Garden and implementing the central government's orders.

For the homeowners, December 5 was another day on which their hopes of saving their homes were smashed. That day, the General Headquarters of the National Flood Control and Drought Resistance (Guojia fangxun kanghan zong-zhihuibu) cabled a circular about demolishing Waitan Garden to the Hubei provincial and Wuhan municipal governments. Unfortunately, and paradoxically, during the next three months of back-and-forth between the homeowners and the local government, none of the homeowners ever saw a word of this fateful circular.[63] As Han Junru, the reporter living in Waitan Garden, later observed, the fact that the circular never made it to the homeowners demonstrated that the official status of the homeowners was too low for them to be informed. The circular infuriated many homeowners, including Han. It was their homes that were to be destroyed by order of the circular, but they had no right to see it. "Because the government is both the property owner and the demolisher," Han said, "it only needs to know itself and disregard the fact that Waitan Garden is the private property of the homeowners."[64] The circular further reflected the die-hard habit of the CCP that favored arbitrary administrative orders rather than law in dealing with the Chinese people and their properties.[65]

The only official notice justifying the eventual demolition of Waitan Garden was, ironically, a collection of opinions entitled "The Implementing Opinions of the Relocation and Settlement of the 'Waitan Garden' Buyers" ("'Waitan huanyuan' goufanghu banqian anzhi shishi yijian"), which was issued by the Hanyang District government. Why issue "implementing opinions" instead of an administrative order? Indeed, the collection was evidently not a legal document, and the opinions could not be used to justify the removal of Waitan Garden homeowners. In hindsight, however, the move was a tactical masterpiece of the Hanyang District government and the Wuhan municipal government. The "opinions" were not an order and seemed negotiable. In that case, even though the homeowners disagreed with the opinions, they could not base a lawsuit on them because they did not constitute a formal administrative order. The local government could thus completely ignore any consequent legal action and continue to use force to evacuate.[66]

In addition to the ambiguous opinions, the local government also possessed the power to unflinchingly carry out any and all orders from their superiors (e.g.,

Premier Zhu Rongji), who themselves had the power to remove the local officials from their positions. According to Li Jun and Joseph Y. S. Cheng, Chinese "government officials cared more about currying favor with their superiors than serving ordinary people" because they were and are well aware that their careers depend on their superiors within the CCP.[67]

On December 9, the local government finally decided to take action and organized a work team (*gongzuozu*) of dozens of local officials to resolve the issue. In PRC history, sending work teams for specific purposes has been fairly common. In the early 1960s, the CCP Party Central Committee dispatched work teams to rural areas to guide the "Four Clean-Up" (*siqing*) movements whose missions were to encourage class struggle and attack "village cadres for corruption and backsliding."[68] In May 1966, at the beginning of the Great Proletariat Cultural Revolution, Liu Shaoqi (Liu Shao-ch'i), who was both Mao Zedong's lieutenant and the chairman of the PRC, sent work teams to some universities and middle schools in Beijing to quell the disturbances caused by radical students and teachers. But Mao's subsequent criticism of the work teams resulted in Liu's fall.[69]

At first, the work team sent by the Hanyang District sought a frank talk with the homeowners to address questions they might have. On the evening of December 9, many homeowners gathered in the sales office, their routine meeting place for the past week, to discuss how to protect their properties. The work team members stealthily entered the sales office and sat alongside the homeowners. Once the homeowners spotted them, the local officials attempted to maintain a cordial and attentive attitude. Most of the work team members came from a variety of Hanyang District departments, and the head of the work team was a district vice head.

The head of the work team told the homeowners that the team had received orders from the provincial and municipal governments to communicate with them. He noted that the team was ready to listen to whatever thoughts and suggestions they had but that they had to be realistic. He soon found himself being grilled. Some of the homeowners asked whether Waitan Garden would be demolished. He was quite evasive in answering, saying only that it was an "irresistible trend." When the homeowners pushed him for a more direct response, he replied that he was merely following the orders of his superiors. Other homeowners were more direct in their queries. They asked questions like: Why are there policemen in Waitan Garden? Who sent them in? And why is the local government responding to our concerns with force? A few older women even cried, telling the head how difficult it was to buy their apartments. Throughout the evening, the head made no mention of the circular. If such an emotional confrontation continued, the work team risked losing control of a meeting it originally expected to be friendly.

Suddenly, Han Junru stood up and said that there might be two reasons behind the demolition of Waitan Garden—it was required by comprehensive state planning, and the complex had an adverse impact on flood control. He continued, however, that the situation was not covered by state planning and that the construction had not yet been determined to be unlawful. Hence, he claimed, Waitan Garden was legal and should not be destroyed. He also reminded the head of the work team that Li Peng (the head of the NPC who was also responsible for the crackdown on the 1989 student demonstrations) had recently—on December 4, 2001, Constitutional Day (*xianfari*)—reaffirmed "administration in accordance with law" (*yifa xingzheng*).[70] The Waitan Garden situation also required the local government to work within the law. Otherwise, the homeowners would very likely use all available legal means to defend their rights. Administrative litigation was the ultimate licit ammunition the homeowners could use in their defense. Han Junru continued: "The administrative litigation of the Waitan Garden homeowners will be the largest 'commoners suing officials' lawsuit in the new century. The lawsuit may not be a bad thing and it would attain three goals: (1) safeguarding the authority of the law and avoiding legal mistakes; (2) . . . preventing administrative infringement of the law; (3) protecting the legitimate interests of the citizens and forestalling the spiritual and economic losses of the citizens."[71]

Under this pressure, the head of the work team promised the homeowners that he would consider their opinions.

The homeowner Xu Bikang had been a judge for eight years, and he was now working in the Political and Legal Commission (Zhengfawei) of the Hanyang District.[72] Therefore, Xu had access to more details about the government decisions than did most of the other homeowners. As early as November 23, four days after the CCTV criticism of Waitan Garden, Xu had known of the plans to remove and resettle the homeowners. The preferable official plan was to provide homeowners with apartments in other complexes that were comparable in size and market price to those in Waitan Garden. But monetary compensation had been ruled out. To indemnify the developer, the local government proposed reducing future developing and planning fees.

As a seasoned politician and judge, Xu told the homeowners that they should present a united front and not speak with representatives of the local government on their own. He suggested the immediate formation of the Waitan Garden Homeowners Committee (Waitan huayuan yezhu weiyuanhui) to negotiate with the local government. But some homeowners were wary of such an organization. Han Junru questioned the legitimacy of the committee. Even if it were established, it would still need to apply for a license from the government. "Will the government recognize it?" he asked. "If it will not be recognized by the government, that would be bad." Instead, he said, it might be a better option to simply elect several homeowner representatives who would hold talks with the government on behalf of the Waitan Garden community. This idea got the support of the homeowners, and Xu was invited to serve as the legal adviser to the representatives.[73]

Despite the initial intense confrontations between the homeowners and the work team, the mission of the latter was not hindered. Even before the work team arrived at Waitan Garden, its members had been divided into several small teams, each headed by a leader of a Hanyang District department or bureau. Each small team was responsible for one Waitan Garden unit, and the pressure was immense. According to Zhang Lijun, the project manager of the Waitan Garden developer, if the mission of any small team was not accomplished, its head would lose his post. Moreover, the work team members were instructed not to fight back if attacked.[74]

However, tension was mounting as more officials converged on Waitan Garden. To prevent the homeowners from using the sales office as a meeting space, the work team decided to close and seal it. This arbitrary action infuriated the homeowners, and they broke the seal. The work team also sent informers to the homeowner meetings to collect information. Yan Fengjun, who had been identified by the work team as the "No. 1" female target, described the informers as people with short hair (policemen typically wear their hair short). One of the informers followed her every day. When the suspicious Yan asked her pursuer in which unit and room she lived, she dodged the questions. The local police began monitoring the cell phones of key homeowners. For example, Yan could not figure out how the local police knew where she went until she found out that her cell phone had been monitored. In 2004, two years after the destruction of Waitan Garden, one of the antiriot policemen who had joined the work team in late 2001 told Yan that he knew her from the surveillance footage taken by cameras installed by the police. The police monitored her home, saw her smoke on her balcony every day, and could even tell the color of her clothes. Since her leadership caused the police and the work team many headaches, she was nicknamed "old witch" (*laowupo*).[75]

The homeowners also quickly discovered that the local government had blocked their petition letters to major public media in China and Hong Kong and that the photocopy stores in Wuhan were ordered not to print materials related to Waitan Garden. More annoying were the intrusive home visits by work team members. The officials of the work team, without legal documents or administrative orders in hand, knocked on all the homeowners' doors and asked them to move before a certain deadline. Some angry homeowners exchanged sharp words with them, and others simply refused to open their doors.[76]

As the local officials and police increased the pressure on the homeowners, the homeowner representatives met to debate possible responses. Xu Bikang worked out an outline for a potential dialogue with the work team that covered the following points:

1. We are the lawful homeowners of Waitan Garden, and we steadfastly oppose its demolition.
2. To protect the legal interests of all the homeowners, we have elected Yan Fengjun and other eight representatives to talk to the government.
3. We hope that the government will "administer in accordance with law" and that the homeowners will "protect their rights in compliance with law" [*yifa weiquan*]. . . .

4. The demolition of Waitan Garden will cost hundreds of millions RMB. There should be ample demonstration that Waitan Garden obstructs flood control. With the exception of demolition, is there any other remedy? If any part of the complex blocks flood control, the whole complex should be unconditionally destroyed. To consolidate the levee, all the homeowners are willing to donate 10,000 RMB.

5. If the government insists on demolition, it should fully protect the human and property rights of the homeowners. The right to know the truth [zhiqingquan] is a key component of human rights. We demand clear responses of the following questions:

   a) Who is ordering the demolition?
   b) On what law will the demolition be based?
   c) On what grounds does the government define Waitan Garden as illegal?
   d) Who made the mistake [of approving Waitan Garden]? Who will bear responsibility?

6. The property rights of all the homeowners should be guaranteed:

   a) Their apartments and decoration should be assessed in accordance with market value.
   b) The losses of the homeowners should be unconditionally reimbursed, including emotional loss, law-violation loss [weifa sunshi], moving fee, etc.
   c) The homeowners demand cash compensation. . . . If the two sides cannot resolve the dispute, it is recommended that both submit their grievances to the mediation department or the people's court.

In the end, Xu Bikang wrote: "Private properties are holy and cannot be violated." Being a judge for eight years and a homeowner himself, it is not surprising that he fully imbibed the notions of human and property rights that had been reintroduced from capitalist states after China initiated reforms in 1978.[77] Xu also understood that the best and, indeed, the sole weapon of the homeowners in the fight to protect their legal rights was the law. Yet he had more experience with China's problematic legal system than did the other homeowners. When a homeowner representative asked him, "If the government refuses to talk to the homeowners, should we sue the government in court?" he was extremely pessimistic about the prospect of such a lawsuit being pursued successfully. The biggest problem would be finding a good lawyer willing to take the case. Although there were eight lawyers among the homeowners, Xu did not believe that any of them dared to sue the government.[78]

Xu's fear was not groundless. Chinese lawyers tend to flock to lawsuits regarding civil, commercial, and criminal cases. But few take administrative litigation because most do not want to risk their careers and personal freedom by confronting officials in the court. In 1998, the *Southern Weekend* reported that a lawyer in Foshan, Guangdong, helped a worker accuse the Guangdong Committee for Collecting Donations (Guangdong mujuan weiyuanhui) of wrongfully denying that it had sold him a winning lottery ticket. Despite a warning from his firm that a local official had chastised him for pursuing the suit, the lawyer insisted on representing the worker. He was then fired by his firm and ultimately unable to find a job at any other law firm in the city. To make matters worse, he lost the suit two years later. The *Southern Weekend* quoted the head of a law firm as saying: "While Foshan has forty to fifty law firms and hundreds of lawyers, only Li Jinsong [the lawyer in question] dares to repeatedly accuse the local government."[79]

The lawyers of Waitan Garden had legitimate reasons to worry that their fate would be akin to that of the Foshan lawyer if they sued the government. "If no homeowner lawyer dared to accuse the government," Xu argued, "the homeowners could sue the government themselves because the case is not very complex."[80] Xu's words, experience, and courage greatly inspired other homeowners. Many of them determined to sue the government if their demands were not satisfied.

While Xu was working with the homeowner representatives on the outline for future dialogues, the officials of the work team were also busy. Still without any legal documents or administrative orders, they continued to knock homeowners' doors. When asked whether they had documents, they replied no. When asked whether they had legal justification, they cited the Flood Control Law but refused to produce a copy of it. Their job was to persuade the homeowners to relocate before the Spring Festival. If any homeowners were willing to move out before January 1, 2002, the incentive would be 3,000 RMB. When the homeowners threatened to sue the local government, the officials were not afraid and told them to go ahead, pointing out that their homes would still be demolished while their suit went forward. When the homeowners asked for monetary compensation, the officials said that the local government did not have much money and wished the homeowners to understand their difficulties. Whatever questions the homeowners asked, the work team stuck to the bottom line—Waitan Garden had to be demolished, and there would be no monetary reimbursement.[81]

In the evening of December 10, the homeowners assembled in the sales office again. This time, there was also a brave photographer who came to take pictures of the meeting. This was encouraging to the homeowners, who wanted to see photos of their meetings publicized by national newspapers so as to draw more outside attention and support. In the meeting, the representatives told the homeowners that they had no other option except "administration and rights protection in accordance with law," which meant that all the homeowners' activities had to be within the bounds of the law. Otherwise, their legitimate demands would become illicit. They might have to let their apartments be demolished, but that had to be done with a clear explanation. When the representatives talked about the administrative litigation, one lawyer mentioned the legal term *retroactive force* (*zhuisuli*). For example, the Flood Control Law became effective in early 1998, but the Waitan Garden project was first approved in 1995. Therefore, it could not be said to have violated the Flood Control Law. The lawyer's clarification of the legal term emboldened the homeowners to take their lawsuit to the government. When the representatives asked the lawyer whether he dared to take the case, he agreed, saying that safeguarding the justice of law and the legal rights of clients was his duty.[82]

Suddenly, news came that, when the photographer was leaving, the plainclothes police tried to stop him on the stairs and take his camera. The homeowners accompanying him clashed with the police and escorted him to another building. The police followed them but could not locate the apartment in which the photographer was hiding. One policeman called for reinforcements, and soon more than ten police vehicles came with scores of policemen. The doors to the building were not forced open, but the building was surrounded, and all exits and entrances were blocked. Even though the outside temperature in early December was freezing, the police stayed and guarded the building. Seeing that it was impossible for him to get out of the building, the photographer removed the film from his camera and put in a blank roll. He then randomly took pictures in the room. At about 2:00 or 3:00 A.M., Yan Fengjun opened her door and told the police that the photographer was inside the building but that the homeowners would not surrender him. Unless the police broke down the door of each apartment, the photographer would continue to stay where he was. One police officer claimed that they did not want to arrest the photographer and that all they wanted was the film in his camera. If he surrendered the film, they would immediately leave. Yan did not trust the word of the police. She required a pledge that they would leave after they had the film. After receiving confirmation, she let the police come into her apartment. The photographer pretended to reluctantly hand the police his camera. They then opened it, destroyed the fake film, and left as promised.[83]

Despite the uneasiness they caused, the work team's visits went on. On the morning of December 11, team members knocked on Han Junru's door. Unlike some other homeowners, Han opened the door and recognized the visitor, who was a head of the Hanyang District. The official took a short tour of the apartment and praised its beautiful decoration. Then he warned Han that individuals could not overcome the government. He thus suggested being flexible rather than stubborn in this case. "The demolition of Waitan Garden," he said, "is irreversible." Han responded that, if Waitan Garden had to be demolished, the demolition must be in compliance with the law. He also said that he wanted monetary compensation and not a comparable apartment. But the official told him that it was not possible because the government had made its decision and it could not be altered. Before he left, the official admonished Han as a friend that he should not be a leader of the homeowners. At this point, Han realized that the government had been monitoring his activities.[84]

But the official warning did not deter Han. He drafted a lengthy article on behalf of all the homeowners. Its title was "A Life-and-Ruin Memorandum of the Wuhan Waitan Garden" ("Wuhan waitan huayuan shenghui beiwanglu"). Because none of the local print shops dared to take the job, Han had to ask a friend to type up the article. Working throughout the night, the friend finished by dawn and made a number of printouts. One copy was delivered to Li Peng, the head of the NPC. The rest were mailed to major public media throughout the country.

The article began by describing the current situation of Waitan Garden, including the arrival of the official work team and the agitation and frustration that the homeowners were experiencing. It also pointed out that the work team had failed to show any evidence of the illegitimacy of Waitan Garden. It told tragic stories related to the demolition. For example, one woman suffered a heart attack in the midst of a discussion with the work team officials; some old people became so distressed that they wanted to die. One frustrated homeowner said: "Yesterday, [the advertisement said that] I will give you the Yangzi River; today, [the government] pushes me into the Yangzi River." The article reaffirmed that the homeowners were innocent and still did not know the reason behind this disaster. Their biggest affliction was not just the loss of their property but the tremendous emotional trauma. As a powerless homeowner, Han Junru attributed his suffering to the government and the work team:

> It has been seven years since the initiation of the Waitan Garden project. . . . The developer has the required "five permits," and the homeowners have "two certificates"[85] to stay lawfully. After the CCTV *Focal Interview* report, which lacks comprehensiveness and impartiality, . . . the lawful homes became "illegal." Within twenty days, the work team arrived, and the destruction will start on New Year's Day, and homeowners must leave before the Spring Festival. . . . Who should be blamed? Where is the fault? Where is the law? Is this a heavenly disaster or a human-caused calamity? . . . The government said in the past that [Waitan Garden] was legal and now says that it is illegal; the government in the past constructed Waitan Garden and now wants to send a work team empowered to demolish it.

As a final plea, the article said that Waitan Garden was in a critical moment between life and ruin. It hoped that the government would not act rashly, in order to protect the authority of the law, the image of the government, and the fundamental interests of the people.[86]

Like previous letters, this article also expressed the homeowners' feelings of betrayal by the government. After all, the government played two opposite roles in the case of Waitan Garden: legal advocate and law violator. But the dire situation faced by the homeowners was different from the situation faced by the government. The government did not lose anything because compensation, as the homeowners argued, would come from the taxpayers—including the homeowners themselves. But the emotional toll on the homeowners, the time and energy they had spent, and the attractive location they cherished could not be reimbursed. Despite holding all the cards, local officials adopted traditionally unconstitutional and arbitrary means, such as ordering the work team to harass homeowners and sending the police to seize lawful materials, seal off the sales office to prevent public meetings, seize film, threaten to arrest innocent homeowners, and monitor the phones and activities of the homeowner representatives.[87] If the local government had violated the Flood Control Law in 1998 (i.e., by approving the second stage of Waitan Garden construction in 1999), it again took illegal action in late 2001 to correct its earlier mistakes. In that regard, those in power—the local government and the law enforcement officials—had no respect for the law.

Government Intimidation Intensified

The officials of the work team had not expected such obstacles in persuading homeowners to relocate. The homeowners they tried visit either refused to open their doors or asked for legal documentation or "red-header documents" (*hongtou wenjian;* i.e. formal administrative orders). The work team usually responded that they would soon have the official documents. The homeowners would then tell them to come back when they had the documents. After many frustrating days, the work team shifted its tactics to a more illegal but more intimidating and effective way to deal with the homeowners. It now turned its attention to the family members and superiors of the homeowners. This new method caused immense psychological and physical pressure on the homeowners, and most of them were forced to surrender to the government, including some of the homeowners most active at the beginning. Of the initial four-hundred-plus homeowners, only about one hundred finally joined the collective administrative litigation against the local government.

The linchpin of the new method was the concept of *danwei*—working units. While some Chinese have seen increasing social mobility and less difficulty in changing careers since the 1978 reform, most of those in the cities at the turn of the twentieth century were still working in their individual *danwei*. In fact, the concept of *danwei,* which originated in the 1930s in Shanghai, involved much more than the working unit.[88] In the words of David Bray, *danwei* is a "generic term denoting the Chinese socialist workplace and the specific range of practices that it embodies." Bray further argues that *danwei* is the foundation of urban China, providing employment and material support for most city dwellers. It also "organizes, regulates, polices, trains, educates, and protects them." *Danwei* is so important that, if someone does not have a *danwei*, he or she is considered to be "suspicious or even dangerous."[89]

As indicated earlier, most Waitan Garden homeowners had decent occupations and belonged to the middle or the upper middle class. When the work team found that its direct approach was not productive, it chose an indirect one. It began motivating the homeowners' superiors to exert additional pressure. As one of the homeowners said in an interview, every homeowner had a *danwei,* and every *danwei* had leaders. Those *danwei* leaders were in charge of the political and occupational future of the homeowners. The local government pressed the leaders of each *danwei,* and, in turn, those leaders pressured the homeowners to abandon their homes.

As the primary target of the work team, Yan Fengjun was the first to face direct pressure from the leadership of her hospital. In China, all public hospitals are under the control of the city or district health bureaus (*weishengju*). Yan—who worked at a hospital in the Qiaokou District, north of Hanyang District—noted that leaders of the Land Planning Bureau (Tudi guihuaju) and the Police Bureau, including the vice head of the Qiaokou District, visited the health bureau of the Qiaokou District urging the bureau and the hospital to dissuade her from making trouble (*naoshi*). They also told the head of the health bureau that her leadership among homeowners had resulted in extremely harmful consequences. They urged him to consider the political seriousness of the case. They claimed that, if Yan was allowed to agitate, the social stability prioritized by the CCP would be in danger.

On hearing the news that Yan was the crucial Waitan Garden organizer, the head of the district health bureau was astonished. He could not believe that the seemingly quiet and gentle female doctor was making trouble. The health bureau quickly ordered the leaders of Yan's hospital to have a conversation with her. The talk was held at a lunch in the hospital, and Yan was asked to step down as an organizer. However, she remained undeterred. She was persuasive in defending her actions to protect her property—so much so that her arguments could not be refuted.[90] Another homeowner who happened to be present during the talk later said that Yan looked composed but that the hospital leaders had grave expressions.[91]

In addition to pressuring Yan through her employer, the work team even went to Hubei University and asked Yan's daughter, who was a sophomore there, to persuade her mother to stop.[92] Yet this method would also prove unsuccessful. If the hospital leaders could not dissuade Yan from continuing to lead the homeowners, it was even less likely that her own daughter could do so.

Another homeowner representative who was a writer had an experience similar to Yan's. After receiving countless calls from the heads of the Wuhan Federation of Literary and Art Circles (Wuhanshi wenxue yishu lianhehui), a government-controlled organization, he found that it was impossible to avoid a confrontation with his superiors. As soon as he arrived at his *danwei,* the Party vice secretary came to meet him and told him that four officials of the Wuhan municipal government had contacted both him and the Party secretary. The writer asked who the four city officials were, but the secretary refused to tell him. The secretary asked the writer if he had taken the lead in the Waitan Garden homeowner organization. The writer replied that he did not know what the meaning of *lead* was. The secretary implied that it meant that the writer had talked at the homeowner meetings. The writer responded that there were many homeowners who had talked at the meetings and not just him. Seeing that the writer was not forthcoming about his "improper" deeds, the secretary went on to remind him that he had talked twice and had received applause each time. The writer was surprised that the secretary knew such details, but he still quibbled that it might have been because his talks were more rational and well organized. At that moment, the secretary and the writer had some tacitly mutual understanding, and they smiled at each other. The secretary then turned solemn and kindly warned the writer: "The Party organization hopes that you will not take the lead due to your reputation. Your name has been recorded in the city [Wuhan]. You should realize that your appearance in public would have a huge impact [on the homeowners]."

Undoubtedly, the writer was fully aware of the good intentions of the secretary. Yet, as a homeowner who was facing the grave threat of losing his treasured apartment, he did not want to heed the gentle admonition. Before letting the writer leave, the secretary demanded a promise as the four city officials were waiting for the results of the conversation. Knowing that he could not leave without a verbal oath, the writer told the secretary that he would not be the leader of the homeowners. With the pledge from the writer, the secretary seemed satisfied. Suddenly, he said that one of the city officials had told him that the homeowners planned to sue the local government in court. The writer retorted that a lawsuit was the right of every citizen in China and that he could not stop the homeowners from lodging their suit. "If you cannot stop it, you can refuse to sign your name [in support of it]," the secretary noted, stepping up the pressure. "Moreover, the owner of your apartment is your wife and not you." Given the pressure from the head of his *danwei*, the writer chose silence, which was commonly interpreted as assent.[93] The writer did not keep his verbal promise as he continued to fight for his own property and the properties of the other homeowners. He not only signed his name on the lawsuit but also became one of the homeowner representatives.

Yan and the writer were just two of the homeowners whose superiors attempted to intimidate them. Many other homeowners also had similar experiences but refused to move out. To force more homeowners to leave Waitan Garden, the work team intensified and expanded its intimidation. The local government created the Headquarters for the Relocation and Settlement of Waitan Garden (Waitan huayuan banqian anzhi zhihuibu) and appointed a vice mayor of the Wuhan municipal government to be the head. Other members of the headquarters included department heads in the Hanyang District. With the vice mayor of Wuhan in charge, the work team was able to greatly increase its power and pressure. Aside from asking their superiors to impose more pressure on the homeowners, the work team probed into potential weaknesses of some homeowners and used these to intimidate them. For example, according to one female homeowner, the work team had been investigating her business's track record and told her that she should think about what would make her wealthy. "It is the Party's good policy that makes you rich," she was told. "Now the Party wants you to move out, but you will forget the pain after the wound is healed [*haole chuangba wangletong*]. Do you still have any conscience?"

The work team threatened another homeowner who, like Xu Bikang, was a government official. The team members pointedly asked how he was able to buy such an expensive apartment given his moderate government salary. When he replied that he had a mortgage of more than 100,000 RMB, they asked, "Where did you find the down payment on 100,000 RMB? Have you not eaten or drunk anything in these years?" One homeowner had used his daughter's name to register. The work team wanted to know why he had not registered in his own name, insinuating that he was holding the property illegally as unidentified excess income. They then attempted to bribe him by saying that, if he agreed to move out, the government would stop the investigation. To the work team's surprise, the homeowner was not deterred. He said to go ahead and investigate further because he had legally bought the property for his daughter. Homeowners who were businessmen were asked, "In your many years of doing business, have you ever evaded payment of taxes?" Those who were silent in the face of the question were offered forgiveness if they promised to move out. Those who continued to challenge the government order found tax bureau officers dispatched to their businesses to investigate any potential tax evasion. "Once any tax fraud has been located," the work team threatened, "the government will not be lenient [in dealing with the case]." It asked one homeowner who had several real estate holdings in Wuhan: "We have heard that you have several properties; do you know anything about the 'unidentified possession of property in excess of legitimate income' [*ju'e caichan laiyuan buqing*]?"[94]

Not only were such questions undisguised threats, but they also violated the constitution and citizens' personal freedom. If the homeowners were involved in any illicit activities such as taking bribes, evading taxes, or stealing public funds, it should be law enforcement officers, and not the work team, conducting the investigation and meting out proper punishment in accordance with the law. If the homeowners who had violated the laws agreed to move out of Waitan Garden, the work team still had no power to absolve them of their crimes. Otherwise, the work team would either abuse its power by substituting as law enforcement or violate the law itself. However, what seems unthinkable in a country with a relatively sophisticated democracy and rule of law, is quite normal in China. As we have argued before, there is no separation of powers in the PRC, and thus all the main political entities such as executive administration (the government), the judiciary, and the legislature (the people's congress) have been under the firm control of the CCP. Because the work team was led by a vice mayor of Wuhan, it could mobilize the police—the primary tool of the government—to seize leaflets from the homeowners, threaten to arrest them, and forcibly separate the homeowners from the people's delegates. It is also not difficult to understand why the work team felt justified in exceeding its power by offering pardons to homeowners who confessed crimes so long as they agreed to leave Waitan Garden. If the law enforcers violate the law, who can stop them?

The overall treatment that most Waitan Garden homeowners received from the all-powerful work team was lenient and less drastic when compared with that faced by other social groups with less power and privilege. Most of the homeowners in Waitan Garden were educated people of the middle and upper middle classes. Some of them were famous lawyers, doctors, businessmen, professors, and writers. A few of them were government officials. Those homeowners had powerful social connections, and some of their petition letters reached the hands of influential government officials. Because of this, the work team had to proceed cautiously. Government policies and actions toward people belonging to the lower social classes would have been harsher and more inhumane.

During an interview, the head of a Wuhan demolition company (*chaiqian gongsi*) said that the company was in fact a quasi-official organ as his duty was to coordinate with the local government and the police. After the demolitions that it ordered in the 1990s had triggered a dramatic increase in skipping-level petitions (*yueji shangfang*),[95] the government has learned to use private companies to deal with such issues. Once land has been sold to a developer, that developer is then responsible for paying the demolition company to do the dirty work of forcible demolition. If any person is dissatisfied with the compensation and incentives offered by the company and refuses to move, the demolition company will first adopt severely coercive and harassing methods such as cutting off the water supply and electricity, sending people to knock on the homeowner's door daily, ignite thunderous fireworks at 2:00 A.M., etc. If all those measures are still not successful, the company will send workers and bulldozers to forcibly destroy the home in question.[96] In angry response, the aggrieved person will most likely petition the local government or even sue the company in court. But, with a tacit agreement between the local government and the demolition company, no government, court, or police entity will accept such a petition or lawsuit. The local media are also warned beforehand not to report any petition cases. If the person insists on taking natural resistance methods such as lodging "illegal" skipping-level petitions to the provincial and even the central government in Beijing, both the provincial and the central government will simply pass the petitions back down to the local Wuhan government. Worse, the agents or local thugs hired by the company will "retrieve" the petitioner and send him back to Wuhan after beating him.[97]

However, the strengths of Waitan Garden homeowners had the potential to also become their weaknesses. As Mao argued in the 1930s, the middle class has innate reasons for refraining from joining the revolution. The relatively affluent conditions and high social status of most Waitan Garden homeowners made them less likely to continue their fight. Unlike lower-class people, the homeowners had more to lose if they persisted in resisting the powerful and unlawful government. One female homeowner, after being repeatedly harassed and intimidated by the local police and the work team, hopelessly lamented to her husband, an activist of the homeowner organization: "Let them [the government] demolish and blow up our home. Let's move out. We should not continue to resist because we can never win. . . . Our living is not too bad. We at least have an apartment to live in, and we are much better off than many impoverished workers and farmers."[98]

This opinion was representative of most homeowners in Waitan Garden. One by one, those with the most to lose decided to move out and gave up resisting the government. Some of the homeowners did not want to surrender without a decisive fight. They still had some faith, however dubious, in the law and the judiciary.

2

Waitan Garden

Law, Law Enforcement, and Lawyers

The "Implementing Opinions" and the Open Letter

For more than two weeks, the local government in Wuhan had not shown any legal documents to justify their attempts to relocate the homeowners. On December 14, 2001, the full contents of the official document were finally made public, as demanded by the homeowners and promised by the work team. From that date on, until the demolition of Waitan Garden, the "Implementing Opinions of the Relocation and Settlement of the Waitan Garden Buyers" was the only "red-header" (i.e. official) document to justify demolition. As mentioned earlier, the document was neither a formal administrative order, nor a court ruling, but simply a list of opinions.

The "Implementing Opinions" was issued by the Hanyang District government. At the very beginning, it noted that the aim was to relocate the Waitan Garden homeowners in light of the PRC Flood Control Law and the gist of the circular from the General Headquarters for National Flood Control and Drought Resistance. It promised to safeguard the economic interests of the buyers. The principle used in the relocation of the homeowners was equal value (*dengzhi*), which meant that the compensation would be equivalent in value to the purchase price of the original property. The "Implementing Opinions" suggested that buyers be relocated to other, comparable residential projects, such as the Oriental Waltz (Dongfang huaerzi), Parrot Garden (Yingwu huayuan), and some others throughout Wuhan. If any buyer had a mortgage from a bank, the bank would sign a new mortgage contract after the buyer chose a new apartment. Most homeowners were concerned about whether their decorating expenses would be reimbursed. Addressing that concern, the "Implementing Opinions" allowed for compensation to be paid in cash after specialists had evaluated the cost. Buyers who settled in a residence provided by the Hanyang District government or in a newly constructed residential complex within the levee would be rewarded with a 10 percent discount on the market value. During the period between moving out of Waitan Garden and moving into a new residence, the government would provide a temporary settlement subsidy. It also vowed to take care of the school transfers of the homeowners' children. The moving fee and temporary settlement subsidy would be determined in accordance with the standards set by the Wuhan Price Bureau (Wuhan wujiaju).[1]

Xu Bikang, the former judge, discussed with his fellow homeowners how furious he was when he saw the "Implementing Opinions": "I told the work team member who gave the document to me: 'You are all my acquaintances [in government]. If you were strangers, I would grab your collar and kick you out [of my home].'"[2] In contrast to the other homeowners, Xu was in a peculiarly awkward situation. As a Party member and a current government official in the Political and Legal Commission, he was expected to take the lead when it came to abiding by the "Implementing Opinions." But, as a homeowner who loved his Waitan Garden apartment, he did not want to move.

The homeowner representatives held a meeting to discuss how to respond to the "Implementing Opinions." They decided to draft an open letter (gongkaixin) criticizing it. The letter, completed on December 15, was a masterpiece, pinpointing the many unlawful and improper policies in the "Implementing Opinions." To begin with, it noted sarcastically: "[The] Hanyang District government bashfully issued the '[Implementing] Opinions' on December 14." All the homeowners were appalled by the government's action of "using power to replace law [yiquan daifa]." "[The] '[Implementing] Opinions' neither understands nor follows the law, and it is neither reasonable nor sympathetic as well as neither sensible nor modest."

The letter denounced the use of the term buyers (goufanghu) in the "Implementing Opinions" as a way to deny the legitimacy of the homeowners. It argued that only the developer could call the homeowners buyers. "The homeowners did not buy their properties from the government; how could they become the buyers of the government?" it asked. Another problem with the "Implementing Opinions" was that it claimed to have followed the Flood Control Law. But the letter questioned that assertion: "Who has the power to follow the Flood Control Law? With which articles has the '[Implementing] Opinions' complied?" The letter answered its own question: "None; there are no such articles." Furthermore, it cast doubt on the legality of the Hanyang District government's demolition order: "First, it [the Hanyang District government] had no right in the past to approve the project and land planning of Waitan Garden; second, it has no legal 'demolition order'; third, it fails to say that Waitan Garden is an illegal construction project. If [Waitan Garden] is not against the law, it should be considered to be legal; if it is legal, the demolition will be a blunder, and all the homeowners can ignore the ['Implementing Opinions']."

The letter also questioned the district government's promise of "not affecting the economic interests" of the homeowners and accused it of being a trap.

The "Implementing Opinions" said that the compensation of the homeowners would be calculated on the basis of their apartments' original purchase prices. But, according to the law, the homeowners were the property owners after they had bought their apartments. The government had no right to forcibly purchase homeowners' properties offering only their original purchase prices: "[The] correct way is . . . that compensation for the properties in Waitan Garden should be determined in accordance with an evaluation of the current market price, location, environment, and grade." Indisputably, the letter's arguments were reasonable, for Waitan Garden was several years old, and the market prices of its units would have risen since construction. It would certainly be inappropriate for the government to use original purchase prices when determining compensation.

Another "trap" of the "Implementing Opinions" was the 10 percent discount on the new properties to be bought by the Waitan Garden homeowners. The 10 percent figure was based on the market price. The reality was that other residential complexes in Wuhan had recently sharply raised their prices. For example, one, with a price of 2,600 RMB per square meter in November, had just raised its price to 3,000 RMB per square meter. Even with a 10 percent discount, the homeowners would still be paying 2,700 RMB per square meter. In that regard, the Waitan Garden homeowners would have to absorb a loss of more than 100 RMB per square meter when purchasing their new homes. Meanwhile, the letter noted that the "Implementing Opinions" failed to take into account the fact that the market value of Waitan Garden properties had also increased in the past several years.

Owing to its many unlawful and problematic points, the open letter finally flatly rejected the "Implementing Opinions" as a useless piece of "blank paper" and indicated that all the homeowners would ignore it. Waitan Garden would remain a legal construction project. Until the Supreme Court decided that it was illegal, "no one has the right to issue a demolition order." The letter warned: "Whoever issues such an order will violate the law and whoever demolishes [Waitan Garden] will have to bear the historical responsibility."[3]

The open letter was filled with professional legal points, and it was clear that Xu Bikang was the chief drafter. As Xu had noted before, he opposed any forms of violence and wanted the homeowners to defend their rights within the limits of the law. "If Waitan Garden must be demolished," he told another homeowner representative, "the destruction has to conform to the law."[4]

When the open letter was completed, the homeowner representatives mailed copies of it to seven major newspapers in Shanghai, Beijing, and Shenzhen. None of those cities were located in Hubei Province because, as the homeowners well knew, the public media there would not risk publishing the letter. To prevent the government from tracking them, the homeowners used fake names. Obviously, they wished that one courageous newspaper would publish their letter and that it would draw more favorable attention to Waitan Garden. Besides the public media, some homeowners took advantage of their extensive social connections by sending a short version of the letter to the secretaries of such CCP leaders as Jiang Zemin and Li Peng. The secretaries all pledged to forward the letters to the leaders. While many other ordinary Chinese petitioners would envy such social connections, the results might not be very different. As shown in other studies, even direct interventions by top leaders do not necessarily mean the redress of grievances.[5]

On the night of December 15, the homeowners again gathered for a meeting. Someone soon spotted the head of the Hanyang District government, who had somehow sneaked into the meeting. The homeowners immediately surrounded him, directing their complaints at him. But he tried to evade their questions. When pressed as to the fate of Waitan Garden, he admitted that he also did not want to see it demolished. "Waitan Garden is in Hanyang; do we [the Hanyang District government] want to destroy it?" He continued: "As you know, the provincial and the Wuhan governments also do not want to demolish it. But the order came from the General Headquarter for National Flood Control and Drought Resistance on December 5, so we have to obey, have to enforce [the order]." At that moment, one homeowner interrupted and questioned the legal grounds of the demolition. Instead of providing a direct answer, the head told the homeowners that he understood their sentiment and the time and energy they had spent on beautifying their homes. But he again confirmed that he had no other choice.

The head's talk triggered more sharp queries from the homeowners. Many of them were about the importance of Waitan Garden and their compensation. One homeowner was so disgruntled at the police presence in Waitan Garden every day that he asked the head to discontinue it. When the head replied that the police were there to protect the safety of the residents, another homeowner demanded that he explain the stalking and monitoring of her and Yan Fengjun. "Are [those policemen] protecting the safety of me and doctor Yan?" she asked mockingly. That was a question the head was not able to answer. One homeowner handed him a copy of the open letter. Before he could finish reading it, a policeman came to escort him out of the meeting.[6] Because of the embarrassing experience, no local head was willing to come and talk to the homeowners after that.

The courage and patience of the district head in holding a dialogue with the angry homeowners should be applauded. While he could not provide good news to the homeowners or answer any of their questions, he had at least tried to listen to their concerns and voice his sympathy. In addition, the relatively high social, economic, and political status of most Waitan Garden homeowners might be another reason behind this face-to-face meeting. If the homeowners had been ordinary workers, farmers, or rural transients who "were denied basic civil and even human rights,"[7] he might not have come in person to talk to them. In one confrontation that took place on April 13, 2010, hundreds of people in Zhuanhe City, Liaoning Province, kowtowed in front of the city government offices, hoping that the mayor would tackle village corruption. But he refused to meet them.[8]

Moreover, the district head's personal visit might also have been meant to head off public, radical action on the part of the homeowners that could have undermined political stability, the top priority of the CCP in the reformed era. Unlike Mao Zedong, who proclaimed "the right to rebel" during the Cultural Revolution,[9] the CCP leaders after him tended to be wary of any social upheaval. Mao's successor, Deng Xiaoping (Deng Hsiao-ping), addressed the issue in early 1989, right before the Tiananmen demonstrations, proclaiming the importance of political stability above all else. "In China, the overriding concern is stability," he said. "Without a stable environment, [the CCP] cannot accomplish anything and may even lose what has been gained."[10] The district head was probably worried that, if he did not meet the homeowners, they might resort to active protests or collective petitions to the local government. If the social and political stability were impaired, his superiors would very likely blame him for not resolving the issue and thus demote him in rank.

"The Lawyers' Ten Points"

As the local government stepped up the pressure, the Waitan Garden homeowners were also hurriedly preparing a countermeasure, an administrative litigation. Xu Bikang was again the driving force behind it because the head of the Hanyang District government had demanded local officials living in Waitan Garden to relocate first. To extend the moving time and protect his own property, Xu drafted another important document, this one entitled "The Lawyers' Opinions" ("Lüshi yijianshu"), whose main target was still, as with the open letter, the "Implementing Opinions." In the prelude, Xu wrote that the "Implementing Opinions" had intensified the confrontation between the local government and the homeowners. The local government asserted that the demolition was in compliance with the Flood Control Law. Yet the homeowners countered that the Flood Control Law came into effect only in 1998, whereas the Waitan Garden project was approved by the Wuhan municipal government in 1994. The homeowners were all legal residents of Waitan Garden, and therefore the demolition was illegal.

Xu also repeated a key point in the open letter—that the government actions "seriously violated the legitimate rights and economic interests of the homeowners." He further accused the government of violating the law: "The government administration [zhengfu xingzheng] is unlawful, and its legal grounds for demolition are inadequate, which is a typical reflection of using power to replace law. . . . The homeowners unanimously agree that, before the Supreme Court issues any statement that Waitan Garden is 'illicit,' the government has no right to demolish."

Xu declared that the homeowners would take two interrelated steps concurrently. On the one hand, they would ask the government to act in accordance with the law; on the other hand, they would "defend their rights through the law" and prepare to sue the government. "Once the lawsuit is to be accepted," Xu wrote with almost impractical optimism, "it will be the largest lawsuit of 'commoners suing officials' in the history of the PRC." Here, he went further than Han Junru, who had said only that the potential litigation would be the biggest in China in the new century.

Even though he had been a judge for eight years, Xu had no grounds to be optimistic about the upcoming administrative litigation. Had he checked the historical records of administrative litigation since 1990, he would not have been so sanguine. According to court records from 1990 to 2003, the success rate of first-time administrative lawsuits varied between 11 and 21 percent, which is phenomenally lower than that in the Republic of China (1912–1949).[11]

"The Lawyers' Opinions" was later summarized, reduced to only ten points that were to become the guidelines that the homeowners followed when negotiating with the work team:

1. The "[Implementing] Opinions" can be ignored as they are just opinions and not laws or administrative orders.
2. We are lawful homeowners and not buyers. The government . . . wants to evade its legal and economic duties.
3. Why relocate? By what order should the homeowners relocate? The "[Implementing] Opinions" deliberately deprives the homeowners of their right to know the truth.
4. Who is going to be responsible for the demolition? The "[Implementing] Opinions" sidesteps the question. . . . The person who makes mistakes should be responsible.
5. The "[Implementing] Opinions" claims to guarantee the economic interests of the homeowners. It is really a trap. . . . The homeowners will suffer big losses.
6. If the Supreme Court finds that Waitan Garden is illicit, the relocation must follow the principles of the market economy. Both parties will designate qualified real estate assessors to evaluate the prices of both properties and decorations in Waitan Garden.
7. The [government] must provide either cash or completed apartments for the relocation.
8. The party who is responsible for the relocation must be liable for compensation.
9. The homeowners must not trust the promises of the Hanyang District government because its total annual budget is not sufficient to cover the compensation.
10. If the two parties cannot reach a consensus on the points listed above, the homeowners suggest that the government file lawsuits against them and let the people's court resolve the disputes.[12]

Most of the points were similar to those made in the open letter. But the last point was creative and brilliant. The homeowners encouraged the government to sue them if the two sides could not reach an agreement. They knew that the government would not fall into their trap and take them to court because they understood that they lacked a legal basis to do so. The "Implementing Opinions" was based on neither laws nor administrative orders, and it certainly could not be used to charge the homeowners. If the government could not sue them, the homeowners could ignore the "Implementing Opinions" and stay in Waitan Garden.

However, "The Lawyers' Ten Points" put the district government in an awkward position. If, like many other workers and farmers, the homeowners simply demonstrated and petitioned, the Hanyang District government would still be able to deal with them. Yet, if they turned to the law and the courts, it would not. On learning the contents of "The Lawyers' Ten Points," the head of the work team was reportedly furious and dispatched local police to track down the author. As a matter of fact, the district government had already notified all the lawyers in the district (including those living in Waitan Garden) not to help the homeowners. "Whoever helps [the homeowners] will be punished," the government warned. "Whoever dares to take the Waitan Garden case will think about the fate of his or her law firm." One lawyer in Waitan Garden revealed that the heads of the Wuhan Justice Bureau (Sifajü)[13] had a special meeting with her during which she was told that the city leaders had said that, if any homeowner lawyer (*yezhu lüshi*) in Wuhan sued the government, the heads of the justice bureau would be fired.[14]

However, despite all the terrifying threats, someone who was familiar with the law was still able to draft "The Lawyers' Ten Points," and the work team was unable to identify the author. According to a lawyer in Waitan Garden, after the vice mayor in charge of Wuhan demolitions heard about the "Ten Points" and other materials, he severely reprimanded the work team: "Are the more than one hundred officials [in the work team] all morons? Who has drafted those materials? Why have you not located the authors?" When a policeman on the work team replied that a lawyer might have written the materials, the vice mayor ordered that the lawyer be detained. Another policeman interrupted, saying that the author might have been a writer. The vice mayor then told him to arrest the writer.[15]

Had these internal workings not been exposed, no one would have believed that the threats to close the law firm and detain any lawyer or writer came from the head of the justice bureau and a top city official. Those threats were absolutely incompatible with President Jiang's oath to construct the rule of law in 1997 and Li Peng's call for administration to be in accordance with law. Since Deng Xiaoping addressed the need to firmly "grasp democracy and the legal system" in 1979,[16] the CCP has taken solid steps to create hundreds of new laws and in 1986 launched a movement to enhance people's legal consciousness.[17] The pace of legal reform escalated in the 1990s as more laws and regulations had been enacted by the people's congresses. The legal reform culminated in 1999 when the construction of the rule of law was added to the PRC constitution.

After more than two decades of reforming the legal system, however, many, if not most, PRC officials had yet to embrace the rule of law. Unfortunately, what their threats regarding Waitan Garden lawyers demonstrated was that the local officials in Wuhan continued to act as if they were above the law, a bad tradition dating back to the Cultural Revolution (1966–1976) when the "authorities of the constitution and law were almost vanished, and . . . the constitution and law were willful trampled."[18] The inferior position of the court and lawyers to the administration helped lay the foundations of an almost unbridled administrative power.[19] That is the main reason behind the official intimidation. As some of the homeowners later recalled, when they heard that the vice mayor ordered the detention of the authors of those materials, all they could do was bitterly smile.[20] Indeed, in the face of the almighty government, the homeowners possessed few means, if, indeed, any, to check government power and defend their legal and political rights.

To be sure, the threats of the city leaders also mirrored their fear of the law, which could be interpreted as one of the accomplishments of legal reform. Such fear might have been inconceivable in most of PRC history before 1989. Despite the essential ineffectiveness of the Administrative Litigation Law, it has generated fear among CCP officials. Without administrative litigation, the situation of the Waitan Garden lawyers could have been much worse.

Although "The Lawyers' Ten Points" was just some suggestions, it had vigorously boosted the spirits of most homeowners and given them an impression that the lawyers in Waitan Garden had initiated the litigation process.

Law versus Power: Continued Fights

The brief happiness of the homeowners brought on by "The Lawyers' Ten Points" was shattered on December 18, 2001, when the sales office that they had used for their meetings was forcibly taken over by the local police, who transformed it into the site office of the Headquarters for the Relocation and Settlement of Waitan Garden (Waitan huayuan banqian anzhi zhihuibu xianchang bangongshi). It was evident that the government could no longer tolerate homeowners meetings. The homeowners were outraged but chose to remain silent. They knew that it was useless to argue with the police.

Some homeowners placed their hopes on reporters from Beijing and Hong Kong who had visited Waitan Garden that morning, including representatives of the Beijing-based *Sanlian Life Week* (*Sanlian shenghuo zhoukan*) and the Hong Kong–based *Ta kung pao*. Yet only *Sanlian Life Week* eventually published an article on Waitan Garden. While *Ta kung pao* is based in Hong Kong, it was established by the PRC and thus does not have the courage to criticize the PRC.

To protest the closing of the sales office, Zhang Lijun, the brave project manager, wrote the work team a letter entitled "A Letter of Sympathy to the Waitan Garden Demolition Work Team" ("Zhiwaitan huayuan chaiqian gongzuozu de weiwenxin"). In it, Zhang mocked the officials on the work team for "defying the cold winter and visiting each homeowner with all their strength." He expressed deepest regrets to them because they "have been compelled to do [such work]." Many homeowners had said that "the officials on the work team are also humans and they have no other options."

Zhang then repeated the arguments made in earlier materials, such as that Waitan Garden had obtained numerous permits, approvals, and evaluations from the government and specialists after it was approved in 1994 and that it had endured the tests of the disastrous 1998 and 1999 Yangzi River floods. The cost of the demolition of Waitan Garden, including compensation, would total around 400 million RMB. The huge amount was nothing but the hard-earned money of taxpayers. Zhang questioned the legality, rationality, and reasonableness of the demolition order. Furthermore, he emphasized the importance of law after China's entry into the WTO and the CCP's stress on "administration in accordance with law." While he blamed the work team for using administrative rather than legal means to deal with the homeowners, he attributed its lack of legal consciousness to the tradition of the planned economy (*jihua jingji*) in the Mao era, during which the law was disdained as either a tool of the state or something belonging to capitalism.[21] After scoffing at the unlawfulness of the work team, he promised that the homeowners would like to work with its members to make the case for Waitan Garden as a vivid and impressive lesson in legal education.

In conclusion, however, Zhang expressed his deep disappointment with the unexpected closing of the sales office. This is how he interpreted it: "[The work team] locked the masters [homeowners] outside and took the sales office. Because the work team is afraid of the homeowners, it has committed mistakes one after another. Is the work team's [action to shut down the sales office] too weak? [The work team] must know that [the sales office] is the property and home of the homeowners! You [the work team] are too ignorant of the law and too arrogant."[22] Unlike previous letters from the homeowners that still held out hope, Zhang sharply chastised the work team for illicitly occupying the sales office, a property belonging to all the Waitan Garden homeowners. The letter also showed its naïveté by asking the local government to make their own judgments and defy the orders of their superiors. As we have argued before, as were officials in the dynasties, officials in the PRC are appointed by their superiors, not elected by the people. They can ignore people's complaints and opinions but not the orders of their superiors. For that reason, the officials in the Hanyang District government will never dare challenge their superiors, who can deprive them of their posts and power.

Good news arrived on December 18. One homeowner, Li Xiuying, received a fax from a friend of the newly enacted Regulations Regarding the Management of Urban Housing Demolition (Chengshi fangwu chaiqian guanli tiaoli). The new law was enacted on June 6, 2001, and became effective on November 1, eighteen days before the CCTV Waitan Garden exposé and more than one month before the local government sent the work team. The law came just in time as the

Waitan Garden homeowners were preparing to sue the government and desperately needed legal support. It provided many homeowners with fresh hope that they might get a better deal if they had to relocate.

Chapter 2, Article 6, stated: "Before conducting demolition, the demolisher must have a permit of demolition." According to the new law, the demolition planned by the Headquarters for the Relocation and Settlement of Waitan Garden and the work team was undoubtedly illegitimate. This was because they had no permit and, to support their position, only the "Implementing Opinions," clearly not a legal document. Article 10 was even more favorable to the work team. It stipulated: "[The] managing department of housing demolition (*fangwu chaiqian guanli bumen*) cannot be the demolisher and cannot be entrusted to demolish." However, the Hanyang District government should be the managing department, which was forbidden by the new law to be the demolisher. In that case, the work team sent by the district government had actually infringed the law.

Article 8 indicated that, when the managing department of housing demolition was issuing a permit of demolition, it should simultaneously publicize the name of the demolisher, the range of the demolition, and the deadline of demolition indicated in the permit. But the Hanyang District government and the work team had done none of that. The first item of Chapter 3, Article 23, discussed the form of compensation, which could be either cash or kind (*shiwu*). The third item stated that the person whose property was to be demolished had the right to choose the form of compensation.[23] Unfortunately, the Waitan Garden homeowners had no such option since the work team had offered them only comparable properties and no cash compensation.

The new law gave the homeowners fresh ammunition to charge the work team and the local government with law violations. It also gave them more options in terms of compensation in their future negotiations with the work team. However, the prospect of defending their properties or at least gaining increased compensation was not hopeful. Despite all the good laws in China, most, if not all, could not be enforced because, in most cases, the lawbreakers were the law enforcers. Even though the work team could turn a blind eye to the new law, they were the law, and that fact could make it harder to deal with the homeowners, a group of specialists. As one homeowner later recalled, he came to understand why the work team's mission had been so difficult and why it had to resort to such means to relocate the homeowners. It was because no law justified its efforts; all it had was its power. And most of the homeowners had a good education, many of them holding doctoral or master's degrees. There were even eight lawyers and some reporters, government officials, and teachers. They could read and could understand the law. They could also file indictments accusing the local government in the people's court or write petitions and send them to public media inside and outside China.[24]

The new law reenergized the homeowners. But they still had to find a lawyer willing to take their case. Even though the former judge Xu Bikang had drafted

"The Lawyers' Opinions," he was not a lawyer and could not take the case to court. After the CCTV report aired, none of the eight lawyers in Waitan Garden had stood up and volunteered to represent the homeowners, the government pressure not to do so being too hard to bear. They all had families, and the government, and especially the justice bureau, could determine their future careers. In China, one the most daunting things an individual citizen can do is oppose the government. Most Chinese fully understand the meaning of the well-known saying, "An arm is no match for the thigh [gebo niubuguo datui]." Unless their vital interests or very survival is threatened, few Chinese have the courage to challenge the government.[25]

Hu Yan, the only lawyer who had drafted the first "The Voices of Homeowners," had disappeared since then, only later explaining why she had stepped back from the case. She lived in the Waitan Garden unit that was to be demolished first. The police and the justice bureau had repeatedly visited her home and asked her to move out. The police warned her "not to place a bit of hope that her home would not be demolished" and reminded her that "China is governed by the CCP." She defied them responding: "Does China not belong to the people? Why do the police take charge of this [demolition]?" The pressure from the justice bureau was more noticeable and direct: "Lawyers are not free-lancers. They have organizations, leaders, and directing agencies." As the directing agency of lawyers, the bureau implied that Hu could lose her job if she refused to relocate. Undeterred, she told the police that she would not move out until they had satisfied two preconditions: (1) The provincial and city officials had to give her an explanation for demolishing Waitan Garden. (2) If she finally had to relocate, she required compensation in cash, not in kind.

However, neither the justice bureau nor the police had taken Hu's preconditions seriously. Neither explained the demolition or offered her cash compensation. In fact, Hu had secretly relocated to an apartment provided by the work team, without telling any of the other homeowners. The homeowner who talked to her after she had moved out commented in an interview: "[Hu Yan was] the first lawyer who has stood out but also the first lawyer who had moved out."[26] Ultimately, Hu chose her career over her Waitan Garden apartment.

The relocation of Hu Yan was just one of the successes of the work team. Slowly and quietly, many homeowners had moved out of their Waitan Garden properties under different pressures and intimidations. Yet, despite its hard work, the work team learned that many homeowners continued to plot against the government and wrote incendiary materials such as "A Life-and-Ruin Memorandum of the Wuhan Waitan Garden," "The Lawyers' Opinions," "The Lawyers' Ten Points," the open letter, and "A Letter of Sympathy to the Waitan Garden Demolition Work Team." Among them, "The Lawyers' Ten Points" and the open letter were the most vexing for the work team. The city government of Wuhan ordered it to ferret out the authors and detain them.

Officials from both the city of Wuhan and the Hanyang District came to visit the homeowners who were lawyers, writers, teachers, and reporters. Those home-owners, the officials believed, could be the authors of the anonymous material. On December 21, four police officers from both the city and the district paid a visit to a writer's home. They suspected him of being one of the authors. One officer, who was the head of the city police bureau, first handed the materials to him and asked him whether he had seen them before. The writer looked at the open letter and said that he had seen it. The officer then told him that Waitan Garden had to be demolished in accordance with the Flood Control Law. To intimidate him, the officer asked him to abide by the "Implementing Opinions." "You eventually will know that you cannot win [the battle against the government]," the officer said. "I urge you to look for another apartment soon. . . . It is impossible for the government to pay you cash [as compensation]. Even if you petition a central leader in Beijing, he will not write a note asking the local government to pay you cash alone."

The writer admitted that he was one of those homeowners who demanded cash as compensation. "To me," he said, "the spiritual loss is bigger than the economic loss." But the officer replied that the local government had no money. When the writer tried to remind him that the city of Wuhan and Hubei Province should have money, the officer became impatient and warned him not to get entangled with this issue. He then asked the writer who he thought could be the authors of the material in question, stepping up his threats: "Those materials are provocative and unlawful. We are currently trying to find [the authors]. Once we track the authors down, we will punish them. According to the Regulations on Administrative Penalties for Public Security [Zhian guanli chufa tiaoli], we can detain the authors for 15 days."

The writer immediately knew that the threat was real, but he insisted that he did not know who the authors were. And, even if he knew, he would not tell the officers because he did not want to betray his fellow homeowners.

Seeing that the attempt at intimidation was not working, the officer told the writer that those materials seemed to be written by one person who had some special writing skills. He looked at the writer and said: "I think the author must be a writer." The writer quickly denied that he was the author and said that he could not write such specialized material, especially "The Lawyers' Opinion," which required legal knowledge. The officer did not keep pressing the writer but turned to another issue: whether the homeowners wanted to hire lawyers to sue the government. The writer said that, if the issue could not be solved through administrative methods, the homeowners would in fact sue. He also assured the officer that he would be involved in the lawsuit. The officer was not at all annoyed by the threat of a lawsuit. Being the head of the city police bureau, he knew more about the nature of the Chinese judicial system than did the writer. He told the writer: "Even if the homeowners hire ten lawyers, it will still be in vain. You know what the final outcome will be." Before the officer left, the naive and warmhearted writer tried to persuade the police officers not to use force against the homeowners: "You are all police officers, and most ordinary people are afraid of you because sometimes you can use whatever means you want. But this time, [I hope] you will not take drastic actions against the homeowners. . . . The reason that the Chinese people have always been afraid of the officials is that the officials have power. To the Chinese people, the police are more terrifying than the officials. Please do not scare them and hurt them."[27]

The threat of detainment was reminiscent of the notorious and brutal literary inquisition in the Ming and Qing dynasties and also in the Cultural Revolution, when numerous writers were tortured and killed because of their alleged antigovernment or antiorthodox writings.[28] As law enforcers in the PRC, the police officers should have been familiar with citizens' constitutionally guaranteed rights to write, protest, and publish. In fact, none of the slogans, petition letters, and lawyers' opinions authored by homeowners had violated PRC law. Conversely, they were protected by the constitution. The threats made by the police officers to search out the authors and detain them for fifteen days were not only unabashed but also unconstitutional. In addition, the police officers' repeated harassment of people in their homes also violated personal freedom. However, the nature of PRC law is that there exists in it a "legal asymmetry" between the government and the citizens. The Chinese government or the law enforcers (e.g., the police) can violate the law without fear of punishment because they are the law enforcers. But, ironically, regular citizens have to be very cautious and adopt only lawful means to defend their rights. If they violate any law, the government will quickly enforce it. As Yuanyuan Shen correctly argues: "The failure of law to transcend politics [in China] has been most evident in instances when the enforcement of law conflicted with the Party's authority and interests."[29] Indeed, the CCP, or the Chinese government, is the biggest obstacle to law enforcement in China. Its intervention in law is not infrequent, and it becomes more frequent in cases that involve the central or local government.[30] Moreover, the CCP's "unwillingness to submit to legal regulations and strictures that may compromise its political power and interests" spurs the blatant arrogance of the police officers and worsens the legal asymmetry in China.[31]

Not surprisingly, the writer was not the only homeowner who had been visited and coerced by the police. They had also visited with and talked to some other activist homeowners. Ye Shousheng, a retired teacher, lived in the third unit of Waitan Garden. From the outset, he had encouraged his fellow homeowners to take action to protect their interests. He had also assisted the homeowner representatives in drafting numerous materials questioning the CCTV report. Because of his leadership, courage, and prolific writings, he had endeared himself to the other homeowners and was known as "Ye, the Productive Person" (*Yeduowei*). When the police asked him who had written those materials, he readily admitted that he had written the article entitled "Please Let the [CCTV] Focal Interview Do the Interview Again" ("Qingjiaodian fangtan zaifangtan"). But, like the writer, he refused to tell the police who had written the other materials. "Even if I know [who they are], I will not tell you," Ye said. "Otherwise, the other homeowners would curse my mother." He mildly scolded the police for not allowing people to pursue their grievances: "Right now, neither reporters nor leaders from the city and province will come to visit Waitan Garden. Both the municipal and the provincial media have been blacked out. The homeowners have nowhere to air [their grievances]. All they can do is to write such materials. Why do you want to find out [who the authors are]? What can you find out?"

The police then told Ye not to attend any activities organized by the homeowners. To their surprise, he responded that he was inclined to lock his door and leave Waitan Garden. This threat scared the police immensely. If everyone followed Ye's lead, the work team would not be able to carry out the demolition as it would be impossible to break into the homes and blow up the properties, unauthorized entry being illegal and, thus, likely to intensify the tension between the police and the homeowners. The police begged Ye not to take such action. The triumphant Ye then said that he would continue to attend the homeowners meetings.[32]

Unlike the writer and Ye, many homeowners refused to open their doors to the police and the work team. They also harassed the work team. To lessen the tension between the homeowners and the work team, Yan, Han Junru, and Ye had persuaded the recalcitrant homeowners to open their doors because the officials of the work team "are also human beings." "Why should we be afraid of the work team?" they asked. "We have a hundred [legitimate] reasons to persuade them, and we should give them a good legal education." The effort at "legal education" proved to be successful among at least some officials, helping to raise their legal consciousness. One of the officials in the work team later admitted to the homeowners that his job was like "lawbreakers asking the law-abiders to relocate."[33]

The Second "Lawyers' Opinions"

On December 21, the hard work of the homeowners in spreading the word of their grievances finally paid off. The *Oriental Daily,* a Hong Kong–based newspaper, published a half-page report on the current situation in Waitan Garden that not only publicized the whole second "The Voices of Homeowners" but also disclosed that the homeowners had upbraided the government for frequently changing the rules and were prepared to sue the local government. It focused on a particular case involving a Hong Kong resident who had bought a Waitan Garden apartment in March 2001 for 500,000 RMB and just moved in. Before purchasing the apartment, she had carefully checked all the legal documents and permits from the city government and the provincial Department of Water Resources. The government now suddenly informed her that Waitan Garden was illicit, something that it was hard for her to accept as she could not believe that the local government would and could change the existing laws at will. She expressed further concern over the local government's promise of foreign investment and thus asked the Hong Kong government to provide assistance. Although the newspaper was based in Hong Kong and not in mainland China, many homeowners were overjoyed and hoped that newspapers in China would follow up and that the increased media exposure would allow them to protect their property.[34]

Emboldened by the media coverage, the project manager, Zhang Lijun, planned to write more material exposing the unlawful activities of the work team, and Xu Bikang was composing the second "Lawyers' Opinions." After fighting the government for a month, Yan Fengjun, the primary target of the work team, remained upbeat over the prospect of the upcoming administrative litigation. She noted heroically: "Once the court accepts the lawsuit [against the local government], either victory or failure will not be important. If [the lawsuit] is victorious, it will be the victory of Chinese law; if [the lawsuit] is unsuccessful, the homeowners of Waitan Garden will still win. Waitan Garden homeowners will be the paving stone of China's road to the rule of law and let people behind us step on it. I believe that this lawsuit will be a vivid textbook in the history of Chinese law."[35] When one of the homeowners expressed his concern that the people's court would not accept the lawsuit, Xu affirmed that it would. He said: "The Administrative Litigation Law is right there; how can the [court] not accept the case?" Because he was the only judge and legal specialist among the homeowner representatives, his words inspired confidence. He was, however, proved wrong. No court accepted the lawsuit.

The Waitan Garden case was not the only one rejected by the court. As a matter of fact, rejection of administrative litigation is quite common in China, and getting court acceptance has been a thorny issue faced by many litigants. As Kevin O'Brien and Lianjiang Li have aptly argued: "The toughest battle of most [administrative] litigants is persuading a court to accept a case."[36] In addition, as we have argued above, even if the court had taken the case and ruled in the homeowners' favor, the local government would very likely not have enforced the verdict.

Zhang Lijun was a quick writer, and his promised article was completed the next day with the title "Correctly Dealing with the Waitan Incident, the Government Must Not Commit Mistakes One After Another" ("Zhengque chuli waitan shijian, zhengfu qiemo yicuozaicuo"). Like his earlier "Letter of Sympathy," this article severely denounced the work team for its unlawful administrative policies and warned its members that the homeowners would rebel if they did not change their coercive tactics. Zhang listed four major "facts of the illicit policies" of the work team.

First, the work team did not comply with the procedures of the Regulations Regarding the Management of Urban Housing Demolition. Because the "Implementing Opinions" had no legal validity, it could not substitute for a government order. In addition, it was unlawful for the Headquarters for the Relocation and Settlement of Waitan Garden to sign contracts with homeowners because it was not a "legal person (faren)." The contracts were thus also rendered illegal.

Second, the "Circular Regarding the Illegal Construction of the Hanyang Waitan Garden" failed to indemnify the homeowners in accordance with the State Compensation Law (Guojia peichangfa).[37] If the construction of Waitan Garden was allowed to proceed because of an administrative error, the government responsible for the oversight did not want to admit that fact, let alone compensate the homeowners.

Third, the methods outlined in the "Implementing Opinions" had, in many respects, severely violated the legitimate rights of the homeowners. For example, it had glossed over the reasons for the demolition and deprived the homeowners of their right to know. It had also used force to relocate homeowners and thus deprived them of the option of cash compensation. That compensation was based on original price paid was extremely detrimental to their economic interests. The developers asked by the government to provide alternative properties had either increased their prices or sought excuses to resist, which further damaged the interests of the homeowners.

Fourth, the work team had "token illicit means" (mingyi weifa fangshi) to accomplish its goals. Without any legal or official documents, the work team of close to two hundred persons had paid countless visits to the homeowners and encouraged the children, parents, relatives, friends, superiors, and colleagues of the homeowners to put pressure on them. Its threats to investigate how the homeowners had afforded their properties had seriously violated their privacy, disturbed their normal life and work, and caused them spiritual harm. In addition, it had pressured the lawyers in Waitan Garden to be the first to relocate, an attempt to prevent them from being involved in the litigation. And it had sent the police to track down the authors of the first "Lawyers' Opinions" and the open letter. Some homeowners had been monitored, followed, enticed, and coerced. The meetings at which the homeowners discussed the relocation had been determined to be illegal. What had been more outrageous and unlawful was the forced takeover of the sales office, which by law belonged to all homeowners. But it was now taken over by the work team.

Taking advantage of the latest media reports in Beijing and Hong Kong, Zhang Lijun cautioned the work team that the media outside Hubei Province had already become aware of the pending demolition of Waitan Garden. Once more details were released, the public image of Wuhan would be adversely affected, discouraging especially financial investment. As the homeowners had already threatened, Zhang reminded the work team that the proposed lawsuit would be the largest since China had entered the WTO. He ended his long article with the suggestion that the local government had to correct its previous mistakes and follow the law: "Only after [the local government] complies with the law," he noted, "could it correctly resolve the Waitan Garden incident. We understand but do not support the radical rhetoric and actions of some homeowners, . . . but how to 'pacify' the homeowners hinges on the government's response. The government should not force the homeowners to rebel."[38]

Unlike the authors of earlier documents, Zhang used the phrase *some homeowners* at the bottom of the article instead of *all homeowners*. This change reflected the sad fact that some homeowners had abandoned Waitan Garden. To revitalize the morale of those who remained, Zhang found himself compelled to use contentious language. Otherwise, as Xu Bikang had warned, the homeowners would "suffer a rout like a landslide" (*bingbai rushandao*).[39]

Zhang was not a lawyer. The primary purpose of his article was to point out how the work team had violated the law by threatening administrative litigation. Some of his criticisms, such as that the work team had deprived the homeowners of their right to know the truth, were not based on any specific Chinese law. The State Compensation Law that he mentioned had yet to have taken effect. In the well-known case of the so-called virgin prostitute (*chunu piaochang'an*), which took place in early 2001, an eighteen-year-old girl named Ma Dandan was falsely charged by two local policemen in Shanxi Province with prostitution. The policemen had not only tortured her for twenty-three hours but also sexually harassed her. After a local hospital proved through a test that Ma was a virgin, she sued the local police and asked for 5 million RMB (roughly $600,000) as spiritual compensation.

The court, however, demanded a second test to demonstrate Ma's virginity, which might have caused further damage to the girl's spirit. When the second test confirmed her innocence, the court ordered the local police to pay a compensation fee of a mere 76 RMB (roughly $8.00 in 2001). The reason was, as a Beijing law professor argued, that the State Compensation Law had fundamental flaws and could not be implemented.[40]

While the work team was not concerned about Zhang's article, that was not the case with the second "Lawyers' Opinions," which was drafted shortly thereafter. The author remains unidentified but most likely was Xu Bikang. After the first "Lawyers' Opinions" was distributed among the homeowners, the local government and the work team worked hard to search out the author, but all their efforts were fruitless. The second "Lawyers' Opinions" was inspired by the recently promulgated Regulations Regarding the Management of Urban Housing Demolition. The new law, which became effective on November 1, 2001, tried to regulate urban demolition, a focal point of social tension.

In the first place, the second "Lawyers' Opinions" stated that, if the local government could not obtain an administrative order, the demolition of Waitan Garden would be unlawful. Because the government refused to recognize its mistakes and indemnify the homeowners, it had violated the State Compensation Law passed by the NPC on May 12, 1996. The second "Lawyers' Opinions" accused the local government of infringing the Regulations Regarding the Management of Urban Housing Demolition as it failed to offer the homeowners current market price for their properties. It stated that the current tactics of the local government to adopt the so-called "house substitution" (*fangwu zhihuan*) had violated the new law. The new law clearly stipulated that the substitution had to be based on current market price. In addition, it reminded the homeowners that the "decorative evaluation" (*zhuangxiu pinggu*) proposed by the local government was a trap that, once fallen into, could not be escaped.

For instance, the local government had acquired the property contracts of and records of the transaction prices paid by the homeowners. If it also obtained information about the compensation rate of the decorative evaluation, it would have all the data it needed. If any homeowner refused to move out, it "could relocate all the furniture of the homeowner and take a record before it forcibly demolished the apartment."

This reminder was quite professional, and it could prevent some homeowners from stepping into the government trap. What would be a legal demolition procedure? Issuing a demolition order, working out lawful compensation methods, discussing housing evaluation and compensation, and finally negotiating decorative evaluation and compensation. If the homeowners "reverse the procedural order," the second "Lawyers' Opinions" warned, "there will be a blunder."

The second "Lawyers' Opinions" concluded with a condemnation of the local government and a recommendation to the homeowners: "The so-called relocation of Waitan Garden is nothing but unlawful administrative action by some government officials who have tried to protect their official posts at the expense of the homeowners. [We] suggest that, before accepting any legal relocation orders, all Waitan Garden homeowners close their doors to those visitors intent on 'decorative evaluation.' This action is legal and does not violate the law."[41]

Unlike the first "Lawyers' Opinions," the second retreated from the earlier stance and omitted the demand for cash compensation. This showed that the homeowners had realized that the local government was steadfast in rejecting any cash compensation and that they had no choice but to accept the compensation in kind. Some homeowners had indicated a willingness to accept another apartment as compensation; all they asked in return was for city and provincial leaders to come to Waitan Garden and offer some good words (*shuohaohua*) to the homeowners. One general manager of a company had even claimed that he would donate his property in Waitan Garden if the government would simply ask him to make that sacrifice. Although these claims seem to be exaggerations, they mirror the strong desire of the homeowners to have an opportunity to meet the local heads in person.

As in the past, the second "Lawyers' Opinions" was sent to the homeowners secretly. It caused more fear in the work team and more anger among top local heads. Yet, try as it might, the work team still could not locate the author. Yan Fengjun found that the police had recently set up as many as eighteen posts in Waitan Garden, and one vice mayor censured the work team for failing to identify the writer. Yan ascribed the failure of the work team to the conscience of the police and not their incompetence. "I think it does not mean that the police could find out the author," she later said. "It might be because the police did not try their best. Some of the policemen agreed with the contents of those materials. . . .

[They] were not illiterate barbarians. Many of them were college graduates, and their ideas were modern and excellent. Meanwhile, they would not have sympathy for the homeowners. The exquisite human nature always situates in the hearts of most people."[42]

Yan may have some unrealistic views of the police. She probably forgot that they were one of the state apparatuses of the CCP. While it may be true that some policemen have retained their consciences, the nature of their job requires them to follow CCP orders or, in the words of Michael Dutton, to be "100 percent Party."[43] After all, the policemen who chased Yan and threatened to arrest her, the policemen who detained her for almost a whole day simply because she had attempted to petition at the meeting of the people's congressmen in Wuhan, and the policemen who illegally took over the sales office and made it the headquarters of the work team certainly had only orders in their minds and not conscience or sympathy.

GROWING PRESSURE AND THE FIRST INDICTMENT

The combination of threat, coercion, and enticement allowed the work team to make headway. The activists felt depressed at seeing more and more homeowners sign contracts with other developers in Wuhan and then leave. Worse, some homeowners did not want to lose their homes but did not have the courage to join the rights protection movement lest they offend the government. Accordingly, they chose to straddle the line between the work team and the homeowner rights protectors. If the latter failed, they would quickly bow to government conditions and leave Waitan Garden; if they prevailed, they would get to stay in their beautiful scenic apartments. As Han Junru sorrowfully noted:

> The reality is that many people would like to be bystanders at first. If there were any benefits, they would hope to take their fair share; if there were any problems, they would expect someone else to deal with them. For years, many Chinese have practiced such human intelligence very adroitly. I would say that not all Chinese have cultivated such "ultimate smartness." There are always some stupid people. The stupidity can serve as a foil for the smartness. The problem is that the number of stupid people is too small in contrast to that of the smart ones. The small number of stupid people often feel that they do not have sufficient supporters and thus cannot accomplish any good thing.[44]

Ye Shousheng, the brave but "stupid" retired teacher, said that one lawyer in Waitan Garden had been among the first to look at alternative residences in other complexes and had already signed contracts with the work team. But that lawyer, who had never attended any homeowner meetings, told Ye that there was no intelligent person in Waitan Garden. No matter how hard those homeowner rights protectors worked, they were still like a blind man riding a blind house. The lawyer claimed that, if he led the lawsuit against the local government, he would definitely win. Ye jeered and asked him why he had not stood up and taken on the lawsuit as the homeowners had been longing for someone to do so. Yet he refused to take the lead. When Ye then asked him how to file the lawsuit, the lawyer "appeared to be highly enigmatic" and did not say anything.[45]

On Christmas Eve, a shrinking number of homeowners assembled again in a makeshift meeting place. The representatives distributed the second "Lawyers' Opinions" and Zhang's article. The homeowners noticed the Regulations Regarding the Management of Urban Housing Demolition. Although the complete text of the new law had not yet been made available, many homeowners were encouraged and felt their hopes revive. The new law eventually served to unite the homeowners behind a future administrative litigation, and they were sure, although unrealistically so, that the new law had provided them with a "magic weapon to win the lawsuit."[46]

Unfortunately, the new law signed by Premier Zhu Rongji neither lessened the pressure to relocate nor slowed down the pace of the work team. On December 25, Xu Bikang told other representatives that he had been to look at an apartment in another residential complex. This decision on the part of one of the staunchest homeowner activists to submit to the government was a shocking blow to the Waitan Garden rights protection movement. According to Xu, nine high-ranking government officials and one district head met him the day prior and tried to persuade him to move out. "As a Party member myself on top of the serious encouragement of the Party," he said, "I have to obey the order."[47] Yet he still drafted the first indictment and handed it over to the other representatives. Apparently, he wished them to continue the legal fight.

The defendant in Xu's indictment was Jia Yaobin, the head of the Hanyan District government, and the plaintiff was any Waitan Garden homeowner. The indictment asked the people's court to make four determinations: (1) the defendant's demolition of Waitan Garden had violated the PRC Regulations Regarding the Management of Urban Housing Demolition; (2) the defendant's illegal administrative action ordering the demolition of Waitan Garden should be revoked; (3) the defendant should apologize to the plaintiff; (4) the defendant should pay a spiritual compensation of 1 RMB (US$0.12) to the plaintiff.

The indictment then provided four facts and reasons (*shishi yu liyou*) to support its requests. First, it argued that the defendant was not qualified to order or oversee the demolition. When the plaintiff bought an apartment in Waitan Garden, all five lawful permits had been obtained. But now the local government claimed that Waitan Garden was an illicit construction and demanded its demolition. If so, who had initially approved the construction of Waitan Garden? The plaintiff believed that the party responsible for the mistake should correct it. Undoubtedly, the Hanyang District government was not the original approver and thus was not in a position to correct the error.

Second, the indictment argued that the demolition of Waitan Garden was unlawful as it had deprived the homeowners of the right to know the truth. On December 9, 2001, the Hanyan District government sent a work team of more than 180 people to Waitan Garden. Without showing any identification, documents, or notice, they repeatedly knocked on doors and told homeowners that Waitan Garden was an illegal construction and would be demolished and asked the homeowners to relocate. The plaintiff believed that the demolition of an illegal construction had to comply with relevant laws and regulations, in other words, that the administration had to function in accordance with the law. When the plaintiff and other homeowners tried to fight for their right to know the truth and legally expressed their views, the Hanyang District government surprisingly used the police to investigate and coerce the homeowners, a serious violation of the personal and property rights.

Third, the demolition order had damaged the property rights of the plaintiff and other homeowners. Even after the homeowners had vehemently demanded that the defendant administer in accordance with law, the Hanyang District government issued the "Implementing Opinions" and used it to legitimize the demolition order. The "Implementing Opinions" had seriously encroached on the property rights of the plaintiff. For example, the use of original contract price when determining compensation was unfair and unjust. Equally unfair and unjust were the defendant's refusal to pay cash compensation and the unilateral appointment of the evaluating organ to measure the decorative costs. Moreover, the developers that the defendant had designated ostensibly promised a 10 percent discount to the plaintiff and other homeowners. But in fact this was a trap as those developers had secretly raised their prices, worsening the situation of the plaintiff and other homeowners. Furthermore, the "Implementing Opinions" had dodged such questions as: Who had ordered the demolition of Waitan Garden? Who had been wrong? And who should be held responsible?

Finally, the financial capability of the Hanyang District government was questioned. The indictment argued that the demolition of Waitan Garden probably needed 400 million RMB, which was more than the annual operating budget of the government. For that reason, the plaintiff did not believe that the defendant had sufficient financial reserves. At the end of the indictment two further pieces of evidence were attached: the "Implementing Opinions" and some homeowner testimonies.[48]

After reading Xu Bikang's indictment, one of the representatives disagreed with the first request. He argued that the primary request should be the second request, that the defendant's illegal administrative action in ordering the demolition of Waitan Garden should be revoked. Another representative questioned Xu's request of 1 RMB as compensation. He argued that, according to the State Compensation Law, all homeowners should be indemnified. Why ask for only 1 RMB? The law also stated that, if people had suffered more than one form of damage, they could make multiple compensation requests. Because the homeowners had endured both spiritual and economic losses, they should be able to ask for compensation for both losses. However, the questions were flatly brushed aside by Xu. He asserted that it was impossible for the court to compensate the homeowners.[49] Despite queries, the indictment won the support of most representatives. This was just the first step in suing the local government. The homeowner representatives also discussed whether the people's court would accept such a suit. As usual, Xu was very confident that it would do so, and his rationale was that the Administrative Litigation Law would be useless if it did not. If that was going to happen, it was, he thought, better for the NPC to repeal the useless law. The impatient Xu finally told the other homeowners: "Just file the lawsuit as I have written it; the court will accept it." Because Xu was a former judge and the only legal specialist among the homeowners, his view was cogent and authoritative. Some homeowners decided to throw in their lot with him.[50]

While the homeowner representatives were discussing Xu's indictment, another homeowner came to tell them that the work team had shifted its tactics from coercing the homeowners to leave to seeking their comments on the "Implementing Opinions." Ye Shousheng was one of the homeowners who had been approached. However, he invoked four points from the open letter and the two "Lawyers' Opinions": the homeowners wanted to meet with the city and provincial leaders, the evaluation of the properties had to be based on the market price, the compensation should be in cash, and the government had to explain the reason for the demolition clearly.

Additionally, Ye reported that several policemen had paid his home a visit two days ago. One of them—the head of the local police bureau—pretended to ask him for his poems. Ye understood that this was an attempt to find out whether he was the author of those poems against the local government. He declined, saying that he could write some poems but that all of them were in his heart. Once the situation calmed down, he would write all the poems and give them to the police. Infuriated by the repeated harassment, he told the police that he would no longer treat them as he would his friends. If they continued to knock on his door, he would charge them with disturbing his private life. On being given this warning, the policemen left.[51]

Before the homeowners could sue the local government, they faced another seemingly simple but actually thorny problem: typing and photocopying the indictment. Xu Jianping, a young homeowner who had unfortunately experienced three relocations in the past five years, was asked to type and copy the indictment. But, after inquiring at five or six printing shops, he found that none dared take on the job. He then had to ask another homeowner whose company had copiers to help him.

The homeowners also desperately needed the assistance of a lawyer. Up to that time, none of the eight lawyers in Waitan Garden had voiced their support. If they hired an outside lawyer, how much would they be charged? If the fee was too high, that could be another, possibly insurmountable problem.

FINDING A LAWYER

In the short history of the PRC, the lawyer system has experienced several ups and downs. After the PRC was created in 1949, the CCP abolished all GMD legal systems, including its lawyer system. In the mid-1950s, the Justice Department of the PRC decided to reestablish the lawyer system. The first PRC lawyers were not professionals. Most came from the people's courts or the government and enjoyed salaries similar to those of government officials of the same rank.[52] On April 2, 1956, to mitigate its financial burden, the Shanghai municipal government promulgated a provisional method for Shanghai lawyers to charge their clients fees.[53] Although the fees were nominal, Chinese lawyers could no longer rely totally on the government for their income. After the Anti-Rightists Movement in 1957, the lawyer system was gradually cut back in size and importance. It was not until the late 1970s that it once again became a significant entity as part of the sweeping legal reform. In 1979, both Beijing and Shanghai had approved lawyer associations. As the reform deepened, the lawyer system gained momentum and thrived in the 1980s and 1990s. By the end of 1997, there were 8,441 law firms in China, and the number of lawyers exceeded 100,000.[54]

Despite the rising number of lawyers, many who were defending sensitive criminal and administrative cases faced increasing government pressure and intervention. Aside from the tragic fate of the Guangdong-based lawyer Li Jinsong mentioned earlier, many other renowned lawyers, such as Zheng Enchong of Shanghai, Gao Zhisheng of Shandong, and Li Zhuang of Beijing, had been arrested and incarcerated by the CCP court or the government owing to their insistence on defending cases against local governments.[55]

The reason that no lawyers in Waitan Garden had stood up to defend the homeowners, including themselves, was simple: they did not want to offend the local government and risk their careers. If they wanted to survive in Wuhan, they had to maintain good relations with the local government. The female lawyer Hu Yan is a good example. She had championed the homeowners' rights at the beginning. However, her enthusiasm quickly waned after unbearable official pressure. She ended up being one of the first homeowners to move out. Ultimately, the homeowner representatives were forced to turn to lawyers elsewhere, especially in Beijing and Shanghai,using personal connections whenever possible.

The first homeowner who had taken tangible action to find a lawyer was Lu Jianrong. Believing that Beijing lawyers would be a better choice for the Waitan Garden homeowners, she went to Beijing alone in hopes of finding a suitable lawyer. A lawyer whose first name was Tu from the Beijing Jingtai Law Firm told her that he would like to defend the homeowners,but he disagreed on the aim of the lawsuit. He said that the lawsuit should not have anything to do with the demolition of Waitan Garden because that was a done deal and there was no way to alter it. He then suggested that the homeowners sue both the city and the provincial governments and not the Hanyang District government. "The district government is too small," he argued. "There will be no good results [if it is the target]. It is because the administrative litigation consists of two instances. Even the biggest litigation will be solved within Hubei Province."[56] In other words, if the homeowners insisted on accusing the Hanyang District government, the Hubei High Court would make the final decision, and the result would very likely be favorable to the district government. Tu did not reveal the fee that he would charge.

On December 26, Li Hanying, another female homeowner, told the representatives that she had found a very famous lawyer in Beijing willing to take the case but that he charged a high fee—10,000 RMB (US$1,200) per day. This was both good and bad news. At least there was a renowned lawyer who wanted to defend the homeowners. Yet the expense could tear the homeowners apart. As Han Junru asked: "What should we do if the lawsuit lasts for six months? The problem is that the lawyer will charge a fee per day no matter what the results will be."[57]

Once again, the homeowners were forced to look to the lawyers in Waitan Garden, hoping that, because they were homeowners themselves, they might not charge a high fee. The next day, the representatives and a few other homeowners met to discuss the issue. Li Hanying brought good news to the meeting, saying that one of her friends working in the Hubei High Court said that the court would accept the administrative litigation. Those attending the meeting decided to persuade Wu Liang, a lawyer in Waitan Garden, to defend them. The biggest dispute in the meeting was whether to request the court to declare that Waitan Garden was an unlawful construction. One of the homeowners argued that, with the increased media attention that would accompany the lawsuit, the demolition of Waitan Garden would become increasingly problematic. But Zhang Lijun dismissed that view as too optimistic because the demolition decision came from the central government, which was beyond the reach of the local courts. He said that the removal of the request would make it easier for the provincial court to accept the lawsuit. Zhang asked those homeowners who backed the request a simple question: "Do you want to include the request and have the court refuse to accept the lawsuit or exclude the request and have it accept it?" To most representatives and homeowners, the top priority was of course to have the court accept their lawsuit. It was decided to delete the request.[58]

On December 29, several representatives met again, this time in a restaurant to evade police monitoring. Xu Bikang, who had had to relocate under government pressure, also attended. It was decided to print out the letter of authorization (*shouquan weituoshu*) and ask the homeowners who were willing to join the lawsuit to sign it. The authorized persons would be a lawyer and the homeowner representatives. The homeowners would elect seven to nine representatives. The meeting also suggested that the representatives meet Wu Liang, a lawyer in Waitan Garden, who had agreed to take the case. But no one knew whether he would ask for a fee and, if so, how much it would be. Optimistically, they calculated that the fee would be at least 10,000 RMB per family. Xu believed that any fee paid to a lawyer was excessive, and he suggested that they not hire one at all. No one else agreed.[59]

A general assembly of the homeowners was held the following day in a vacant apartment. The homeowners were encouraged by the news that a lawyer was going to file a lawsuit against the local government on their behalf. Many of them were optimistic that they would prevail. As Han Junru noted, most thought that they had the truth on their side and did not believe that the court would decide against them. The progress of legal reform over the past twenty years seemed to have confirmed their optimism. The Administrative Litigation Law passed ten years earlier was to provide the commoners with a legal weapon against the officials. If the homeowners did not take the weapon, it was they who had given up their legal rights, and they would have no one but themselves to blame. The speech of a homeowner named Wang Yanbo was probably most representative. As he put it: "The lawsuit is in fact to defend our human dignity [*rende zunyan*], and it does not matter whether the result will be successful or not. Any lawful struggle of the little people [*xiao laobaixing*] will make a certain contribution to China's legal construction and push China's law to move one step forward. Just because of this point, we should engage in this lawsuit."

The term *human dignity* was first introduced from the West via Japan in the late Qing period. Since then, it has been instilled in the hearts of many Chinese and has been used frequently as one of the basic features of a citizen.[60] It was more intriguing that the homeowner used the derogative term of *little people*, which has a long history in China. In the dynasties, Chinese rulers, the sons of heaven, liked to refer to the commoners as "stupid people" (*yumin*) or "child people" (*zimin*).[61] The commoners used to call themselves "little people" or "grass people" (*caomin*). This tradition persisted into the republican period when Sun Yat-sen, the interim president of the ROC, announced in early 1912 that all Chinese people were to be emperors in the republic.[62] In the mid-1940s, more than three decades after the Chinese people gained citizenship, many commoners continued to call themselves *little people* in their petitions to Chiang Kai-shek, the republican president.[63] In the pre-1978 PRC, the CCP and Mao had launched a series of political movements such as the Anti-Rightists Movement and the Cultural Revolution in which students and commoners had organized to struggle with school leaders and officials. Consequently, few people had recently used the term *little people*.[64]

The homeowner who used the term *little people* had a relatively better living and better social connections than did most commoners in Wuhan. Like commoners in the dynasties and the republic, the homeowners were profoundly helpless in the face of the unchecked power of the government. If the affluent homeowners could not defend their legal rights, then other, less privileged commoners could not do so either.

More questions were raised at the meeting. One homeowner asked whether the court would accept the lawsuit. None of the representatives could guarantee this. All they could say was that it would be meaningless for the court not to accept it. The court could decide against the homeowners, but it could not refuse to accept the case. Doing so would deprive citizens of their rights. But the representatives also warned the homeowners that they should be prepared for the worst-case scenario: "Accepting a lawsuit is the fundamental standard of the law. If this fundamental standard disappears, we [the representatives] have to surrender completely." To make the point more clearly, the representatives said that, if the provincial high court turned down the lawsuit, they would capitulate.[65]

Another homeowner reminded everyone that the lawyer's fee remained an unresolved issue. If the fee were too high, some homeowners would probably back away from the lawsuit. Although around seventy homeowners had endorsed the lawsuit, that number was a small portion of the four-hundred-plus homeowners in Waitan Garden. The fact was that most had decided to relocate so as to avoid a direct confrontation with the government.

After the meeting, the representatives consulted with a homeowner lawyer on the lawsuit. The lawyer, who had never attended any homeowners' assemblies, told them that the court would not accept the suit if the defendant was the government. He argued that the "Implementing Opinions" had actually been drafted by the city government, which could not be sued. Any lawsuit at the district or city court level was meaningless because both levels were ready to defeat the homeowners.

"Let us think," the lawyer said. "Can the city and district courts make verdicts against the city and district governments?" To the lawyer, the ideal place to file the lawsuit was in the provincial court. The problem was that the provincial court would not accept any case that was not well-known in the nation. The lawyer did not believe that the Waitan Garden case was an influential one in China, and he further frustrated the representatives by saying that the timing was not ripe for such a lawsuit. The representatives expressed their concern that the unity of the homeowners would fall apart if the lawsuit was postponed. The lawyer did not reply, but he cautioned them that his fee would be prohibitively hight: 30,000 RMB for each family, three times the rate of the famous Beijing lawyer.

There is no doubt that the representatives would not agree to such a high fee. Even if they themselves accepted it, the majority of homeowners would not. Another lawyer had to be found. The next one they contacted was the head of a law firm in Wuhan. He first talked about the complexity of the case, and he also demanded a legal fee. When one representative asked him how much he would be charged on the basis of his 300,000 RMB apartment, the lawyer said that the fee would be 12,000 RMB. If he won the case, the charge would be 20,000–30,000 RMB, a price similar to that of the other lawyer. After bargaining, he agreed to reduce the fee to 3,000 RMB per family but hinted that he might withdraw from the lawsuit if the pressure from the government to do so became too heavy. Even with the reduced fee, the total charge for one hundred homeowners would be 300,000 RMB. Yan voiced her worries that she dared not file the lawsuit because the representatives would take the blame if the case was eventually lost.[66]

Yan Fengjun recommended Wu Liang, the first homeowner lawyer who dared take the case. Wu opposed any lawsuit that sought to halt demolition, which he believed was not pragmatic. Instead, he felt that the homeowners' best hope was seeking better compensation. He also suggested that the first lawsuit should be filed with the Wuhan Intermediate Court. If it lost there, he would go up to the provincial court and eventually to the Supreme Court. Like Xu Bikang, Wu said that he would surrender if the provincial court refused to accept the case. When asked why he wanted to defend the homeowners, he spoke passionately about how lawyers also had sentiment and were democratic fighters (*minzhu doushi*). If the goal of the lawsuit was only to repeal the illegal administrative action, he would have had little interest in it; if he were to file a lawsuit, he wanted the case to be an exemplar of the progress of the post-WTO Chinese legal system. He assured the representatives that he would fight for them to the end but also cautioned that he could not guarantee success.

Despite all his passionate words, Wu Liang told the representatives that his firm would charge a fee of approximately 30,000 RMB per family, which was similar to the head of the law firm in Wuhan. So far all the lawyers had required a fee too high for most homeowners to accept.[67]

Before the representatives began to search for a lawyer, their biggest worry had been that no one would dare defend the homeowners. After several consultations, they found that there were in fact lawyers willing to take the case but that all of them were too expensive and none could guarantee a positive outcome.

Why were the lawyers so willing to help the homeowners file administrative litigations? Did they not fear government reprisal? It is our contention that their willingness to take the case does not mean that they wanted to challenge the government. As seasoned professionals,[68] they knew a great deal about the law and the Chinese legal system. Most of them were aware that such lawsuits were unlikely to be accepted by the courts and, if they were accepted and were successful, would not be enforced by the government. That could probably explain why all the lawyers, including the Waitan Garden lawyers, demanded a fee from the homeowners no matter what the result would be. Whereas a judge's income is a fixed salary, a lawyer's income relies on various fees. Even if the lawsuits failed, the lawyers would still collect a fee from the homeowners, meaning that they had nothing to lose. In comparison, the homeowners wanted the lawyers to guarantee a court victory before agreeing to any fee. Unless a Waitan Garden lawyer was willing to take the case for free or for an acceptable fee, the homeowners would be faced with the choice of paying a substantial fee or moving out of Waitan Garden.

As negotiations with lawyers continued to fall through, the representatives became increasingly impatient and downcast. They began to lose their confidence and did not know what to do next. On New Year's Eve, the homeowners held a celebration meeting during which the representatives were questioned on the progress they had made finding a lawyer.

About fifty policemen surrounded the assembly venue. Ye Shousheng spotted several local police department heads there, and he went to greet them. He told them not to be nervous about the meeting because all the homeowners were law-abiding citizens. One of them wanted him to be responsible for any disturbances. He retorted that whoever broke the law that night would be responsible and no one else. While the number of homeowners was diminishing, the work team still worried that the remaining homeowners might create trouble.

He Feng, a young accountant and one of the representatives, opened the meeting with a New Year's greeting in which he urged the homeowners to unite behind justice and the progress of the Chinese legal system. The representatives assured the homeowners that the next step would be an administrative litigation against the local government. But some homeowners again expressed their concerns about the lawyer, the legal fee, and the court's acceptance of the lawsuit. The representatives promised that the lawyer was from Beijing and that they would initiate the lawsuit right after New Year's Day. This was apparently only half true, but the representatives felt compelled to make such a statement in order to pacify the homeowners. As a promising sign, the wives of two Waitan Garden lawyers, Sun Gexin and Huang Jiancheng, attended the celebration, which indicated that their husbands might be willing to take the case. Han Junru later recalled that this turned out to be the biggest gain and in fact a turning point for the representatives that night.[69]

The New Year celebration party was touching and rewarding. Some homeowners gave inspiring speeches that helped strengthen the unity and courage of the homeowners. The writer focused his speech on the importance of human dignity and legal rights: "Tonight, everyone has dignity. It is only because we have dignity that we can live like real men. If we discard the dignity and rights bestowed by law, we will have an ignoble life. . . . After we have adequate clothes and food, our dignity and rights have become the top priorities; this is particularly true for us Waitan Garden homeowners. . . . In that sense, while we are defending our individual dignity and rights, we are also like the soldier who is defending the dignity of law." Zhang Hua, a former bodyguard for CCP leaders and the husband of Li Hanying, stated: "We do not fear anything, especially the policemen. What we want is justice. We want something that we deserve, including both economic and political interests."[70]

3

Wuhan's Showdown
at the Supreme Court

Individual Complaints

Almost two months after the CCTV report criticizing Waitan Garden, the homeowners' rights protection movement finally drew the attention of the central media. On January 5, 2002, the Xinhua News Agency, one of the CCP's key mouthpieces that had recently returned to "the leading position in Chinese media,"[1] issued a report on Waitan Garden entitled "Many Homeowners of the Wuhan Waitan Garden Are Accusing the Local Government of Inconsistency and Using Power to Replace Law" ("Wuhan Waitan huayuan dapi yezhu konggao defang zhengfu chuer faner yiquan daifa"). The report mentioned the legal permits that the homeowners had obtained and their upcoming lawsuit against the local government. At the beginning, it indicated that Waitan Garden, which had once been a model project of the "Yangzi River urban garden" (*Changjiang chengshi huayuan*) in Wuhan, was recently ordered demolished. As many as 105 homeowners from China and overseas had publicized open letters and lodged collective petitions. They were also charging the local government with frequently changing policies, using power to replace law, and "slapping their own faces" (*ziji daziji zuiba*).

The Xinhua report went on to provide an overview of Waitan Garden. It cited "angry" petitioners' comments that all the homeowners possessed lawful permits for their properties. The Hanyang District government had no legal right to order the demolition since it had neither the power to approve the project nor a legitimate demolition order. Moreover, it was wrong to destroy the legal Waitan Garden. Those views apparently came from the open letter and the two "Lawyers' Opinions." The report also interviewed Jia Yaowu, the Party secretary of the Hanyang District government, who admitted that Waitan Garden had indeed been approved by the local government. Yet, after media (i.e., CCTV) criticism, both the provincial and the Wuhan governments made clear decisions to demolish the project and protect the basic interests of the developer and the homeowners. The irony was that Jia reportedly claimed that the emotions of most homeowners were stable (*qingxu wending*). Undoubtedly, he was not telling the truth, but the rhetoric he used is typical among Chinese officials as a way to pacify their superiors and protect their own posts. However violent and drastic a situation may be, most Chinese officials will claim that people's emotions are stable and that the situation is under control.

The report also looked into a collective protest carrying 120 signatures in which lawyers such as Sun Gexin, Huang Chengjian, and Deng Tao argued that the demolition order was illicit as the Hanyang District government had not issued it. The demolition order violated both the State Compensation Law and the Regulations Regarding the Management of Urban Housing Demolition, signed into law in June 2001. "The so-called demolition," the lawyers said, "is nothing but grave lawbreaking and wrong administrative behaviors by which the local officials try to protect their posts and transfer the loss to the homeowners." In a stunning but pro-homeowners tone, Xinhua invoked the words of a retired cadre: "Needless to say, the simplest thing is that the government must issue an order to demolish. From the inception, Waitan Garden has existed for seven years. First-term homeowners have lived here for three or four years, and they have complete permits from the developer. . . . Just because of a seriously false [CCTV] report, local officials in Wuhan reverse their policies overnight and want to change a legal home into an illegal one. This is too hasty and unreasonable."[2]

The author of the report was one of the three journalists who visited and interviewed homeowner activists in December 2001. Thanks to its status as one of the primary central media and thus beyond local control, Xinhua is able to publish such a relatively objective report that skews toward sympathizing with the homeowners.[3] In contrast, none of the local Hubei newspapers dared report on Waitan Garden because they are all under the leadership of the Hubei Propaganda Department.

The publicity given the protests and petitions of the Waitan Garden homeowners by the Xinhua report failed, however, to force the local government to shift its policies and stop its law violations. The new hope it gave the homeowners quickly vanished. As the central power of the CCP trickled down to the local government during the reform era, the popular saying, "Heaven is high above, and the emperor is far away" (tiangao huangdiyuan), once again proved true.[4] The "decentralized authoritarianism" significantly enhanced the power and independence of local governments, which made them less likely to fear media criticism.[5] Additionally, although the central government did not authorize the local government in Hubei to take the illegal action of demolishing Waitan Garden, the fact is that orders originally came from the central government that could easily be interpreted by local officials as a green light to adopt any and whatever methods.

As the deadline for the demolition drew closer, the homeowners encountered more unlawful violence from the work team and the police. To protect their legal properties, many homeowners had elected their representatives and prepared for a lawsuit against the local government. A few wrote down their personal experiences of official violence and sent individual petitions to various public media and upper-level governments.

On January 6, one homeowner, Li Hanxiong, condemned the local government for forcing him to relocate without cash compensation. He was particularly enraged by local officials' notion that the homeowners should share the loss with the local government. If the homeowners had all the legal permits, why did they have to bear the loss? Li questioned the local government: "The core of President Jiang Zemin's 'Three Represents' is to represent the most fundamental interests of the masses. Yet can we say that the relocation work [by the work team] embodies the spirit of the 'Three Represents'? How can [the local government] explain the loss of the mass? I do not understand. Therefore, I plead that, to truly reflect President Jiang's 'Three Represents,' the compensation [of the homeowners] should be in compliance with certain state laws or regulations in order to ensure that the interests of the masses will not be harmed."[6]

In another individual petition letter, Fu Yuanyuan, the courageous homeowner who defied the government order to stop the decoration of her apartment, voiced her anger at official threats and coercion. According to Fu, to buy the Waitan Garden apartment, she had sold her property in a remote city in Heilongjiang Province. Before the decoration was finished, she and her husband had to sleep on the floor of her company. Beginning in mid-December, a group of officials came to her apartment trying to stop the workers from decoration. When Fu's husband pointed out to the officials that the apartment had all the lawful permits, the officials acknowledged the fault of the government in approving the project. But they said that Waitan Garden had to be demolished and that the government would try to minimize the homeownerss losses. The official account prompted Fu to question why the homeowners were being forced to cover the government losses if it was not their fault. One of the officials warned her and her husband that they must be pragmatic because the Chinese legal system was not perfect. In other words, China's imperfect legal system gave the officials an excuse to ignore the law in dealing with the impractical couple. Fu's husband retorted: "China has joined the WTO; if China's legal system is still imperfect, is it [the Waitan Garden case] not a good chance to improve the legal system?"

Seeing that Fu Yuanyuan refused to stop decoration, the local officials threatened the workers several times and accused them of "daring [to proceed] against the government['s orders]." The coercion not only forced the workers to slow down their work but also severely disturbed Fu's life and work. She quoted her father-in-law, a vice president of a Party school (*dangxiao*) and congressman in Heilongjiang, as saying: "All places in China have been working hard to ameliorate their investment environments and stress the construction of democracy and legal system. Why do such notoriously ungracious things take place in Hubei, which has long had a reputation of being highly open?"

As a legal specialist himself, Fu's father-in-law also criticized the legal procedure followed in the Waitan Garden case. If the government had made mistakes in approving the project, the correct legal procedure was that the people's court and not the government or leaders adjudicate. The CCTV interference was a typical case of "using power to replace law" in modern civilized cities (*xiandai wenming dushi*). The congressman continued that the principle to be followed in this case was to let the lawbreakers compensate. The homeowners should not bear the loss.

Fu Yuanyuan ended her petition letter with a caveat to the local government: "Anyhow, our property was bought with lawful money and it has all five required permits, yet we have still suffered unexpected threats, harassment, and loss. My husband vows to take action. If it is not possible to sue the government in Hubei Province, he will go to Beijing to file a lawsuit; if Beijing is still not successful, he will appeal to a court in another country. I definitely support his decision."[7] Local officials of course recognized this as sheer bravado and much less menacing than the other collective lawsuits guided by professional lawyers. With the court and the police under control, the government need not take Fu seriously.

Xiao Wenjian was one of the homeowners who had been publicly harassed by the police. Unlike most other homeowners, he had the police abuse of power more forcefully imprinted in his memory. On January 13, as more and more homeowners had exercised their constitutional rights by petitioning city and provincial governments, the local police became very sensitive of any petition. In the morning, when Xiao walked out of the Waitan Garden gate, a police car suddenly blocked his way, apparently suspecting that he was on his way to petition. Several policemen asked him to come into the car for a talk, and the following exchange ensued:

The Police: Where are you heading?
Xiao Wenjian: It is none of your business. Do I not have the freedom to walk?
The Police: We want to check your belongings.
Xiao Wenjian: You have no right to check.
The Police: Do you have an ID?
Xiao Wenjian: You can ask any person in the street for his or her ID. You are here with some mission. Are you carrying your IDs?
The Police: If you do not have your ID, we have to inspect you.
Xiao Wenjian: You are acting against the law. You are violating my human rights!
The Police: We are carrying out an order, and the police have the right to check you.
Xiao Wenjian: You can inspect me, but we should go to the Wuhan Police Bureau, and you can check my belongings in front of the police head.
[At this suggestion, the police hesitate.]
Xiao Wenjian: You are feeling guilty. Let's go to the headquarters of the work team in Waitan Garden, and you can find out what law I have violated.

The Police: We did not say you have broken the law. All we want is an inspection.

Xiao Wenjian: How can you check me? Which law can be used to justify your inspection?

The Police: The Police Law.

Xiao Wenjian: Does the Police Law say that the police can search any person at will?

The Police: As long as a person is suspicious, the police can conduct the inspection.

Xiao Wenjian: Why do you suspect me? Have I committed murder, arson, or robbery?

The Police: We suspect that you have committed murder.

Xiao Wenjian: As a people's policeman, you should be responsible for your words. Whom have I murdered? You have to explain it to me. Otherwise, I will accuse you of making a false charge.

The Police: OK, go ahead and sue me.

Xiao Wenjian: I have never seen any policeman search people at will. Do we not have personal freedom? If you cannot be reasoned with, I believe that there should be somewhere that I can speak freely.

Both sides refused to give in for half an hour. Finally, Xiao allowed the policemen to check his belongings under the condition that they had to tell him their names. The policemen found nothing but an umbrella. Before they left, one of them cursed him: "You need to live longer and not to let a car to kill you."[8]

In this case, Xiao had done nothing wrong, and he simply wanted to go to work. But the policemen first blocked his way and then asked to search his belongings. Although in some countries (e.g., France and the United States) it may be legal for the police to stop and check the IDs of suspicious people,[9] they must first show their own IDs. But the Wuhan policeman showed Xiao no ID before asking to check his belongings. This was an absolute infringement of a citizen's rights. In addition, Xiao was harassed for over half an hour, a violation of his personal freedom. According to the latest PRC Constitution: "Article 37: The Personal Freedom of the citizens of the People's Republic of China is inviolable. . . . Unlawful detention or deprivation or restriction of citizens' personal freedom by other means is prohibited, and unlawful search of the citizens is prohibited. Article 38: The personal dignity of citizens of the People's Republic of China is inviolable. Insult, libel, false accusation or false incrimination directed against citizens by any means is prohibited."[10]

Without a doubt, the behavior of the local policemen had violated both Article 37 and Article 38 of the PRC Constitution. Xiao was right to question their actions. More frighteningly, the policemen, as the enforcers of the law, did not even know or care about the PRC Constitution and had no fear even if they were breaking the law.

Instead of writing petition letters, a handful of talented homeowners composed petition poems and distributed them among the homeowners or sent them to various media outlets. In one poem, a homeowner who chose to be anonymous wrote:

Opposing administrative corruption,
Indemnifying my apartment and money.
The muddled mayor should step down,
The lying district head should resign.
Illegal demolition and merciless handling,
[The government is] transferring crisis but cannot escape punishment.
Government's lie is bigger than heaven,
Where is the law? Where is the reason?
The homeowners' grievances are as deep as the ocean,
Under heaven, homeowners defend their rights with tears and blood.
More than one hundred homeowners cry to the Yangzi River,
Long live the law, one year the lawbreakers![11]

In this desperate plea, the poet denounced the government's abuse of power and shameless violations of the law. With a bit of exaggeration, he called for public attention to the tremendous grievances of the homeowners. If power was in the hands of the government and the government was also the enforcer of the law, no one would be able to come to the aid of the homeowners even if the homeowners had the law behind them.

Extralegal Petitions

Petitions have a long history in China. Prior to the establishment of the ROC in 1912, the difference between petitions and the judiciary had often been blurry. The republic for the first time separated the petition system from the judiciary and created the administrative court as the judicial petition system. In the early PRC, the petition system became the letters and visits system (*xinfang zhidu*) and gradually developed into a comprehensive system.[12] In his study of the PRC letters and visits system, Carl Minzner argues that it is an extralegal institution that overlaps with the formal judicial system.[13] Aggrieved Chinese prefer petitions to lawsuits because they believe they cost less and are sometimes more effective.[14]

Shortly after the local government in Wuhan began pressuring Waitan Garden homeowners to move out, some homeowners thought about petitioning the provincial and central leaders. Like petitioners in the dynasties, they hoped that the state leaders would hear their grievances and intervene. The first, most detailed petition letter was sent to Premier Zhu Rongji on January 1, 2002, a time when the homeowners were facing the daunting task of finding a good lawyer. Taking advantage of New Year's Day, the letter accused the work team of gravely infringing the law, using the "Implementing Opinions" alone as justification in its attempts to relocate the homeowners. And, of course, the other, by-now familiar complaints were recounted. "The people have grievances," the petitioner wrote, "but the local government arbitrarily persists in its false policies." When the homeowners took moves to protect their rights, the police intimidated them, saying: "Do you not know China's [legal] system? It will be useless to hire even ten lawyers." "Is it real that Chinese people have no way to defend their rights?" the petitioner asked the premier.

Just like dynastic petitioners, who always eulogized the emperor as their loving and just father while criticizing local officials, the Waitan Garden petitioner then praised the premier for his kindness and compassion. While he was not sure whether the letter would ever reach the premier, he still implored him to listen to the homeowners' grievances.[15] Before the petitioner mailed his letter, a friend had suggested that he add one sentence saying that more than one hundred homeowners would petition Beijing if the local government did not properly tackle the Waitan Garden issue. But he declined on the grounds that doing so could be regarded as threatening and thus being disrespectful to the premier, whom he wanted to read his letter and intervene. Still, he did note: "If you cannot help us, we will have to depend on the law."[16]

In mid-January, while the hundred-plus homeowners were anxiously waiting for responses from the Hubei Provincial High Court and the Supreme Court, they simultaneously petitioned a number of central and local leaders. President Jiang Zemin, the highest-ranking official in China, unquestionably became their priority. If he would hear their petition and intervene, they would be able to protect their properties. At the beginning of the short petition they sent on January 17, the "distressed" homeowners wrote that they were encountering an "extremely serious issue, the imminent demolition of Waitan Garden and the residences of the homeowners." They charged the local government with willfully infringing their "lawful rights" and "living rights" (*shengcunquan*). Cleverly invoking the slogan of the "Three Represents," which Jiang introduced in 2000, they argued that the actions of the Wuhan municipal government had departed from the basic spirit of the initiative. Furthermore, they criticized the Wuhan government for severely damaging the Party image among the masses. Finally, they urged the president to save them: "In the face of [the violations of the local government], we (the homeowners) are feeling angry and helpless! Now is the season of deep winter, and the Spring Festival is close; the four-hundred-plus homeowners (more than one thousand people) will soon have no place to live. Most urgent! President Jiang, please spend a little time rescuing the people from water and fire!"[17]

Apparently, however, Jiang did not respond to the petition, let alone take any action to save Waitan Garden. According to the homeowners, the letter might have reached his secretary. But, even if the president had received the letter, it was never likely that he would intervene. This was because the order to demolish Waitan Garden had come from Premier Zhu Rongjin, both his protégé and a longtime colleague in Shanghai.

Besides central leaders, the homeowners had also petitioned Yu Zhengsheng, Party secretary of Hubei Province. Yu, who currently is the head of the Chinese People's Political Consultative Conference, became Party secretary on December 7, 2001, only fifteen days after the CCTV report on Waitan Garden. The homeowners hoped that the new leader of Hubei would help them. Compared to the petition letter to Jiang Zemin, the tone of the letter to Yu Zhengsheng was a bit tougher and more peremptory.

The petition stated that the homeowners wanted to inform Yu of some of the latest developments in the Waitan Garden case. The first was that the homeowners had been resisting the illegal demolition of their properties by the local government. After the local government rejected their request for lawful administration, 130 homeowners decided to sue the Wuhan and Hanyang governments in court. Second, Sun Gexin, Huang Chengjian, Qian Yiping, Wan Zhihong, and Liu Tao, lawyers from the Hubei Dongfangzhou Law Firm, had formed a legal team to represent this first commoners-against-officials case since China had joined the WTO. The lawyers submitted their suit to the Hubei Provincial High Court on January 11, 2002. The petition listed a number of violations committed by the local government. For instance, the local government was faulted for having illicitly approved the Waitan Garden project in 1995, which had plagued the homeowners spiritually and economically.

The work team created by the Hanyang District government had employed all kinds of illegitimate methods, such as intimidation, coercion, tracking, and mobilizing the leaders, friends, and relatives of the homeowners in order to pressure them. It had also tried forcing them to relocate by threatening loss of employment, suspension of duties (*tingzhi*), failure to pass job performance appraisals (*kaohe buchengzhi*), tax inspection (*chashui*), closure of their businesses (*guanbi yezhu jingji shiti*), damaging the political careers of homeowners' relatives (*lianlei yezhu qinren zhengzhi qiantu*), and so on. "Those illegal means," the petition said, "have gravely infringed the personal rights of the homeowners." In addition, on January 12, the work team, producing no legal documents, began to demolish two buildings in Waitan Garden and cut off the gas supply, which resulted in clashes between the homeowners and the construction workers. On January 13, while some homeowners were petitioning during the meeting of the Wuhan People's Congress, the police detained seven of them for twelve hours. On January 14, the legal team informed the work team that it intended to open its office inside Waitan Garden, but the police deemed such a move illegal, and removed all traces of the legal team's presence. On the same day, the work team ordered the homeowners to relocate by January 17.

On January 17, a large number of police, workers, and engineering trucks came into Unit 1 of Waitan Garden, forcing the remaining homeowners to relocate. When other homeowners and lawyers went to help, the police blocked them.

On January 18, the workers began demolishing Unit 1, working around the clock. The homeowners denounced this as an unlawful demolition because no court order allowing it had been issued. Some homeowners who were suing the local government were also forced to move out, and a few homeowners from Taiwan and Hong Kong rushed to Wuhan after their properties had been demolished.

The petition ended with a plea and a warning to Yu Zhengsheng:

> Dear Party Secretary Yu:
> The degree of the illegal administration of the Wuhan government has reached an astounding level. In a megacity boasting eight million people, how can the local officials run wild and ignore Party regulations and state laws? How can they neglect President Jiang's "Three Represents"? The homeowners will hold those individual city and district officials accountable. For the moment, the Waitan Garden homeowners are passionate about going to Beijing to petition for justice. Because you are the Party representative in Hubei, all the homeowners wish the Party to stand out at this critical moment to swiftly curb all the illicit activities of the Wuhan government, restrict the behaviors of the local leaders that were against Party principles, and avoid any further deterioration in the situation.[18]

Unlike Jiang Zemin, who might not have heard about the struggles of the homeowners, Yu would surely have been aware of them. But, as Party secretary, he had an excuse to give a green light to local officials and ignore the grievances of the homeowners. The homeowners received no response to their petition. Instead, what they saw were more intensified and forcible violations of their legitimate rights in the final days of Waitan Garden.

The homeowners complained more widely than just to central leaders. Some petitioned central organs such as the *People's Daily,* one of the principal propaganda tools of the CCP, and the Central Commission for Discipline Inspection (Zhongyang jilu jiancha weiyuanhui), the primary *internal* disciplinary and *watchdog* organization of the CCP.

The letter to the *People's Daily* was sent on January 27, 2002, two days after the work team demolished Unit 1, and the homeowners sued the local government through the Supreme Court. Clearly, the intent of the letter was that the Party newspaper would publicize the agonies of the homeowners and expose the legal violations of the local government. The complaint tried first to arouse the sympathy of the *Daily* by censuring local officials for blacking out all local news and using police to track down homeowners. On January 25, one homeowner knelt in front of the debris of Unit 1, crying and singing for two hours. People who listened were all touched and burst into tears. On the same night, after watching the consistently false CCTV reports claiming that the local government was "passionately handling the case and properly relocating the homeowners [*youqing caozuo tuoshan anzhi*]," exasperated homeowners smashed the windows of the work team headquarters. The letter also accused the local government of providing homeowners with apartments that had no property ownership certificate and were priced higher than market value. Worse, the local government did not even mention the latest Regulations Regarding the Management of Urban Housing Demolition, which required the government to offer cash compensation to the homeowners and calculate property values in accordance with market prices.

The homeowners called for all honest men and unbiased media to expose the unlawful administration of the Wuhan and Hanyang governments during the process of demolishing Waitan Garden. They also told the *People's Daily* that, shortly after the Hubei Provincial High Court turned down their administrative litigation, 130 homeowners had appealed to the Supreme Court on January 27. All that the homeowners expected was sufficient media exposure to allow them to defend their legitimate rights from infringement.[19]

As the central watchdog of the CCP, the Central Commission for Discipline Inspection was established in 1977 in the wake of the end of the Cultural Revolution. The original aim of the commission was to strengthen discipline among Party members and restore internal democracy within the Party. During the reform era, the commission engaged more in investigating misconduct among the cadres.[20] According to the Statutes of the CCP, the main tasks of the commission are to "uphold the statutes and the other important rules and regulations of the Party, to assist the respective Party commissions in rectifying Party workstyle, and to check up on the implementation of the Party's line, principles, and policies."[21] Since 2002, the head of the commission has been one of the members of the Politburo Standing Committee, the most powerful decision-making organ of the CCP. Recent movements aimed at "beating big tigers" ("tigers" being high-level officials), such as former Party leaders Bo Xilai and Zhou Yongkang, have all been conducted by the commission. The importance of the commission makes it a popular venue among aggrieved Chinese petitioners.

Like many other petitioners, the Waitan Garden homeowners also sent one of their complaint letters to the commission, hoping that it would interfere in the case and punish the local officials. The petition was sent on February 1, 2002, when the homeowners had probably lost all hope that the Supreme Court would accept their appeal. The petition, which was the final one, showed that the homeowners had placed their last hope with the commission.

Citing major newspaper reports, such as those appearing in the *Labor Daily* and the *Legal Daily* (*Fazhi ribao*), that the demolition of Waitan Garden had "seriously shattered the image of the rule of law among commoners" as well as the invested environment of Wuhan, the petitioners questioned why no person or department had borne the legal liability for the demolition. "On the contrary," the petitioners wrote:

> The same officials who originally approved the Waitan Garden project
> are now becoming the demolishers. And their demolition has from the

outset been illegal administration with no official order and procedure. The officials have adopted methods such as coercion, threatening, using police, and restricting personal freedom to force the homeowners to accept unfair terms for their relocation. More seriously, the local officials compelled about ten homeowners in Unit 1 to move out without signing any contract. Even now, some homeowners are still homeless. In fact, the local officials are trying to use a more dangerous illegal action to camouflage their previous unlawful administration. . . . This action has seriously smeared the images of the Party among the masses and resulted in extremely bad consequences in Wuhan.[22]

The petitioners did not forget to notify the commission that they had first filed a lawsuit in the provincial high court and then, when that was rejected, filed another one with the Supreme Court. As they did in the petition letter to President Jiang Zemin, they appealed to the commission to investigate those local leaders who had repeatedly violated the Party regulations and state laws. They said—invoking language traditionally used by the CCP—that they were confident that the "Great Party" (*weidade dang*) and the "Wise Central Government" (*yingming zhongyang zhengfu*) would certainly back the people because the Party would not allow its image to be tarnished.[23]

Unfortunately, neither the *People's Daily* nor the Central Commission for Discipline Inspection was responsive. The *Daily* never supported the homeowners or questioned the legality of the demolition. In stark contrast to the *China Youth Daily*, which has the courage to expose government corruption and champion the "little people,"[24] the *People's Daily* remains the main voice of the Party and, owing to its continuing CCP subsidy, feels no need to heed popular grievances. The central commission, which has been criticized for abusing its power and itself breaking the law, may have been used as a tool in power struggles among CCP factions.[25] The commission's recent highly acclaimed anticorruption movement has allegedly been being utilized by top CCP leaders against their political foes.[26] The best example of the impotence of the central commission when it comes to redressing commoners' grievances is the case of Guo Guangyun, a former Shandong local official who had been persecuted by the provincial Party secretary. Despite the direct intervention of the head of the commission, Guo had spent eight years petitioning various central organs against the most powerful official in Hubei Province. In that particular case, Guo, an official himself, could reach the head of the central commission through personal connections. How many petitioners are lucky enough to have such important and powerful connections? In fact, even though Guo did have such a connection, it was of no avail.[27]

In the United States, aggrieved people can contact their congressional representatives for help, and those representatives must respond.[28] In China, while the constitution stipulates that the people's congresses at both central and the local levels are the most powerful organ in the country, they are essentially useless because the congressmen are generally appointed by the Party and not, as the constitution states, elected directly by the people. The experience of the homeowners on November 28, 2001, when their congressmen paid no attention to their complaints, was particularly acute, further demonstrating that the congressmen felt that they could not side with the people against the government.

For that reason, the homeowners had refrained from petitioning the NPC. They had petitioned only the Office of the People's Congress in the City of Wuhan (Wuhanshi renda bangongting), on January 18, 2002. The petition letter began with a short description of recent official actions in Waitan Garden, charging the local government with illegally ordering the demolition. Since January 7, 2002, the local government had allegedly taken the following unlawful actions: frequently cutting off the supply of gas, detaining elderly people during their morning exercises, and using force during the process of demolition. Government actions had "damaged the environment of the community, disturbed the order of homeowners' lives, and threatened the lives and properties of the lawful homeowners." The letter warned the congress that the consequences could be dire if the conflicts between the homeowners and the work team lingered.

The petitioners continued to argue that they had all acquired the required legal permits prior to buying their properties in Waitan Garden and that the project proved to be effective in terms of flood control. They demanded that the city congress respond to three requests as soon as possible. First, they wanted the local government to immediately stop its forcible demolition of Waitan Garden and the work team harassment. Second, arrange for specialists to appraise the impact of Waitan Garden on flood control and make convincing conclusions. Was it possible to preserve rather than demolish Waitan Garden through some kind of structural modification enhancing flood control since compensation for decoration would cost at least 200 million RMB? Third, the homeowners had the right to know what went wrong with Waitan Garden and why it had to be demolished. "In the meantime, the [local government] must correct its previous mistakes and conform to legal procedure," the petition noted. "The only way to correctly resolve the Waitan Garden incident is to comply with the law." In addition, it indicated that the demolition of Waitan Garden should follow certain articles of the Regulations Regarding the Management of Urban Housing Demolition and that compensation needed to be in accordance with the State Compensation Law.

It was not surprising that, being a ceremonial and, thus, powerless legislature, the city congress of Wuhan did not respond to the petition.

Natural Resistance

Most of the time, the homeowners had tried to use lawful means to address their grievances. In early 2002, as the situation became increasingly dangerous, some of them felt compelled to adopt methods of "natural resistance." Unlike "rightful resistance," which normally invokes laws and regulations as the basis for their charges and operates through established legal channels,[29] natural resistance operates outside existing laws and regulations. In Chinese history, appealing to both religious and secular principles such as the concepts of a loving and powerful heaven and Confucian *minben,* adherents of natural resistance "often consciously or unconsciously ignore the laws and regulations that required them to proceed through lawful steps in seeking justice for official malfeasance."[30]

According to the 2005 Regulations Regarding Letters and Visits (Xinfang tiaoli), all petitions must be valid and lodged step-by-step; no more than five people can deliver a petition; attacks on government organs and the interception of public vehicles (*gongwuche*) were prohibited. Although the regulations outlaw official suppression of petitioners and the taking of revenge against them, they fail to say what punishment those in violation of the regulations will face.[31] Seeing that lawful resistance was having no effect, some homeowners began resorting to natural resistance. On January 13, the city congress of Wuhan was holding a conference. Fearing an attempt to disrupt the meeting, the government dispatched a large number of antiriot police to Waitan Garden to ward off any collectively delivered petitions. In the morning, pretending to go to their workplaces, Yan Fengjun and some other homeowners left Waitan Garden individually to avoid police attention. Afterward, they headed to the conference venue. The police there were attentively monitoring the crowd. No sooner had Yan taken out a banner and started chanting slogans than the police detained her. Some homeowners rushed into the conference room and spread out a long scroll with slogans such as "Defending rights in compliance with the law" (*yifa weiquan*), "Administration in accordance with the law," and "Down with Tu Yong" (Tu being the Wuhan vice mayor in charge of demolition) on it. They also distributed copies of the official permits they had obtained when purchasing their properties to the congressmen. Unfortunately, none of the congressmen acted in their support. The police came in and detained all of them. They remained in police custody for almost a day but were allowed to leave after 9:00 P.M.[32]

In this case, the homeowners had violated the 1995 Regulations Regarding Letters and Visits because their number exceeded the legal limit of five. Moreover, the law also banned such attacks by petitioners. This time, the local police seemed to have a legitimate reason to detain the protesters.

Undeterred, the homeowners persisted in practicing natural resistance. Three days later, Yan and another homeowner secretly went to Beijing to petition, traveling separately to avoid suspicion. According to one account, the other homeowner carried only a small bag and, after leaving home, went first to her office. She stayed there for about half an hour and then stealthily took a bus to the airport. Later she recalled that the three-hour waiting period before the plane left was the most nerve-wracking time of the mission. While waiting at the airport, she constantly worried that the police might discover her whereabouts and take her into custody. After she boarded the plane, she became more terrified because, if the police came at this time, all her efforts would be in vain. It was not until takeoff that she finally relaxed since she knew the plane could not be stopped now. In Beijing, she met Yan, and they both went to the Central People's Radio Station (Zhongyang renmin guangbo diantai). Several reporters there admitted that they had all heard about the Waitan Garden incident, but none of them felt that they could do anything to help. A friend introduced them to a CCTV reporter. They gave her a detailed account of the case, including the falsity of the 2001 CCTV report. She promised to write a report in the evening and give it to the head of CCTV the next morning. They also met a reporter from the renowned program *Half Hour at Noon,* which was broadcast by the Central People's Radio Station. Like the CCTV reporter, this reporter promised that he would report the case to the head of the station.

While in Beijing, Yan and her companion wrote another petition letter to President Jiang Zemin, imploring him to interfere in the Waitan Garden case and order the local government to stop the illegal harassment. The letter supposedly arrived in Jiang's hands thanks to personal connections. However, no response was forthcoming. Nor were they ever contacted again by the CCTV reporter. Yet another attempt to save Waitan Garden had failed.[33]

As we have shown earlier, the Waitan Garden homeowners had the advantage of connections with powerful people. But the case involved Premier Zhu Rongji and the flood control law, and neither the media nor any leaders were willing to get involved. Faced with such difficulty in getting their grievances redressed, Yan and her compatriot decided to take a skipping-level petition to Beijing, which was against the 1995 law.

On January 16, the same day Yan and her compatriot went to Beijing, the homeowners sent an urgent petition to the public media. It highlighted recent law violations by the local government, such as the continual intimidation of the homeowners, the cutting off of the gas supply to Unit 1, and the destruction of two other units without legal justification. On January 14, the work team had prohibited the lawyer team, led by Sun Gexin, to open its office in Waitan Garden and ordered the remaining homeowners in Unit 1 to relocate before January 17. Infuriated homeowners chanted the slogan, "Live and die with Waitan Garden," escalating the conflict. The petition ended with the threat of a massive petition in Beijing: "The situation is now very severe and urgent! Over four hundred home-owners and one thousand people have been pressured to the brink of a mountain of swords and a sea of flames [*daoshan huohai*]. At this critical moment, if the provincial and city leaders still ignore them and do not take quick action to solve their problems, the homeowners will organize a petition team of one thousand people that will travel to Beijing!"[34]

The threat of mass petition would, if implemented, certainly infringe the Regulations Regarding Letters and Visits, which permitted at most five petition-ers. Moreover, the petition to Beijing would be a skipping-level petition if the homeowners did not first petition the district, city, and provincial governments.

Seeing that more homeowners were taking the course of natural resistance, the local government was afraid that the petitioners in Beijing would cause it trouble. According to a document issued by the National Bureau of Letters and Visits (Guojia xinfang jü) circa 2003, any magistrate confronted with a collective petition of more than fifty people should resign, and the official in charge of the local letters and visits office should be fired. Another secret order from the central government noted that any counties from which collective petitioners traveled to Beijing would not be considered "advanced," which meant that the magistrate would not be promoted.[35] If more Waitan Garden homeowners petitioned Beijing, the local officials feared that their political careers would be compromised. To prevent this from happening, they increased their monitoring of Waitan Garden, and especially of a handful of homeowner activists.

On January 21, ten days after the Waitan Garden lawyers filed their lawsuit against the local government with the provincial high court, the five homeowner representatives went to the court inquiring about the result. But the court police refused to let them in. When they called the Case Filing Chamber (Li'anting), reminding its members that the Supreme Court required courts to make decisions on whether to accept cases within seven days, one associate leader responded that the provincial high court had no such regulations. The homeowner representatives were befuddled by this response, and they wondered whether the Supreme Court had revised its order or whether the interpretation of the provincial high court took precedence over the Supreme Court order. After a quarrel at the provincial letters and visits office and a threat to petition Beijing, the representatives finally met Huang Jianshe, the "honorable" vice head of the high court. Huang told the representatives that the provincial high court did not accept collective lawsuits. He suggested that they lodge a suit with the Wuhan Intermediate Court. The representatives were astonished at this because the lawyers had told them that only the provincial high court could accept collective lawsuits.

The representatives then decided to go to Beijing to petition. They made an appointment with a Beijing reporter. One of them, He Feng, gave three others a ride to the train station. Fearing that the local police might track him, He got out of the car early and walked to the station. He bought a ticket to Beijing and walked to the waiting room. As soon as he arrived there, a dozen policemen besieged him. He immediately realized that he had lost his personal freedom and could not go to Beijing as planned. He recorded the detailed conversation between himself and the police that ensued:

Police: Are you He Feng?
He Feng: Yes.
Police: Where are you going?
He Feng: Beijing.
Police: Why do you want to go to Beijing?
He Feng: I want to know if you want to stop me by force.

Police: No, absolutely not. We just want to chat with you.

He Feng: I think your action is very disgusting. I no longer want to go [to Beijing].

He Feng then walked straight to the square in front of the train station and called another homeowner, asking him not to bring him a ticket. Suddenly, a policeman rushed forward and dragged him by the collar, yelling at him: "You cannot leave. You must stop." He Feng asked: "What do you want?" The policeman said peremptorily, "Nothing, but you cannot go." He Feng became angry: "Do you want to use force today?" The policeman did not reply. He Feng went on: "If you want to use force, please show your ID. What you have done in public is outrageous. If you do not want your face [i.e., reputation], I still want mine. Are you treating me like a criminal?"

He Feng later wrote that he was quite nervous at the time because the police outnumbered him. Had they used force, he would have resisted. More seriously, he had an important document in his bag which he planned to give to a Beijing reporter and could not be confiscated by the police. After a short standstill, one official from the work team smiled and said that they wanted a chat and nothing more. Seeing that he had no choice, He followed the police to the headquarters of the work team in Waitan Garden. There, a vice head of the Hanyang District Police Bureau interviewed him for an hour, denying that police had violated the law by restricting his personal freedom, and warning him to cease his involvement with the homeowner representatives: "You are one of the five representatives, and that does no good to you. Why do you want to challenge the government? Central leaders have already approved the demolition of Waitan Garden, and there is no chance for it to survive. You will gain nothing by challenging the government." He then tried to entice He to drop his involvement in the lawsuit: "If you have any requests, we can help you solve them. But we can take care only of you and not other homeowners. If you feel that dropping the lawsuit will cause you to lose face, we can also help you. All your personal requests will be considered."

Like other representatives, He certainly did not want to betray the homeowners. He told the police head that, if Waitan Garden had to be demolished, he and the other homeowners needed to know that the action was in fact legitimate. "We bought our Waitan Garden properties with clear [legal documents]," he said, "and we also want a clear explanation of relocation." He asked the police head why the local government could not conform to the Regulations Regarding the Management of Urban Housing Demolition. He regarded the lawsuit as legitimate and believed that it would not be rejected. He also rejected the offer of help. He then said that his mother suffered from heart disease and that he needed to leave and look after her.

Seeing that He could not be bought off and that the train to Beijing had left, the police head decided to let him leave. But first he asked him whether he thought that the police had unlawfully detained him, reiterating that they merely wanted to "make a friend" of him. He Feng sneered but replied politely: "The fact is there, and you really did not allow me to board the train. Despite the fact, I personally would not think that way because we had a good conversation tonight." After leaving the room, He Feng saw many police outside. There was no question that he could not have left without the consent of the police head. He was relieved afterward that his composure helped protect the important document in his bag.[36]

In this case, He Feng was "retrieved" by the local police, a common occurrence in China during the past two decades. To protect their official posts and ensure their promotion, local officials in Wuhan, and almost all regions in China, have tried myriad means to stop petitioners from going to Beijing. Indeed, the police were generally polite to He Feng and used minimal force, as was not the case with individuals who had no strong connections in the government and the public media.[37] He Feng and most other Waitan Garden homeowners were relatively well-off and better educated. If the police used force, He and his fellow homeowners might have the ability to disclose that fact to the national media or, through personal connection, to the central leaders.

Those cases in which Waitan Garden homeowners practiced natural resistance were typical of "legal asymmetry." That is, it was the homeowners, and not the police, who had to obey the law. Once the homeowners violated the law by "attacking" the local congress, bringing skipping-level petitions to Beijing, or pursuing collective petitions with more than five people, the local police would detain them and place them in custory or detain them at the train station. But the laws prohibiting the police abuse of power would not be enforced. The reason was simple: the police were both lawbreakers and law enforcers. Moreover, they had the backing of the local government.

LAST HOPES DASHED

None of the petitions that the homeowners filed had been successful. The Waitan Garden lawyers filed their first administrative litigation with the Hubei Provincial High Court on January 10, 2002. The plaintiffs were the five representatives, and the defendant was the Wuhan municipal government. The plaintiffs accused the defendant of illegally approving the Waitan Garden project and transferring responsibility for its mistake to the plaintiffs. They made a total of five requests to the court:

1. Confirming that a number of the defendant's administrative actions in approving the Waitan Garden project were unlawful.
2. Confirming that the defendant's actions in relocating Waitan Garden homeowners are illegal.
3. Ordering the defendant to relocate and compensate the Waitan Garden homeowners in accordance with the law.

4. Ordering the defendant to openly apologize to the plaintiffs.
5. Ruling that the defendant must pay all litigation expenses.

The plaintiffs then provided a detailed explanation justifying their requests. First, they discussed the legal permits that the homeowners had acquired from the Waitan Garden developer. All the permits corroborated that the defendant had undoubtedly approved the Waitan Garden project. After CCTV criticized Waitan Garden as an illegal construction, however, the approvers of Waitan Garden suddenly transformed themselves into demolishers. The work team of over two hundred members entered Waitan Garden and began relocation. Without any legal documents, the work team had mobilized a large police force to intimidate dissatisfied homeowners, threatening them by checking whether their income was legal and whether they had paid their taxes, using relatives, superiors, and friends to exert pressure, occupying the rooms belonging to the homeowners, obstructing their meetings, and not allowing Wuhan lawyers to defend them. In addition, the plaintiffs charged the defendant with preventing the public media from interviewing homeowners and suppressing homeowners' efforts to use legal means to protect their properties.

The homeowners had been forced to accept the "Implementing Opinions" of the Hanyang District government. After some naive homeowners signed their contracts with the local government, they realized that they had fallen into a trap. Not only did the apartments in the other complexes designated by the local government sharply increase their prices, but those properties were also either not available or difficult to resell.

The plaintiffs argued that those actions of the local government had devastated both the plaintiffs' "deep passion" (*shenhou ganqing*) for the Party and their faith in the defendant's ability to correct its own mistakes. They had suffered great spiritual harm and economic loss. They pointed out that, while Wuhan had begun to take advantage of China's entry into the WTO and tried to become an international metropolis, it was inconceivable and intolerable for the defendant to take illegitimate actions to correct its own mistakes.[38]

The lawyers, of course, were Sun Gexin and his colleagues. After waiting for about two weeks, the provincial high court turned down the lawsuit on the grounds that it was a collective one. This result surprised neither the lawyers nor the plaintiffs. On January 25, 2002, the plaintiffs appealed to the Supreme Court, as planned.

The Supreme Court lawsuit had the support of 130 Waitan Garden homeowners, which arguably made it the largest collective litigation after China entered the WTO. Its requests were the same as those of the high court suit. The plaintiffs and their lawyers waited several more weeks for the court decision. Meanwhile, homeowners tried to petition various central and local leaders and governments, hoping for a miracle. A few used their connections to contact friends on the Supreme Court and provided additional documents. Unfortunately, all the last-ditch efforts were of no avail. The Supreme Court, like the provincial court, refused to accept the lawsuit.[39]

As Xu Bikang and the homeowner representatives had said earlier, the Supreme Court was their last hope and they would give up the fight if it refused the case. However reluctant, the homeowners had to accept defeat after nearly two months of courageous resistance and horrendous living conditions. They now had a better understanding of the Chinese saying, "The arm is no match for the thigh." Despite similar admonitions from their friends, relatives, and other homeowners, the representatives had at first an obstinate and unrealistic faith in Chinese law. They insisted on believing that the Administrative Litigation Law, the central leaders, and China's entry into the WTO would be the best ammunition with which to defend their legal rights. Accordingly, they had refrained from natural resistance until their lawsuits suffered setbacks. For some time, they had failed to recognize the crucial but cruel fact that in China the law is inferior to power. The experience of a legal fight against the local government helped smash their original naive belief in Chinese law and courts.

Fortunately, most of the homeowners in Waitan Garden had decent jobs and incomes. In that regard, they were more fortunate than thousands of other impoverished petitioners and thus would be less likely to become desperate and take extreme measures, such as self-immolation, attacking local government buildings, or wandering homeless in Beijing to continue their petition.

As scheduled, Unit 1 in Waitan Garden was blown up on January 25, 2002. Throughout February and March, the remaining homeowners no longer caused trouble or challenged the local government. One by one, they packed up their belongings and left their beloved apartments. Some have ended up in apartments they detest; others have had to wait for a while before moving into new homes. One homeowner later recalled that he had spent almost a year trying to sell his new apartment because it was located in a suburb of Wuhan.[40]

To compensate the developer of Waitan Garden, the Wuhan government gave the company 30 million RMB, which allowed it to thrive once again. Unlike the homeowners, the company heads had never challenged the local government. As a businessman, the manager of the company knew that his business depended on the support of the local government. In other words, the local government acted as his "parents who provide food and clothing" (*yishi fumu*).[41] According to one homeowner, none of the local officials who had been responsible for approving the Waitan Garden project were punished. Li Daqiang, the vice governor of Hubei Province, who advocated for the Waitan Garden project in 1995, was arrested and punished in 2000, one year before the demolition.[42] Instead of being punished, the local officials were in fact praised for their excellent work during the demolition process because they spent much less money than expected to complete their mission.[43]

On June 6, 2002, about two months after demolition was complete, Premier Zhu Rongji came to Wuhan to inspect the debris. He told the provincial leaders: "The construction of Waitan Garden is a bad beginning. But the demolition of Waitan Garden is a good beginning. From now on, no one will dare to build housing within the flood control levee."[44] It seemed that the premier was satisfied with the local officials actions. He totally ignored the plight of the homeowners and the desperate petitions they had sent him. Even if he had received the letters, he probably did not read them. He had also overlooked local officials' widespread and severe law violations of the local officials. According to one account, when the homeowners went to Beijing to tell Wu Yi, the vice premier, who himself came from Wuhan, that Waitan Garden had all the legal permits and should not be destroyed, Wu reportedly told them that it was the premier who had issued the demolition order. "If the premier's orders cannot be implemented, how can he command the world under heaven [*haoling tianxia*]?" he asked.[45] This was tantamount to saying that the premier's orders were above the law. In other words, even if his orders contradict the law, local officials still cannot challenge them. Thus, while they were free to break the law in the Waitan Garden case, they could not ignore the premier's orders. Clearly, China does not have the rule of law. Even the Supreme Court is under the control of the Party and the political leaders.

More than two thousand years ago, after the heir apparent of the Qin broke state law, the great legalist Lord Shang punished him. Shang said: "The reason that the law cannot be implemented is that people at the top violate it."[46] As one of the most prominent legalists in Chinese history, Shang was clearly aware that the law had to be enforced from the top. But Zhu chose to turn a blind eye to the infringements of the local officials. If the historical account of Shang is true, Zhu lags far behind him in his understanding of the importance of the law and the harm that can be done by power.

THE END: POWER TRIUMPHED OVER THE LAW

From November 19, 2001, when CCTV broadcast its skewed report, to March 30, 2002, when the last of the Waitan Garden buildings were torn down, there were a total of 130 days. To most Waitan Garden homeowners, those 130 days were not only miserable and harrowing but also grim and frightful. The resistance of many of them, and particularly their representatives, was courageous and heroic and represented a perfect test of the relations between law and power in the reformed China. The homeowners, who were mostly educated professionals, had, from the beginning, taken rational and legal measures such as meetings, petitions, and lawsuits to protect their properties. They argued cogently that their properties were legitimate and thus could not be destroyed and unfairly compensated. What they demanded from the local government was reasonable and legitimate, and all they wanted was a resolution of the Waitan Garden issue in accordance with recent state laws. After the local government repeatedly rejected their lawful requests and tried to impose a news blackout, they resorted to personal connections to reach out to the public media and high-level government officials. When these efforts failed, valiant Waitan Garden lawyers and over 130 homeowners decided to lodge administrative litigations against the local government. While the odyssey of the homeowners was ultimately in vain, their collective lawsuit has been hailed as the first and largest collective commoners-against-officials lawsuit in twenty-first-century China.

There were several reasons behind the failure of their rights protection movement. First, its opponent, the local government—a microcosm of the Chinese government—was too powerful. The CCP and the Chinese government (both central and local) firmly control the administration, judiciary, and congresses. Even if the central government or the NPC has promulgated certain laws and regulations, the local government can ignore them, and the premier's order was more powerful than the law. Second, to protect their political careers, local officials in Wuhan and Hubei Province, who had approved the Waitan Garden project themselves, performed a quick about-face and supported demolition. The local governments (both Wuhan and Hanyang) gave the police the green light to take unlawful and forcible means to relocate the Waitan Garden homeowners. Other abuses of power included intimidation, harassment, pressuring relatives, friends, and superiors, blocking petitions, seizing materials, threatening to detain activists, and detaining homeowners at train stations. No matter how vehemently the homeowners petitioned and protested, the abuse of power continued. Third, the lack of an independent judiciary made administrative litigation especially difficult. As some scholars have argued, if commoners are to sue officials successfully, a court must accept the lawsuit. In many, if not most, cases, such suits are simply rejected. In the Waitan Garden instance, the refusal of both the provincial court and the Supreme Court to accept the case meant that the homeowners' fight was over.

The case of Waitan Garden reflects the legal asymmetry in the PRC. On the one hand, the homeowners had to follow the law when attempting to protect their properties. The only illegal approaches they adopted were the skipping-level petition in Beijing, collective petitions with more than five people, and chanting slogans in the local congressional meeting. Yet all such actions were taken after all legal means had failed. Local government officials and the police, however, unabashedly ignored and violated what to them were inconvenient laws and regulations. They were clearly aware that, in an authoritarian nation like China, there is no check on their power.

4

Xuzhou

A Teacher versus the Powerful Government

Beginning in 2002, there were many media reports about Wang Peirong, an associate professor at the Chinese University of Mining and Technology in Xuzhou (Zhongguo kuangye daxue), Jiangsu Province. While many Westerners may be familiar with major cities like Shanghai, Beijing, Guangzhou, and Nanjing, they are not familiar with Xuzhou, which is a relatively unpopular city in China today. Historically, however, Xuzhou, whose establishment can be traced back to six thousand years ago, was very important, and its strategic location made it the gateway between north and south. It was also the birthplace of some famous historical figures, such as Liu Bang, the founder of the Han dynasty (202 BCE–220 CE), and Sun Quan, the ruler of Wu (182–252 CE) during the Three Kingdoms (220–280 CE). It was also the capital of Liu Bang's archrival Xiang Yu, the Hegemon of West Chu (232–202 BCE). In early 1938, the GMD army fought with the Japanese aggressors in Xuzhou area and won one of China's greatest victories.[1]

Professor Wang became well-known not because of his scholarship but because of his exceptional courage and perseverance in fighting the local government alone. When I (Qiang Fang) first met him in Xuzhou in late 2003, he was not different from many other people. But I could sense the hazardous situation in which he was involved. The interview was held in the hotel where I stayed because, as he told me, it was dangerous for me to visit his family at that time. A local thug against whom he had been attempting to press charges had placed a 20 million RMB on his head.[2] The interview went pretty smoothly, and I had the chance to get firsthand information from a man who had fought a legal war with the powerful local police, judges, and government. Despite numerous setbacks in terms of administrative litigations filed and especially the beatings from and threats on his life by local gangsters, Wang persisted in his struggle for justice and eventually won the support of the local heads and many other people around the country. His years of working alone have attracted much attention from the public media, yet, up to now, there are only a few serious studies focusing on his legal battles.[3] This chapter offers the first analysis of the asymmetric relations between law and power and between commoners and powerful officials/persons in Wang Peirong's lone legal battles. His case will help us understand more about the nature, practice, enforcement, and fundamental problems of the law during China's current urbanization movement.

Antitheft Doors

What Professor Wang had been fighting for over five years was the antitheft doors of Fenghuayuan, a beautiful residential community similar to Waitan Garden in Wuhan. Wang came to Xuzhou from northwest China in 1995, a time when, like many other cities in China, Xuzhou was experiencing rapid urbanization. In 1999, he and thousands of other faculty and staff bought new homes in Fenghuayuan. The original intention of the local government in building Fenghuayuan was truly good. In an effort to both beautify the city and address the shortage of housing for intellectuals working in Xuzhou, the Xuzhou municipal government initiated a project called People's Heart (Minxin) and invested a total of 300 million RMB (about US$49 million) in it. Most of the apartments in Fenghuayuan were to be sold to renowned specialists who had made major contributions to the scientific, economic, and cultural development of the city. Some central leaders had reportedly stressed the quality of the units' construction.[4] The residential community comprised roughly sixty upscale buildings. After the complex was completed in 1999, many central and local leaders came to inspect it. In 2000, the Fenghuayuan residential community won the title "Exemplary Residential Community of National Property Management" (Quanguo wuye guanli shifan zhuzhai xiaoqu), a prestigious award conferred by the Ministry of Construction (Jianshebu).[5]

Initially, most Fenghuayuan homeowners were very happy with their new apartments, which had modern designs and were fully equipped. Soon, however, they discovered problems with them. The biggest and most noticeable problem was their antitheft doors. Before they had moved in, each had been asked to pay 500 RMB for an antitheft door, a price that was much higher than the market price. More frustrating was that the doors were Three-Noes products (sanwu, meaning no production place, no trademark, and no certification). They were all of poor quality. Some could be opened without keys; others could not be locked or could be unlocked with different keys. According to a contract signed by the Fenghuayuan developer in 1999, the antitheft doors were to be Shengying (lit. "holy baby"), a reliable brand made by a company in Nanjing, the capital of Jiangsu Province. Yet, to the homeowners' dismay, while the doors carried the correct brand name, they were actually made illegally by a factory in Xuzhou. Furthermore, the supplier of the knockoff doors was the Yunlong District Security Company (Yunlongqu bao'an gongsi), whose business license had been revoked in 1998, one year before the homeowners moved into Fenghuayuan.[6]

In April 2000, when one Fenghuayuan homeowner arrived at his home around 11:00 p.m., he found that he could not open his door no matter how many times he had tried. Unwilling to disturb his neighbors, he spent the night in a public bathroom. The next morning, he complained to the property manager, who promised to fix his door for free.[7] Owing mostly to the defective antitheft doors, homeowners lost hundreds of bikes and other possessions. And they began to worry about their personal safety. Other problems gradually came to light. For example, the underground water pipes often leaked, and the floors of some apartments had cracked. For the first three years Fenghuayuan was occupied, many homeowners complained to a variety of government officials in Xuzhou and elsewhere. But none had been responsive.[8]

Despite the poor quality of construction and the less-than-helpful property manager, the fees that the homeowners were required to pay were higher than those in most other residential communities in Xuzhou. The first Fenghuayuan property manager was Xinyuan Property Management, which took on the job in late 1999. In April 2000, however, Xinyuan was mysteriously replaced by Jialong Property Company, which was associated with the Fenghuayuan developer, the Xuzhou Economical Housing Center (Xuzhou jingji shiyongfang zhongxin), and a local government organ. To the surprise of many Fenghuayuan homeowners, when it assumed the job of property management, Jialong did not have a legal certificate to operate. The certificate that it did have had been forged by the Xuzhou Economical Housing Center. Apparently, the center wanted to make more money by hiring its own company to manage Fenghuayuan. According to Wang Peirong, the extra income found its way into the pockets of some of the local heads. Backed by the Xuzhou Housing Managing Bureau (Xuzhou fangguanjü), Jialong allegedly counterfeited the commission contract of property management (*wuye weituo hetong*) and an official seal. By doing so, it was able to obtain an award for national exemplary property management from the Ministry of Construction.[9]

Two Powerful Local Men

Who should be held responsible for the overpriced and defective antitheft doors, leaking pipes, and cracked floors? How did the manufacturers dare to produce such poor-quality products? And why did the local government openly install the doors and do other work in Fenghuayuan? Who benefited most?

Ultimately, two powerful local individuals were implicated. One was Yan Jiaxun, and the other was Li Hai. Yan was a self-employed person (*getihu*). Owing to his strong connections with the local police, he managed in 1997 to affiliate his own company with the Xuzhou Yunlong District Security Company, which was owned by the local police, meaning that it was recognized as a business department of the security company. The benefits of being a government-backed company were clear: "the power to mobilize social resources" and make "unlawful profits."[10] For Yan, the cost of affiliating with a government company was an annual charge referred to as a "management fee," a small price that he deemed worthwhile.

Not surprisingly, within a year Yan's new company had violated local regulations, and the Xuzhou Industrial and Commercial Bureau (Xuzhou gongshangjü) decided to discontinue its certificate. Yan was not, however, forced out of business. On the contrary, he continued to use his local connections to continue in operation. The lucrative business of making antitheft doors was one of his enterprises. It needed official approval, however, and both the Xuzhou Police Bureau and the Xuzhou Yunlong District Police Bureau reportedly provided the required permits. Losing his official certificate had turned to Yan's advantage since he was not required to pay any taxes on his illegal operations. This meant an extra bonus for him and his supporters in the local police.

To further assist him, the local police unlawfully allowed Yan to buy a police car marked "public security" (gong'an). Along with his connections with the local police, that car helped him successfully win contracts to make antitheft doors for Fenghuayuan. The total amount was 1.5 million RMB, a sizable sum. Invoking the PRC Criminal Law, Wang Peirong argued that Yan's crimes—illegally producing products, selling Three-Noes goods, and evading taxes—warranted a sentence of fifteen years to life in prison.[11] But would Yan's allies in the local police bureau and courts enforce the law?

Yan was also conspiring with Li Hai, whose father was the former vice Party secretary of Xuzhou, the former head of the Xuzhou Organizational Department (Zuzhibu), and the former head of the Political and Legal Commission. Li not only collaborated with Yan in producing the defective antitheft doors, but he was also responsible for buying and installing the defective gas meters, water meters, and water pipes. According to the homeowners, the price of their shoddy water meters was five times that of the regular ones. Some of the gas and water meters also had serious leakage problems, and, while water leaks were wasteful, gas leaks were potentially fatal. To make more money, Li and Yan raised the price of each antitheft door from 390 RMB to 500 RMB, totaling 370,000 RMB in revenue.[12] It was clear that Li's connections helped him secure the Fenghuayuan contracts. He and Yan chose to work with local companies in order to increase their profits. Also because of their connection, Li and Yan were not concerned by homeowners' complaints. Had it not been for Wang Peirong, who persisted in his petitions and administrative litigations, the government could simply have ignored the problems.

First the Villain Sues His Victim

From the inception of his struggle to obtain justice, Wang Peirong, unlike natural resisters, who resort to extralegal or even illicit means to address their grievances, was determined to use only legitimate methods. As early as spring 2000, before he began his petitions and lawsuits, some Fenghuayuan homeowners had petitioned the local government and newspapers. On July 18, 2000, the *Pengcheng Evening News,* a local newspaper, publicized petition letters from Fenghuayuan homeowners that complained of the shoddy and overpriced antitheft doors.[13] In November 2001, Wang had begun mailing petition letters to the local government. His efforts quickly won the support of most Fenghuayuan homeowners, who formed a committee and elected him head. On November 9, 2001, Wang submitted a lengthy petition letter to the Letters-and-Visits Office of the Xuzhou municipal government, accusing both Yan Jiaxun and Li Hai of illegal activities. The letters and visits offices were first created in the 1950s, shortly after the establishment of the PRC. CCP leaders made clear that the mission of state apparatuses such as the courts, the police, and the procuratorates were to deal with class enemies, whereas the letters and visits offices would resolve disagreements among the people.[14] From the late 1950s through the 1970s, almost all counties and townships had founded the Letters and Visits offices.[15]

When interviewed by a newspaper reporter, Wang said that he could not recall how many government units he had petitioned. To gather evidence, he had traveled between Xuzhou and Nanjing, a distance of over one hundred miles. But all his petitions were to no avail. Although some central, provincial, and municipal leaders had ordered that the case be investigated, no one in Xuzhou took it serious and thus took no action. "I have to continue my petitions," Wang noted. "I have not counted how much money I have spent. It is estimated to be at least 20,000 or 30,000 RMB."[16] Ridiculously, one of Wang's petition letters to the central government ended up in the hands of the local police whom Wang had charged. Brandishing the letter in front of him, one policeman informed Wang that it was useless for him to petition the central government. The letter remained in the hands of the local police, and the central leaders would not satisfy Wang's grievances.[17]

It is not surprising that the central government offices do not have sufficient personnel to deal with all the petitions filed by aggrieved citizens and must therefore pass the petitions on to local governments. In some cases, petition letters will be directed to the officials accused in them.[18] But Wang's constant petitioning finally caught the attention of some local public media. On January 14, 2002, for example, the *Metropolitan Morning News* (*Dushi chenbao*), a popular newspaper based in Xuzhou, reported on the high prices charged for the antitheft doors and electricity in Fenghuayuan.[19] Three days later, the morning channel of Xuzhou TV also reported on the defective antitheft doors.[20]

To Wang's surprise, while he was busy petitioning on behalf of the homeowners, he received a subpoena from a local court on May 10, 2002. The accuser was none other than Yan Jiaxun. Why did Yan take this action? There was no denying that he had been vexed by Wang's petitions to the local, the provincial, and even the central government. His allies on the local police force were also worried that Wang's petitions would adversely affect their careers. The Yunlong Branch of the Xuzhou Police Bureau allegedly helped Yan forge several official documents. One was to legalize Yan's purchase of the police car. To stop Wang from petitioning, Yan put on 20 million RMB bounty on his head. When Wang asked the local police for protection, no action was taken. Yan had also attacked Wang. In February 2003, as Wang was walking one day to the gate of Fenghuayuan, Yan robbed and beat him. After the police were called in, Yan was not intimidated, going so far as to beat Wang in the presence of the police, and the police did not interfere. The next year, Wang had asked the local police many times to retrieve the property that Yan had stolen, and the police refused to assist him. Their inaction greatly emboldened Yan and put Wang's life in danger.[21]

The local police, the court, and Yan also reportedly worked together to fabricate clumsy and clearly perjured cover stories. One was supposedly proof from the Nanjing Shengying Security and Protection Company, the authentic manufacturer of the antitheft doors. But Wang saw through it in court and argued that the manufacturer was actually the Nanjing Public Security Technological Industrial Company. In addition, Wang pointed out in court that Yan's "proof" was a photocopy with clear man-made marks and not the original. The "proof" was then retracted from evidence. Another piece of fabricated evidence was Yan's occupation, which the local police had secretly changed from worker in the Yunlong District Security Company to cadre working at the Yunlong branch of the Xuzhou Police Bureau.

On July 18, 2002, Wang submitted tapes in which a head of the Xuzhou Police Bureau said that the sale of all antitheft doors in Xuzhou had to be registered with the Xuzhou Police Bureau. Yet both the production and the sale of the antitheft doors installed in Fenghuayuan were not registered, a clear violation of the order. Also, the head said that all antitheft doors had to pass muster with inspection centers in either Beijing or Shanghai. Otherwise they could not be sold. Wang also displayed evidence from as many as thirteen witnesses to Judge Li Xiumei that Yan Jiaxun had brutally beaten him at around 6:30 P.M. on June 7, 2002. Another important evidence was a letter written by a witness who had charged Yan Jiaxun with bribery. The judge, an alleged ally of Yan's, chastised Wang for submitting the evidence, and Wang responded, but a transcription of the ensuing dialogue was not included in court records, which further raised Wang's suspicion that the judge intended to protect Yan.

More outrageous was that the judge ordered the court police to detain Wang when he asked to duplicate the documents fabricated by local police. His request was legal, and he had made an appointment to meet the judge in her office, but "to prevent Wang from copying the perjuries" Li Xiumei ordered the court police to datain him. During the court debates, Li also "frequently" interrupted Wang's testimony.

The court's deliberate favoring of Yan meant that it was predetermined that Wang would lose his case. The court verdict indicated: "The activities of the defendant (Wang Peirong) have exceeded the boundaries of accusation and criticism and they should be regarded as humiliating and slandering other people by taking advantage of accusation. [Wang's] activities have constituted an infringement of [Yan's] reputation."[22]

The court also required Wang to pay 2,000 RMB to Yan as compensation for his emotional loss. Wang, of course, did not accept the biased and unjust judgment. He told the judge that it was only after the local police had failed to ensure his personal safety that he had exposed Yan's unlawful activities. All he wanted was to tell Fenghuayuan homeowners the truth. The defiant Wang quickly appealed to the appellate court, the Xuzhou Intermediate Court.[23] In an open letter to the public, Wang denounced the corruption of the Xuzhou Police Bureau and the local court. He charged them with severely sabotaging the socialist rule of law, the image of the Party, and the social ethos. He pleaded with the public media and every honest person in China for help so as to draw the attention of the central leaders to this case.[24] National and local media, such as the *Law and Life,* the *China Youth Daily,* the *China Social Newspaper,* the *Modern Swift News* (*Xiandai kuaibao*), and the *Jiangnan Times* (*Jiangnan shibao*) all reported on Wang's petitions and trials.

Given the increased public pressure and intervention by city leaders, Wang's chance of winning a second trial was promising. On August 12, 2003, the Xuzhou Intermediate Court annulled the verdict of the local court and rejected Yan's requests. It also concluded that Yan was behind the production and sale of the bogus antitheft doors. It did not, however, support Wang's request that Yan transfer his income from sales of the antitheft doors to the local procuratorate and police bureau. Still, the favorable decisions were Wang's first victory and demonstrated that, while the so-called people's court had been a tool of the Party, some judges could still make impartial decisions, especially in cases where the defendants were not powerful officials. Despite being backed by the local police and the court, Yan was not a government official. In contemporary China, the police are usually more powerful than the court, and the heads of the police are often the heads of the political and legal commissions, which, as we have seen, are in charge of the Party's "knife hilts."[25] Given Yan's connection with the local police, it was not surprising for the local court to favor him. Yet the intermediate court was beyond the jurisdiction of local police, and that was why it could accept Wang's lawsuit and rule against Yan. Wang's case was different from that of Waitan Garden in that the latter involved both the Hubei provincial government and Premier Zhu Rongji, which made it extremely difficult for the court to accept the case.

WANG'S INITIAL ADMINISTRATIVE LITIGATIONS

Wang Peirong did not anticipate that Yan Jiaxun would file a lawsuit against him. If Yan, the criminal, could sue him, why could Wang, the victim, not sue Yan? Shortly after losing his case to Yan in the local court, Wang decided to file his own administrative litigations against the local government. On October 8, 2002, he filed a lawsuit against the Xuzhou Price Bureau (Xuzhou wujiajü) with the local court. This would be the first of his six consecutive administrative litigations. In his indictment, He argued that the price bureau needed to refund the 500 RMB for each antitheft door and 65 RMB for each heat installation that it had charged in Fenghuayuan. He also requested that the price bureau apologize to Fenghua-yuan homeowners for its administrative inaction (*xingzheng buzuowei*). The local court accepted the suit. During the trial, the price bureau argued that in 1999 decisions about prices were within its jurisdiction. To better deal with the case, the court drew on evidence from a third party, the Xuzhou Economical Housing Center. It ruled that the price bureau had failed to provide evidence that the anti-theft doors met quality standards and to explain the basis on which it set the price of the doors. On April 29, 2003, the court backed Wang's request and ordered the refund. This was Wang's first and only administrative litigation victory.[26]

On October 25, 2002, about two weeks after he sued the Xuzhou Price Bureau, Wang brought the Xuzhou Police Bureau to the Xuzhou Yunlong District Court. Unlike the price bureau, the police bureau was much more powerful and directly involved in this case. In his indictment, Wang asked the court to make three judg-ments: (1) the approval of Yan's use of a police car by the Yunlong Branch of the Xuzhou Police Bureau violated state law; (2) he (Wang) was justified in accusing Yan of unlawful possession of a police car; (3) the police bureau should apologize to him for its administrative inaction (*xingzheng buzuowei*). The police bureau submitted its defense response (*dabianshu*) on November 6, 2002. The court did not render a verdict until ten months later (the verdict was printed in late Sep-tember 2003). During the ten months, the court had allegedly fabricated a verdict that it had not made and a session that it had not opened in order to dupe Wang and protect the police bureau. To press the court for a speedy verdict, Wang peti-tioned many central and local courts, including the Central Disciplinary Com-mission. When the verdict was finally passed down, he questioned Zheng Jifeng, the court judge who was in charge of the case, why state law had not been fol-lowed. Article 57 of the Administrative Litigation Law clearly indicates: "The peo-ple's court should make its initial judgment within three months after it accepts a lawsuit." The judge did not respond. When Wang asked him to make a forensic appraisal of the printing time, he dodged the request, saying only that the original verdict was made on November 19, 2002, and that it was kept in the court.

The belated court verdict first argued that it was illegal for Wang to ask the police bureau to produce documentation of its approval of Yan's use of a police car because the principal party was the Yunlong Police Branch and not the Xuzhou Police Bureau. Second, recognizing the justice of his action, as Wang requested, was not within the court's power. Third, the use of police vehicles was an internal affair. If Wang appealed the decision, the court would not be able to consider the matter. Finally, the court rejected Wang's request that the Xuzhou Police Bureau apologize to him. Therefore, according to the forty-first article of the Administra-tive Litigation Law and the forty-fourth article of the Supreme Court's interpre-tation of the Administrative Litigation Law, it dismissed Wang's requests. Worse, the court ordered him to pay a 100 RMB litigation fee.[27]

Again, Wang was disappointed by the court verdict. Soon after receiving it, he appealed to the Xuzhou Intermediate Court, which had backed him against Yan the previous year. To the initial requests Wang added five more. (1) Owing to the administrative inaction, the defendant (i.e., the Xuzhou Police Bureau) should publicly apologize to him in the national public media (e.g., in the *People's Daily* and on CCTV) as well as in the major provincial and municipal media. (2) The defendant should pay the litigation fee. (3) Because the longtime administrative inaction of the defendant had inflicted spiritual and physical harm on the plaintiff, the Xuzhou Police Bureau should pay him 1 RMB as a nominal indemnity. (4) Because the Yunlong District Court had allegedly violated legal procedure by making its ruling before opening the court debate and put off rendering its verdict for ten months, the intermediate court should overturn the district court verdict. (5) If the intermediate court could not free itself from the control of criminals, make just rulings, and hold the local court accountable for intentionally rendering a false judgment, Wang threatened to appeal to the Jiangsu Provincial High Court or the Supreme Court in Beijing. In addition, he warned that, because some leaders in the police bureau had become the protectors of certain local criminals, the court should by law transfer important evidence from the defendant, the police bureau, to responsible government departments.

Wang was not bluffing. He did in fact take his suits to the provincial high court, an action that had great public impact and put immense pressure on local officials.

Unfortunately, Song Xinhe, a judge in the intermediate court who took charge of the case, was ruder and more insulting to Wang than the former local judge had been. When Wang asked him to find that the local court had not rendered its verdict in the legally proscribed time frame, he made "all sorts of excuses" in an attempt to shirk his responsibility. On November 20, 2003, the court opened its session. According to Wang, Song's attitude was very nasty throughout. After Wang criticized his bad attitude, Song refused to put forth any reason or legal basis (*falü yiju*) for his judgment at all. Wang then demanded an interpretation from the court. Song told him: "I will not reason with people like you, let alone give you the legal basis." He rejected Wang's further requests.

The final ruling was undoubtedly unfavorable to Wang. Like the local court, the intermediate court also cited a number of state laws to justify its decisions. As a result, Wang lost his second suit.

The two judges that Wang had encountered in the local and the intermediate courts had hardly acted professionally. The local judge had (allegedly) made up his mind even before the trial began, which, if true, was clearly against the law. And the judge in the intermediate court had insulted Wang in court. More incredible was that the local judge was named one of the ten "best judges" in Xuzhou in 2003.[28] He Weifang, a law professor at Peking University, had in 1998 attempted to draw attention to the poor quality of the judges. He argued against the use of military veterans, most of whom had little formal legal training as the main source of court judges: "For people who have spent many years in the military, compliance has become their second nature, and it is very difficult for them to transform into an independent judge."[29] Although legal education in China experienced an unprecedented expansion in the 1990s and the Judge Law was promulgated in 1995,[30] many judges, especially those working in cities in central China, were still either military veterans or people who had little legal training.

Despite their unprofessional and even unlawful behavior, both courts in Xuzhou had at least accepted Wang's suits. Moreover, they had based their verdicts on relevant state laws and not on personal opinions. This may be one of the notable changes that have occurred during China's current legal reform. If Wang had accused the local police during the Cultural Revolution or the Anti-Rightist Movement,[31] the judges or military cadres would have not accepted his case; even worse, he would likely have been charged with being a counterrevolutionary or a rightist and might have been punished.

Indeed, Wang was certainly aware of the danger inherent in challenging the local police. In November 2002, not long after he had brought his first suit, some officers in the Xuzhou Police Bureau threatened to fabricate a charge as a pretext to send him to *laojiao* (reeducation through labor). According to H. L. Fu (Fu Hualing), the Chinese police often used *laojiao* to punish "minor offenses"— punishment for which was determined by the police—"summarily." Unlike *laojiao, laogai* (reform through labor) was "subject to limited judicial review," and its application was determined by the courts, not the police.[32] This means that the local police had the power to sentence Wang to two years' *laojiao*. In PRC history, the extralegal *laojiao* was first used to punish tens of thousands of rightists in 1957, and it had frequently been practiced as late as 2013.[33] It was obvious that the local police wanted to abuse their power to take revenge on Wang for his accusations.

Fortunately, the leaders of Wang's university vehemently opposed police intimidation. One was quoted as saying: "So long as I am the president of the university, no faculty or students will allow the police to use 'false charges' to *laojiao* Wang Peirong. ["Before the police can *laojiao* Wang], they must arrest me first."[34]

As a scholar, Wang had some trust in the legal reform and the law; as a homeowner representative, he wanted to use the law to defend the legitimate rights of the homeowners who had elected him. The failure of his administrative litigations did not intimidate him. In fact, long before he received the verdict from the intermediate court, he had filed a bolder and larger lawsuit.

THE TUG-OF-WAR BETWEEN LAW AND POWER

On July 7, 2003, while the local court purposely procrastinated, Wang decided to take five major local governments to the Xuzhou Intermediate Court for their administrative inaction. In addition to the Xuzhou Police Bureau, the defendants also included the Xuzhou municipal government, the Xuzhou Quality and Technology Inspection Bureau (Xuzhou zhiliang jianduju), the Jiangsu Provincial Industrial and Commercial Administrative Bureau (Jiangsuzheng gongshang xingzheng guanliju), and the Xuzhou Price Bureau (second trial).

When a reporter asked him why he chose to charge the five local governments, Wang noted that he felt compelled to take that move:

> In the past several years, I have sent complaint letters to the municipal, provincial, and central governments. The heads of both the Ministry of Construction and the provincial people's congress have written official comments on my petitions; the Xuzhou mayor and the head of the Provincial Industrial and Commercial Bureau have issued orders; and some other departments have promised to investigate the case. But none of them have taken any tangible action. The person who made the poor-quality antitheft doors is still at large and driving his police car. The safety of my family cannot be guaranteed. Hence, I feel it necessary to accuse all the relevant governments in the court.[35]

His requests were similar to those made in his previous lawsuit against the police bureau. One major difference was that he sought a court ruling that the five governments had failed to take timely action in dealing with the defective antitheft doors. The real goal of his lawsuit was not to penalize the governments but to use court pressure to prod them to solve the problem. Therefore, he asked for only a single Chinese yuan and an apology from the five governments as token compensation for all the injustices he had suffered and the time he had spent. In his words, if he asked for greater compensation, the money would come from the taxpayers rather than from the government. He certainly did not want to waste tax money on local government misconduct.[36]

In court, Wang reaffirmed that the Fenghuayuan antitheft doors had been made and installed by Yan Jiaxun's company. Because its license had been revoked in 1998, it had no legal right to produce the doors, much less register them with the local police bureau. Yet Yan's illicit activities had obtained the support of the Xuzhou Police Bureau. In June 1999, some leaders of the police bureau and its Yunlong branch authorized Yan to buy a police car. The police car provided a legal cover for him and greatly helped his business. On July 28, 1999, he was allegedly driving his police car and using his nonexistent company as cover to close a deal with a local private company to produce antitheft doors. Moreover, Wang expressed concern for his family's safety. He testified in court that Yan had threatened him dozens of times and also beaten and robbed him in the presence of the local police. Whenever Wang called the local police for help, no officer had ever investigated. Also, the local police had not yet returned to Wang the property that Yan had stolen from him. All phone records in the case, including those of Wang's calls regarding Yan's attacks, had gone missing.

Again, the biggest problem with administrative litigation—as identified by Kevin O'Brien and Lianjiang Li—and the one faced by the Waitan Garden representatives did not exist in Xuzhou.[37] The Xuzhou Intermediate Court accepted Wang's administrative litigation against the five governments, the first multiple administrative litigation in China.[38] The 1989 Administrative Litigation Law allows each party in a lawsuit to submit its indictment. Unlike many governments in other cases that had refused to show up in court,[39] almost all the governments charged by Wang had at least submitted a written defense. This represents further progress in the process of Chinese legal reform.

The Xuzhou municipal government was the first to offer its defense. As the highest and most powerful government in Xuzhou, it argued that the city had consistently met its legal obligations. Since 2001, some city leaders had issued orders dealing with the case. In November 2001, Zhuang Huaping, the vice mayor of Xuzhou, asked certain departments to investigate the Fenghuayuan antitheft doors. On April 11, 2002, Mayor Pan Yonghe commented on Wang Peirong's petition letter and ordered the Xuzhou Price Bureau to take care of the issue. On April 17, 2003, the municipal government convened a meeting specifically about the Fenghuayuan antitheft doors. Officials from the police bureau, housing management bureau, economical housing office, and inspection bureau attended the meeting. Therefore, the city government said, it had actually paid serious attention to the matter and had taken responsible action in accordance with the law.

The city government then tried to excuse its shirking of its duty: "According to the Chinese Constitution and the Organizational Law [Zuzhifa], all local governments have adopted the cadre responsibility system [shouzhang fuzezhi]. The system requires the principal administrators to direct government affairs, their main duty being to guide the work of the departments within the unit and the inferior governments. Thus, the city government has the power to lead all the municipal departments but no power to deal with particular cases. In resolving each case, the municipal departments will be the main law enforcers."

The Xuzhou municipal government seemed to have forgotten that, as the top administration in the city, it had the responsibility to supervise the work of all the city and district departments. If those departments failed to conduct meticulous and timely investigations of cases, the city government was required to hold the department heads responsible and even demote or dismiss some of them. Using state laws as an excuse merely convinced many that the city government attempted to evade its legal and political obligations.

The city government further repeated that it had made many comments on the issue brought up by Wang Peirong. And Wang himself had confirmed that it had fulfilled its duties. There were many causes for the slow pace at which the issue was resolved. For example, the power boundaries of administrative departments were very strict. When an administrative department was performing its functions, it had to comply with the principle that "nothing can be done without conspicuous legal authorization." The city government believed that Wang had misunderstood the administrative functions. According to feedback from other departments dealing with the case, those departments had followed the orders of the city government by initiating the procedure to solve the problem. As for the specific details of the case, the court should ask the other government defendants. In so doing, the city government cleverly relieved itself of any responsibility in the case. It finally asked the court to reject Wang's "erroneous" charges against it.

The response of the Xuzhou Police Bureau differed from that of the city government in its threatening and terrifying rhetoric and attitude. Yet, like the city government, the police bureau also cited state laws to justify its actions. To begin, it argued that under the terms of the eleventh article of the Administrative Litigation Law it could not be charged with administrative inaction. According to the article, administrative inaction occurs only when a citizen "appeals to an administrative department to fulfill its legal obligations in terms of safeguarding physical and property rights" and "the department refuses to take action or to respond." One of the preconditions for a finding of administrative inaction was that the appeal of the private party (*xiangduiren*) was the objective factual basis (*keguan shishi jichu*) for the administration to exercise its lawful duties. After Fenghuayuan was completed in December 1999, the police bureau claimed that it had not received any appeal or notification regarding the poor quality of the antitheft doors. For that reason, the police bureau deemed it inappropriate to charge the bureau with inaction.

Next, the police bureau argued that it had no legal responsibility to investigate the antitheft doors. Thus, Wang's requests in his lawsuits had no legal support. Even though his suit outlined criminal activity that fell within police purview, it was still beyond the jurisdiction of administrative litigation.

The police bureau then turned to Yan Jiaxun's bribery, his use of a police vehicle, and his reprisals against Wang. It argued that those criminal charges should not have been included in the administrative litigation and that the court should therefore not accept it. The police bureau would be unwilling to defend itself and provide the necessary evidence if it were. In the meantime, however, it lodged a countersuit against Wang. It noted that, while Wang was making his accusations, he had to base his charges on the evidence and correctly explain the facts of the case. However, Wang took advantage of the petitions and accusations and attacked state administrative organs (i.e., the police bureau). It accordingly asked the court to impose draconian restrictions on Wang's attacks and turn down his appeals.[40]

As we noted earlier, the police bureau was different than the city government. The police were arguably the most powerful component of the political and legal commission that supervised the court, the procuratorate, and the police. The head of the police was usually the head of the political and legal commission. Accordingly, the police bureau did not fear the court and dared to ask it to forbid Wang from attacking it. In addition, it dodged any charges Wang made regarding its alleged collusion with Yan Jiaxun. It simply told the court that those charges were improper and should not be accepted them. It implied that, if the court insisted on investigating, it would not cooperate. This brazen response not only showcased the power of the police bureau and its contempt of the court but also proved that the bureau had in fact colluded with Yan.

The third defendant was the less powerful Xuzhou Quality and Technology Inspection Bureau. The bureau, of course, rebuffed all Wang's accusations. It first argued that, after Wang had petitioned it about the inferior antitheft doors, it conducted a preliminary investigation and found that those doors had been installed more than two years previously. According to the Administrative Punishment Law (Xingzheng chufafa), the complaint should have been filed earlier, and the producer could therefore not be held responsible. Hence, the bureau did not accept Wang's charges and refused to offer an explanation. It insisted that what it had done was completely in accordance with the law and that there was no administrative inaction. "On the contrary," it indicated, "it would be an unlawful action and administrative trespass if we accepted and investigated the case." On May 21, 2002, one of the associate heads of the bureau had led a team to Fenghuayuan to conduct an inspection and provided Wang with a detailed explanation and response.

Next, if the plaintiff needed an opinion on the quality of the antitheft doors, the only way to obtain one was to conduct an inspection. But the bureau said that it was not empowered to do so.

Third, the bureau contended that the plaintiff's requests lacked legal bases. For example, the request to be paid a single Chinese yuan had no legal basis because the bureau had done nothing illegal or anything contributing to the plaintiff's financial loss. Thus, the bureau should not be required to pay compensation of any kind. In addition, according to the plaintiff's petition, the case involved criminal offenses, which were not within the bureau's purview. Moreover, no law required the bureau to apologize to the plaintiff. As for Wang's last request, that his actions be recognized as just and righteous, the bureau again reasoned that it had no a legal basis.[41]

In general, the response of the Xuzhou Quality and Technology Inspection Bureau was similar to that of the municipal government. Both flatly rejected all the requests of the plaintiff but refrained, as the police bureau had done, from attempting to intimidate Wang. The arguments of the bureau were apparently problematic. If it said that it could not take action because of time limitations, why was an investigation not conducted immediately after Wang's petition in 2001? Such a delay clearly demonstrated that the bureau had been unresponsive, a key indicator of administrative inaction.

While Wang was fighting the local governments in the court, his administrative litigations and exceptional courage won the support of many including lawyers and journalists. In a phone call to a local newspaper, one urbanite in Nanjing expressed his admiration of Wang and criticized the Xuzhou governments:

I am touched by Professor Wang; he is definitely not stupid. For the administrative departments [in Xuzhou], it should be easy to resolve issues like the antitheft doors in Fenghuayuan if they really want to. Yet some government organs have always been slow in taking actions. Their slogan is, "Wait a minute, and we will surely deal with [the problem]." No one knows how long the delay will be. When commoners are facing such [government delays], they will be angry, but most of them do not know what to do. Professor Wang teaches us that we need to use the available legal weapons to protect our rights and interests.

Some legal professionals praised Wang as the first commoner in China who had accused five governments. They also expressed worries that such litigation might not go smoothly in China.[42]

One month after Wang filed his lawsuit against the five local governments, Wang received a verdict from the intermediate court saying that the Jiangsu Provincial Industrial and Commercial Administrative Bureau, one of the five government defendants, disputed the court's jurisdiction and that that issue must be resolved first. The verdict quoted a Supreme Court interpretation of enforcement of the Administrative Litigation Law as saying that the case must be terminated.[43] In other words, while the intermediate court had accepted the case, it had now decided to proceed no further with it. No one knew whether the court had actually faced political pressure. But, in the Chinese legal milieu, it was not surprising that it could not stand up to such pressure. In the Waitan Garden case, both the Hubei Provincial High Court and the Supreme Court refused to accept the administrative lawsuit lodged by the homeowner representatives. The biggest obstacle, as has already been noted, was pressure from the provincial and central governments.[44]

On August 18, the indomitable Wang petitioned the intermediate court and other relevant departments demanding that the case be reopened. But the court refused to give him an answer. In the meantime, he emailed public media in Nanjing and law firms around China asking for help. A few lawyers voluntarily offered legal assistance. Three lawyers from Nanjing, the capital of Jiangsu Province, formed a team to assist him. Pei Guosheng, a lawyer, replied to Wang that the court verdict was wrong. According to a Supreme Court interpretation, when a party disputes jurisdiction, the people's court should investigate. Then, if the dispute is valid, the case should be transferred to the court that does have jurisdiction; if it is not, the court should reject the dispute but not terminate the case. One famous lawyer argued that it was anticipated that the court would suddenly terminate the case, a very shrewd tactic. Doing so would deprive the plaintiff of the right to appeal to the appellate court because the termination had no time limitation. He went on to say that it was too difficult for the Xuzhou Intermediate Court to deal with a case against the local government in the same city in which it was itself located. The best venue for this case was the Jiangsu Provincial High Court.[45]

As in the Waitan Garden case, there were some lawyers and judges who were willing to put social justice before personal interest. The lawyers in Nanjing who had been deeply impressed by Wang's audacity in his lone legal fight offered him free legal aid. As one of them reportedly said, the lawsuit Wang had filed was for the "public good" (*gongyi*), which did not meet the requirement for legal aid (*falü yuanzhu*). But he had decided to help Wang anyway because he was a "citizen" (*gongmin*) and not a "subject" (*chenmin*). Wang was also a "vulnerable person," and no local Xuzhou lawyer had dared take his case. But his spirit was "something the society needs to champion."[46]

Obtaining the assistance of lawyers and winning the lawsuit were two very different issues. In the face of power, both the law and the courts seem weak. The argument that it was better to take this case to the provincial court was correct. In China, local governments usually control the coffer, service, and benefits of the local courts, meaning that those courts find it hard to "try cases fairly where the economic and political interest of the local governments and officials are at stake."[47] In addition, local Party committees were always more powerful than the judges. Since the early years of the PRC, judges had been required to ask the Party committees for advice or approval of their adjudications.[48] Moreover, the promotion of court judges was in the hands of the local Party committees. As Pei Minxin, a political scientist, argues, the CCP's control of the most senior judicial appointments "profoundly affects how judgments are determined by the courts."[49] Likewise, Zhu Suli, a law professor at Peking University, observes that Chinese judges tend to see themselves as civil servants rather than independent professionals. He argues that they "are more likely to defer to rather than confront existing political and administrative hierarchies in which they themselves are embedded."[50]

Wang Peirong's next move was to appeal the termination because the dispute of the Jiangsu Provincial Industrial and Commercial Administrative Bureau had passed the submission deadline (*tijiao qixian*) stipulated by law. In a confidential discussion between Wang and several court judges, it was suggested that Wang withdraw his lawsuits and accuse each of the five local governments separately instead. If he would do so, the judges agreed to charge him for only one lawsuit. However, Wang did not take this advice. In his view, accusing the five local governments together would prevent them from passing the ball to each other. Cui Wu, one of the lawyers who offered Wang help, told him that he had the initiative to file a lawsuit. Wang could scrap his charge of the Jiangsu Provincial Industrial and Commercial Administrative Bureau and accuse the other four governments in the Xuzhou court.[51]

To Wang's surprise, on September 30, 2003, the intermediate court informed him that it would reopen the case owing to the "disappearance of the cause for termination (i.e., the dispute over the extent of jurisdiction)."[52] Just one month earlier, the same court had used the extent of jurisdiction as a pretext to terminate Wang's lawsuit. Now, it suddenly decided to take the case up again without offering a convincing explanation as to why. Shortly afterward, however, the court again reversed its decision and closed the case. The reason was the same as was given in August: "Dispute over the extent of jurisdiction." The chameleon-like court quickly drew criticism from the public media. On October 23, the court finally rejected Wang's requests.

The next day, an editorial in the *Jiangnan shibao* (lit. *River South Times*), a newspaper owned by the *People's Daily*, criticized the Xuzhou Intermediate Court for its inconsistency in Wang's case, noting sarcastically that the so-called "disappearance of the cause for termination" was not a joke but a formal legal document. But the legal document was repudiated as a trick. "How was the drama of the inconsistency played out in the first-class (*yiji*) people's court (i.e., the Xuzhou Intermediate Court)?" the editorial questioned:

> Oh, the fact is that the obstacle that Wang Peirong has been facing is too big. Where does the obstacle come from? It certainly does not come from the ordinary people. Therefore, can we extrapolate that the Xuzhou Intermediate Court has, at least initially, tried to withstand the pressure and eliminate the "causes for termination." Later, the court resumes the "causes for termination" because it cannot resist the pressure. Does the intermediate court make a fool of the "professor commoner" Wang Peirong or the law? Can the law be used as both shield and spear?[53]

The editorial raised a crucial question that made manifest the paradoxical relations between law and power in the PRC. Having no judicial independence, the Xuzhou Intermediate Court could not withstand the pressure from the local governments that had been accused by Wang Peirong. But it also tried to follow the law by accepting Wang's lawsuit. Despite repeated calls for the rule of law by CCP leaders in the 1990s, the inconsistent decisions of the intermediate court testified to the awkward role of law in a country dominated by an omnipotent Party.

On October 30, 2003, taking the suggestions of some upright lawyers who voluntarily offered their help, Wang filed his lawsuit against the five governments with the Jiangsu Provincial High Court. Like the intermediate court in Xuzhou, the provincial high court accepted the case.

VICTORY FOR LAW OR POWER?

Even before Wang Peirong appealed to the provincial high court, something favorable to him and his fellow Fenghuayuan homeowners had quietly surfaced. It seemed that his years of repeated petitions and lawsuits had finally come to fruition. The first promising sign arrived on the afternoon of September 3. That day, Xuzhou mayor Pan Yonghe told Wang that the city government was very attentive to the issue of the antitheft doors and had arrived at a total of five solutions. For example, the mayor would uphold Wang's lawsuits against the five governments and wished the court to make impartial judgments. He would accept responsibility for not acting to resolve the antitheft door issue. The Xuzhou Party secretary and a few other top leaders would be in charge of the issue. The mayor also promised Wang that the city government would not only investigate the anti-theft door problem but also punish any officials who had been involved in their production and sale.[54]

For almost two years, Wang had expected this day to come. But why did the mayor become humble and make those promises at this time? Without a doubt, it was Wang's ongoing lawsuits that triggered the mayor's actions. It seemed that for once law would prevail over power.

On September 16, 2003, the Xuzhou Economical Housing Center put up a poster in Fenghuayuan, notifying the homeowners that their antitheft doors would be replaced on September 20. The public notice did not mention anything about the mayor's new conciliatory stance, let alone Wang's lawsuits. It simply noted that the center had signed contracts with legitimate producers of antitheft doors and that the quality would be guaranteed.

On the following day, in an interview with journalists, Xuzhou mayor Pan Yonghe reiterated his support of Wang's lawsuits: "This case of commoners against officials is normal. The government should not and has no right to intervene. I also come from a common family, and I believe that the government becoming a defendant will help us improve our working attitude and service to the people. As for addressing people's difficulties, I back Wang Peirong in his charges against the governments, including the municipal government. We need to win back people's trust and support by resolving this case." He also warned that the city government would thoroughly track down the persons and officials who had been responsible for the problem and would bring them to justice.[55]

This was not the first statement of the mayor's regarding Fenghuayuan, and it was certainly not the last. As Wang had said earlier, some city officials, including Pan, had mentioned the issue of the antitheft doors many times, but they had taken no action afterward. That failure was the main reason behind the frustrated Wang's lawsuits.

After hearing the good news, Wang felt relaxed. He was first of all grateful to the mayor. During an interview, when asked whether he felt guilty for bringing charges against the mayor, he replied that he would have preferred not to have had to. But he had no choice because the issue remained unresolved.[56]

Wang may be right that it was the lower-ranking departments that had failed to follow the mayor's orders. This has happened many times in the short history of the PRC. At the beginning of the Cultural Revolution, Mao Zedong complained that the Beijing municipal government did not respect and abide by his orders.[57] In the case of Guo Guangyun, an official who had fought the corrupt but powerful Hebei Party secretary for eight years, the orders of CCP leaders had been totally ignored by local officials.[58]

But we should also fault the mayor because he did not make sure his orders were implemented. Had he paid more attention to the plight of the homeown-ers and to Wang's petitions, he would have assumed personal responsibility for the case and punished the officials who had repeatedly ignored his orders. His new promises after Wang charged the city government were, at most, an action taken under pressure. The combination of government power and the bureaucratism (*guanliao zhuyi*) censured by Mao in the 1950s had exacerbated and prolonged the woes of the homeowners.[59] In fact, the bureaucratism stemmed from the nature of the flawed PRC bureaucratic system, in which officials are appointed by their superiors rather than elected by the people. Most officials in China, if not all, accordingly care more about the opinions of their superiors than about the citizens. While Wang was a professor, he was still a commoner and had no political power. That was why the local officials could ignore his petitions and the local police could fold their hands and watch Yan Jiaxun beat him.

However, old habits die hard. Despite the government notice and the mayor's new orders and admonition, no action had been taken by September 20, the day by which the Xuzhou Economical Housing Center promised to replace all the antitheft doors. The cause of this government inaction was the bureaucratism or, more precisely, irresponsible local officials. After Wang's provincial high court suit on October 30, the local government felt compelled to take action. On November 6, the housing center announced to the homeowners that it would start the next day to gradually replace the antitheft doors. The announcement quickly spread among the homeowners. Wang Peirong made several appreciative calls to the *Jiangnan shibao,* the municipal government, and especially Mayor Pan Yonghe for their valuable efforts. Given the government inaction after the September order, Wang also expressed concern to the public media about the implementation of the latest order.[60]

Unfortunately, Wang's concerns turned out not to be unfounded. The new antitheft doors were of even poorer quality than the old ones. As soon as this became known, many homeowners refused to allow their old doors to be replaced. The whole project was thus forced to stop. Wang felt compelled to complain to the mayor again. Pan agreed to deal with the problem after he returned from a trip abroad. One of the deputy mayors in Xuzhou visited Fenghuayuan on November 22 and was appalled by the poor quality of the new antitheft doors, which he felt would further damage the image of the city. He also assured the homeowners that the municipal government was capable of solving the problem, which satisfied the homeowners.

As he had promised, when he returned, the mayor convened a meeting on November 29 specifically targeting the antitheft doors. He told officials that, when he was out of the country, many friends and former classmates had blamed him for failing to resolve such a small issue. He claimed to have been actually been attentive to the matter, making many comments about and issuing orders with regard to it. He even ordered the Xuzhou Police Bureau to create a special case unit (*zhuan'anzu*). Yet all his efforts had been in vain, and he felt deeply sad and regretful. He then ordered the officials to investigate the case and to hold the responsible persons accountable.[61]

Almost two months after the repeated promises of the mayor and the vice mayor, the problems that the homeowners, including Wang Peirong, had complained of for almost four years remained unresolved. The government had issued no new orders, and the homeowners still lacked security. The patience of Wang and the other homeowners finally wore out. On January 21, with the support of over four thousand homeowners, Wang sued the Xuzhou municipal government again in the provincial high court. His current requests were similar to his previous ones, mainly seeking a court judgment regarding the inaction of the municipal government. But he did add one new request, asking that the city government probe those inside the Xuzhou Police Bureau who were cooperating with the city's criminal element.

This second lawsuit to the provincial high court prompted the leaders of the Xuzhou government to take swift actions to solve the problem. This time, Xu Ming, the Party secretary and the highest-ranking official in the city, convoked a meeting on January 30, 2004, at which three decisions were made. First, the homeowners should be reimbursed in full for the money they spent on the anti-theft doors. Second, the police bureau needed to look into the production and sale of the shoddy doors and any criminal activities associated with this case. Third, the revenge attacks on Wang should be investigated.

Unlike Pan Yonghe, who had failed to ensure that his orders were enforced, Xu Ming made sure that his orders were. Within days, an amount totaling 1.6 million RMB was returned to the homeowners. In the evening of January 30, Yan Jiaxun was detained by the police. On March 15, the Xuzhou Procuratorate formally arrested him on criminal charges. Wang's years of petitions and lawsuits seemed to have been rewarded. The Fenghuayuan homeowners were also satisfied with the results. Wang decided to drop his lawsuit against the city government. In addition, he told Li Fuquan, the deputy mayor who had succeeded Pan Yonghe, that he would like to offer a pennant to the city government as recognition of its swift solution of the problem. But the deputy mayor politely turned down the offer as he felt guilty that the problem had lingered for four years unresolved. Wang respected the new mayor and did not press the issue.[62]

For the second time, a lawsuit against the Xuzhou municipal government with the provincial high court effectively forced city leaders to take speedy and direct action to solve an issue they had long failed to act on. It seems that law dwarfed power in this case. The lawsuit, however, still might not end up with a verdict favoring Wang, or the court might again terminate the session because of its potential enormous impact on the local officials, whose inattentiveness and incompetence would be exposed and future promotions affected. Their superiors in both Jiangsu Province and Beijing would certainly be unhappy should the Party image be tarnished.

To be sure, Wang's persistent administrative litigation also reflected the problems endemic to the PRC judicial and political systems. Although the law may have played an important role in pressing the local governments to solve the problem, we would argue that power was decisive in the final solution of the case. Prior to 2004, Wang had taken the local governments to court several times, including once to the provincial high court. But they had repeatedly failed to take effective action. The latest lawsuit against the city government in the provincial high court had yet to produce any verdict. Thus we could not say that law triumphed over power. Indeed, it was the fear of losing favor with their superiors that most likely forced local officials to act. In that regard, the power of their superiors, and not the law or the courts, subdued them. After all, even if the provincial court sided with Wang against them, enforcing the verdict would be extremely difficult, if not impossible.[63] Additionally, no Xuzhou official/policeman had been punished for malfeasance or covering Yan Jiaxun in this case.

On February 26, 2004, invoking the words of Xuzhou Party secretary Xu Ming, the *Xinhua Daily,* the most important official newspaper in Jiangsu Province, attributed the long-lasting problem of the antitheft doors to the bureaucratism afflicting the government: "For the problem of the Fenghuayuan antitheft doors, a memo of the city government last September clearly distributed the responsibilities, workloads, and coordination among certain city departments. But, owing to endless blame games, the replacement of the doors had to be suspended."[64] This seemingly critical article had in fact protected the local officials by making its target the bureaucratism, a systemic problem in the PRC that no single official should be punished for.

WANG'S CONTINUING LEGAL FIGHTS

After the police arrested Yan JiaXun and compensated the homeowners, most people in Fenghuayuan thought the case was over. Wang Peirong, however, did not want to stop his lawsuits and legal fights. For the moment, thanks to his historic and audacious challenges to the powerful local governments, he had won immense sympathy and support across the country. On October 21, 2004, two graduate students in the law school of the Peking University offered him free legal aid. They jointly submitted an administrative litigation to the Beijing First Intermediate Court against the Ministry of Construction charging it with designating Fenghuayuan as an exemplary residential community of national property management in 2000. Wang, the plaintiff, requested that the court order the ministry to withdraw its award to Fenghuayuan and to pay all the legal costs associated with the suit. For most of the Fenghuayuan homeowners who had been troubled by the defective antitheft doors and many other problems, not only was this award undeserved, but it had also resulted in their paying a higher fee for property management. According to the regulations of the Xuzhou Price Bureau, only with such a national award could a residential community charge the residents a first-class fee. In August 2004, Wang surveyed Fenghuayuan homeowners, and 97.62 percent of them were dissatisfied with the security of the community, and almost all of them disliked the high property management fees. The *China Youth*

Daily discovered that Fenghuayuan won the national award from the Ministry of Construction even before it won a similar award from Jiangsu Province, a scenario that was very unusual. When a reporter asked the Xuzhou Housing Managing Bureau (Xuzhou fangguanju) how Fenghuayuan had won the national award, no one could answer the question.

"This award has been won because of deception," said Wang. If the ministry would withdraw the award, the Fenghuayuan homeowners would pay lower property management fees. The Beijing court did not accept Wang's lawsuit on grounds that the decision of the ministry had no "interest relationship" (*lihai guanxi*) with Wang. But Wang was not at all disappointed by this court ruling. Before the court gave its verdict, officials from the local construction department had promised Wang that they would immediately repudiate the award if Wang withdrew his lawsuit. On January 23, 2005, the Ministry of Construction announced that the awards of sixteen residential communities had been canceled, that of Fenghuayuan among them. The ministry gave no explanation for its decision. For Wang, this was another example of losing a battle but winning the war.[65]

The Beijing court lawsuit was similar to the one that Wang had lodged against the five local governments in 2003. While the Beijing court refused to accept it, the fact that he brought it in the first place was certainly instrumental in the ministry's decision to cancel its previous award to Fenghuayuan. But it remained the case that courts dare not accept litigation directed against central leaders, the police, or organs of the government.

A victorious Wang attempted to move forward. His next lawsuit, his fifth administrative litigation, targeted the Xuzhou Housing Management Bureau. It was filed on May 8, 2005. This time, the court was the Gulou Court, a district court in Xuzhou. Wang wanted the bureau to withdraw the certificate of property management (*wuye guanli zizhi zhengshu*) that had been issued to the Xuzhou Jialong Property Company in 2000. In the indictment, he argued that the company had forged a contract to manage Fenghuayuan with its main shareholder, the Xuzhou Economical Housing Center. The contract was illegal because the company had neither business license nor qualification certificate (*zhizhi zhengshu*). Apparently, the company, like Yan Jiaxun, collaborated with the local government in taking over the lucrative property management of Fenghuayuan. The housing center was under the supervision of the Xuzhou Housing Management Bureau, which arguably failed to do anything to stop the illicit activities of the company and, on the contrary, issued a qualification certificate one month after the company's unlawful management of Fenghuayuan. Wang accused the bureau of providing the illegal activities of the company with "legitimate garb" (*hefa waiyi*).

The district court accepted the lawsuit and opened the session on May 23. This case was said to be the first one of its kind in China. During the court debate, the bureau rejected every charge and asserted that it had done nothing illegal. It also displayed a commission contract between the housing center and Jialong. But Wang quickly dismissed the contract as a fabricated one in that the seal on it was not official and it had been issued in a fake name. However trenchant his arguments had been, the court rebuffed Wang's charges because there was no "interest relationship" between him and the bureau, a decision similar to the one made by the Beijing court.[66]

In July 2005, the dissatisfied Wang appealed to the appellate court, the Xuzhou Intermediate Court. As he did in 2003, he again made multiple charges. The accused governments included the Xuzhou municipal government, the Xuzhou Housing Management Bureau, and the Quanshan Housing Management Bureau. While Wang acknowledged in his written statement that the city government had actually paid attention to the problems caused by Jialong and ordered the housing management bureau to deal with them, so far nothing had been resolved, and the city government had failed to respond to the Fenghuayuan homeowners committee of which Wang was the elected head. Wang accordingly asked the court to rule that the city government had committed administrative inaction. Furthermore, he blamed Jialong for not transferring all the property-related material, including that about rental income, to the homeowners committee. And he charged both the city and the district housing management bureaus with failing to supervise Jialong. Wang's latest—and also his last—administrative litigation was backed by the signatures of thousands of Fenghuayuan homeowners. However, the court chose not to accept the case.

To either demonstrate that he was not a pettifogger or express his willingness to compromise, Wang wrote to the Xuzhou Party secretary three days after bringing his lawsuit against the city government. In his petition letter, he explained that the ongoing lawsuit of the homeowners committee had been necessitated by the inaction of the Xuzhou Housing Management Bureau. Ignoring numerous orders from the city government, the bureau had consistently refused to solve the problems of Fenghuayuan. When the homeowners committee criticized it for being unresponsive, it argued that it reported only to the Party secretary. If the committee wanted a written response from the bureau, it should ask the Party secretary for one. As an effort to shirk its responsibility, the bureau said that the city government had deprived it of its ability to enforce the state laws and the orders of the Ministry of Constructions. In other words, the homeowners should seek a solution to their plight with the city government and not the bureau as the bureau had no power.[67] Unfortunately, the city government did not respond to Wang's petition.

THE FORMIDABLE POLITICAL POWER

For four years, Wang Peirong had been fighting a legal war against some of the most powerful local governments. His series of administrative litigations during the height of the Chinese urbanization movement and legal reform came to an end having achieved a mix of success and failure. Apart from one favorable decision (the rejection of Yan Jiaxun's accusation of him by the intermediate court), his lawsuits had generally been unproductive. Nevertheless, he and his fellow Fenghuayuan homeowners may have lost the battle in the courts, but they won the war in in that their major problems were resolved. Some of Wang's lawsuits, especially those to the provincial high court, had prompted the city leaders to act speedily to seriously address the problems of the homeowners. It was vital that the courts at both the city and the provincial levels had accepted most of his lawsuits. Had they not, city officials might still have used bureaucratism as an excuse for their lack of response.

In comparison with the Waitan Garden case, the administrative litigations that Wang had filed better manifested the complicated relations between law and power in the contemporary PRC. It was the fact that the Waitan Garden case unusually entailed central governments and leaders (e.g., Premier Zhu Rongji) that made it extremely difficult for local and central courts to accept the homeowners' lawsuits. The case of Wang Peirong and Fenghuayuan was more common in China as the lawsuits were mainly targeting local governments. Unlike many other cases in which the courts refused to accept administrative litigation, the courts in Xuzhou and Jiangsu not only accepted Wang's cases but also opened sessions that forced the powerful local governments to defend their policies. However minimal the progress, the actions taken by the local courts in Wang's case represent a promising step by the CCP toward the rule of law.

The long and tough legal battles that Wang had fought also mirrored the ferocious obstacles Chinese law has been facing. It is clear that political power poses the single biggest hurdle to the rule of law in China.[68] Although most of the local courts accepted Wang's administrative litigations, almost all sided with the local governments and rejected his lawsuits. The only favorable court judgment was in the case of the lawsuit against Yan Jiaxun. Even though the local courts had supported Wang's charges, the enforcement of their verdicts would be another daunting task. It was true that the decisions of the city leaders to arrest Yan and compensate the homeowners were made after Wang had taken five governments to the provincial court. But, as we have argued earlier, it was also true that it was the city government and not the provincial court that resolved the problems of Fenghuayuan and detained Yan Jiaxun. More frustrating was that no government official had been held responsible or punished for the serious corruption and misconduct involved in the case.

The initial successes of Wang and the Fenghuayuan homeowners, as well as the arrest of Yan, did not mean that the case was over and that power would succumb to law in the future. In fact, even before public attention to and interest in the case receded, the local government as well as the local judicial apparatus had begun to play a legal game with Wang. Local officials were well aware that protecting Yan was tantamount to protecting themselves. If Yan were punished for the crimes of which Wang accused him, the involvement of many local officials and police would be made public. Throughout the trial, the police had refused to provide the court with complete evidence of Yan's activities in bribing officials and evading taxes. In September 2004, eight months after his detainment, the Quanshan court in charge of the case sentenced Yan to eighteen months in prison for making inferior products and fined him 200,000 RMB. For the 1.5 million RMB that Yan had charged Fenghuayuan homeowners for the antitheft doors, the court recognized only 130,000 RMB, which helped alleviate his crime. In addition, it held that only some of the doors were defective. When Wang questioned those decisions, the judge allegedly said that they had been made not by him but by his superiors. His frankness revealed that the court had no discretion. The superiors in question were most likely the local police or government officials, two powerful elements that few judges in China dare challenge. In December 2004, the prosecutor in charge of Yan's case told Wang that the local police had refused to provide the court with the requested material.[69]

Moreover, the local court did not take any action against Li Hai, who was much more powerful than Yan. In addition to collaborating with Yan in producing the defective antitheft doors, Li was also responsible for supplying shoddy water pipes, heating units, and water meters. According to Wang Peirong, the total amount that Li had deceitfully seized from the homeowners was in the tens of millions, a sum much larger than Yan had grabbed. On March 11, 2003, the *Grand Portrait* (*Daxiezhen*), a popular program on Jiangsu Provincial TV, reported that, instead of buying cheap and well-constructed antitheft doors, Li had chosen to buy Yan's more expensive and inferior doors, allegedly having accepted a 100,000 RMB bribe. Owing to his connections, Li remains a free man and will likely never be prosecuted.[70] The case clearly shows that, in the absence of judicial independence, power will almost always triumph over law.

As the incident of the antitheft doors wound down, Wang Peirong did not content himself with simply returning to his research, instead continuing his crusade against corruption.[71] His extraordinary bravery and success in safeguarding justice have drawn the attention of various legal scholars. For instance, Jiang Ming'an, a law professor at Peking University,[72] once praised Wang for his dexterous utilization of existing legal resources such as administrative reconsideration (*xingzheng fuyi*), lawsuits, and petitions to local and state leaders. Moreover, Wang has used the public media and the Internet and appeals to legal specialists to exercise tremendous pressure on lawbreakers. Jiang argues that it was especially difficult for Wang to take only institutionalized paths (*zhiduhua tujin*) to defend justice within the current political and legal environment:

> Owing to the systemic problems of our country, the institutionalized path for citizens to defend their rights usually presents obstacles. Even if a case meets all the requirements, the court may not want to accept it. Even though you have indisputable evidence, the court verdict goes against you. What you can do? Under the existing circumstance, all we can do is to adopt more nonsystemic means to make up for the deficiencies of the institutionalized path. . . . Although Wang lost his lawsuits, we

can find that the local governments have been secretly correcting their unlawful behaviors under public pressure.[73]

Yet what Jiang has not made explicit is the cruel fact that power normally prevails over law in China. As clearly shown in Wang's six lone legal battles, despite more than two decades of legal reform and CCP leaders' calls for the rule of law, the judiciary was still a "knife hilt" of the Party, a situation not very different from that in the 1950s. Without legal supremacy, Chinese courts, be they local or provincial, will have no courage to challenge their peer administrations. Before the CCP genuinely accepts accountability to the law or adopts a supremacy of law, the rule of law will be nothing but a dream in the PRC.

5

Professor Wang's Costly Battle against Local Power

18-Month Captivity

From late 2012 to the spring of 2014, the once highly active and seemingly indomitable Professor Wang Peirong seemingly went missing. All efforts to contact him were futile. At first, it seemed likely that he might have decided to return to a normal private life after his widely publicized battles with the Xuzhou government. But, in May 2014, eighteen months after disappearing from public view, he suddenly returned, claiming that he had been imprisoned on false charges of libel. One of the local officials among his accusers was Liu Yongxiu, who once served as the head of the neighborhood committee (*juweihui*) of Fenghuayuan at the same time Wang Peirong served as the head of the homeowners committee (*yezhu weiyuanhui*). The key distinction here is that the neighborhood committee is "the lowest [form of government] of the Chinese Party-state,"[1] while the homeowners committee is a nongovernment organization that has no legal status. According to Article 6 of the PRC Organizational Law of Urban Neighborhood Committees (Zhonghua remin gongheguo chengshi jumin weiyuanhui zuzhifa), the "establishment, abolition, and scale adjust" (*guimo tiaozheng*) of neighborhood committees shall be decided by the local governments. Article 17 states that the local governments shall decide on and earmark both the managing funds of neighborhood committees and the range, standard, and source of committee members' living allowances.[2] The law clearly shows that a neighborhood committee is not so much an informal mass organization as a part of the local government.

As Xu Feng has correctly argued, the neighborhood committee is, "in theory, an even smaller-scale mass organization under the leadership of the street committee." "In practice, it still acted as an arm of the government."[3] In that regard, Liu Yongxiu was a government official, albeit at the lowest level of power. Who was he, and how did he become the leader of the neighborhood committee? How and why did Wang get involved in a protracted and dangerous feud with him? Why did Liu bring charges against Wang and succeed in having him incarcerated for such a long time? Did he have any backing in the local governments or courts? We are going to provide in-depth answers to these questions in this chapter. The bloody and costly fights between Wang and Liu made headline news some national media and drew tremendous attention from the public in general as well as local urbanites in Xuzhou. More important, the confrontation further reflects the weakness of law in the face of powerful officials.

FROM ALLIES TO FOES

To the surprise of many people, Wang Peirong and Liu Yongxiu had originally been allies and "battle companions" (*zhanyou*) in the 2003 fight against the Feng-huayuan property management company. Whenever the homeowners committee had disputes with that management, Liu would always side with Wang, the head of the homeowners committee. Mainly for that reason, Wang had been grate-ful for Liu's staunch support, and the two men became good friends. However, the seemingly firm friendship quickly deteriorated into hostility shortly after Liu became the head of the neighborhood committee in 2005. In 2006, the relation-ship between the two was so bad that they actually saw each other as archenemies.

The root cause of the hostility was a dispute over the proper distribution of the revenues derived from renting out Fenghuayuan properties. As noted in the previous chapter, Fenghuayuan is a nationally renowned residential commu-nity in Jiangsu Province, and most of its homeowners are high-level intellectuals working in local universities or research centers. The community has more than ten thousand residents and owns over eighteen thousand square meters of public buildings and facilities. Yet, before 2004, all the public buildings and facilities had been occupied by a property management company, and the homeowners had no access to them. Most homeowners had not even been aware that they should be the real owners of those facilities and thus reap the benefit derived from their rental. Right after being reelected as the head of the homeowners committee in late 2003, Wang Peirong tried to regain control of those public facilities and the revenue they generated. In July 2004, after struggling with the property man-agement company for several months, the homeowners committee managed to regain the control of almost all such facilities in Fenghuayuan.

The question then became how best to use the public facilities to benefit the homeowners and the community as a whole. Wang felt that the best option was to rent them out and thus generate revenue. He first tried to open a bank account in the name of the homeowners committee. But the bank told him that the commit-tee was not a legal entity and thus could not have a bank account. If the commit-tee could not have a bank account, how could it collect and save the rent money? Then Wang planned to register the committee at the local civil service bureau (*minhengju*). But a lawyer told him that the bureau would not accept his applica-tion as there was no existing law in China under which he could do so. Worse, the lawyer warned him that, should the committee need to take a tenant to court, no court would accept the case.[4]

The desperate Wang had no choice but to contact Liu Yongxiu and ask that the neighborhood committee open a bank account and invoice tenants in the name of the homeowners committee. Negotiations went pretty smoothly, and Liu assured Wang that he would keep the rent his committee collected and other revenues generated by the public facilities clear and safe for the homeowners. "No matter when you or any other homeowners want to inspect the accounts," he pledged to Wang, "they will be ready, and I will not let you down." For Wang and most other Fenghuayuan homeowners, letting the neighborhood committee take charge of the public facilities was akin to putting the money in a safe. They had reasons to trust Liu. During the last election for the head of the neighborhood committee in March 2005, Wang and many Fenghuayuan homeowners voted for him. No one else on the committee was considered more trustworthy than Liu.[5]

However, Liu did not fulfill his promise. Taking advantage of the situation, he and his cohorts allegedly began siphoning off the revenue. In late 2005, a resident brought a contract between the neighborhood committee and a Xuzhou technology company to Wang's attention. Instead of charging the local company for renting the Community Center of Cultural Activities (Shequ huodong zhongxin), the committee allowed the company to use the facility for free and asked to "donate" 500 RMB (about $80.00) every month to the committee. Had the company paid rent, the funds would have had to be transferred to the homeowners committee. But, if the rent took the form of a donation, the committee would have been able to do what it liked with the money, a violation of Liu's legal agreement with Wang.[6]

After reviewing the contract, Wang realized that something had gone wrong. He chose not to expose what was going on before collecting more evidence. He and some other homeowners therefore launched a clandestine investigation of Liu and the neighborhood committee. With the help of the committee's accountant, Wang discovered that it had used money owed the homeowners committee to pay members' telephone, air-conditioning, and heating bills. In September 2005 alone, 4,000 RMB had been disbursed as subsidies—as much as 680 RMB for each of the five committee members. Outraged by the theft of their money and the infringement of a contract, in late 2005 Wang and the homeowners committee demanded that Liu allow the homeowners committee to supervise all accounts. But, on the pretext that he was extremely busy at the end of the year, Liu put Wang off until early 2006.[7]

In March 2006, three months after Wang's request, Liu still refused to give him access to the accounts. Through a contact on the neighborhood committee, however, Wang managed to collect evidence of Liu's embezzlement. It turned out that, between May 2005 and March 2006, the committee had in fact taken in about 270,000 RMB in rental income. Wang decided to make this misappropriation public. In addition, he felt compelled to quell the rumors that he and Liu had conspired to seize public revenue. On April 3, 2006, Wang publicized his denunciation of Liu in a big-character poster (dazibao), a wall-mounted poster handwritten with large-sized Chinese characters and used as a means of protest, propaganda, and popular communication since imperial times. He claimed that, since the homeowners committee had entrusted Liu to manage the public facilities of Fenghuayuan eight months ago, the neighborhood committee had misappropriated and split among themselves as much as 100,000 RMB of the public revenue. "These activities of [Liu and his committee] are a betrayal of the trust of the homeowners," Wang argued. Before he warned Liu not to continue to deceive the kind homeowners, he insisted that the neighborhood committee release all its accounts and return the public revenue it had illegally appropriated.[8]

After posting his accusation in Fenghuayuan, Wang went straight to Liu's office and demanded to review the committee accounts. Liu refused. So Wang called the Xuzhou Tax Bureau and reported that the neighborhood committee had used false contracts to escape taxes. The next day, Wang brought copies of his evidence to the reporting center (*jubao zhongxin*) of the tax bureau. On April 7, the bureau informed him that it had decided to investigate Liu and his committee. On April 29, under immense pressure from the tax bureau and the homeowners, Liu reluctantly opened the accounts, which showed that, from May 2005 to March 2006, the neighborhood committee had taken in revenue totaling 245,000 RMB through renting Fenghuayuan public facilities. In the same period, its overall expenses exceeded 110,000 RMB, most of the money going to pay for the committee's managing fees and members' personal expenses, such as phone bills, air-conditioning, heating, and office facilities. Wang contended that those expenses should not be paid for by the public revenue because the local government was responsible for paying the salaries of Liu and his colleagues and the managing expenses of the committee.[9] The neighborhood committee had misappropriated almost one-third of the total public revenue.

In May 2006, the two committees at Fenghuayuan held a meeting to resolve their disputes. The hardened stance of Liu made negotiation impossible. During a break in negotiations, the local tax bureau sent a note to Wang that its investigation had revealed that the neighborhood committee had evaded paying over 40,000 RMB in taxes and that it had decided to fine the committee 1,025 RMB, essentially substantiating Wang's claims. To step up the pressure on Liu to yield, Wang and other homeowners notified him that the committee had to move out of its office in Fenghuayuan as its occupation was "forcible and illegal" or be removed by force.

Not surprisingly, Liu refused. So Wang locked the neighborhood committee out of the office. Liu immediately called the police, but they could not persuade Wang to open the office. The Quanshan District government, which had jurisdiction over the neighborhood committee, intervened and asked the committee to move out of Fenghuayuan. But the defiant Liu, who had his supporters among district government officials, suspended committee operations for three months. In June, the Taishan Subdistrict Office (Taishan jiedao banshichu), the committee's immediate superior, convened a meeting attempting to mediate the dispute. Unfortunately, the effort ended with an even more violent confrontation as one irritated accountant on the neighborhood committee threw her tea in the face of one of the homeowner representatives.[10]

In August 2006, the situation turned increasingly intense and incendiary. Liu remained firm in refusing to return the money to the homeowners, while Wang intensified his public charges against Liu and his committee and was poised to take more decisive action. He sent an ultimatum in the name of the homeowners committee to Liu on August 25 demanding his committee to move out of Fenghuayuan before August 30, charging Liu again with embezzling four-fifths of the roughly 250,000 RMB revenue that the committee acquired through managing Fenghuayuan's public facilities. He also denounced Liu for repeatedly ignoring the earlier order of the Quanshan District government, pointing out that the neighborhood committee was renting out its former office space while occupying the Fenghuayuan office for free. "[Liu]'s continual occupation of the Fenghuayuan office not only has shut down the neighborhood committee for almost four months but also makes it difficult for the homeowners committee and the property management team to run [the complex]," Wang remarked. The ultimatum finally ordered Liu and his committee to move out of the Fenghuayuan office before August 30. "Otherwise," Wang threatened, "the homeowners committee will use force to move all belongings of the neighborhood committee out of its office, and Liu must be responsible for the consequences."[11]

To avert further violent clashes between the two committees, on August 28 the subdistrict office forcibly moved the neighborhood committee out of Fenghuayuan. Liu felt shamed and was infuriated with Wang. He believed that the neighborhood committee was a lawful organization and had the right to use the Fenghuayuan office. Some top Xuzhou officials shared his opinion. One of them accused Wang of seeking homeowner self-rule, which was taboo under the Party state. "For the time being, [homeowner self-rule] is not viable," he said. Why support Liu over Wang? There is no doubt that with his accusations against the five local governments in 2003 Wang made a nuisance of himself. As one local official told a journalist in 2007: "[Wang is] a crazy man repeatedly exposing [official misgovernment or corruption] [*jubao kuangren*]."[12] Given his support in the local government, Liu decided to teach Wang a lesson.

A BLOODY ATTACK

On the evening of September 6, 2009, when Wang was posting a note inside Fenghuayuan telling homeowners to remember to pay the 400 RMB maintenance fee, three persons suddenly rushed out and attacked him: Liu, holding a large champagne bottle, his wife, holding a wooden pole, and their daughter. "Beat the thief," Liu's wife yelled, hitting Wang in the left hand with the pole. In the meantime, the daughter grabbed Wang's legs while Liu struck him in the head with the champagne bottle. Bleeding profusely after several blows, Wang tried to crawl away and call for help, but Liu's son-in-law, a powerful local police head, blocked his path and, despite the attempted intervention of a Fenghuayuan guard, continued to beat Wang. The wounded Wang wanted to call the police, but he found that his cell phone had been taken by Liu's wife. He then asked the guard to call the police. Liu and his family continued to beat Wang, who fell to the ground and lost consciousness shortly after the first police car arrived. Later, Wang heard that the police, the guards, and some homeowners had protected him from further violence on the part of Liu's family and sent him to a hospital.[13]

According to the hospital report, Wang had suffered injuries to his head, left knee, and chest. Hearing that Liu's family was responsible, more than eight hundred angry homeowners signed a letter demanding that they be severely punished. However, because Liu's son-in-law was a local police head, the police were reluctant to conduct a serious investigation, even though roughly twenty people had witnessed the beating. Liu, his wife, and their daughter had confessed to the attack, and some witnesses reported that the son-in-law had joined in. One policeman even claimed that the son-in-law was not present during the attack.

The next day, Wang's wife called the local police asking for an appraisal of Wang's condition (*shangqing*) by a legal medical expert and was told that such an appraisal could be made only after Wang had recovered. Yet, according to the Appraisal Standard of Minor Physical Injury (Renti qingweishang jianding biaozhun) issued by the Ministry of Public Security in 1997, all minor injuries had to be assessed before they healed. Appraisal afterward would not reveal their true extent. Wang's wife petitioned the Xuzhou Municipal Police Bureau, and a supervisor investigated. Under pressure, the local police gave Wang's wife a trust deed for injury appraisal. But the legal medical expert refused to conduct the appraisal because the trust deed was improperly prepared. Wang's wife had no choice but to go to the local police for another trust deed. The medical expert rejected this one as well, for the same reason. In the meantime, Wang's wounds were healing, a fact that would certainly undermine the result of the appraisal.

On September 14, eight days after and having recovered from his injuries, Wang went to the local police for a new trust deed of appraisal. But the police head declined his request. Wang brought with him the signatures of eight hundred homeowners and petitioned the district, the municipal, and even the provincial police departments. Seeing that the petitions might cause trouble, the local police head sent two officers to accompany Wang to the office of the legal medical expert. To Wang's great surprise, the two policemen first talked privately with the expert, who then allegedly asked Wang a preposterous question: "Can you negotiate with the local police and not conduct the appraisal?" Wang said no. On September 16, ten days after the incident, the legal medical expert finally issued an appraisal, which did not implicate Liu's family, noting simply: "Due to disputes between Wang and Liu's family, Wang was hit by people with something similar to a bottle and a wooden rod resulting in injuries to his body and head." That is, Wang's injuries were the result of a fight, not a purposive assault.

Wang later questioned the credibility of the appraisal. It was clear that it was inaccurate as it did not mention Liu's son-in-law and then attributed Wang's injuries to a mutual family hostility. It also misrepresented the seriousness of Wang's injuries, which it indicated were "inconsiderable" (*qingweishang*) and not "minor" (*qingshang*). But Wang contended that the medical appraisal was made almost ten days after he was beaten, when most of his injuries had already healed, and that it ignored the hospital report from September 6. According to the Appraisal Standard of the Human Body (Renti qingshang jianding biaozhun) jointly promulgated by the Supreme Court, the Supreme Procuratorate, the Ministry of Public Security, and the Ministry of Justice, any wound longer than six centimeters should be regarded as a minor injury. As shown in the initial hospital report, the wounds on Wang's head alone were longer than six centimeters. Also, if other wounds were present, the degree should be considered minor.[14] Wang petitioned the Xuzhou Municipal Police Bureau, which did not respond. Given the fact his connections and the reputation of the Xuzhou police,[15] Liu had little to fear.

Although Wang did not obtain justice from the local police, he had won the hearts and minds of most, if not all, of the Fenghuayuan homeowners. During his stay in the hospital, groups of homeowners voluntarily came to visit him. Seeing how serious his wounds were, one homeowner was so moved that he told him not to fight Liu owing to his power and strong government network. "You are no longer young, Mr. Wang," the homeowner said. "Please do not fight Liu anymore. Can we just not ask [Liu] to return our money? We [the homeowners] will not blame you."[16] Another homeowner described Wang's return to Fenghuayuan from the hospital: "Almost all the homeowners lined up to welcome him, and the scene was like welcoming home a hero. Most of the homeowners wholeheartedly support Wang Peirong."[17]

LAW VERSUS POWER IN IMPEACHING LIU YONGXIU

The sympathy and warm support of the homeowners deeply touched Wang, who felt that all he had suffered in the fight against Liu had been repaid. But he did not want, they suggested, to capitulate to Liu, his violence and his power. While in the hospital, he had discussed with some of them their next step, which would be to impeach Liu and elect a new neighborhood committee head.

On September 9, 2006, just three days after Liu's attack on Wang, the homeowners committee posted "A Proposal to Impeach Liu Yongxiu" ("Bamian Liu Yongxiu changyishu") in Fenghuayuan and asked supportive homeowners to sign their names. The proposal argued that the total revenue owed the homeowners was about 332,952 RMB and that the undisputed, lawful expenses (taxes etc.) of the neighborhood committee were 41,573 RMB. The revenue from the rent alone would be over 100,000 RMB. But none of the remaining revenue had yet been transferred to the homeowners. The proposal accused Liu of stealing the public funds to pay himself subsidies, a practice that he had earlier characterized as illegal. The proposal went on:

The immoral Liu is still the head of the neighborhood committee who has corrupted the social morality and discredited the committee. He is the shame of both the committee and Fenghuayuan. . . . Liu assumes that he has the power to take public funds whenever he needs without consulting with the homeowners committee. He also claims that, if anyone questions his accounts, he will not return the original deposit of 80,000 yuan that belongs to the homeowners committee. How arrogant Liu Yongxiu is! Do the homeowners have no means to take him down? The most effective means would be to impeach Liu as the head of neighborhood committee.[18]

Within days, more than sixteen hundred households in Fenghuayuan had signed their names in support of impeaching Liu. As stated in the Organizational Law of Urban Neighborhood Committees, if one-fifth of the residents call for a meeting—and sixteen hundred households was well above one-fifth of the total thirty-five hundred households in Fenghuayuan—the neighborhood committee must convene and oversee it. (The residents meeting has the power to impeach or elect committee members.)[19] In an interview with *Jiancha ribao* (Jiancha daily), an official publication of the Supreme Procuratorate, Wang summarized three reasons for impeaching Liu. (1) The election of Liu's committee was illegitimate because, during the last election (in March 2005), Liu was both the head of the election committee and a candidate, which was inappropriate. (2) Liu was unqualified to head the committee, and two of the five committee members had already resigned owing to his undemocratic behavior. (3) The accounts of the committee were sloppy.[20] In the interview, Wang did not mention that he had been friends with Liu and that he had voted for him in the last election.

When Liu Yongxiu heard about his impeachment, he downplayed the proposal as "provoking the public opinion" (*shandong minyi*) and "disturbing social order," two charges that were potentially frightening because they had frequently been adopted by state media or politicians against their opponents.[21] Liu called the local police to stop the so-called farce. Yet, when the police arrived, they did not intervene because there was no sign of disorderly conduct. Nevertheless, Liu still had the support of his superior. He dismissed the impeachment as a "water-injected [i.e., diluted] public opinion" (*zhushui minyi*) and refused to follow the law and convene a residents meeting.[22] None of his superiors intervened.

Officials at the Taishan Subdistrict Office told reporters that the office had paid serious attention to the impeachment proposal. It had asked over seven hundred homeowners about the accounts of the neighborhood committee. During the auditing, many homeowners had reported new problems with the accounts. The office promised the reporters that it would convene a meeting of the residents soon after the audit was completed. Zhang Yunhui, an official at the subdistrict office, said that the office asked Liu to hold a homeowners meeting but that Liu did not want to do so. Liu, however, offered a different explanation. He argued that his superior told him that it was his choice to convene a meeting of the residents. Contra Zhang's report, Liu asserted that he did want to hold a meeting of the residents and invite officials from the subdistrict office and the district bureau of civil service but that his superiors dared not come owing to a fear of Wang. Liu's account cannot be independently confirmed as it contradicts the report in the popular magazine *Jiating*.[23]

Without mentioning anything about Liu's infringement of his agreement with the homeowners committee, a vice head of the subdistrict office testified that both Wang and Liu had no economic problems and that the office had taken efforts to resolve their dispute, albeit unsuccessfully. He ascribed the failure of the efforts to the lack of power. "The office does not have effective means to intervene," he said. "It can only guide the neighborhood committee and cannot cross the line."[24] Sui Liangjin, the Party secretary of the Fenghuayuan community, who had alledgedly received sizable monthly subsidies from Liu to pay his utility bills, sided with Liu and opposed the impeachment. "We believe that the impeachment is incongruous with the facts," he noted. "Therefore the community Party committee decides not to support the impeachment." He also admitted that he disagreed with his superiors (i.e., the subdistrict office) in assembling a residents meeting.[25]

Like Sui, some officials in the subdistrict office and upper-level governments also allied themselves with Liu and tried to shield him from prosecution. After Wang and the homeowners committee submitted the Quanshan Audit Bureau evidence, "certain audit officials" allegedly took advantage of their power and the people's trust and used all kinds of means to assist Liu, including the fabrication of fake invoices and receipts totaling 250,000 RMB. Two leaders from the subdistrict office also forged "A Response to the Problems in Wang Peirong's Petition," which provided faked copies of property certificates in order to prove that a supermarket in Fenghuayuan belonged to the developer and not, as the homeowners committee had consistently argued, to the homeowners. The "Response" also alleged that Liu's neighborhood committee had the right to rent out its official office and spend the rent money. On hearing the contents of the "Response," Wang angrily charged the subdistrict office with complicating the case and deceiving the district and municipal governments.

On February 5, 2007, Wang petitioned the Quanshan District government demanding a reexamination of the "Response" and asking for lawful and convincing evidence that the neighborhood committee had the right to rent its official office and that the supermarket belonged to the developer and not the homeowners. Despite his repeated petitions and requests, he never received a reply.[26]

In May 2007, a desperate Wang had lost any confidence in his petitions to the local governments. As he did in 2003, he escalated his fight by filing an administrative lawsuit against four local governments—the Taishan Subdistrict Office, the Quanshan District Bureau of Civil Service, the Quanshan District government, and the Xuzhou Municipal Bureau of Civil Service—with the Xuzhou

Intermediate Court. In his indictment, he made five requests. (1) Because the sub-district office protected Liu and the other three government organs failed to super-vise him, Wang asked the court to declare that the four governments were guilty of administrative inaction. (2) Because the Fenghuayuan homeowners demanded a meeting to impeach Liu but the lack of supervision of the four government defen-dants made that impossible, Wang again asked the court to declare them guilty of administrative inaction. (3) After two-thirds of the households in Fenghuayuan signed a petition asking for a meeting to impeach Liu, the inaction of the four gov-ernments postponed the meeting and the implementation of state laws. (4) Wang requested the court to enforce state laws and convoke a homeowners meeting within a month. (5) He also asked that the defendants pay the indictment fees.[27]

On May 15, the court informed Wang that the lawsuit was beyond its pur-view. In a written notice, it argued that the neighborhood committee was a self-managing, self-educating, and self-sufficient organization. It only received "guidance" from the city, district, and subdistrict governments, not "orders." According to the Several Interpretations of Enforcing the Administrative Liti-gation Law (Guanyu zhixing xingzheng susongfa de ruogan jieshi) promulgated by the Supreme Court, one of the litigations lodged by any citizen, legal person (faren), or other organization that cannot be regarded as administrative is the nonforceful administrative guiding activities (buju qiangzhili dexingzheng zhidao xingwei). Because the four government defendants provided Liu's neighborhood committee only with "guidance," Wang's administrative litigations against them lacked legal foundation.

Unsatisfied with the court verdict, Wang decided to resort to petitions, which would be his last hope. On May 23, a judge at the intermediate court unexpect-edly called Wang and said that, after some further investigation of his lawsuit, the court deemed it suitable for administrative litigation. All Wang would have to do would be to pay the 50 RMB administrative fee. However, just a week after Wang had paid the fee, the court once again reversed itself and turned down Wang's litigation.

Outraged, Wang appealed to the Jiangsu Provincial High Court. Yet, on July 20, 2007, that court rejected the appeal. It argued that the four government defendants could not be held accountable for the delay in the meeting and that there was no proof of administrative inaction. As had his 2003 lawsuits, Wang's second round of administrative litigation failed. He expressed his frustration to a reporter: "Fenghuayuan homeowners have signed a petition for a meeting to impeach Liu Yongxiu. Their action is in tune with the law, and some local govern-ments have also agreed. We have contacted the Xuzhou Municipal Bureau of Civil Service many times and demanded a meeting organized by homeowners them-selves. But the bureau replies that the meeting will be invalid unless it is convened by the neighborhood committee under the guidance of the subdistrict office." As a result, the impeachment cannot be initiated. "Why is there no one who will take responsibility?" Wang asked.[28]

Who has violated state law? If the law allows one-fifth of the households in a community to convene a meeting, the call for a residents meeting was legal, and any government effort to postpone or derail the meeting was illegal. Both courts' decisions were also problematic. If neighborhood committees were self-managing nongovernmental organizations, why did the local government pay Liu 500 RMB every month and provide his committee an official office? Furthermore, as both Anne-Marie Brady and Xu Feng have argued, neighborhood committees are at the bottom of the PRC's political hierarchy.[29] The Party secretary of the Fenghuayuan community, Liu's superior, made a decision not to call the meeting. This was clearly an order, not "guidance." It was the backing of his superiors that gave Liu the power to ignore the impeachment proposal and refuse to call a meeting. If his superiors could give neighborhood committees orders, why was Wang unable to lodge administrative litigations against them?

A *Jiancha ribao* report also questioned the Xuzhou court ruling. Invoking specialists' views, it argued that the ruling obstructed democratic development at the local level. "Any rights without [legal] remedy are incomplete," it commented. "Without legal safeguards, people's democratic rights and the local democratic autonomy will be merely a castle in the air [*kongzhong louge*]."[30]

Power behind a Fraudulent Election

After repeated setbacks at both the local and the provincial levels, Wang had no better choice than to wait for the upcoming neighborhood committee elections, scheduled for late 2008. Meanwhile, Liu—clearly disliked by many Fenghuayuan homeowners—understood that his reelection would not be easy. To make sure that his followers would continue to support him, Liu had attempted twice—in January and July 2008—to call for early elections so as to utilize his power to appoint his friends as candidates for the next committee head. But both attempts were foiled by massive homeowner boycotts.

On October 20, 2008, Liu pushed for a third election. Learning from their previous failures, Liu and his allies took more forceful means to warrant a favorable outcome. In the past elections, the head of each building unit in Fenghuayuan would be in charge of the fixed ballot boxes (*guding toupiaoxiang*) and distribute ballots to the homeowners living in the unit. Yet, because many unit heads had signed the proposal to impeach him, Liu distrusted them and decided to scrap the traditional rules.

According to Yang Gongzhan, a homeowner representative who had petitioned many local governments and leaders about Liu's "fraudulent election," Liu's powerful allies in the Taishan Subdistrict Office and the Quanshan District government selected dozens of officials, most of whom came from other subdistrict governments. They also hired student volunteers from the local colleges. Together with Liu's other supporters they numbered more than two hundred. The local governments also sent many policemen to Fenghuayuan ostensibly to maintain order but actually to help Liu and his proposed candidates. Each person was reportedly to receive 30 RMB as a daytime stipend and 60 RMB as an evening stipend. No matter when homeowners wanted to post anything on the community walls, Liu's supporters and the policemen would stop them and tear the posters down. If any homeowners complained, Liu's supporters and the policemen would yell at them and intimidate them. In one account, Yuan Chenglan, a renowned writer living in Fenghuayuan had hardly voiced her complaints at one of the ballot boxes when a man in his thirties came straight up to her and yelled: "Who are you? Where do you live? What is your name?" No other homeowners wanted to endure such a confrontation. Among more than a dozen posters in Fenghuayuan, about half of them threatened to punish any activities adversely affecting the election. Some homeowners reportedly said: "This is nothing like an election. It is so terrifying that it seems like the comeback of the political campaigns [in the Mao era]."[31] Those officials or volunteers had the list of candidates in their hands and coerced homeowners to vote for them. If any homeowner did not want to vote, his or her ballot would be taken away. The presence of scores of policemen also placed immense psychological pressure on the voters. Undoubtedly, the election was filled with fraud and threats. Infuriated, Yang complained that this election was rare and unprecedented in China in that it "both sabotages the democratic and harmonious atmosphere and damages the images of local Party and governments."[32]

Additionally, many homeowners sharply criticized the procedure used in the allegedly fraudulent election and pointed out that it had violated the Organizational Law of Urban Neighborhood Committees. Article 9 of the law states that all neighborhood committee meetings must be attended by more than half the adult residents or representatives elected by residential units. And any decision made at the meetings must have the support of more than half the attendees.[33] Yet Liu's team and its allies did not at first publicize voting procedures and sought suggestions from the residents. Later, they rejected the voting procedures stipulated by law. What they eventually did was to use a "simple majority" (*jiandan duoshu*) to elect future committee members, a voting procedure that, in Yang Zhangong's words, "not only infringed the state law but also had no acknowledgment from the majority of the homeowners."[34]

Another of Liu's tricks was to intentionally pick two workdays as voting days and avoid weekends, when most homeowners were free to cast their ballots. For Yang Zhangong, this tactic revealed the "evil minds" of a few people who wanted to manipulate the election. "Asking people who left home at 8:00 A.M. for work to come back [to Fenghuayuan] to cast their ballots, who can guarantee that those 'specially-trained' election staff do not play devils in the darkness?" he asked.

In a standard election, the location of the ballot boxes should remain fixed, and the head of each building unit were responsible for seeing that they weren't moved. But Liu's allies established twenty-seven movable ballot boxes, undermining the credibility of the election because "criminals" would easily evade supervision and use the movable boxes to cast fake ballots. Many homeowners asked to return to the old, legal system, but they were ignored.

The biggest violation of law in this election was the abuse of power by many local governments and officials. The Quanshan District government and the Taishan Subdistrict Office were directly engaged. They were behind most important decisions, including sending police, picking candidates, and "usurping Party's name" to forcibly send "An Open Letter to All Party Members" into every home. When Wang Peirong and his homeowners committee made public announcements on October 23 and 24 lambasting such unlawful activities and refusing to accept the election results, the Taishan Subdistrict Office further abused its power by issuing an official order dismissing Wang's announcements and attempting to intimidate him into issuing a retraction.[35]

Wang and his committee did not give in. In a defiant response, they argued that their announcements "merely told the truth, exposed our views, and expressed our stand of point" and that none of the announcements had any binding force (*yueshuli*) on the homeowners. "Do you not allow [us] to expose the problems in this election? Are you afraid of hearing any criticism?" they sarcastically asked. "What should be dismissed is the "election committee, which has neither legal foundation nor the support of most homeowners. No power can alter the facts and evidence, and no administrative order can revoke [people's] opinions and attitudes."[36]

To the abhorrence of Wang Peirong, Yang Zhangong, and many other homeowners, Pan Zengkui, one of the handpicked candidates, was even a criminal suspect. He was a former vice head of the Xuzhou Salt Administration Bureau and had been charged with scalping (*daomai*) salt and dividing the spoils. In 2003, the Yunlong District Procuratorate began investigating his case and summoned him for interrogation many times. He was eventually accused of abusing his power and conducting illicit business. In 2007, while allegedly on parole, he was appointed by the Taishan Subdistrict Office as the Party vice secretary of the Fenghuayuan community. Now he was the candidate for vice head of the neighborhood committee. With the backing of the local governments and Liu Yongxiu, along with the excessive use of government power, the police, and intimidation, all the official candidates were elected despite the opposition of most homeowners. One leader at the Taishan Subdistrict Office reportedly dismissed the opposition and said that no election would satisfy everyone. After the election, Yao Guihua, the vice head of the Quanshan District Bureau of Civil Service, reported to his superior that the election was "very smooth and successful."[37]

The unabashed and fraudulent election deeply infuriated homeowners like Yang Zhangong. He denounced it as "undemocratic and manipulated" and petitioned many local governments. But, like all Wang's complaints, his too were in vain. The *Jiancha ribao* report discussed neither the accusations of fraud nor the complaints of Yang Zhangong and Wang Peirong. It merely mentioned that no former members of the neighborhood committee, including Liu, had been reelected, which, in Wang's words, "represented the will of the residents."[38] As an official publication, the *Jiancha ribao* had refrained from criticizing the local governments too harshly, much less invoking the complaints of Yang Zhangong.[39]

THE PRICE OF FIGHTING FOR JUSTICE: BEING BEATEN, SLANDERED, AND FIRED

Fighting for justice is never easy, especially in China, where law and political power are strongly intertwined. While many people and the public media often laud those who do fight for justice, few know the pressure they have endured and the price they have paid. As we have mentioned before, the Shanghai lawyer Zheng Enchong, who had defended aggrieved people whose properties had been dismantled or taken by officials, was imprisoned for three years in 2003. In 2012, another lawyer and rights defender, Chen Guangcheng, was forced into exile after several years in prison.[40] In 2014, Xu Zhiyong, a Beijing-based lawyer who had helped defend complainants and led them to protest, was sentenced to four years in prison for "damaging and disturbing public order."

Unlike these lawyers, Wang Peirong mainly fights for the rights of his fellow homeowners and does not draw much international attention. Still, he pays a high price for his legal battles. Even after Liu Yongxiu and his family beat him in September 2006, no one has been punished, including Liu's son-in-law, a police official. During the subsequent movement to unseat Liu, Wang continued to experience violent reprisals from Liu and his allies. According to his account, on the morning of January 3, 2008, Liu again hit and robbed him. After the police arrived, Liu was not afraid and still threatened to beat him in front of the police. In the afternoon, Liu and his followers tried to make trouble at Wang's university. On February 22, 2008, one of Liu's colleagues on the neighborhood committee took off his shoe and beat Wang. Both of them were later taken to the local police bureau for further interrogation. On hearing the second incident, Liu rushed to the police bureau. Once there, he "not only cursed Wang but also struck him." But the police only "criticized and educated Liu and his colleague."[41]

Aside from beating and robbing Wang, Liu and his allies tried many means to slander Wang, for starters charging him with embezzling sizable amounts of public money. The first attempt came in May 2006 when a big-character poster headlined "Wang Peirong and Others Have Grafted One Million Yuan from the Homeowners Committee" ("Wang Peirong dengren tanwu yeweihui baiwanyuan") appeared in Fenghuayuan. The poster prompted Wang's wife to ask him whether the charge was true. Wang assured her that he had retained all receipts and breakdowns of the accounts. Several days later, Dong Feng, the vice president of the Chinese University of Mining and Technology and also the Party secretary of the Quanshan District government, harshly criticized Wang at a university staff meeting. "Some teachers focus on crooked things rather than on teaching and research. [They] will mislead students," Dong said.

Who was Dong Feng? Why did he side with Liu and oppose Wang? Liu once claimed that Dong Feng was one of his relatives.[42] That might explain why the district and the subdistrict governments worked so hard to protect him and supported his allies.

On May 23, 2006, Liu's committee continued to defame Wang. In a new poster headlined "The First Part of Wang Peirong's Economic Problems" ("Wang Peirong jingji wenti diyi bufen"), Liu asserted that his committee had quickly discovered many problems after Wang had transferred the money from the homeowners committee to Liu in 2005. One of them was a payment of 10,000 RMB to the Jialong Property Company for the utility bills owed by the Zhang Hong Research Unit (Zhang Hong yanjiu suo). Liu argued that his committee had discovered that, while the research unit claimed to have paid the homeowners committee, the committee had never paid Jialong. Thus, Wang and Meng Zhen, one of the representatives on the homeowners committee, were charged with embezzling 20,000 RMB (the 10,000 RMB owed Jialong and the 10,000 RMB received from the unit) and forging fake accounts. The poster concluded: "Wang Peirong and Meng Zhen are persons who have economic problems. We cannot give our original materials to people with problems to destroy them. We will speak the truth and continue to expose [the economic problems of Wang]."[43]

In the next few days, Liu and his committee issued similar posters alleging that Wang and Meng had "economic problems." To defend their reputation among the homeowners, Meng and Wang opted to file a lawsuit on July 2 to a local court charging Liu and his committee with slander. The lawsuit was in the name of Meng Zhen, who submitted three requests to the court: (1) the defendant should stop libeling, restore the plaintiff's reputation, and openly apologize; (2) the defendant should pay a compensation of 10,000 RMB to the plaintiff; (3) all fees incurred as a result of the lawsuit had to be paid by the defendant. In his written indictment, Meng Zhen reasoned that the neighborhood committee had since May 23 produced and distributed a series of posters accusing Wang and Meng of embezzling public money belonging to all homeowners. As we have seen, the May 23 poster blamed Wang and Meng for stealing 20,000 RMB by fabricating fake accounts in the case of the Zhang Hong Research Unit. The May 24 poster accused them of secretly withdrawing a donation of 1,744.5 RMB, a donation that had never been made. The May 25 poster said that the rent that Wang and Meng had collected from the research unit from May and June 2004 was only 7,946 RMB, 3,720 RMB less than what was actually owed, meaning that Wang and Meng had embezzled 3,720 RMB.

In addition, on June 12, 2006, Liu's committee posted an article entitled "What Is the Purpose of the Fake Articles regarding Fenghuayuan" ("Guanyu fenghuayuan de jiawenzhang mudi shishenme") on a popular local Web site. The article noted among other things how one utility fee of 7,019.94 RMB and the 10,000 RMB cash that the research unit had paid had vanished from Wang and Meng's accounts. In other words, both Wang and Meng had embezzled the money.

In conclusion, Meng wrote that those groundless charges had damaged his reputation among Fenghuayuan residents. He had taken photos of all the posters as evidence and reported them to the police.[44]

It was not until December 2006 that the Quanshan court finally settled the case. Instead of investigating and then rendering a verdict, it played the role of mediator between Liu Yongxiu and Meng Zhen. Its report stated that the neighborhood committee's charges against Meng were incompatible with the reality of the case. Hence, the neighborhood committee had to apologize to Meng for its false accusations. In return, Meng would withdraw his indictment. According to Wang Peirong, although the neighborhood committee agreed to apologize to Meng Zhen, Liu rejected any public apology. He also refused both to compensate Meng for his loss of reputation and to pay the indictment fee. Ironically, the court did not compel him to do either even though he admitted that he had committed slander. To appease and avoid offending Liu, the court simply told Meng that he did not have to pay the fee but that he should also not ask Liu to pay it.[45]

Why did the court not accuse Liu of slander and, as it did in late 2012 in a similar case against Wang, sentence him to prison time? Meng Zhen had hard evidence of the defamation, but that was not enough. Considering this case in combination with Wang's earlier lawsuits against four local governments for inaction suggests that Liu's backers and relatives might have played some role in the court decisions. After all, as we noted in previous chapters, Chinese courts are not independent, and their budgets and Party membership are subject to the control of local governments.

Virtually unscathed, Liu remained aggressive and hostile to Wang. In the late summer of 2007, he and his committee launched a new wave of libelous accusations against Wang and Meng. On August 2, in a new poster headlined "The Economic Inside Story of Wang's Homeowners Committee" ("Wang Peirong deyeweihui jingji neimu"), they argued that in December 2006 Wang and Meng had displayed a handwritten receipt to the Quanshan court saying that Wang had returned a deposit of 10,000 RMB to Zhang Hong. Yet the court discovered later that the receipt was counterfeited. Zhang did not receive the deposit, and the account of his research unit had no record of it. By asking "honest" homeowners to find out where Wang and Meng had hidden the money, the poster hinted that Wang and the homeowners committee had embezzled it.[46]

On September 7, Liu's committee posted purported evidence of the economic problems of Wang's committee, but they had allegedly been "covered" by Wang. Three days later, it posted another poster claiming that it would offer more evidence at the request of many residents. In fact, no hard evidence had been offered, as had been pledged in the second poster, but two "doubts" were shared. The issue was again the research unit. The first doubt was the claim that Zhang Hong had paid Jialong the 10,000 RMB deposit before the establishment of Wang's homeowners committee. If Wang had never received the 10,000 RMB deposit, why did Wang and Meng return the money to Zhang? The court investigation showed that Zhang had not written the receipt for the deposit, nor had anyone in his unit. Moreover, Zhang and his accountant never received the 10,000 RMB supposedly returned by Wang's committee. The second doubt was that Meng allegedly used the supposedly nonexistent receipt to withdraw the money on March 15, 2005. As the August poster did, this one asked Wang and Meng: "Where did you hide the 10,000 RMB?" Finally, it admonished Wang not to withhold evidence and promised the homeowners that Liu's committee would bring to light even more evidence of Wang's economic problems.[47]

Liu's committee also hung banners outside the neighborhood committee office and the community police unit denouncing Wang and his colleagues as "evil force" and "gangsters."

Despite the public personal smears and attacks, Wang and his colleagues did not take further legal action against Liu. It may be because Wang had a profound distrust of the local court's ability to render justice impartially. But it is more likely that he was overwhelmed by an ongoing fight against Dong Feng, one of Liu's key official backers. Since late 2006, Dong's distraught wife had provided Wang with evidence that Dong had many mistresses and had taken bribes from dozens of officials. Initially, Wang chose the traditional means of forwarding those materials to local governments. But several months had lapsed, and no government official had contacted him. So, on July 6, 2008, Wang determined to use the public media and the Internet to expose Dong. In addition to posting pictures of Dong and his mistresses, he also sent over a thousand emails to journalists in the employ of the major Chinese media. Under immense public pressure, Dong's superiors and the local prosecutors dismissed and arrested him within days. The success quickly made Wang a national celebrity.[48]

However, while Wang's success in combating corrupt officials such as Dong Feng and local power like Liu Yongxiu brought him national fame, the leadership of his university was not at all kindly disposed toward him. Shortly after he had exposed Dong, he was asked to stop teaching for a year. This was not the first time that he had been deprived the right to teach, and it would not be the last. Before the Dong Feng affair, he had reportedly been ordered by the university to stop teaching for one semester owing to his having exposed the dealings of a corrupt municipal leader. On August 18, 2009, the university threatened that it would bar him from teaching if he did not stop his Internet accusations of a more powerful vice mayor of Xuzhou. In late September, after he refused to yield, he once again lost his teaching position. One university leader had praised Wang's record as a teacher. But, mainly because of his political activity, the university felt compelled to punish him.[49] While Wang's charges against Dong Feng had sidelined a powerful backer of Liu Yongxiu, his other charges against more formidable Xuzhou leaders had sowed the seeds of misfortune for him in the coming years.

A Lost Battle

After Liu Yongxiu and his committee admitted the slander against Meng Zhen and Wang Peirong and especially the arguably fraudulent reelection of the neighborhood committee in 2009, many, if not most, people in Fenghuayuan would have thought that the fight between Wang and Liu had ended, especially since Wang seemed to have shifted his attention to higher-ranking and more powerful local officials. To many people's surprise, however, it lingered and even intensified in late 2012 when Liu along with three other people lodged a lawsuit against Wang with the Quanshan court charging him with slander. The result of the lawsuit was even more inconceivable as Wang, the legal fighter and a longtime victim of libel, was convicted and sentenced to eighteen months in prison.

According to the verdict of criminal charge of the Quanshan court, four retired homeowners in Fenghuayuan—including Liu Yongxiu, Xue Changling, the Party secretary of the neighborhood committee, Liu Bosheng, Wang's colleague and the vice head of the homeowners committee, and Zhang Zhixiong, a homeowner—accused Wang of smearing them as gangsters, corrupt, and embezzlers. Because neither Wang nor the defendants accepted court mediation, an open trial was held on November 30. About forty people attended, among them representatives of the local people's congress, teachers at the Chinese University of Mining and Technology, Fenghuayuan homeowners, and journalists.[50] During the trial, the plaintiffs argued that since 2006 Wang had adopted a number of means of attacking and abusing them with "fabricated and fictitious facts." They provided the court with photocopies, testimonies, and electronic data corroborating their charges. They argued that Wang's slander had greatly damaged their reputations, affected their families, and inflicted psychological trauma on them. They believed that he had violated the "246th Article of the PRC Criminal Law" and asked the court to penalize him.

Rejecting all those accusations, Wang contended that all he had done was to expose Liu as a gangster, a corrupt official, and an embezzler of public revenue and that he had the evidence to prove it. He criticized the report of the Quanshan Audit Bureau for fraudulently shielding Liu's crimes. He also said that all his denunciations of Liu had been made in the name of the committee to inform other homeowners. Therefore, the plaintiffs should sue only the homeowners committee, not him. In addition, he noted that one of the accusations against Liu entitled "Strongly Condemning the Scoundrelly Activities of Gangster Liu Bosheng" was attached to a formal poster of the homeowners committee asking the homeowners to safeguard their interests. That poster, he said, simply told the "ironclad" (*tiede*) truth and should not be treated as slander.

With regard to his poster charging Xue Changling with tampering in the reelection of the neighborhood committee in 2008 and backing the gangsters, Wang argued that the only candidates on offer had been handpicked by local officials and were not qualified. Xue and the reelection committee also used recommendations (*tuixuan*) made by one or a few powerful local officials as substitutes for the lawful nomination made through legal process. In order to conceal the truth, Xue "took all means" to destroy all documents produced by Wang and the homeowners committee exposing the fraud. Wang claimed that many videos could testify that Xue had upheld gangsters like Zhang Zhixiong, an embezzler who had also committed such other violent crimes as robberies and beatings. He gave the court more than 250 pages of documents as well as videos demonstrating that his charges were true.

After all the statements were given, the judges collected the copies of evidence and displayed them. The plaintiffs also offered supporting testimony from two people. Two were Liu's allies, one was the vice head of the Quanshan Bureau of Civil Service, and the other was the head of the Taishan Subdistrict Office. All denied that Liu was a gangster who had embezzled public money. They also denied that Xue had manipulated the reelection in 2008 and confirmed, from the government point of view, that the proceeding had been legal. To the dismay of Wang, three of his colleagues on the homeowners committee reportedly testified that he had "monopolized" the official seal of the committee since 2011, which meant that the homeowners committee would not be responsible for the posters supposedly defaming the plaintiffs. The judges did not tell Wang how they had acquired the testimonies, and Wang was not permitted to confront the witnesses because none of them showed up in the court.[51]

When the judges asked Wang whether he was responsible for the posters and the Internet postings, he admitted that he was. But he denied that his activities were illegal because all his charges were true and backed by hard evidence. Unmoved, the judges discounted all his evidence and told him that the plaintiffs and their lawyers had argued that the evidence was irrelevant to this case. For example, the pictures showing a bloodied Wang in September 2006 could not prove that Liu was responsible. All that was clear was that Wang and Liu had had personal disputes. As for Wang's accusations that the plaintiffs had sabotaged the 2008 reelection, the judges said that the evidence was insufficient. They also told Wang that his charges against the plaintiffs were "counterclaims" (*fansu*), which were actually criminal accusations (*konggao*) and would not be accepted by the court.[52]

The final decision of the court read as follows:

By ignoring state laws and social order, defendant Wang Peirong has long purposely fabricated facts and displayed them in both big-character and small-character posters as well as on the internet openly accusing [the four] plaintiffs of organized criminal activity, corruption, embezzlement, and beatings and robberies. Wang's activities have derogated the dignity and tarnished the reputation of the plaintiffs. In particular, after certain local governments have investigated the content of his reports and provided him with feedback, Wang continues to fabricate and spread fictitious facts. Wang's longtime slanders against other people have had a detrimental effect. Wang's activities have constituted the crime of slander.

The court rejected Wang's defense that what he had done was to report crimes and not to slander. The local police had already investigated his reports and concluded that they were groundless. "The state laws protect citizens' rights to report crimes," the court ruling indicated, "but they do not allow any person to smear others on the basis of personal conjectures or assumptions [*tuice yiduan*]." Therefore, according to Articles 246 and 64 of the PRC Criminal Law, Wang was sentenced to a term of eighteen months in prison. Moreover, his "criminal tools," including his computer, were to be be confiscated.[53]

Neither Wang nor the plaintiffs were satisfied with the court decision. Wang was sure that his charges were not slanderous, whereas the plaintiffs deemed punishment too lenient. Both sides appealed to the appellate court, the Xuzhou Intermediate Court, which convened on December 30, 2012, exactly one month after the Quanshan court had rendered its verdict. Again, both parties refused mediation. Giving as its reason that all the supporting evidence was clear, the appellate court decided to close the trial to the public.

The intermediate court trial employed essentially the same documents as had the Quanshan court. The accounts and evidence presented were essentially the same. Wang asked the court to reverse the ruling of the Quanshan court and declare him not guilty, contending (1) the first trial did not allow him to confront the witnesses; (2) the lower court violated due process by concealing evidence; and (3) all his charges were backed up by evidence and thus were not slanderous. He also asked the court to look into the perjury of the plaintiffs.

The court did not accept any of Wang's requests or rationales. Its verdict indicated that the results of its investigation were in tune with that of the lower court. It could accept neither Wang's defense nor his evidence, and his punishment would not be altered. As for his argument that there was no legal foundation for the lower court to confiscate his "criminal tools," the court invoked Article 64 of the Criminal Law, which said that the decision was correct. It also rejected the plaintiffs' request to augment Wang's punishment.[54]

Wang's sentencing has provoked differing reactions. After auditing his first trial, a local congressman told a journalist from the *Legal Daily*, the most influential newspaper covering the law in China, that the case could deter others from taking legal means to protect their rights.[55]

Gu Zhijian, a human rights activist based in Suzhou, Jiangsu Province, regretted that Wang admitted to the veracity of the plaintiffs' charges. "Have Liu Yongxiu and others acknowledged that they have ever attacked you?" he asked. "The Quanshan court would never pay attention to your evidence about their crimes. Your confession opens the way to prison. I do not believe that you are an honorable person [*gaoshang*]." He then blamed Wang for his naïveté. "Yet, in

China, evil is the pass [i.e. nature] of evil persons [*beibi shi beibizhe de tongxing-zheng*], so why do you not understand?"[56]

Why did Wang resort to displaying posters accusing Liu Yongxiu and the other plaintiffs? Did the Xuzhou courts make just rulings in this case? Was Wang's sentence justified? While some of his accusations may have gone too far, he was clearly forced to use posters because the governments, at both the local and the higher levels, had either turned down his administrative litigations or ignored his petitions. According to Wang, all his petitions against Liu to the provincial and central leaders eventually fell into the hands of Han Xiude, the Party secretary of the Taishan Subdistrict Office and Liu's superior.[57] Believing that he had hard evidence as well as the responsibility to serve the homeowners, he posted his charges. Both local courts had mainly accepted the testimony of the plaintiffs and the evidence provided by the local governments or officials before ruling against Wang.

Ever since he was sentenced in late 2012, Wang had petitioned the Xuzhou and Jiangsu disciplinary departments, questioning the court decisions. He complained that, when he presented the judges with hard evidence, they refused to verify it and claimed that it was pertinent only to a "countercharge" and that the trial was dealing with his purported slander alone. Any further accusations against the plaintiffs must be reserved for a later lawsuit. Wang later compared the trial to a boxing match in which "the referee allows your opponent to beat you but forbids you to defend yourself."[58]

Is there anyone who might be behind the trial and punishment of Wang? According to Wang, during his imprisonment in the Xuzhou Tongshan detention center, he was notified many times that, if he would stop reporting the corruption of Li Rongqi, the Xuzhou mayor, he would be immediately released with impunity and the four plaintiffs would be sentenced. But he rejected such offers because he would "never bow to corrupt officials."[59] His account, if true, gives us clues to answer such questions as why Liu Yongxiu unexpectedly sued Wang in late 2012 and why the local courts refused to verify Wang's evidence and harshly punished him. Since 2009, Wang had posted evidence of Li Rongqi's corruption on the Internet. Li had used his power to pressure the university to fire Wang in 2009 and to have him kidnapped in August 2012, less than two months before Liu Yongxiu sued Wang and three months before the local court sentenced him.[60]

Although Wang's accounts could not be independently confirmed, some human rights activists in China would rather trust him and fault the government. For instance, Gu Zhijian expressed strong suspicion of the government's intent in imprisoning Wang. As he put it: "Wang Peirong won the top prize in science and technology of Chinese universities in 2010. Had it not been because of rights protection and anticorruption, he would have been a full professor long ago. However, instead of being promoted, Wang has lost his job and even his personal freedom. On the surface, the victim in this case seems to be Wang, but in reality the case targets all Internet commentators. When our comments are deemed to threaten [[CCP] rule, they will immediately take action [against us] without mercy."[61]

Another prominent human rights activist, Sun Wenguang, is a retired professor who taught at Shandong University. Like Gu, Sun is also highly critical of the punishment of Wang. He argued after Wang's trial that college professors should be encouraged to use the Internet to stand up to corruption, a move that the Chinese people would also welcome. The court's decision to punish Wang was actually a move by the government to stifle the anticorruption movement among the people. "[Wang's punishment] is a violation of human rights," Sun remarked. "I hope the judiciary will safeguard justice and correct the verdict." Sun believed that the Chinese government was afriad of certain intellectuals, specifically those "who are working in colleges and collaborating with anticorruption forces in society." Once some outspoken intellectuals went on the offensive against corruption, the government would attack them. "The likely pretexts used by the government to attack intellectuals," as Sun noted, "are slander and fraud. "If what [Wang] has exposed is basically true, [the government] should support him. It will be very despicable for the government to use the judiciary to strike [Wang]."[62]

Conclusion: Powerless Law

In 2010, one Fenghuayuan homeowner called Wang a "lone fighter" (*gudude doushi*).[63] As a matter of fact, he is not just a lone fighter but also a legal fighter. During his battle with Liu Yongxiu, he worked, as he did in 2003, through legal channels. Only if there was no response would he post his evidence on the Internet. Unlike many other such informants, however, he never posted under an alias. He once told a reporter that he had evidence to back up all his reports: "If [someone] wants to accuse me of slander, I am waiting for him/her to charge me."[64] Unfortunately, he failed to understand the "legal asymmetry" inherent in Chinese law in which the officials or people with government backing often enjoy certain legal privileges or immunity, whereas commoners, no matter how credible and cogent their evidence, cannot obtain justice in the face of political power. In many cases, powerless commoners are likely to become the victims of powerful people and their allies. The biggest lesson Wang should have learned from his imprisonment is that he is living in a country where law and the judiciary are merely the knife hilts of the ruling Party.

6

Shanghai and Chongqing

The Winner, the Loser, and the Prisoners

After discussing several nationally notable legal cases in Wuhan and Xuzhou in which many aggrieved commoners used law against powerful local governments, we now want to shift the focus to high-ranking CCP cadres and see how they treated the law and how they reacted when their power conflicted with the law. The two cadres to be examined in this chapter are Chen Liangyu and Bo Xilai. Chen had been the Party head of Shanghai, once China's largest city and still its financial center, while Bo Xilai was the former leader of Chongqing, a city that was made directly subordinate to the central government in 1997 and has since then become the most populous city in China. During their tenure as heads of their cities, both Chen and Bo were members of the CCP Politburo, the most powerful governing organ in the PRC. More important, both have been potential candidates to enter the seven-member Standing Committee of the Politburo, which governs the PRC. This chapter will examine the Chinese criminal justice system, including legal processes, court hearings, torture, the use of force, and prosecution, using the two cases as examples. It aims to show that, while both Chen and Bo had violated laws in dealing with powerless commoners, lawyers, and businessmen, they eventually became the victims of those more powerful than they themselves were and the lack of the rule of law. Additionally, this chapter seeks to identify major problems facing Chinese courts and procuratorial reforms and the opposition from law enforcement to these ongoing judicial changes.

LEGAL REFORM AND PERSISTING PROBLEMS

In the wake of the 1989 Tiananmen massacre, instead of slowing down the pace of the economic reform and urbanization movement, the Chinese government chose to hasten it. It began to realize the importance of an urbanized country governed by the rule of law where city residents and power-interest groups are treated and held equally responsible. From 1995 to the present, the Party Center has sped up legal reform to achieve its goals of making the rule of law "the principal tool to govern the country."[1] President Jiang Zemin announced in 1997 that China would construct the rule of law. Since then, many new laws have been adopted covering a wide range of issues such as legislation law in 2000, property rights, the administration of lawyers, and labor relations in 2007, the administration of lawyers and the handling of emergencies in 2008, and access to public records and incidental responsibilities in 2009.

During the early years of the twenty-first century, the legal profession became increasingly institutionalized, marked by an expansion in legal education and a growing awareness on the part of the citizenry of their rights under the law. Many judges now wear robes instead of military uniforms, and they increasingly wish to have their courts separate from other branches of the Party-state. Court discussions and decisions have morphed from enforcing Party policy to maintaining neutrality in order to resolve disputes. The new requirements for the selection of judges reflect a change from a primary reliance on political background to legal education and professional experience.[2] In the twenty-first century, procuratorial bodies have paid special attention to political scandals, corruption, and mismanagement in the government and the Party. Many cases involved the collection of bribes for the procurement of licenses or the manipulation of regulations.

These reforms have had a strong impact on the criminal justice system, and tremendous changes have taken place in courtrooms, law firms, and prisons. Because of a societal environment increasingly supportive of legal reform, more and more people have become aware of their rights as citizens and want to use law to protect them.[3] Three interesting but somewhat contradictory trends can be observed: first, the separation of the law from the state; second, bringing the state back in to reinforce the new rule of law; and, third, the law used as an institutional tool in political power struggles against certain urban interest groups. The first restrains the state's power, while the second and third press the government to use its power to pursue justice. All these trends, however, appear to serve the purpose of promoting constitutional rights over the state itself.

As discussed in previous chapters, more and more urban dwellers have now turned to legal sources for assistance in solving problems with their landlords or the authorities. By 2012–2013, Chinese courts handled more cases than at any previous time, with those studying the subject noting that the country was facing a "litigation explosion."[4]

In the meantime, however, little structural change has been made in the Constitution, which, as a result, has a number of intrinsic deficiencies. For example, enforcement of court decisions is limited, and few legal sanctions exist for official violators. As an international human rights organizations pointed out: "The Party's continued dominance over, and interference with, judicial institutions, as well as the weak and inconsistent enforcement of judicial decisions means that overall, the legal system remains vulnerable to arbitrary interference and remains a tool of the CCP."[5] Moreover, it is difficult to implement the rule of law because Party leaders and government officials are supposedly morally superior and above the law. Party members, the self-proclaimed vanguard of society, are also required to use laws to protect the achievements of the socialist revolution against class enemies or the foes of the people.

In China today, as in the late Republican period (1927–1949), because rights and civil liberties are a gift of the authorities, they can also be withdrawn by them. Currently, the dominant CCP perceives the laws as a malleable tool to strengthen its power and magnify its interests. The country is still ruled by the law of the Party and its officials, particularly the local Party chiefs. The Party per se and its local leaders are still above the law, and their failures are attributed more to the loss of political and factional struggles than to violations of law.

The Shanghai Gang: The Rise and Fall of Chen Liangyu

Jiang Zemin finally decided to retire in 2003 after nearly fourteen years in power, and in 2004 Hu Jintao became the new Party chairman and the country's president and the chairman of the Central Military Commission. Hu also designed his "scientific development" concept, entrenching it in the Party's constitution as an official guiding ideology. He emphasized political and social harmony by nurturing good relations with central and local governments as well as supporting the growing professionalism and interest groups inside and outside the government.

Nevertheless, the growing diversity within the CCP leadership and the dynamic interdependence among competing factions were emerging at this time. From different cities such as Shanghai and Chongqing, several interest groups of younger, ambitious, and capable leaders aggressively and skillfully fought political battles for control of the Party and the government. They proposed alternative missions to change some causes of the Party to provide opportunity for its evolution and new development. The two most powerful camps were *tuanpai* (former leaders of the CCYL) and princelings (children of the first or second generations of CCP leaders). Their increasing factional struggles have constrained Hu and Wen Jiabao (1942–), premier of the PRC, from making new domestic and foreign policy initiatives.

Factional politics, which have been particularly noticeable during the current power transition, have resulted in new struggles, scandals, and even more crises for the new Hu-Wen leadership. The two continued the simulacrum of legality, which was still under control of the Party, whose priority is to maintain the central authorities. Whenever there was a local challenge or a political threat to Beijing, the Party Center was able to employ the legal system as an arbitrary means to defeat its political rivals.

One major case was the arrest and sentencing of the former Shanghai Party Committee secretary Chen Liangyu in 2006. Chen, who was said to have directly challenged Wen Jiabao, was charged with corruption and misuse of the city's pension fund.[6] The Shanghai Party Committee and the city government put pressure on the prosecution in Chen's case, including a threat to remove the chief prosecutor from his office. But the prosecutor won the case, and in 2007 Chen was dismissed from all his posts in the Party and city government. The court then agreed with the prosecutor to relocate the case from Shanghai to the northern city of Tianjin. In November 2008, Chen was convicted and sentenced by the Tianjin Court to eighteen years in prison.

Born in 1946 in Niingbo, Zhejiang Province, Chen joined the PLA in 1963 and became a member of the CCP in 1980. During his service, from 1963 to 1968, he enrolled in the PLA Academy of Logistic Engineering. After leaving the army in 1970, he worked at the Shanghai Pengpu Machine Factory for thirteen years as a worker, an engineer, and then the deputy director of the factory. His political career began when he was promoted to Party secretary of the Shanghai Electrical Appliances Corporation in 1984.

The Electrical Appliances Corporation belonged to the First Bureau of Electrical Machinery of the Shanghai municipal government. The political scientist Cheng Li points out: "From the mid-1980s through the entire 1990s, officials from that bureau formed a powerful network and dominated the top leadership posts of the Shanghai branch of the CCP and the Shanghai municipal government."[7] Among the notable figures from the First Bureau were Huang Ju and Hua Jianmin, who later became Party secretary and vice mayor of Shanghai, respectively. The First Bureau was also under the leadership of the Ministry of the Electronic Industry of the PRC, which was headed by Jiang Zemin. Therefore, in the 1980s, the "Shanghai Gang" became the most powerful urban elite group in Chinese politics—and Chen became part of it.

In 1985, when Jiang Zemin served as mayor of Shanghai, Chen Liangyu was, at thirty-nine, appointed director of the Retired Officials Bureau of the Shanghai municipal government. He was then on the fast track of career advancement, serving as deputy Party secretary and director of Huangpu District from 1987 to 1992, deputy secretary-general of the Shanghai municipal government in 1992, deputy Party secretary of Shanghai in 1993, and deputy mayor in 1996. On at least three occasions, Jiang played a crucial role in helping him advance his political career in Shanghai.

At the CCP Fifteenth National Congress in Beijing in 1997, Chen became an alternate member of the CCP Central Committee, one of the youngest members of this powerful organization. In 2002, he became the mayor and Party secretary of Shanghai. At the CCP Sixteenth National Congress in 2002, he became one of the three youngest members of the Politburo. His ascent to political prominence was largely attributable to Jiang's patronage.

Chen's problems began when he took over the position of top leader of the Shanghai Gang. In November 2002, when Jiang retired, Hu Jintao became chairman of the CCP at the Sixteenth CCP National Congress. In March 2003, he was elected president of the PRC at the Sixth National People's Congress.

LAW VERSUS POWER IN THE CASE OF ZHENG ENCHONG

Even though his biggest patron had retired, Chen continued the predatory policies in Shanghai by forcibly relocating thousands of people from central Shanghai to remote suburbs and then allegedly transferring their land to friends or businesses for huge profits. Most of the relocations were in the name of "Renovating the Old Town" (Jiucheng gaizao). From 2001 to 2002, the Shanghai municipal government had approved the redevelopment of 301 lots of land. Over the next three years, approximately six hundred lots of land had been approved for redevelopment.[8] One group of eight lots was called *dongbakuai* (lit. eight lots in the east) and located in the center of Shanghai. Two of the lots reportedly went to Zhou Zhengyi, the so-called richest man in Shanghai and a good friend of Chen's brother. The other six lots belonged to powerful officials or their relatives and Li Jiacheng, a Hong Kong business tycoon who had close connections with CCP leaders.[9]

Given reasonable compensation, the renovation of the old town should have been a welcome policy to many Shanghai residents living in the ghetto-like homes. It would also greatly ameliorate the image of the old town as well as of Shanghai. However, to generate greater fortunes for themselves and their allies, Zhou and his backers, including Shanghai Party boss Chen Liangyu, like local officials in Wuhan, coerced the residents to abandon their homes and accept the relatively lower compensation offered by the city government. In the words of Zheng Enchong, a Shanghai lawyer who had defended complainants against local officials, the local governments in China looted residents' homes under the name of law:

> In China, the government makes all the decisions about confiscating land and relocating homes. It is because the Chinese government monopolizes all land. The residential land is always controlled by a small number of people in the government. If the government wants you [a resident] to leave, you must leave; if the government wants to relocate your home, you must do so. The governments use the law to rob you, and you must cooperate. The knife hilts [law enforcers], guns [military], media, and court are all controlled by a small number of people in all local governments.[10]

Unsatisfied with their insufficient compensation, hundreds of residents facing violent relocation asked Zheng to help them defend their rights. One of the residents was a young Hong Kong woman named Shen Ting, whose parents were under government pressure to relocate. Some residents had gone to Beijing to petition the central government in hopes that president Hu would hear and redress their grievances. But the Beijing police had humiliated and beaten them before forcing them to return to Shanghai. The collective lawsuit against Zhou was initially successful after a local court sentenced him to three years in prison. Yet, on June 6, 2003, the local police arrested Zheng and accused him of leaking state news.[11] On October 23, 2003, the Second Shanghai Intermediate People's Court held a closed-door trial of Zheng. According to a former judge, the court was guarded by many police officers that morning, and any passerby was detained without a warrant. At the trial, Zheng reportedly told the judges that all of them knew that he was innocent.[12] Obviously, without the alleged consent of and pressure from the city government (i.e., Chen Liangyu), the police would not have abused their power, and the judges would not have convicted Zheng.

According to the official verdict of the Shanghai Second Intermediate People's Court, on May 23, Zheng was informed by a policeman of a "collective incident" (*qunti shijian;* i.e., a demonstration) at the First Shanghai Yimin Food Factory. He then recorded it and, on May 28, faxed it to Chinese Human Rights, a nongovernment organization based in New York. What he sent was an internal report entitled "Forced Relocation Resulted in Conflict and Reporters Encountered Assault during Interviews" ("Qiangxing chaiqian yinfa chongtu, jizhe caifang zaoyu weigong") issued by the official Xinhua News Agency. The "forced relocation" involved Zhou Zhengyi. The verdict also indicated that Zheng had written "internal report of the Xinhua News Agency and please reference" before faxxing. After inspection, the Shanghai State Secret Bureau (Guojia baomiju) confirmed that both faxed items were classified as state secrets. The Shanghai Procuratorate charged Zheng with breaking Article 111 of the Criminal Law by leaking state secrets to an overseas agency. While Zheng contended that he had been unaware that the reports were state secrets and that Chinese Human Rights had not received them, the court was not convinced and sentenced him to three years.[13]

Zheng later recalled that, during the court investigation, one judge asked him why he sent the report about Zhou to an external organization. Zheng replied that he wanted the news to be "imported" from outside because the state-controlled media would not allow its publication in China. In addition, Zheng accused Shanghai leaders such as Huang Ju, Chen Liangyu, and Han Zheng of having shielded Zhou in his violent relocation of thousands of local residents.[14]

On November 5, 2013, six journalists made a collective public statement protesting the rationale of Zheng's incarceration. They argued that the Shanghai government had three purposes in bringing the case against him: (1) attacking Zheng's prestige among the public and tarnishing his moral image; (2) reiterating the rationality of the local relocation policy; and (3) wrapping up the case and changing the public's bad opinion of the Shanghai government. What the Shanghai government wanted most was to make sure that the punishment of Zheng Enchong was attributed to his leaking state secrets and not his accusations regarding Zhou Zhengyi or Chen Liangyu. In fact, the journalists wrote that what the court claimed were state secrets were not secret at all, let alone state secrets. Shortly after the case of Zhou Zhengyi became known to the public on May 28, 2013, two national media—the *Twenty-First Century Economic Report* (*Ershiyi shiji jingji baodao*) and the *Financial Times* (*Caijin shibao*)—reported the details of the case. The first had interviewed Zheng before issuing its report. On June 4, another major newspaper based in Guangzhou and a Hong Kong television station also interviewed him. Both interviews focused on Zhou. On June 6, the Shanghai police arrested Zheng. "The most direct reason behind Zheng's arrest by the Shanghai government," the six journalists noted in a joint statement, "is simply to stop Zheng from accepting overseas interviews and disclosing more facts related to Zhou Zhengyi [and, therefore, Chen Liangyu]."

Risking violating the law, the journalists questioned whether the so-called state secrets were really secret. They said that one of them verified as such by the Shanghai Secret Bureau was that a reporter from the Xinhua News Agency had been roughed up while he was interviewing at one relocation site in Yangpu District. The other was that the police had broken up a workers' demonstration in a factory. Both incidents were wrongly considered state secrets, the journalists argued. "They [the journalists] have known from their communications with Zheng Enchong, and they have probably talked to many people." They continued their charges: "Because Zheng Enchong has been convicted, does that mean that we are also suspected of acquiring and leaking state secrets? Furthermore, if the Xinhua reporter or one of the workers who participated in the demonstration talks about his or her experience to overseas [media], has he or she also leaked state secrets? Has he or she also violated the law?"[15]

The journalists finally called on the Shanghai court to try the case publicly. If that was possible, the six journalists said that they would reveal their identities and testify in court.[16] However, the public statement challenging the arrest and sentencing of Zheng never found an outlet willing to publish it..

In 2010, long after Zheng's trial and sentence, Zhang Sizhi, Zheng's lawyer, once again publicly questioned the court ruling. Unlike the six journalists, who were laymen, the lawyer questioned the legal basis of the court verdict. According to Article 11 of the Secret Protecting Law (Baomifa), each level of the state organs should set its degree of secrecy in compliance with the regulations. In that regard, Zhang argued that it was Xinhua that needed to determine whether its report was a state secret, not the Secret Bureau. More important, according to an official certificate provided by Xinhua to the court: "The report of the agency has been published in the seventeenth issue of the *Selected Internal Reports* [*Neican xuanbian*]." If so, how could it have been a state secret?

Zhang also disagreed with the court verdict that the content of the Xinhua report "is relevant to national security and interest." "The report only mirrors the problems involved in a relocation case of a city and that the reporter has been assaulted during interviews," he wrote. "The report concludes with an emphasis on the fact that that city leaders are taking active measures to soften the social contradictions triggered by relocation." "Through what angle can [the court] corroborate that the report is related to or threatens national security and interest?" he asked.[17]

The biggest blow to the Shanghai government, and especially Chen Liangyu, was Shen Ting's book *Who Explodes the Case of Zhou Zhengyi?* which was published in Hong Kong in 2007. As a victim of the forced relocation and a supporter of Zheng Enchong, Shen exposed many details about the relations between Chen Liangyu and Zhou Zhengyi. Fearing that the book would have an adverse effect on their images and political careers, top officials under Chen had warned Shen that they would revoke her permit to return to China if she insisted on publishing her book. But she did not budge, countering: "President Hu Jintao talks about the rule of law, and I do not fear you." But the official who called her said: "Then you need to ask Hu Jintao for your permit. The Communist Party has only one [in China]. It is not a supermarket that can be opened one after another." After the German government awarded Zheng Enchong a human rights prize in 2007, the Shanghai government forbade him to leave China. Shen therefore tried to go to Germany to accept the prize on his behalf. Before she headed to the airport, Shanghai officials continued harassing her, making phone calls, and taking photos. Consequently, the German president reportedly expressed concern for her safety during her stay in Germany.[18]

Like their counterparts in Wuhan, both Zheng and Shen were powerless "little people" when confronting the powerful state mechanism. While her husband was awaiting his court trial in 2003, Zheng's wife, Jiang Meili, appealed for help. In a public statement, she first pointed out that the local government had denied the renewal of Zheng's certificate to practice law because he had often provided aggrieved people with legal advice. "Although he knows pretty well that it is a deep trap to fight corruption," she said, "Zheng Enchong continues to write indictments and evidence confirmations for the commoners. His aims are to uphold the national interests, protect the popular trust [*weixin*] of the Party among the people, and safeguard the dignity of the constitution and the law." Finally, the desperate wife questioned the defected Chinese legal system: "Is it true that the socialist modern society with Chinese characteristics is inferior to a feudal polity in the past? Is it true that the current construction of the socialist rule of law is merely lip service?"[19] Jiang's words may best reflect the asymmetrical yet harrowing relationship between law and power in China today.

FROM POWERFUL TO POWERLESS

Soon after Hu Jintao assumed the top position in the PRC, he found that he faced tremendous difficulties with China's economic and political reforms in the midst of continuous social transition. Even though he and Jiang Zemin had many disputes over specific issues, they reached a consensus on the key objective: China's economic growth and social stability. In the first decade of the new century, however, Chinese analysts worried about the country's macroeconomic instability and its potential problems.

To deal with those problems, Hu first appointed his longtime confidants from the CCYL Central Committee and northwestern and southwestern provinces such as Gansu and Guizhou where he had served as a local official and governor. Second, he strategically shifted China's economic development from a globally oriented policy to one more regionally balanced through macroeconomic readjustment that posed a potential threat to the development of Shanghai and its neighbors.[20] If this policy was implemented, it would be against Jiang Zemin's relatively liberal and decentralized policy as it gave the central government the initiative in curbing the overheated economy. As a result, new problems in the Chinese economy may not respond to old solutions, owing to the failing system and decentralized control. Third, Hu attempted to operate against the backdrop of Jiang's legacies because some of Jiang's "loyalists seem to have difficulties in shifting their loyalty from Jiang to Hu."[21]

Chen Liangyu, however, believed that Hu's new policies had intentionally ignored the interests of Shanghai and the Shanghai Gang and considered them to be a reversal of Jiang's policy. He began leading a criticism wave in 2004 against the new leadership in Beijing. He questioned Hu and his premier, Wen Jiabao, both of whom had advanced their careers mainly in the inland region and did not have experience in handling tough economic issues in coastal cities in an era of globalization. The overseas media widely reported that Chen voiced strong dissent against the macroeconomic control policies of Hu and Wen during a Politburo meeting held in June 2004.[22] Chen reportedly argued that the Hu-Wen administration's macroeconomic control policies would hamper the country's economic growth, especially its booming real estate industry in large cities such as Shanghai.[23] Chen even accused Wen of being responsible for the damaging consequences of the economic policy.

A political battle began over China's economic policy between Hu in Beijing and Chen in Shanghai. Hu quickly organized a strong defense by rejecting Chen's criticism. He initially asked all provincial and municipal governments to respond to his macroeconomic policy in a positive way and to adopt it immediately. All local governments soon showed their political support and loyalty to the Hu-Wen administration by doing so. Chen was isolated, both inside and outside Beijing.

Hu then removed some of the PLA old-guard generals and improved the chain of command of the military by appointing younger officers to the rank of general. After this streamlining, the average age of the PLA top officers significantly decreased. The average age of members of the Central Military Commission was sixty-eight in 1998 but sixty-three in 2004. The average age of military leaders on the CCP Central Committee decreased from 62.3 at the Fourteenth CCP National Congress in 1992 to 58.6 at the Sixteenth National Congress.[24] The newly promoted generals understandably supported Hu and the Party Center while opposing Chen and the Shanghai Gang.

With the military on his side, Hu began negotiating with Jiang Zemin since Chen had been seen as a protégé of the former president. Although Jiang had retired,he still had tremendous influence in both Beijing and Shanghai. As a result of the negotiations, a political compromise was made to remove Chen but save the Shanghai Gang. Chen Li, a political analyst at the Brookings Institute, explains: "Factional politics is becoming less a zero-sum game in which the winner takes all, and more a power-sharing dynamic in which two factions or coalitions compete in certain areas and cooperate in others."[25] To save his power group in Shanghai and keep the rest of his people in their positions, Jiang had to sacrifice Chen by publicly expressing his anger about his "bullying behavior" and "rotten lifestyle."[26]

Finally, having everything under his control, Hu made this fight public by ordering a criminal investigation of Chen on corruption charges, effectively eliminating his main political and policy rival. After the announcement, he moved quickly.

On July 5, 2006, the CCP CCDI began its investigation of Chen on corruption, bribery, and misappropriation of social security funds charges. On August 24, the Standing Committee of the CCP Politburo held a special session and voted to discipline him. On September 24, the Politburo was briefed by the CCDI and reviewed its preliminary investigative report. The Politburo decided on September 25 to remove Chen from all positions in the Party, including the Party secretary of Shanghai, member of the Politburo, and member of the CCP Central Committee. On July 24, 2007, the Shanghai People's Congress held a special session to terminate his term in the National People's Congress, to which he had been elected before the Tenth National People's Congress.

On July 26, 2007, the Politburo held a meeting and reviewed the CCDI final report on the investigation of Chen. The leaders at the meeting believed that Chen had seriously violated CCP laws and committed crimes during his tenure. They agreed to terminate his Party membership and refer his case to the court. According to the CCDI report, Chen was responsible for 3.45 billion RMB (US$439.4 million) being siphoned from the Shanghai Social Security Pension Fund and used for illicit loans and investments. In addition, he was also alleged to have been involved in other serious disciplinary violations, such as "helping further the economic interests of illegal businesspeople, protecting staff that severely violated laws and discipline, and furthering the interests of group members by taking advantage of his official posts."[27] But the report did not mention Chen's role in the case of Zheng Enchong or correct the largely unlawful punishment of Zheng. It should be noted that the misuse of pension funds did not occur only in Shanghai. China first established social security funds in 2000 to deal with the country's aging population. Its Ministry of Labor and Social Security has acknowledged that the embezzlement and misuse of pension funds is widespread within local government. Again, it was used for factional politics. And, again, the law, which has failed to protect the rights and interests of urban citizens, also failed to protect the rights of individual city officials.

During the criminal investigation, Beijing transferred Chen from Shanghai to Tianjin, a city in the north, away from his political base and influence. On

April 11, 2008, he was convicted on two counts, bribery and power abuse. The municipal court of Tianjin then sentenced him to eighteen years in jail. The pension fund scandal and the fall of Chen were major blows to the Shanghai Gang. But, as we have seen, because of the political compromise, almost all other prominent members of the gang have remained in power, and the urban power group has survived.

Ironically, Chen had in 2003 used his power to subdue the law in the case of Zheng Enchong to support his brother and a rich friend. Despite the nationally notable case and widely covered law violations, he emerged intact because of his powerful position and the weakness of the law. Five years later, however, he was unfortunately engaged in a fight with a more powerful person, Hu Jintao. This time, he himself ended up a victim of a compromise between Jiang and Hu. The bully was now the bullied. Had the rule of law been established in China, there would have been no unchecked power. In that case, Zheng Enchong would have not been imprisoned, and Chen would have been punished for authorizing the illicit and forceful relocation of many residents and the subsequent punishment of Zheng, but not for his involvement in an internal power struggle.

WHEN CHONGQING CHALLENGES BEIJING

The years 2012–2014 witnessed one of the greatest challenges the CCP had ever faced. The dramatic escape of a powerful police chief, Wang Lijun, from the city of Chongqing and his attempt to seek asylum in the offices of the US Consulate General in Chengdu shocked the whole world as well as the CCP itself. The significance of the event is, however, broader in that it lead to the exposure of many more scandals within the Party. Wang's boss, Bo Xilai, a member of the Politburo and one of the rising Party stars, is reported to have been deeply involved. His popular campaigns "Singing the Red [Songs]" and "Smashing the Black [i.e. the mafia]" (Changhong dahei) and retaliation against his opponents as well as suspicious relations with the military, huge illegal financial transactions, and even purported murder (and a subsequent coverup) can all be described as obvious signs of defiance of the central leadership in Beijing, which in his eyes was not doing enough to maintain the Party's monopoly on power and betraying the Maoist revolutionary ideology.

Wang was a member of China's princelings power group, and his personal ambition was to become at least one of the top leaders, if not the highest. The Bo Xilai incident, obviously, has become a real challenge to a Party that has been facing more and more challenges in recent years. The events have made many Chinese (its top leaders included) believe that long overdue political reform can no longer be postponed.

In early February 2012, news began to spread quickly, at first not via any official Chinese news channels but on the Internet. It was reported, that on the evening of February 6, a popular and powerful police chief of Chongqing City,

160   POWER VERSUS LAW IN MODERN CHINA

Wang Lijun, had fled his own city and entered the US Consulate General's office in Chengdu, a nearby city and the capital of Sichuan Province. Many believed that he was looking to the Americans for asylum. According to some reports, the Chongqing City mayor, Huang Qifan, rushed to Chengdu with up to seventy police vehicles, surrounded the consulate building, and tried to convince Wang to come out voluntarily.[28] According to a US State Department spokesman, Wang left the building "of his own volition" after a night's stay, though he refused to go back to Chongqing. Instead, he was picked up by national security authorities in Beijing on February 7.[29]

On March 15, most Chinese news media announced Party decision: Bo Xilai had been removed from the office of Chongqing Party secretary. Officials of the central government confirmed his removal was owing to the Wang Lijun incident. Bo's photograph, previously frequently displayed on television, immediately disappeared from public view. On March 26, Great Britain confirmed that it had asked the Chinese government to reopen the murder case of Neil Heywood, the English businessman who died in Chongqing in 2011. Soon after that, on April 10, China officially announced that Bo Xilai had been stripped of all his CCP posts and that his wife was under investigation in connection with Heywood's death.[30]

After being appointed mayor of Dalian City, Bo Xilai gradually became well-known—he had been credited with the successes of the city, one of China's cleanest, and with booming economic activities, frequently used to showcase China's economic success after Deng Xiaoping's "Reform and Open-Up" policy was put in place in the early 1980s. Dalian City is also the place where Bo and his police chief, Wang Lijun, began and strengthened their relationship. When Bo was promoted to governor of Liaoning Province, Wang was also moving up. In 2004, Bo became China's minister of commerce and, in 2007, a new member of the Politburo, before moving on to Chongqing City.[31]

Bo Xilai has been described by foreign correspondents as "flamboyant," "charismatic," and "suave," someone who enjoys the limelight with his signature smile in front of cameras, which sets him apart from the typical images of other top Communist leaders in China (his superior, Party general secretary Hu Jintao, was famous for his poker face).[32] His leadership style as well as the policies he tried to put into place also differ from those of other Communist leaders. While serving as Party boss in Dalian and later of the whole province of Liaoning, Bo successfully implemented his policies, attracting foreign investment, beginning construction projects, planting trees and grass (locals call it *Xilai grass*), and making many other popular moves. He also made a lot of enemies. According to some reports, he mercilessly pursued his political opponents. One of these whistle-blowers was the journalist Jiang Weiping, who tried to reveal the Bo family's shady business dealings but ended up being sent to jail for five years.[33] All sorts of people—journalists, common folk, businessmen, and even government officials who were not willing to cooperate with Bo—faced harassment, prison time, and death threats (some of which seem to have been carried out).[34] His actions won praise from the Left and the populace but also raised a lot of eyebrows, especially among top leaders and jurists in Beijing owing to his blatant abuse of power and violation of law.

The rampant corruption among officials added even more fuel to the fire. The last time the Chinese government published the numbers of mass demonstrations, petitions, or riots in a given year was 2006. In that year, it is reported that more than 85,000 such events took place across the country. According to scholars' estimates, 2011 saw more than 180,000 such incidents.[35] Clearly, such incidents have become major concerns of the Party leadership because "maintenance of stability" has been the priority of the Party since the beginning of the current century. Deng's popular 1980s–1990s policies of "Getting rich is glorious" and "Letting some get rich first" seem to have accomplished their mission, and other policies are badly needed to keep the Party's control over power and society.

For people on the Left who are nostalgic for the Mao years or resent the unbridled government corruption, Bo Xilai's "Chongqing model" seems to offer an alternative, or, more optimistically, viable, solution to the problems facing China today. Taking full advantage of his revolutionary bloodline as one of the princelings, he began putting into practice a number of populist campaigns as far back as his days in Dalian but mostly during his time in Chongqing, one of the several municipalities directly controlled by the central government. A campaign that he launched in Chongqing demonstrated his smart appropriation of modern technology and people's yearning for the simpler, supposedly less corrupt Mao years. Bo personally sent out mass text messages to the city residents with his favorite Mao quotations, calling on people to keep in mind the old but much valued Communist ideals of earlier times in the newly developed economy. He also personally promoted the Singing the Red campaign. Tens of thousands of people—factory workers, students, government employees, and so on—were convinced to band together in singing groups, learn the old revolutionary songs, and compete among one another. Bo even personally took some of the winning groups to perform in other regions of the country, including Beijing. In Chongqing, all prime-time commercial television advertising was banned, replaced by revolutionary movies, patriotic songs, or other propaganda programs promoting revolutionary spirit. Untold numbers of trees were planted in and around the city (called *Xilai trees*), low-income public housing projects sprung up, and the city's infrastructure was improved.[36]

Alongside the Singing the Red campaign is the Smashing the Black campaign, a movement aimed at cracking down on the organized crime that had been disrupting the city and its residents for quite some time. As the Party boss of the city, Bo and his police chief, Wang Lijun, beefed up the police force, provided more police services, and used the newly reformed police force in his anticrime campaign. According to one official report, from 2009 to March 2012, when Bo was relieved of his official positions, the Chongqing government had investigated more than eighty organized crime rings and prosecuted and convicted 1,297 people, a number of whom were sentenced to death.[37] Among the condemned were members of the parvenu, the group that has caused people's hatred or jealousy of wealth accumulated in a short time.

Personal property, businesses, and cash worth hundreds of millions of dollars were confiscated. Some was used to modernize the city's police force and its infrastructure projects, but a large amount of it simply disappeared. Bo's political enemies were particularly targeted. For example, the former vice commissioner of public safety, Wen Qiang, was sentenced to death for corruption and for providing protection criminals. It is still not clear how many people were actually guilty and how many simply got in Bo's way.

LAW AS DOUGH KNEADED BY POWER AT WILL

From the very beginning of the Smashing the Black campaign, Bo and Wang made sure that the law buttressed rather than bound their crackdown. With law becoming the knife hilt of power, Wang could pursue any means—legal or illegal, lenient or harsh—to extract confessions from his prey. In many cases, Wang gave the green light to torture, which clearly violated the 1996 Criminal Procedure Law, Article 43 of which states that judges, procurators, and interrogators should adopt legal proceedings to collect evidence and that torture is strictly prohibited.[38] Unfortunately, while many PRC laws have, since the early 1950s, prohibited it, torture remains an immense problem in the PRC owing to its embedded tradition and the disrespect of law. In the dynasties, torture was a largely legal means of extracting confessions from suspects.[39] In the early 1930s, according to the late historian Gao Hua, armies loyal to Mao Zedong mercilessly tortured masses of his political adversaries, the AB faction.[40] Torture continues in the reformed period despite a progressive campaign to modernize the Chinese legal system. The recent instances of torture in the widely publicized cases of Du Peiwu and Ma Dandan, the virgin prostitute, are just two unfortunate examples.[41]

However, torture in Chongqing was much larger in scale and more serious in degree. It also won the support of the top police head, Wang Lijun, and to some extent Bo Xilai. To fill their coffers, Bo and Wang allegedly fabricated charges against many local businessmen, accusing them of organized criminal activity. If they denied the accusations, they would be tortured. According to the *New York Times,* before Li Jun, one of the wealthiest magnates in Chongqing, eventually fled China, he had become a target of the local police as "a black society boss" and endured three months of "beatings, torture, and relentless pressure to implicate others in nonexistent crimes."[42] In an interview, Li told a *Times* reporter that the police had confined him in the "Tiger Seat," a notorious torture method, for forty hours to force him to confess. Li said that he would rather die.[43] Aside from torturing him, the local government also confiscated from him property worth $711 million.

Li Jun's experience was merely the tip of the crackdown iceberg in Chongqing. In fact, he was just one of 4,781 people who had been arrested in Bo's high-profile campaign.[44] Gong Gangmo, a motorbike mogul in the city, was charged in 2009 by the Chongqing police with such felonies as ordering the murder of a man after a nightclub fight. But Gong rejected the charge and claimed innocence. The police detained him and sent him to Tiepingshan, one of the twenty-four temporary detention centers in Chongqing. He later told reporters that in the center he was hung and beaten for eight days, during which his "urine and excrement fell to the floor." Overwhelmed by torture, he eventually confessed to the crimes that the police insisted on.[45]

Under Wang Lijun's iron fist, no one, or no group, was absolutely safe. Many policemen were arrested and tortured for alleged corruption. For example, in January 2010, Wang Yong, an officer in Wanzhou District, was taken from his office and transferred to a Smashing the Black base. The tormentors put a hood on his head and ordered him to sit on an iron chair. For days, he was unable to sleep. During one session, he was beaten so harshly that one of his clavicles was broken. Afterward, the perpetrator, Wu Jiong, was promoted to head of a local police bureau.[46]

Another policeman named Zhou Wenzhou, who had been on the force for thirty years, and his wife had a far worse experience. On August 7, 2009, while Zhou was watching television at home, he received a phone call from his bureau asking him to help solve a drug-selling case. He agreed, but hardly had he arrived at the bureau when several men surrounded him. One of them told him that Wang had issued an order to detain him. That same night, Zhou's wife was also arrested and sent to another base. In the following days, the couple suffered gruesome tortures. According to the *Nanfang dushibao,* a bold and popular newspaper based in Guangzhou, Zhou's wife was put in the Tiger Seat and her feet shackled. Zhou himself was forced to wear a "thick and filthy" black hood and to sit on an iron chair. Heavy fetters were affixed to his body. In front of him were bright lights that remained on day and night. He was not allowed to sleep. Despite the cold weather outside, the air-conditioning ran continuously, and the cold wind would "blow frantically." After two weeks of such treatment, Zhou's lower body was so swollen that he could barely stand up and part of his hip was ulcerated. "All I wanted then was to find an opportunity to kill myself, and [for me] death was really better than living," Zhou later recalled.[47]

Similarly, a retired cadre of the powerful political and legal committee complained about the torture of his son, Xiao Shaoyong, a decorated police officer, by Wang Lijun. On April 13, 2010, Xiao suddenly found himself charged with harboring criminals and being involved with organized crime. The local police detained him and sent him to a secret base. For the next ten days, he underwent excruciating and "fascist" corporal tortures. As Wang Yong and Zhou Wenzhou had been, Xiao was tied to an iron chair and forbidden to put his feet on the floor, move, sleep and rest, close his eyes, or go to the bathroom. As a result, he became seriously dehydrated, and both his legs were swollen. Worse, he was hung and beaten, had cold water poured on him, and was beaten about the head. When he claimed that torture was unlawful and a violation of his human rights and the rule of law, he was informed simply that the direct orders of the police chief, Wang Lijun, were being carried out. "If we torture you to death," he said, "we will say that you have committed suicide in order to escape punishment [*weizui zisha*]. Whatever you do, you will not break the iron chair. I will see how long you can resist."[48] While the fate of Xiao is unclear because there is no further report, one thing is evident: the police have clearly and regularly broken state law.

In early 2012, despite evidence to the contrary, including Wang Lijun's attempt to seek asylum, Chongqing Party secretary Bo Xilai flatly rejected any charge that the local police had used torture. On March 9, 2012, while he was attending the annual National People's Congress meeting in Beijing, he told reporters that no torture had been used during the Smashing the Black campaign.[49] However, as Wang's superior and the initiator of the movement, he could not plausibly deny his involvement.

Aside from attacking and torturing businessmen and policemen, Wang and his adherents also detained and punished people for minor offenses. One such incident involved a scatological blog post. On April 22, 2011, shortly after the lawyer Li Zhuang had been accused by Wang of committing perjury, a Chongqing resident called Fang Hong posted a message on his blog: "Bo [Xilai] has pooped a lump of waste, and he asks Wang Lijun to eat, Wang passes it to the procuratorate, the procuratorate passes it to the court, the court passes it to the lawyer Li Zhuang. But the lawyer says that the person who has pooped should eat the waste and returns it to Dr. Wang Lijun. Wang has to eat the waste of his master [i.e., Bo Xilai]."[50]

The next morning, a local police head called Fang Hong and told him that his blog post had "irritated" him. On April 22, several police went to Fang's home, took him into custody, and confiscated his computers. Fang's initial punishment was ten days' incarceration. But a policeman from the city police bureau said that the punishment should be one year in a labor camp. Fang understood that the police decision could not be altered and thus he resigned himself to a year in a labor camp. To save his father from what was essentially prison, Fang's son contacted rights protectors and foreign media. Under pressure, the local police head warned Fang to stop his son, who might otherwise "be kidnapped or drowned."[51]

The PRC labor camp was created in 1957 when the National People's Congress promulgated the Decision on the Issue of a Labor Camp. But its root can be traced back to the base period during which the CCP sentenced criminals to forced labor.[52] In the early 1950s, and especially during the counterrevolutionary campaigns, thousands of so-called class enemies were sentenced to labor camps or "forced education" (*guanjiao*).[53] Wu Hongda (a.k.a. Harry Wu) published a book entitled *Laogai: The Chinese Gulag* in 1992 recounting his years in a Shanghai labor camp and denouncing the system. Unlike a court sentence, the decision to send someone to a labor camp can be arbitrary, made by several policemen without the approval of either procuratorate or court.[54]

In 2012, Fan Zhongxin, a liberal law professor at Hangzhou Normal University, lashed out at the police decision to sentence Fang Hong to a labor camp. It was, he felt, against democracy and the rule of law: "Let us see: one blog of less than one hundred words resulted in one year of labor camp?" He continued: "Is this what a democratic country should do? Is this what a rule-of-law country should do? Is this what an organ of implementing law for the people should do?"[55]

Throughout the Smashing the Black period, not all policemen agreed with or backed the widespread illegal activities of Wang Lijun, particularly those policemen who had fallen victims of torture. One anonymous policeman who had reportedly witnessed the process had secretly recorded the tortures and other unlawful policies of Wang. In an online book entitled *Witnessing Wang Lijun* (*Jianzheng Wang Lijun*), he questioned the legality of such actions. In 2011, he discussed Wang Lijun with another police officer who had been stationed in three so-called Smashing the Black special units. Both agreed that Wang, a professional policeman who held a college degree in law, was not building up the police force but rather destroying it. Although many policemen hoped that the central government would stop him, they were disappointed when some central leaders visited Chongqing and endorsed him and Bo Xilai.

Using tangible and specific examples, the police criticized Wang's unlawful policies. For instance, under the law, police could only deal with common criminal cases, not those involving state officials. Yet Wang had often put himself above the law by arresting state officials for alleged economic crimes and transferring them to Smashing the Black special units. Second, by law, within forty-eight hours of arrest, the suspect could hire a lawyer, and the police were to cooperate with the lawyer. But, in Chongqing, lawyers had often been banned, and many of them had been punished. Third, despite its unlawfulness, torture was quite common for Smashing the Black special units. When a police chief was under interrogation, Wang allegedly approved all "necessary means." After torture, the policeman's head was bloodied. Some other policemen, such as the aforementioned Wang Yong and Luo Li, had been brutally beaten. Additionally, when, after his arrest, investigators determined that Xiao Shaoyong had not committed any crime and requested that he be released, Wang refused.

As a law enforcer, the courageous police author sensed that the law had been distorted under Wang Lijun. "[I] always feel that law is no longer as precise [*yanjin*] as [what I have learned] from books," he noted. "Law becomes a dough, which can be kneaded by [powerful] people [i.e. Wang] at will and used for any purpose. I have been worried by such a bewilderment."[56]

Powerless Law in the Case of Li Zhuang

Most instances of torture and other law violations under Bo Xilai and Wang Lijun were almost unknown to outsiders until Wang's attempt to seek sanctuary and Bo's subsequent fall. The case of the lawyer Li Zhuang was, nationally prominent, uncovered part of the true color of Bo's campaign, and generated suspicion, at least among legal specialists.

Li Zhuang was a lawyer working in a Beijing law firm. In the summer of 2009, a friend asked him to help deal with a Chongqing case involving a client named Gong Ganghua. After he agreed, the friend brought Gong to Beijing. It turned out that Gong Ganghua's brother, Gong Gangmo, had been arrested and accused by the Chongqing police of involvement with organized crime. But Gong Ganghua concealed the extent of his brother's crimes and told Li simply that the police had discovered an ornamental handgun in Gong Gangmo's home as well as a sizable stash of cash. On November 19, Li suddenly received a call from Gong Ganghua, who deeply apologized and pledged to hire Li as his only lawyer. The initial fee was 200,000 RMB, and Li agreed to take the case.

Soon after Li Zhuang arrived in Chongqing, he realized that the case was not as simple as Gong Ganghua had described. It turned out to involve four murders, ten kilograms of drugs, seventeen guns, and five hundred bullets. The Chongqing police considered the case to be a "major mafia" matter, and the relevant documents comprised 109 volumes, 2,200 pieces of evidence, and 180 testimonies. Despite the extent of the material to be reviewed, the judge told Li that the trial would begin the next day and that he would not brook delay. Once he was able to review the documents, Li found, to his surprise, that he had been given only about one hundred pages detailing the evidence and a few pages of confession and accusation. He also found evidence that the confession was forced. He decided to visit Gong and talk to him face-to-face.

On November 23, Li Zhuang went to the Tiepingshan detention center to meet Gong Gangmo. His talk with his client was monitored by the local police, a clear violation of the law.[57] Article 37 of the Criminal Procedure Law prohibits law enforcement officers to monitor meetings between lawyers and their clients.[58] Li's protests against the presence of the police were to no avail. While he was talking with, two policemen sat behind them. Li told Gong that the evidence offered was sufficient to sentence him to death. Gong burst into tears and said that "he had been hung and beaten for eight days by the police" and that, "although his toes could touch a table, his heels could not." Li became very angry. He told a policeman in the room, who had allegedly beaten Gong: "You should get out because you have committed the crime of torture." Three days later, Li held a second interview with Gong. He encouraged Gong to testify in court that the police had tortured him. To prevent the court from hiring another lawyer who might collaborate with the police, he also told Gong not to allow the court to appoint any lawyer other than him. Finally, he assured Gong not to fear the police in the court and just speak the truth. If necessary, he could use body language (e.g., showing the bruises that resulted from torture). However, unlike the first time, when they simply observed, the local police now recorded the conversation, and the recording later served as evidence when Li Zhuang was charged.

On December 1, Li Zhuang invited several renowned criminal lawyers in

Beijing to testify in the case of Gong Gangmo. This made Wang Lijun and the Chongqing police uneasy. They feared that, by attempting to make this case public, Li would not only derail this particular trial but also reveal that the police had, in fact, employed torture. Wang thus moved swiftly to deal with the situation. First, a vice head of the local court tried to persuade Li to cooperate with local law enforcement. But Li was unmoved because doing so would result in the death of his client. His intransigence enraged Wang. One of the policemen reportedly suggested that they could ask Li to quit the case by paying him more money than Gong Gangmo. But Wang rejected that option lest other lawyers catch wind of the transaction and would have to be likewise bought off. He finally decided to arrest Li on a charge of perjury.[59]

Xiong Feng and Wang Zhi were Wang Lijun's most trusted followers and in charge of Gong Gangmo interrogation. According to Gong, despite the cold weather, Wang Zhi beat him about the head, and Xiong poured cold water on him and turned on the air-conditioning. Xiong encouraged Gong to accuse Li and gave him the phone number of Wang Zhi, the vice head of a local police bureau. Wang Zhi conducted many interviews with Gong and promised not to execute him. To force Gong to cooperate, the Chongqing police went to a Beijing hospital to detain his dying wife. After Gong agreed to betray and accuse his lawyer, Wang Zhi asked Gong to practice his testimony often before appearing in court.[60] In the meantime, Gong's brother also faced police pressure to cooperate. According to the *New Beijing Newspaper,* the Chongqing police arrested him and forced him to accuse Li Zhuang of visiting prostitutes. He later admitted that all his accusations were false: "Gong Gangmo is not Jiang Jie; I am not Xu Yunfeng [two fictional communist heroes]. We could not stand the torture [and had no choice but to accuse Li]."[61]

The day of December 12, on which he paid a visit to Gong's wife in a Beijing hospital, was a disastrous one for Li. To his surprise, a group of Chongqing police, led by Wang Zhi, suddenly appeared and arrested him. He was taken to Chongqing, where he was met by Wang Lijun, along with dozens of policemen. Wang Lijun told Li that nothing could protect him. Li retorted that the law would be on his side. According to a report in the *China News Week,* after the Chongqing police arrested Li, Wang Zhi became the leading interrogator. Wang Zhi told Li: "The top leaders [i.e., Wang Lijun] have determined to sentence you to prison. If you manage to escape incarceration, I will quit my career as a policeman. Even if there is no confession, we will still imprison you." It is clear that law enforcement in Chongqing was not conducted in accordance with the law. As in the Waitan Garden case, it was one of the biggest hurdles to constructing the rule of law in China.

Many lawyers quickly questioned the arrest and accusation of Li Zhuang. A number of them submitted a joint petition to the Ministry of Public Security and the NPC on December 16, suggesting that the trial be transferred to a city other than Chongqing. But the suggestion was ignored by the Chongqing court.

In addition, the Chongqing police detained Li's assistant, Ma Xiaojun, and his wife, depriving Li of a key witness. It was not until the downfall of Bo and Wang that Ma finally disclosed that the Chongqing police had arrested him and coerced him into not testifying on Li's behalf.[62]

During the first court appearance on December 30, 2009, the evidence used by the public procurator (*gongsuren*) to indict Li on a charge of instigating perjury consisted of eight testimonies. One was from Li's client, Gong Gangmo, who allegedly said that the police had not tortured him and that it was Li Zhuang who had encouraged him to say that they had. When Li asked the judge whether he could see the testimonies, meet the witnesses, and watch the videos made in the detention center, this legitimate request was turned down. He was sentenced to two and a half years in prison.[63] At his second court appearance in February 2010, Li agreed to a compromise and confessed his guilt in order to avoid incarceration. But, to his surprise, he was still sentenced to a year and a half in prison instead of being put on probation.[64]

In Li's case, the law was powerless in the face of virtually absolute political power. The legal system could easily be made to serve the needs of political campaigns and even the will of powerful local politicians. To make matters worse, fearing that they might be the next Li Zhuang, many lawyers have become unwilling to accept criminal cases. Chen Guangzhong, a renowned law professor at the Chinese University of Politics and Law, argues that the defense system (*bianhu zhidu*) underwent serious setbacks during the Smashing the Black movement in Chongqing. For him, the greatest lesson of the case of Li Zhuang is a recognition of the state of the legal defense system in China. "A crucial yardstick to measure a country's progress in democracy and the rule of law," he has remarked, "is the extent to which human rights are protected."[65]

THE DOWNFALL OF BO XILAI

Despite its disregard for the law, the Chongqing model, which featured the Singing the Red and Smashing the Black campaigns, apparently met with the approval of quite a number of people, in whose eyes Bo Xilai was a champion of the common folk and a crusader against corruption, greed, and inequality. Many also believed that his actions in Chongqing were a direct criticism of his predecessors in Chongqing, as well as of the Beijing government, for not doing enough to fight the rampant corruption in China.[66] Even after his downfall in 2012, many in Chongqing and other areas still insist that his course of action was the right one. American travelers' reports seem to back up such claims. "Wang [Lijun] gave people a sense of safety and Bo [Xilai] gave us hope," Chongqing folks would say. Such feelings are widespread as many believe that Bo and Wang were "not perfect" but still "really did something."[67] One commentator vividly describes these campaigns. Bao Tong, an assistant to former Party general secretary Zhao Ziyang before the 1989 Tiananmen incident, recently pointed out that Bo actually understands the Party's traditional policy much better than we believe he does. According to Bao, Bo's Singing the Red is good at promoting the Party's absolute control over power, while Smashing the Black can easily be used to eliminate any opposition groups or individuals. As for the common folk, Bao believes, Singing the Red will ensure that the citizens to obey the Party completely, while Smashing the Black only makes them the willing thugs (*dashou*) of the Party. Bo Xilai actually internalized the core ideas of Mao's theories, relying on mass movements to replace the rule of law.[68]

Such campaigns, of course, also established Bo as the symbolic leader of China's New Left group, those who are continuously criticizing the government, especially the central leadership under Hu Jintao and Wen Jiabao, for letting go of the much-valued Communist ideals and promoting the development of a capitalist market economy. Beijing leaders were not happy to see this. They correctly understood that what Bo was doing in Chongqing was actually a direct criticism of their policies—the economic reforms were in deep trouble, and Bo was challenging them by providing a different model, or a way out. Although none of the top leaders openly criticized the Chongqing model, their unease with it can be seen clearly in time many times they gave Bo the cold shoulder. When he took his Chongqing singing groups to perform in Beijing City before the Wang Lijun incident, not a single member of the Politburo attended any performance. By the last day of the 2012 NPC, the news of Wang's defection had already become widespread, and Premier Wen Jiabao openly criticized the Chongqing City government, warning that campaigns in that city could only bring back bad memories of the Cultural Revolution, and predicting that the Chinese people would not allow that kind of catastrophe to happen again. He also made it clear that the Chongqing Municipal Party Committee and government must "reflect seriously and learn from the Wang Lijun incident." The following day, April 10, 2012, the Xinhua News Agency officially announced Bo's downfall. He was stripped of all his Party and government positions, and his wife would go on trial for Heywood's murder.[69]

THE TRIAL OF BO XILAI

On July 26, 2012, less than six months after Wang Lijun's failed asylum attempt, Gu Kailai and her aide, Zhang Xiaojun, were charged with intentional homicide. By August 20, both had been convicted of the murder of the Englishman Neil Heywood in reaction to an "economic conflict."[70]

However, the real story of the murder case remains unclear, even after a trial that offered a great deal of evidence, including witness testimony, none of which has ever been released to the public. It is not clear whether Gu conceived and executed the plot on her own or whether her husband was involved. According to one Chinese American scholar, Chen Liming, Gu let the court know that she told Wang Lijun everything about the murder while seeking his assistance but did not know that he had recorded the conversation. However, no one knows whether Gu informed her husband or what her husband did when he was informed. It is also unclear what Wang did after Gu confessed to him. Rumor has it that he went to see Bo and played him the recorded conversation and that an angry Bo slapped him in the face. Soon after, Wang was removed from office.[71] In *A Death in the Lucky Holiday Hotel,* Pin Ho and Wenguang Huang argue that Wang had backers in Beijing, even among Politburo Standing Committee members.[72]

Whatever Wang had done, his attempted defection may suggest a larger plan by one of the princelings in Beijing to get rid of Bo Xilai. Also, it is said that Wang worried whether he could flee Sichuan Province, which Bo ruled like an independent kingdom. This would explain why he decided to turn to the Americans for protection. With his own life in danger, it seems a good choice: even if his application for political asylum was rejected, his information regarding Heywood's murder would surely arouse the Western media's interest as well as attracting Beijing's attention. In other words, Wang's behavior would surely cause the new Party leadership under Xi Jinping to take action since what Bo was doing in Chongqing was part of his and his supporters' plan to prevent Xi from successfully taking over the Party leadership. Xi and his followers would surely move forward to protect Wang, using him against Bo and his supporters. Wang was a winner, according to Ho and Huang; he saved his own life and ruined Bo's political career.[73]

On August 20, 2012, when Gu Kailai's trial was over, she received a suspended death sentence (which means that, after two years in prison, her death sentence may be converted into a life sentence, according to a tradition in China's legal system).[74] Wang faced his trial in Chengdu. The trial began in secret on September 17 and concluded the following day. Nobody outside the court knows the details. On September 24, Wang was convicted and received prison sentences for defection (two years), abuse of power (two years), bribe taking (nine years), and bending the law for selfish ends (seven years), but the court decided to give a combined fifteen-year sentence. His "political rights" were also stripped for one year.[75]

After the punishment of his wife and former lieutenant, Bo Xilai's fate was sealed as early as April 2012. On April 10, the Xinhua News Agency issued the following statement: "As Comrade Bo Xilai is suspected of being involved in serious discipline violations, the Central Committee of the Communist Party of China has decided to suspend his membership in the CPS Central Committee Political Bureau and the CPS Central Committee, in line with the CCP Constitution and the rules on investigation of the CCP Discipline Inspection Department."[76]

The CCP Discipline Department conducted an initial investigation of Bo. The case was then transferred to Jinan Intermediate People's Court. The court, which is located in Shandong Province, issued a verdict in September 2013 stating that Bo had seriously violated the Party's rules and abused his power while serving in various positions in Dalian City, Liaoning Province, the Department of Commerce, and Chongqing City. His first crime was accepting bribes totaling

21 million RMB from 1999 to 2006. The second crime was corruption. In 2000, when Bo was the helmsman of Dalian, the head of the Dalian Land Bureau gave 5 million RMB to the Dalian municipal government in order to be awarded a construction project. He told Bo that his family could keep the money if no one knew of it. Bo immediately called his wife, and soon the money was transferred to her law firm. The third crime was abuse of power in dealing with Heywood's murder. On January 28, 2012, after Wang Lijun reported the murder, Bo slapped Wang and ordered that the two policemen who had exposed the murder be punished. In addition, he violated the organizational regulation in his decision to strip Wang of his official positions. After Wang's attempted defection, Bo and his wife forged medical proof that Wang suffered from serious depression. On February 8, Bo gave permission to publicly issue the false news that Wang had accepted "holiday treatment." The court verdict ascribed the tardy investigation of Wang's defection to Bo's abuse of power.[77]

In the days following the court decision, most official news channels produced a large number of articles, editorials, and comments pledging to support the Party's decision regarding Bo Xilai. The Chongqing government also issued a statement in support of Beijing's decision. The *People's Daily* even ran an editorial on its front page endorsing the court decision: "In terms of the case of Bo Xilai, the entire proceedings, from investigation to charges, to prosecution, to the opening of the court session, and to court verdict, are based on facts and laws. They also manifest the spirit of the rule of law and judicial justice and reflect the resolute determination and attitude of the Party and country in penalizing corruption in compliance with the law."[78]

Although the government took pains to control the flow of information regarding the case, rumors continued to circulate in China and throughout the world through the spring and early summer of 2012, the information being released puzzling everyone. For example, a rumor about a failed coup in Beijing on March 29 caught the attention of many. Supposedly, some troops loyal to Bo Xilai and his supporter Zhou Yongkang (who is in charge of China's security troops) tried to rescue Bo from custody but failed. The Chinese government moved quickly to delete the story and punished those responsible for spreading it. So far, no further information regarding this supposed coup has been released.[79] It was also reported by the *New York Times* that Bo had run a wiretapping network across Chongqing, his officials listening to phone calls of Party and government officials, including President Hu Jintao. A group of veteran Party members, according to another report, wrote collectively to Hu demanding that he sack not only Bo but also Zhou Yongkang, who was considered to be working behind the scenes to revive a movement to lead China back to Mao's time.[80] Again, it is unclear whether these are simply rumors (*yaoyan*) or "predictions far ahead of their times" (*yaoyao lingxian de yuyan*), as the popular saying goes among the Chinese.

Bo Xilai undoubtedly was dissatisfied with the first court verdict. He appealed to the appellate court, the Shandong High Court. On October 25, 2013, the high court made a final ruling upholding the earlier decision. Throughout the proceedings, Bo reportedly interrupted the judge and disputed the decision and the evidence. For instance, when the judge said that he would be sentenced to seven years for his role in Wang Lijun's defection, Bo told the judge that it was absurd because the defector would be sentenced to only two years. "It shames the Chinese judiciary; it is a step backward in the move to the rule of law in China," he said in court. After the judge finished, Bo could not control himself and shouted: "I am innocent; you want to be the hero of striking the tigers. But in fact you are creating unjust, fake, and wrong cases. This is the retrogression of the rule of law in China."[81]

Who on earth is right about the rule of law in China today? Bo Xilai or the official media? Bo denounced the court decision as against the rule of law, while the official media claimed that his punishment indicated the success of the rule of law in China.[82] There were few scholarly voices in China bold enough to publicly challenge these court verdicts. Some scholars based overseas have questioned the trial of Bo Xilai. Invoking a report in the *Economist,* Yu Churu, a political analyst, argues that the indictment of Bo was "made by the winners and not the judicial apparatus." He agrees that the trial drew more attention than any in the past thirty years. Yet, the trial per se was largely a political performance. From the very beginning, Yu argues, he sensed the backwardness of the rule of law. "If we could put the case of Bo into the large reform milieu of China, the failure of Bo would be more likely the result of a contest between the left and the right factions." He continues: "Obviously, the trial of Bo evaded this important point at the beginning because it avoided the key issue of political course but accused Bo of corruption and taking bribes." Yu notes that the trial is backward if compared with the trial of the "Gang of Four" in the early 1980s, which did not hide the struggle between different political factions.

In regard to the charge that Bo accepted bribes totaling over 20 million RMB, Yu remarks that Bo dismissed it with a smile because such a small amount was not even enough to keep a mistress. The prosecutors had ignored overseas reports that he might have amassed at least 8 billion RMB, chosing instead to accuse him of taking a mere 20 million RMB. In addition, they overlooked more serous crimes. The major one is the massive law infringements during his campaigns against organized crime. These campaigns have not only generated numerous grievances but also resulted many suicides. Yu also points out that the government had violated the law by blocking pro-Bo views during Bo's trial. In one case, Song Yang, a far-Left Maoist, had been detained by the police in consequence of his strong support of Bo. Only an edited transcript of the trial has been made public, further clouding things. Moreover, according to Yu, Bo revealed at the trial that the officers in the Central Disciplinary Department had interrogated him several hundred times and that he lost consciousness twenty-seven times. The prosecutors had threatened that, if he did not cooperate, they would sentence his wife to death and repatriate his son (a student at Harvard University).[83] The torture and coercion employed by the prosecutors against Bo, if true, cannot be squared with the claims of the official media that the trial demonstrates the rule of law in China. After all, the Central Disciplinary Department, and not the procuratorate, acting as the prosecutor is incompatible with the spirit of the rule of law.

No One Is Safe without the Rule of Law

Since China opened its door in the late 1970s, Shanghai and Chongqing have been among its most important cities. On the one hand, Shanghai, the financial center and former largest city, has often been on the forefront of China's reform, especially after 1990. Chongqing, on the other hand, has been the largest city in terms of population and area since 1997. The leaders of the two cities—Chen Liangyu and Bo Xilai—had many things in common. They are Party chiefs in their respective cities and members of the powerful Politburo. Chen, a member of the Shanghai Gang, had strong backers among top CCP leaders such as Jiang Zemin, Zhu Rongji, Huang Ju, and Wu Bangguo. In contrast, Bo was even more prominent as a result of his popular but highly controversial reform in Chongqing.

However, both Chen and Bo had another similarity: using illegal means to deal with complainants or their enemies. For example, to speed up urbanization in Shanghai and also profit his relatives and friends, Chen used force to destroy many homes and gave some of the best land thereby obtained to his friend Zhou Zhengyi. When the poor residents who had lost their homes lodged petitions and hired the lawyer Zheng Enchong, Chen paid no attention to their petitions, and the Shanghai court sent Zheng to prison after an unjust trial. Bo Xilai's initial intent might have been good as he wanted to clamp down on organized crime and improve the life of the poor urbanites. Unfortunately, like Chen, he took a hazardous path to attain his goal. To smash the so-called blacks, he launched a number of high-profile campaigns against organized crime. He gave his lieutenant Wang Lijun a free hand in interrogating and torturing suspects. With his support, Wang established a total of twenty-four antiblacks bases in which the law was largely absent. The police transported many alleged criminals to the bases and inflicted on them a variety of gruesome torture methods to extract confessions. In many cases, those confessions were the only evidence supporting the charges. Because the court, the procuratorate, and the police were the knife hilt of the Party, law enforcement officials in both Shanghai and Chongqing not only failed to question those law violations but also became tools and accomplices of the government.

The downfalls of Chen Liangyu and Bo Xilai have something in common. Both men fell not because of their violations of state laws but because they became the prey of more powerful persons in Beijing. Chen was involved in a direct conflict with President Hu Jintao and Premier Wen Jiabao. As a result of an alleged political compromise between Hu and Jiang Zemin, Chen was tried and sentenced to prison. Bo received a harsher punishment than did Chen, as he was sentenced to life in prison. Before the court rendered its final verdict, Bo reportedly had already endured cruel interrogation and torture, albeit nothing as bad as was dealt out when Wang Lijun still held office. When Bo shouted during his trial that his punishment was unfair and broke the law, he had probably forgotten that many people had suffered far worse fates during his rule in Chongqing. Neither Bo nor Chen may ever realize that no one is safe without the rule of law. When they were in power, they had no intention of respecting the law and often abused their power. When that power suddenly vanished, they finally realized how important legal protection was. But that realization came too late.

Conclusion

The Legal Asymmetry

In this book, we have examined four prominent cases from urban China, each of which has drawn considerable attention from national and even international public media. Using abundant and mostly exclusive primary sources, we have been able to conduct in-depth studies of each of the four, especially the Waitan Garden and Xuzhou cases. All four have one thing in common: they have clearly mirrored the complicated and contradictory relations between law and power in China today, which will surely help us better understand the political and legal nature of the PRC. Our analysis has uncovered three key problematic relationships between law and power in the PRC today: lawless power, powerless law, and legal asymmetry. We first outline those relations and then consider whether they are unique to the PRC or have been endemic to China throughout its history.

LAWLESS POWER

The first problematic relationship between law and power is lawless power, which means that the political or official power is beyond the constraint of the law. In all four cases, lawless power was frequently displayed, whether by local officials, the police, even the courts.

For example, in the Waitan Garden case, local officials and the police put intense pressure on the residents to abandon their homes, ignoring the law and threatening forcible relocation. And, after all their complaints to both local and central leaders failed, more than one hundred homeowners opted to sue the local government, arguing that the decision to demolish Waitan Garden had not been taken legally and that illegal measures had been taken to force them to move out. Despite their cogent articulation of their case, they could not find a court willing to accept their lawsuit, proof that the courts had surrendered to or were collaborating with political power. Even worse was that Zhu Rongji's order proved more powerful than state laws and the legal contracts that the homeowners were forced to enter into in order to buy their properties. In the Xuzhou case, lawless power prevailed because the challenger, Wang Periorng, was a mere college professor and not hundreds of homeowners.

In the Shanghai and Chongqing cases, two highly powerful heads were involved. In Shanghai, Party secretary Chen Liangyu took advantage of the urbanization movement. When hundreds of residents were facing eviction, the government ignored their complaints. They then hired the lawyer Zheng Enchong to help them bring their lawsuits to court, but the police and the court were tools of the local government, and Zheng was arrested and then tried in a closed-door and heavily guarded hearing, charged with leaking state secrets, convicted and incarcerated for three years.

The case of Bo Xilai, the Communist helmsman of Chongqing, China's largest city, and a member of the powerful Politburo, was different. Bo launched a massive crackdown on organized crime. Although many locals supported his efforts, later details surfaced that he and Wang Lijun, the head of the Chongqing Police Bureau, had abused their power and violated state laws by extracting forced confessions from criminal suspects. In the notorious case of Li Zhuang, a Beijing-based lawyer who helped defend one of the so-called criminals also wound up in prison, the victim of police and local court officials who had no choice but to follow the orders of their superiors. The local courts, under the control of the Party, merely accepted the confessions of suspects and dared not conduct independent investigations. Ironically, despite his overt endorsement of police torture and other lawless policies during his tenure as head of Chongqing, Bo chastised the Chinese judiciary as rejecting the rule of law during his own trial in 2013.

POWERLESS LAW

When state apparatuses, such as governments, the police, and the courts, act without regard for the law, the law becomes powerless. As our four cases have shown, even though the victims of power have taken all kinds of legal means to seek justice and have their grievances redressed, they eventually realize that the law is powerless in the face of overwhelming power.

The Wuhan homeowners were initially confident that they would prevail since they had followed the law in obtaining all the necessary certificates and contracts. However, as local officials ignored their arguments and increasingly pressured them to relocate, they decided that further action was required. While some resorted to extralegal natural resistance, most explored legal options. The slogan of the homeowners was, "Administration in accordance with law and using law to defend rights." Even in the face of the unlawful actions taken by local officials and the police, many homeowners still naively believed that by following the law they would prevail. Some petitioned a variety of local, provincial, and central leaders, and others worked diligently to find honest and brave lawyers to take on lawsuits, but none made any headway and were forced to give way before the will of power.

Wang Peirong was not as lucky as he had to fight alone. He adopted methods similar to those employed by the Waitan Garden homeowners, first petitioning, then filing administrative litigations. Only out of frustration when his efforts proved ineffective did he resort to extralegal means. The Shanghai residents who sought sufficient compensation when their apartments were to be destroyed similarly attempted to resolve their grievances through legal channels, only to have their lawyer detained, charged, tried, convicted, and sentenced to prison.

If the law in Shanghai was powerless to safeguard commoners' lawful rights, in Chongqing it found itself in an even worse situation. In order to further his political career, Bo Xilai launched a massive campaign against organized crime that was conducted mostly extralegally. Even Li Zhuang, the lawyer attempting to expose the police torture of his client, found himself a victim of a law enforcement system unconstrained by the law.

Legal Asymmetry

Like two halves of a walnut, lawless power and powerless law are intertwined and difficult to separate. Lawless power inevitably leads to powerless law, and powerless law gives rise to lawless power. Without lawless power, there would be no powerless law. The coexistence of the two can best be described as *legal asymmetry*. In a state of legal asymmetry, people with power, whether direct or indirect, will be less likely to be afraid of violating the law no matter how egregious their activities, while people without power will be punished in accordance with the law no matter how minor their crimes.

In the case of Waitan Garden, local officials and the police were free to disregard the constitution and other state laws and infringed on homeowners' human rights, harassed their families and coworkers, restricted their personal freedom, and blocked their petitions. Most of the homeowners, however, had to be very careful to take only legal action in attempting to protect their property. Otherwise, they invited detention and punishment. The homeowners had the law on their side, but the local officials and the police held the power.

In Xuzhou, both Yan Jiaxun and Liu Yongxiu had close ties with the local police. Yan drove a police vehicle, which obviously broke the law. Liu's son-in-law was the vice head of a local police bureau. As a lower-ranking government official, Liu had strong connections among local governments, and his most powerful backer was Dong Feng, the Party secretary of the Quanshan district government. Taking advantage of their powerful patrons, Yan and Liu were bold enough to beat Professor Wang in the street or even in a local police bureau. More outrageous to Wang was that his petitions to provincial and central leaders against Yan and other local officials had been returned to the hands of the police allies of Yan or the charged officials themselves. Wang's subsequent lawsuits against local governments also ended in failure as most local courts rejected his appeals. Facing insurmountable barriers, Wang had turned to the Internet to expose the corruption and law violations of local officials. Yet, unlike the actions of those powerful police and officials who could freely neglect and infringe the law, Wang's desperate decisions to expose Liu's corruption quickly drew charges from his powerful enemies. He was sentenced to eighteen months in prison, while the real culprits remained at large.

Legal asymmetry was best manifested in the cases of Shanghai and Chongqing, in which the Party secretaries Chen Liangyu and Bo Xilai were able to do almost anything they wanted. Chen in Shanghai could neglect the law by taking land from legal inhabitants and disregard their complaints and lawsuits. When a lawyer attempted to challenge their power and criticized the local government during interviews with both domestic and external media, Chen's knife hilts acted swiftly to detain the lawyer and indicted him on trumped-up charges. Thus, a commoner's minor crime, if the accusation were indeed true, would be easily tracked and punished by law enforcement officials, while the government could have a virtually free hand in violating people's lawful rights. Similarly, Bo Xilai and his longtime supporter Wang Lijun, who had full control of the police, the procuratorate, and the court, had widely abused their power and taken numerous illicit and grisly means such as torture, intimidation, arrest without warrant, entrapment, and perjury in their campaigns against the so-called local mafia or blacks. In the meantime, if any commoners or persons with few government connections in Chongqing had crossed the lawful line, they would be quickly detained, tortured, charged, and punished in the name of law.

The root of legal asymmetry in urbanized China is almost omnipotent political power. As we have seen, Montesquieu warned people about the adverse consequences of a union between legislative power and judiciary power. Because the CCP dominates the three principal state powers, it is actually above the law. The lack of judicial independence and thus enforceable constitutional law further strengthens the CCP's power and makes the law merely its knife hilt.

The Rule of Law and the Party-State

After Xi Jinping became the new CCP leader in 2013, some people hoped that he would support a constitutional government and restrain the power of the Party. But subsequent developments quickly shattered that dream. Like his predecessors, Xi continues to talk about the significance of the rule of law. On February 23, 2013, for instance, he noted: "All organizations or persons must act within the law. All citizens, social organizations, and state apparatuses must use law as their standard of conduct [xingwei zhunze] and exercise their rights or power and fulfill their obligations in compliance with the constitution and the law." On another occasion, invoking the words of the legalist Han Feizi of the Warring States Era, he remarked: "A state will not be governed well unless its law has been implemented." He went on to warn law enforcement agencies in China to have a firm belief in law and to strictly implement the law.[1]

Xi's statement about the rule of law and law enforcement is not different from what former president Jiang Zemin said in 1997 at the Fifteenth Party Congress when for the first time he declared that the CCP would construct the rule of law in China.[2] However, while he has verbally stressed the rule of law and law enforcement, Xi has never, as Xie Yanyi, a Beijing lawyer, has argued, made it clear that he supports a "constitutional government," a political concept embracing both judicial independence and a government under the law.[3] In fact, as long as he is the Party head, he will not back a constitutional government in China. It is because in a constitutional government law is supreme and independent and the CCP would be bound by the law. As a *People's Daily* editorial frankly admitted in early 2014, both the judiciary and the law enforcement agencies were the knife hilt of the CCP and had to be placed under the absolute control of the Party.[4] The status of law under the CCP has been consistent since at least the early PRC. The notion that law should be independent and above the Party or political power generally have long been denigrated by the Party as a Western capitalist idea that is incompatible with "Chinese characteristics." Since his rise to power, Xi has launched political crackdowns to "silent dissent."[5] Many of them are reportedly politically oriented and largely ignore the law. For example, owing to his persistent and troublesome protests, his call for political and legal reforms, and his defense of the rights of aggrieved petitioners, Xu Zhiyong was sentenced to four years in prison.[6] In the summer of 2015, another crackdown on rights lawyers whose scale and scope were far greater than that in which Xu was caught up in was launched by the CCP. More than two hundred lawyers have been detained and interrogated. The crackdown immediately drew intense criticism from rights groups and the Western media.[7] Xi's anticorruption campaigns have been quite popular among ordinary Chinese. Yet, reminiscent of Bo Xilai's campaign in Chongqing, many of them have involved illegal torture and interrogation.[8]

It may be inappropriate for Xi, the paramount state and Party leader, to openly announce that the Party is above the law. Local Party leaders would find it much easier to talk about the "true color" of the CCP's rule of law. For example, a recent article ostensibly authored by Zhang Chunxian, the Party secretary of the turbulent Xijiang Uighur Autonomous Region, overtly lashes out at the Western principle of judicial independence and positions the CCP above of the law: "While the rule of law is a crucial fruit of human civilizations, it never has just one pattern. The key difference between China's rule of law and the Western constitutionalism is the organic unity [*youji tongyi*] of upholding the Party's leadership, people as state masters, and using law to govern a state. Our rule of law is not the one of 'separation of three powers,' and it should not follow Western ways of 'judicial independence' and 'judicial neutrality' [*sifa zhongli*]."[9]

He Weifang, another liberal law professor at Beijing University, notes that the rule of law and judicial independence can restrict the power of government.[10] Indeed, although most CCP leaders in contemporary China have frequently pledged to respect the law and construct the rule of law, none have taken the further step of promoting a constitutional government in which law will be supreme and independent. The reason is quite simple: the CCP mainly considers the law to be a tool with which to consolidate its power and does not want the law to confine its power and actions. Not surprisingly, without a constitutional government and judicial independence, CCP leaders, for now and in the foreseeable future, will at most be like enlightened dynastic rulers such as Han Wendi and Tang Taizong whose compliance with the law depends solely on their own legal consciousness and cannot be enforced. Hence, in a Party state, political power or anyone who enjoys government/official backing will take advantage of the legal asymmetry, and tragic cases like those of Waitan Garden and Xuzhou will certainly recur for the foreseeable future.

Acknowledgments

Our research for this book spanned the period from the late 1990s to 2013, a time when China experienced the fastest pace of urbanization in its history. We have focused on five cases in four cities—Wuhan, Xuzhou, Shanghai, and Chongqing—that reflect the complex relationship between law and power in the ongoing urbanization movement in China and, to some extent, in many other countries as well. While the unprecedented and massive urbanization movement has improved the living standards of many people and transformed urban landscapes, many urbanites have unfortunately fallen victim to it. One of the purposes of this book is to serve as a reminder their experience.

Our research would have not been possible without generous financial support from grants provided by the University of Minnesota, Twin Cities, and the University of Minnesota, Duluth. These grants include but are not limited to a university grant-in-aid, the Imagine Fund, and the Chancellor's Small Grant. We especially appreciate the University of Minnesota's Institute of Advanced Studies Residential Fellowship, which made it possible for Qiang Fang to complete the bulk of the book. In addition, Qiang Fang would like to thank Ms. Jing Duan for her crucial assistance throughout the writing of this book.

Many people at the University of Central Oklahoma (UCO) have contributed to this project and deserve recognition. First, Xiaobing Li would like to thank President Don Betz, Provost John F. Barthell, Associate Vice President Gary Steward, and Chairperson of the Department of History and Geography Patricia Loughlin. They have been very supportive of the project over the past several years. The UCO faculty merit-credit program sponsored by the Office of Academic Affairs, as well as travel funds from the Office of Research and Grants and the College of Liberal Arts, provided funding for our research and trips to conferences. The UCO Student Research, Creative, and Scholarly Activities grants sponsored by the Office of High-Impact Practices made student research assistants available to us. Special thanks to Michelle Magnusson, who copyedited all the chapters. Annamaria Martucci provided secretarial assistance. Graduate and undergraduate students at UCO who contributed to the book include Gary Johnson, Derek S. Liu, Jiahui Xu, and Lingling You.

We wish to thank Professor Shiping Hua for his scholarly leadership in the "Asia in the New Millennium" series through the University Press of Kentucky (UPK) and Stephen M. Wrinn, former executive director of UPK, Jonathan Allison, interim director of UPK, and Allison Webster, executive assistant to the director of UPK, for their interest and excellent editorial guidance. Any remaining errors in facts, language usage, and interpretation are our own. Finally, we want to thank the three anonymous readers for their invaluable and insightful comments and suggestions.

Qiang Fang
Xiaobing Li

Notes

INTRODUCTION

1. It was reported by the police that Zhang and Pan threw several burning gasoline bottles from their house toward the crew outside before setting themselves on fire.

2. *Jingji banxiaoshi* (Economic half hour), CCTV, November 21, 2008.

3. Among the self-immolation suicides protesting the forced urban removals of 2008–2009 were a young couple in Quanzhou, Fujian Province, on April 3, 2008; a family of three in the city of Fuzhou, Jiangxi Province, on September 10, 2008 (one died, while two were seriously injured); a family in the city of Chifang, IMAR, on February 13, 2009; Zhang Xie in Qingdao, Shandong Province, on October 28, 2009; Tang Fuzhen in Chengdu, Sichuan Province, in November 2009; and Xi Xinzhu in Beijing on December 16, 2009.

4. Li Peilin, *Dangdai zhongguo chengshihua jiqi yingxiang* (Urbanization in modern China and its effects) (Beijing: Shehui kexue wenxian chubanshe, 2013). See also Bai Xuemei, "Zhongguo chengshi zhuanxing dequshi, yingxiang yuzhengce zhixiang" (The trend, influence, and policy direction of China's urban transformation), in *Haiwai xuezhe shiye zhongde zhongguo chengshihua wenti* (The problems of Chinese urbanization from the perspectives of overseas scholars), ed. Tang Lei and Lu Zhe (Beijing: Zhongguo shehui kexue chubanshe, 2013), 3–21.

5. *Han Feizi,* with annotations by Chen Bingcai (Beijing: Zhonghua shujü, 2007), chap. 36.

6. "Xi Jinping qiangdiao yifa zhiguo yifazhizheng yifaxingzheng gongtong tuijin (Xi Jinping stresses ruling, administering, and governing in accordance with the law and moving forward together), Xinhua News Agency, February 24, 2013.

7. Yang Weihan, "Xi Jinping chuxi zhongyang zhengfa gongzuo huiyi" (Xi Jinping attended the central work meeting of the politics and law), Xinhua News Agency, January 8, 2014.

8. "Haobu dongyao jianchi dangdui zhengfa gongzuode lingdao" (Unequivocally safeguard the Party's leadership of politics and the law), *People's Daily,* January 9, 2014.

9. Pitman Potter, *The Chinese Legal System: Globalization and Local Legal Culture* (London: Routledge, 2001), 11.

10. For example, renowned scholars such as Wang Zaoshi and Yang Zhaolong argued in 1957 that the percentage of criminal cases involving false arrests, detainments, and judgments was as high as 34 percent between 1950 and 1957. *Wenhuibao,* June 30, 1957. In another article, Yang Zhaolong noted that many of the new judges, such as veterans, progressive workers, and farmers, had no legal knowledge. He also accused the CCP of violating the constitution. See Yang Zhaolong, "Falujie dedang yufeidang zhijian" (The legal realm between Party and non-Party), *Wenhuibao,* May 8, 1957.

11. "Zhengfa bumen xuyao chedi zhengdun" (The police and the judiciary need thorough revamps), *People's Daily,* December 20, 1957.

12. Zhong Shu, "Dangde daobazi: tongxiang minzhong yuqiege zijiu" (The Party's knife hilt: Stabbing the people and cutting and saving itself), *Cheng ming,* February 2014, 42–44.

13. "Zhonggong dangbao jiguan daobai lunzao tafa" (The argument of knife hilt by Party media is attacked), January 9, 2014, http://china.dwnews.com/news/2014-01-09/59367324-all.html# (link inactive or blocked).

14. See, e.g., Margaret Y. K. Woo, "Law and Discretion in Contemporary Chinese Courts,"

in *The Limits of the Rule of Law in China,* ed. Karen G. Turner, James V. Feinerman, and R. Kent Guy (Seattle: University of Washington Press, 2000), 163–95; Xin Ren, *Tradition of the Law and Law of the Tradition: Law, State, and Social Control in China* (Westport, CT: Greenwood Publishing, 1997), 10; and Josh Chin, "'Rule of Law' or 'Rule by Law' in China: A Preposition Makes All the Difference," *Wall Street Journal,* October 20, 2014 (citing John Delury and Victor Mair).

15. Sinkwan Cheng, introduction to *Law, Justice, and Power: Between Reason and Will,* ed. Sinkwan Cheng (Stanford, CA: Stanford University Press, 2004), 1–21, 3.

16. Cited in Martti Koskenniemi, "Legal Universalism: Between Morality and Power in a World of States," in Cheng, ed., *Law, Justice, and Power,* 46–69, 52.

17. R. W. Carlyle and A. J. Carlyle, *A History of Medieval Political Theory in the West,* vol. 6 (New York: Barnes & Noble, 1936), 1.

18. Cited in Cheng, introduction, 4.

19. Randall Peerenboom argues that there are two kinds of rule of law, "thin" and "thick." See Randall Peerenboom, *China's Long March toward Rule of Law* (Cambridge: Cambridge University Press, 2002), 2–10.

20. F. A. Hayek cited in Woo, "Law and Discretion in Contemporary Chinese Courts," 165.

21. A. F. P. Hulsewé, "Ch'in and Han Law," in *The Cambridge History of China: The Ch'in and Han Empires, 221 b.c.–220 a.d.,* ed. Denis Twitchett and Michael Loewe (Cambridge: Cambridge University Press, 1986), 524–29; Peerenboom, *China's Long March toward Rule of Law,* 36–42; Ye Xiaoxin, ed., *Zhongguo fazhishi* (A history of the Chinese legal system) (Shanghai: Fudan daxue chubanshe, 2002); Ren, *Tradition of the Law and Law of the Tradition,* 20; Ralph H. Folsom, John H. Minan, and Lee Ann Otto, *Law and Politics in the People's Republic of China in a Nutshell* (St. Paul, MN: West Group, 1992), 12; Liu Zehua, Wang Maohe, and Wang Lanzhong, *Zhuanzhi quanli yuzhongguo shehui* (Authoritarian power and Chinese society) (Tianjin: Tianjin guji chubanshe, 2005), 24–26.

22. Ronald A. Cass, *The Rule of Law in America* (Baltimore: Johns Hopkins University Press, 2003), 4.

23. Qiang Fang and Roger V. Des Forges, "Were Chinese Rulers above the Law? Toward a Theory of the Rule of Law in China from Early Times to 1949 CE," *Stanford Journal of International Law* 44, no. 1 (Fall 2007): 101–46.

24. *Shangshu* (The ancient book), ed. Liang Hong. Hunan: Shidai wenyi chubanshe, 2003. See also Wu Gou, "Yiwei gongzhengde faguan weishenme shudao weigong?" (Why has one just judge been attacked), *Nanfang dushibao,* March 17, 2013. For the argument that Gao Yao was the first judge in China, see Yang Jianjun, "Haofaguan deliangzhong xingxiang" (The two images of good judges), *Faxue luntan* 5 (2012): 28–36.

25. Zhu Xi, *Sishu zhangju jizhu* (Annotation of the Four Books) (Liaoning: Liaoning jiaoyu chubanshe, 1998), 2.

26. Karen Turner, "Rule of Law Ideals in Early China?" *Columbia Journal of Chinese Law* 6, no. 1 (Spring 1992): 1–35. For legalists' theory of equality before the law, see Geoffrey MacCormack, *The Spirit of Traditional Chinese Law* (Athens: University of Georgia Press, 1996), 5. See also Fang and Des Forges, "Were Chinese Rulers above the Law?"

27. Qiang Fang, "The Spirit of the Rule of Law in China," *Education about Asia* 13, no. 1 (Spring 2008): 36–41.

28. Ibid.

29. Sima Guang, *Zizhi tongjian* (Comprehensive mirror for aid in government), 294 vols. (Beijing: Zhonghua shujü, 1956), 196:6182.

30. MacCormack, *The Spirit of Traditional Chinese Law,* 22.

31. Sima, *Zizhi tongjian,* vol. 194.

32. Sun Yat-sen, *Sunzhongshan quanji* (The complete works of Sun Yat-sen), 11 vols. (Beijing: Renmin chubanshe, 1981), 10:460. For a similar speech, see John Fitzgerald, *Awakening China: Politics, Culture, and Class in the Nationalist Revolution* (Stanford, CA: Stanford University Press, 1996), 44–45.

33. *Zhengfu gongbao* (Government gazette), 206 vols. (Taiwan: Wenhai chubanshe, 1971), 8: 358.

34. Zhang Sheng, "Minchu daliyuan shenpan duli de zhidu yu shijian" (The independent system and practice of supreme court jurisdiction in the early Republic), *Zhongguo zhengfa daxue xuebao* (Journal of China University of Political Science and Law) 04 (2002):146–52, 149.

35. *Xianxing faling quanshu* (A complete book on the contemporary law), 14 vols. (Beijing: Zhonghua shujü, 1922), 2:268.

36. Philip Huang, *Code, Custom, and Legal Practice in China* (Stanford, CA: Stanford University Press, 2001), 57–61. For the freedom of marriage, see also Susan L. Glosser, *Chinese Visions of Family and State, 1915–1953* (Berkeley and Los Angeles: University of California Press, 2003), 94.

37. Karl Marx, *The Civil War in France* (Gloucester: Dodo Press, 2009), 54.

38. Vladimir Lenin, *The State and Revolution: The Vulgarisation of Marxism by the Opportunists,* 1917, http://www.marxists.org/archive/lenin/works/1917/staterev/ch06.htm. See also Lu Shilun, *Lienin falu sixiangshi* (The history of Lenin's thought) (Beijing: Falu chubanshe, 2000), 117.

39. A similar order was issued by Dong Biwu, the interim chairman of the North China People's Government on March 31, 1949. See Dong Biwu, *Dongbiwu faxue wenji* (Selected legal works of Dong Biwu) (Beijing: Falu chubanshe, 2001), 14–16. For the February order, see "Zhongyang guanyu feichu GMD liufa quanshu hequeding jiefangqu sifa yuanze dezhishi" (The central directive regarding abolishing the GMD's six laws and determining the judicial principles of the liberated regions), February 22, 1949, http://cpc.people.com.cn/GB/64184/64186/66650/4491574.html.

40. "Shanghaishi renmin fayuan chuxing biaozhun" (The Shanghai People's Court's guidelines for coping with cases), December 1949, Shanghai Archives, no. B1-2-308; "Zhongyang renmin zhengfu zuigao fayuan laixin" (Letter from the Supreme Court of the Central People's Government), April 20, 1950, Shanghai Archives, B1-2-308-20.

41. "Guanyu zhenya fanggeming huodongde zhishi" (Directives regarding suppressing counterrevolutionary activities), October 10, 1950, http://cpc.people.com.cn/GB/64162/6416 5/70486/70496/4844076.html.

42. "Shanghaishi renmin fating fangeming panjueshu" (Verdicts against counterrevolutionaries of the Shanghai People's Court), October 1950–March 1951, Shanghai Municipal Archives, no. B1-2-30.

43. "Bixu chedi gaige sifa gongzuo" (Must completely reform judicial work), *People's Daily,* August 17, 1952.

44. Dong, *Dongbiwu faxue wenji,* 123, 159.

45. Huaiyin Li aptly argues that the Cultural Revolution had a different impact on cities that it did on the country. For many rural residents, it was positive as it "offered ordinary villages a new opportunity to express themselves and advance their interest." See Huaiyin Li, *Village China under Socialism and Reform: A Micro-History, 1948–2008* (Stanford, CA: Stanford University Press, 2009), 158.

46. Maurice Meisner, *Mao's China and After: A History of the People's Republic* (New York:

Free Press, 1999), 315. Jonathan Unger argues that the Cultural Revolution lasted between 1966 and 1968. See Jonathan Unger, "The Cultural Revolution at the Grass Roots," *China Journal* 57 (January 2007): 109–37, 113–15. However, we retain the conventional periodization of 1966–1976.

47. Gong Pixiang, ed., *Dangdai zhongguo de falü geming* (The legal revolution of modern China) (Beijing: Falu chubanshe, 1999), 287; Jin Qiu, *The Culture of Power: The Lin Biao Incident in the Cultural Revolution* (Stanford, CA: Stanford University Press, 1999), 16. Recent studies show that during the Cultural Revolution investigators did in some cases followed the law and did not make arbitrary rulings. See Qiang Fang, "Lawlessness in the Cultural Revolution? The Case of a Historical Counterrevolutionary in 1969," *American Review of Chinese Studies* 12, no. 1 (2011): 33–52.

48. Yang Su, "Mass Killings in the CR: A Study of Three Provinces," in *The Chinese Cultural Revolution as History*, ed. Joseph W. Esherick, Paul G. Pickowicz, and Andrew G. Walder (Stanford, CA: Stanford University Press, 2006), 96–123, 122.

49. Meisner, *Mao's China and After*, 355.

50. For example, in 1969, two years after Yu Luoke, a worker in Beijing, argued in the big-character poster "The Class Origin" ("Chushenlun") against the prevailing theory of lineage (*xuetonglun*), he was executed. See Qiang Fang, "Resilient or Decaying? The Case of China's Administrative Litigation," *Modern Chinese Studies* 2 (2014): 93–118.

51. "Zhonggong zhongyang weiyuanhui zhengfawei guanyu diyici yanda chengjiu yiji guihua dierci yundong debaogao" (Report by the Politics and Law Committee of the CCP Central Committee on the achievement of the first campaign of the Strike Hard campaign and planning of launching the second campaign), October 31, 1987," cited in Huang Weiming, *Dangdai zhongguo sixing panjue de biyaoxing* (The value of the death sentence reprieve in contemporary China) (Beijing: Kexue chubanshe, 2007). For a good study of the Strike Hard campaign, see Harold M. Tanner, *Strike Hard: Anti-Crime Campaigns and Chinese Criminal Justice, 1979–1985* (Ithaca, NY: Cornell University Press, 1999).

52. Andrew J. Nathan, "China's Changing of the Guard: Authoritarian Resilience," *Journal of Democracy* 14, no. 1 (January 2003): 6–18.

53. Martin Jacques, *When China Rules the World: The End of the Western World and the Birth of a New Global Order* (New York: Penguin Books, 2012), 277–87, 538, 565.

54. Minxin Pei, "Is CCP Rule Fragile or Resilient?" *Journal of Democracy* 23, no. 1 (January 2012): 27–42.

55. Bruce J. Dickson, "Cooptation and Corporatism in China: The Logic of Party Adaptation," *Political Science Quarterly* 115, no. 4 (Winter 2000–2001): 517–43, 531.

56. Bruce J. Dickson, *Wealth into Power: The Communist Party's Embrace of China's Private Sector* (Cambridge: Cambridge University Press, 2008), introduction.

57. Bruce J. Dickson, "Updating the China Model," *Washington Quarterly* 34, no. 4 (Fall 2011): 39–58.

58. Kellee S. Tsai, "Adaptive Informal Institutions and Endogenous Institutional Change in China," *World Politics* 59 (October 2006): 116–41, 118.

59. Kellee S. Tsai, *Capitalism without Democracy: The Private Sector in Contemporary China* (Ithaca, NY: Cornell University Press, 2007), 15.

60. Randall Peerenboom, "Law and Development of Constitutional Democracy: Is China a Problem Case?" *Annals of the American Academy of Political and Social Science* 603 (January 2006): 192–99, 192.

61. Ibid., 193.

62. David Shambaugh, "The Illusion of Chinese Power" *National Interest,* June 25, 2014,

www.nationalinterest.org/feature/the-illusion-chinese-power-10739. See also David Shambaugh, "The Coming Chinese Crackup," *Wall Street Journal*, March 6, 2015; Dexter Roberts, "Almost Half of China's Rich Want to Emigrate," *Bloomberg Business News*, September 15, 2014; and Sophia Yan, "Rich Chinese Overwhelmed U.S. Visa Program," *CNN Money*, March 25, 2014, http://money.cnn.com/2014/03/25/news/economy/china-us-immigrant-visa.

1. Urban War at the Yangzi River

1. William Rowe, *Hankow: Conflict and Community in a Chinese City, 1796–1895* (Stanford, CA: Stanford University Press, 1989), 1, 16.

2. "'Changjiang qingzhang zhalou' jinchen daxiang" (The cleanup and demolition of the buildings began this morning), *Xinmin wanbao*, January 25, 2001.

3. "Wuhan waitan huayuan ganga qibao" (The embarrassing demolition of the Wuhan Waitan Garden), *Jinghua Times*, January 26, 2001.

4. "Zhachu 'weifalou,' Wuhan shimin jiaohao" (Wuhan residents applaud the blowup of the "illegal building"), Xinhua News Agency, January 25, 2002.

5. According to "Plans for the Development of the Press and Publication Industries in Year 2000 and Year 2010," issued by the State Press and Publications Administration, newspapers were to raise the percentage of advertisement revenue in their total revenue from an average of 60 percent in 1996 to 70 percent by 2000 and 80 percent by 2010. See Yuezhi Zhao, "The State, the Market, and Media Control in China," in *Who Owns the Media? Global Trends and Local Resistance*, ed. Pradip N. Thomas and Zaharrom Nain (London: Zed Books, 2005), 179–212, 186–87. See also Guo Ke, "Newspapers: Changing Roles," in *New Media for a New China*, ed. James F. Scotton and William A. Hachten (Hoboken, NJ: Wiley-Blackwell, 2010), 43–60. For the *China Youth Daily*, see Qiang Fang, "Chinese Media and the Rule of Law: The Case of the *China Youth Daily*," in *Modern Chinese Legal Reform: New Perspectives*, ed. Xiaobing Li and Qiang Fang (Lexington: University Press of Kentucky, 2013), 27–58.

6. "Wuhan zhalou: weihu falu zunyan" (Blowing up building: Safeguarding the dignity of the law), Xinhua News Agency, January 25, 2002.

7. "Fanghong hedaoli debieshu" (The villas built on the riverbed of flood control), in *Xinwen beihou* (Behind the news), 140–42 (Beijing: Renmin wenxue chubanshe, 2005), http://read.jd.com/392/17168.html.

8. Wang Sixin and Chen Xie, "Wuhan waitan huayuan buneng 'yizha bailiao'" (Wuhan Waitan Garden should not end with an explosion), *Workers' Daily*, January 29, 2001.

9. Huang Guangming and Chen Hai, "Yige 'guaitai'de shengyusi" (The birth and death of a "freak"), *Southern Weekend*, January 24, 2002.

10. For the theory of rightful resistance, see Kevin O'Brien and Lianjiang Li, *Rightful Resistance in Rural China* (Cambridge: Cambridge University Press, 2006); Kevin O'Brien, "Rightful Resistance," *World Politics* 49, no. 1 (October 1996): 31–55; and Kevin O'Brien and Lianjiang Li, "The Politics of Lodging Complaints in Rural China," *China Quarterly*, no. 143 (September 1995): 756–83. For the theory of natural resistance, see Qiang Fang, *Chinese Complaint Systems: Natural Resistance* (London: Routledge, 2013), and "Hot Potatoes: Chinese Complaint Systems from Early Times to the Late Qing (1898)," *Journal of Asian Studies* 64, no. 4 (November 2009): 1105–35.

11. The Shanghai Bund was built after the first Opium War (1840–1842). Over the following hundred years, the occupying foreign powers had built numerous European-style buildings that helped make the bund a tourist destination and the financial center of Shanghai.

12. "Wuhan waitan huayuan ganga qibao."

13. Permits provided by homeowners. See also Huang and Chen, "Yige 'guaitai'de shengyusi."

14. Interviews with anonymous Waitan Garden homeowners, 2010–2013; documents provided by Waitan Garden homeowners, 2011–2013, no. 5.

15. Huang and Chen, "Yige 'guaitai'de shengyusi."

16. "Changjiang 'Waitan huayuan'shi ruhe jianshede" (How the Yangze River 'Waitan Garden' was constructed), 2010–2013, documents provided by Waitan Garden homeowners. For the legality of the first stage of construction, see also "Wuhan waitan huayuan ganga qibao."

17. "Guanyu Wuhanshi Hanyangqu changjiang daqiao shangshou hanyang waitan huayuan xiaoqu weizhang shigong detongbao" (A circular regarding the illegal construction of the Hanyang Waitan Garden on the upper part of the Wuhan Hanyang Yangzi River bridge), May, 2000, documents provided by Waitan Garden homeowners.

18. Huang and Chen, "Yige 'guaitai'de shengyusi."

19. He Renmin, "Wuhanren danzizhuang, zhuzhai jianzai changjiangshang" (Wuhan residents are bold and build residence on the Yangze River), *China Economic Times,* December 23, 2000.

20. Huang and Chen, "Yige 'guaitai'de shengyusi."

21. Interviews with anonymous Waitan Garden homeowners, 2010–2013; documents provided by Waitan Garden homeowners, no. 48.

22. "Wuhan waitan huayuan ganga qibao."

23. Mao Zedong, "Zhongguo shehui gejieji defenxi" (An analysis of China's social classes), December 1925, in *Maozedong xuanji* (Selected works of Mao Zedong), vol. 1, http://www.qstheory.cn/zl/llzz/mzdxjd1j/200906/t20090630_4006.htm.

24. Mao Zedong, "Lun fandui riben diguozhuyi decelue" (The tactics against the Japanese imperialists), December 27, 1935, in *Maozedong xuanji,* vol. 1, http://www.qstheory.cn/zl/llzz/mzdxjd1j/200906/t20090630_4031.htm.

25. "Hedaoli jianqi shangpinlou" (Commercial buildings were constructed on the riverbed), *Jiaodian fangtan* (Focal interview), November 19, 2001, http://www.cctv.com.cn/news/china/20011119/425.html.

26. "Fanghong hedaoli debieshu."

27. Interviews with anonymous Waitan Garden homeowners, 2010–2013;.

28. Brigid Harrison and Thomas Dye, *Power and Society: An Introduction to the Social Sciences* (Boston: Cengage Learning, 2013), 138. See also Yanzhong Huang, *Governing Health in Contemporary China* (London: Routledge, 2013), 13.

29. Documents provided by Waitan Garden homeowners, no. 5.

30. Interview with Han Junru, June 19, 2013; documents provided by Waitan Garden homeowners, no. 85.

31. "Waitan huayuan jiben qingkuang" (Basic information about Waitan Garden), November 22, 2001, documents provided by Waitan Garden homeowners.

32. Interview with Yan Fengjun, June 20, 2013; interview with Tang Hanqing, June 20, 2013.

33. Interview with Han Junru.

34. Interviews with anonymous Waitan Garden homeowners, 2010–2013; documents provided by Waitan Garden homeowners, 9.

35. See *People's Daily,* August 27, 1998.

36. Interviews with anonymous Waitan Garden homeowners, 2010–2013; documents provided by Waitan Garden homeowners, 42.

37. There have been short periods in the history of the PRC, such as the spring of 1957,

when many prominent scholars criticized the CCP and its policies, the late 1970s, when newspapers like the *Guangming Daily* challenged Chairman Hua Guofeng's "Two Whatevers," and the late 1980s, when the public media enjoyed unprecedented freedom. But many critics of the Party were later denounced and punished. For the earlier periods of press freedom, see Richard H. Solomon, *Mao's Revolution and the Chinese Political Culture* (Berkeley and Los Angeles: University of California Press, 1971), 272–95. For the 1989 press freedom, see Hui Wang, *China's New Order: Society, Politics, and Economy in Transition* (Cambridge, MA: Harvard University Press, 2003), 64.

38. For the rise of Internet broadcasting, see James F. Scotton, "The Impact of New Media," in Scotton and Hachten, eds., *New Media for a New China*, 28–42. For public criticism of CCTV, see Jinghao Zhou, *China's Peaceful Rise in a Global Context: A Domestic Aspect of China's Road Map to Democratization* (Lanham, MD: Lexington Books, 2010), 122.

39. Interview with Yan Fengjun.

40. "Yezhu husheng" (The voices of homeowners), November 25, 2001, copy in authors' possession.

41. Interview with Yan Fengjun; documents provided by Waitan Garden homeowners, no. 9.

42. Interview with Jin Baoqiang, June 18, 2013; documents provided by Waitan Garden homeowners, no. 10.

43. Interview with Yan Fengjun.

44. The Constitution of the People's Republic of China, December 4, 1982, http://english.people.com.cn/constitution/constitution.html.

45. He Weifang, *In the Name of Justice: Striving for the Rule of Law in China* (Washington, DC: Brookings Institution Press, 2012), 67–68.

46. Montesquieu, *The Spirit of Laws* (New York: Colonial Press, 1900), 151–52.

47. According to the Chinese scholar Lin Qian, Aristotle was the first person in the West to propose the idea of the separation of powers, which for him included discussion (*yishi*), administration (*xingzheng*), and adjudgment (*shenpan*). John Locke, another influential Enlightenment philosopher, wrote of the importance of the separation of powers in his *Two Treatises of Government*. See Lin Qian, *Chuantong zhongguode quanyufa* (The power and law of traditional China) (Beijing: Falu chubanshe, 2013), 20; and John Locke, *Two Treatises of Government* (London: Whitmore & Fenn, 1821), 313–14.

48. Thomas Lundmark, *Power and Rights in US Constitutional Law* (Oxford: Oxford University Press, 2008), 8.

49. Interview with Yan Fengjun; documents provided by Waitan Garden homeowners, no. 10.

50. In 1998, when Fang was a graduate student in the Shanghai Teachers University, hes was asked to vote for one of three candidates to be a delegate to the National People's Congress. Two of the three candidates were university leaders, and the other was a student cadre who had obviously been picked by the university administration. When one graduate student stood up and denounced the fakeness of the election, he was subsequently criticized by the department head.

51. Sharon Lafraniere, "People's Congress Gets to Work in China," *New York Times,* March 4, 2010.

52. William C. Jones, "The Constitution of the People's Republic of China," in *Law in the People's Republic of China: Commentary, Readings, and Materials,* ed. Ralph H. Folsom and John H. Minan (Leiden: Martinus Nijhoff, 1989), 39–49, 40. For the defects of the Chinese people's congresses, see also He, *In the Name of Justice,* 119.

53. See, e.g., Peerenboom, *China's Long March toward Rule of Law,* 12.

54. Keping Yu, *Globalization and Changes in China's Governance* (Leiden: Brill, 2008), 244.

55. Documents provided by Waitan Garden homeowners, no. 11.

56. Former president Jiang Zemin first presented his theory of "Three Represents" in 2000. It focused on the future role of the CCP as "a faithful representative of the requirements for the development of advanced productive forces in China, the orientation of advanced culture in China, and the fundamental interests of the broadest masses of the people in China." Jiang Zemin, *Jiang Zemin wenxuan* (Selected works of Jiang Zemin) (Beijing: Renmin chubanshe, 2006), 2–3.

57. "Yezhu husheng."

58. See O'Brien and Li, *Rightful Resistance in Rural China.*

59. Although in both 1963 and 1982 the CCP issued guidelines for dealing with people's petitions, neither version was made public, and both were circulated only among government officials. But in 1995, as a part of the CCP's efforts to construct the rule of law, the 1995 Regulations Regarding Letters and Visits was for the first time publicized by state media in the PRC, and ordinary citizens had a chance to learn the details of the regulations. See Fang, *Chinese Complaint Systems,* chap. 6.

60. For the complete history of petitioning in China, see Fang, *Chinese Complaint Systems,* and "Hot Potatoes." Carl Minzner argues that the PRC petition system is a quasi-formal one that overlaps with the judicial system. See Carl Minzner, "Xinfang: An Alternative to the Formal Chinese Legal System," *Stanford Journal of International Law* 42, no. 1 (2006): 103–79.

61. "Waitan huayuan wenti qingzhengfu sansier houxing" (The government needs to fully reconsider the issue of Waitan Garden before taking action), December 1, 2001, documents provided by Waitan Garden homeowners, no. 14.

62. "Zhonghua renmin gongheguo xingzheng susongfa" (The Administrative Litigation Law of the People's Republic of China), April 4, 1989, http://www.law-lib.com/LAW/law_view .asp?id=5641.

63. Some homeowners eventually got wind of the circular by chance. In fact, the circular seems to have been distributed only among various government agencies. But the governments at the state, provincial, and city levels saw no need to reveal its contents to the homeowners. Documents provided by Waitan Garden homeowners, no. 19.

64. Interview with Han Junru.

65. For the CCP's longtime history of violating and neglecting the law, see Alison W. Conner, "True Confession: Chinese Confessions Then and Now," in Turner, Feinerman, and Guy, eds., *The Limits of the Rule of Law in China,* 132–62, 155; Woo, "Law and Discretion in Contemporary Chinese Courts," 166, 170; He, *In the Name of Justice,* chaps.1, 4; and Fang, *Chinese Complaint Systems,* chaps. 5–6.

66. Documents provided by Waitan Garden homeowners, no. 105.

67. Li Jun and Joseph Y. S. Cheng, "Cadre Performance Appraisal and Fabrication of Economic Achievement in Chinese Officialdom," in *China: A New Stage of Development for an Emerging Superpower,* ed. Joseph Y. S. Cheng (Hong Kong: City University of Hong Kong Press, 2012), 117–48, 129. See also Godwin C. Chu, *The Great Wall in Ruins: Communication and Culture Change in China* (Albany: State University of New York Press, 1993), 143; and Fang, *Chinese Complaint Systems,* 153.

68. The "Four Cleanups" movement started in late 1962. Its aim was to clean up politics, thought, the economy, and organizations. See Jonathan Unger, *The Transformation of Rural China* (Armonk, NY: M. E. Sharpe, 2002), 55; Hok Bun Ku, *Moral Politics in a South Chinese Village: Responsibility, Reciprocity, and Resistance* (Lanham, MD: Rowman & Littlefield, 2003), 73; and Fang, *Chinese Complaint Systems,* chap. 5.

69. For the details of the work team, see Roderick MacFarquhar and Michael Schoenhals, *Mao's Last Revolution* (Cambridge, MA: Harvard University Press, 2006), 66–85.

70. Li Peng's position on "administration in accordance with the law" is consistent with President Jiang Zemin's 1997 call for the establishment of the rule of law in China. In 1999, the rule of law was added to the newly revised PRC constitution. For legal reform under Jiang Zemin, see Qiang Fang, "Legal Reform under Jiang Zemin," in *Evolution of Power: China's Struggle, Survival, and Success,* ed. Xiaobing Li and Xiansheng Tian (Lanham, MD: Lexington Books, 2013), 227–50.

71. Interview with Han Junru.

72. The Political and Legal Commission was created in the early PRC under the State Council, and Dong Biwu was the head. The commission has overall authority over China's police, courts, and procuratorate. In the 1980s, it underwent several reforms but gradually became more powerful in the 1990s as its head became one of the members of the Standing Committee of the Politburo. For the Political and Legal Commission in the 1980s, see Willy Wo-lap Lam, "Zhao Ziyang's Contributions to Reform in Historical Perspective," in *Zhao Ziyang and China's Political Future,* ed. Guoguang Wu and Helen Lansdowne (London: Routledge, 2008), 151–63, 153.

73. Documents provided by Waitan Garden homeowners, no. 27.

74. Interview with Yan Fengjun; documents provided by Waitan Garden homeowners, no. 28.

75. Interview with Yan Fengjun.

76. Documents provided by Waitan Garden homeowners, no. 29.

77. Similar Western notions first came to China in the late Qing. But the CCP repudiated them as capitalist in the early PRC.

78. Interview with Yan Fengjun; interview with Han Junru; documents provided by Waitan Garden homeowners, no. 30.

79. "Gaoguan lushi wunai piaobo" (The lawyer who accuses officials has to wander aimlessly), *Southern Weekend,* February 7, 2002.

80. Documents provided by Waitan Garden homeowners, no. 34.

81. Documents provided by Waitan Garden homeowners, no. 32.

82. Interview with Yan Fengjun; interview with Han Junru.

83. Interview with Yan Fengjun; documents provided by Waitan Garden homeowners, nos. 32–33.

84. Interview with Han Junru; documents provided by Waitan Garden homeowners, no. 34.

85. The two certificates are the property ownership certificate (*fangchanzheng*) and the land use certificate (*tudi shiyongzheng*).

86. "Wuhan waitan huayuan shenghui beiwanglu" (A life-and-ruin memorandum of the Wuhan Waitan Garden), December 13, 2001, documents provided by Waitan Garden homeowners, nos. 39–40.

87. *Traditionally* refers to the arbitrary policies historically employed by the CCP, including, but not limited to, the political campaigns in the early 1950s, the 1957 Anti-Rightists Movement, the Four Cleanups in the early 1960s, the Cultural Revolution, and the treatment of political dissidents after 1978.

88. Wen-hsin Yeh, "Republican Origins of the *Danwei:* The Case of Shanghai's Bank of China," in *Danwei: The Changing Chinese Workplace in Historical and Comparative Perspective,* ed. Xiaobo Lü and Elizabeth Perry (Armonk, NY: M. E. Sharpe, 1997), 60–90, 82.

89. David Bray, *Social Space and Governance in Urban China: The Danwei System from Origins to Reform* (Stanford, CA: Stanford University Press, 2005), 2–5.

90. Interview with Yan Fengjun.

91. Interview with Han Junru.

92. Documents provided by Waitan Garden homeowners, no. 45.

93. Documents provided by Waitan Garden homeowners, no. 49.

94. Interview with Han Junru; interview with Yan Fengjun; documents provided by Waitan Garden homeowners, no. 75.

95. For instance, in the first half of 1995, petitions resulting from urban demolition in Beijing alone constituted 43.2 percent of the total number of petitions in that city. In August 2003, a Shanghai official acknowledged that the problem of urban demolition had become the top issue in collective petitions. For the increase in petitions in Beijing, see Sidney Tarrow, "Prologue: The New Contentious Politics in China: Poor and Blank or Rich and Complex?" in *Popular Protest in China*, ed. Kevin O'Brien (Cambridge, MA: Harvard University Press, 2009), 1–10, 4; and Zhao Ling, "Chaiqian shinian beixiju" (Ten years of tragedies and comedies of urban disposal), *Southern Weekend*, September 4, 2003. For Shanghai, see Ling Bo, "Huajie dongqian maodun yicheng dangwu zhiji" (The top issue is to dissolve the contradiction of urban disposal), *Shanghai xinfang* 10–12 (2003): 11, 8, 10. See also Qiu Dengchang, "Wosheng xinfang gongzuo mianlin de xinxingshi" (The new complaint situation in our province), *Xuexi luntan* 2 (2000): 39–40. Like Henan, Shannxi also experienced large-scale illegal collective complaints. See Zhou Hulin, "Zengyang ladong qunzhong jifangde zhidong lianhuan" (How to pull the braking hoop of the mass collective complaints), *Minqing yuxinfang* 2 (2000): 21–27, 25.

96. In 2003, seeing that cutting off the water supply and electricity could not force Pi Shufeng, an older woman, to leave her home, the Dongcheng District government of Beijing sent workers and bulldozers to raze two of her other homes. No matter how and where Pi petitioned, no one came to her aid. See Fang *Chinese Complaint Systems*, chap. 6.

97. Interviews with the head of a demolition company in Wuhan, 2013. For a study of "retrievers" of petitioners, see Lianjiang Li, Mingxin Liu, and Kevin O'Brien, "Petitioning Beijing: The High Tide of 2003–2006," *China Quarterly* 210 (June 2012): 313–34.

98. Documents provided by Waitan Garden homeowners, no. 106.

2. WAITAN GARDEN

1. "Waitan huayuan goufanghu banqian anzhi shishi yijian" (Implementing opinions of the Waitan Garden buyers), December 13, 2001, documents provided by Waitan Garden homeowners, nos. 50–51.

2. Documents provided by Waitan Garden homeowners, no. 52.

3. Interview with Han Junru; documents provided by Waitan Garden homeowners, nos. 54–55.

4. Documents provided by Waitan Garden homeowners, no. 51.

5. In the case of Yang Xiaoming, who had been murdered in 1982 by a criminal from a powerful family, the final redress arrived only after repeated interventions by Party secretary Hu Yaobang. In another case, Guo Guangyun, who in 1995 had accused the Party secretary of Hebei Province of corruption, succeeded in obtaining two direct interventions from Wei Jiangxing, the head of the Central Commission for Discipline Inspection (Zhongyang jilu jiancha weiyuanhui), and a member of the powerful Standing Committee of the Politburo. But their actions still did not produce any positive result. It was only after the retirement of the Hebei Party secretary that Guo's grievances finally were satisfied after eight years of petitioning. For the details of both cases, see "Falü de shengli" (The triumph of the law), *China Youth Daily*, November 13, 1985; and Guo Guangyun, *Wogao Chengweigao: Yige gognmin yu yige shengwei*

shuji de zhangzheng (I accuse Cheng Weugao: A war between a citizen and a provincial party secretary) (Beijing: Dongfang chubanshe, 2004).

6. Documents provided by Waitan Garden homeowners, no. 59.

7. Dorothy J. Solinger, *Contesting Citizenship in Urban China: Peasant Migrants, the State, and the Logic of the Market* (Berkeley and Los Angeles: University of California Press, 1999), 5, 87, 135.

8. "Liaoning zhuanhe minzhong zhengfu menqian xiagui" (People from Liaoning Zhuanghe knelt down in front of the government gate), *Nanfang dushibao,* April 13, 2010.

9. Maurice Meisner, *The Deng Xiaoping Era: An Inquiry into the Fate of Chinese Socialism, 1978–1994* (New York: Hill & Wang, 1996), 52.

10. *Deng Xiaoping wenxuan* (The selected works of Deng Xiaoping), 3 vols. (Beijing: Renmin chubanshe, 1938–1992), 3:284–85.

11. The percentages are based on a number of sources. Figures from 1989 to 1992 come from "Mingaoguan shinian pandian" (A ten-year study of people accusing officials), *China Youth Daily,* April 16, 1999. Others come from *Zhongguo falü nianjian, 1987–1997* (The encyclopedia of Chinese law, 1987–1997) (Beijing: Zhongguo falü nianjianshe, 1998), 835–91; and *Zhongguo falü nianjian, 1989* (The encyclopedia of Chinese law, 1989) (Beijing: Zhongguo falü nianjianshe, 1988): 1082; *Zhongguo falü nianjian, 1999* (Beijing: Zhongguo falü nianjianshe, 1998): 1023; *Zhongguo falü nianjian, 2000* (Beijing: Zhongguo falü nianjianshe, 1998), 1211; *Zhongguo falü nianjian, 2001* (Beijing: Zhongguo falü nianjianshe, 2000): 1258; *Zhongguo falü nianjian, 2002* (Beijing: Zhongguo falü nianjianshe, 2001): 1240; *Zhongguo falü nianjian, 2003* (Beijing: Zhongguo falü nianjianshe, 2002): 1321; *Zhongguo falü nianjian, 2004* (Beijing: Zhongguo falü nianjianshe, 2003): 1055. For a more recent chart of administrative litigations, see Bin Liang, *The Changing Chinese Legal System, 1978–Present: Centralization of Power and Rationalization of the Legal System* (London: Routledge, 2008), 47; and Fang *Chinese Complaint Systems,* chap. 6.

12. "Lüshi yijianshu" (The lawyers' opinions), December 7, 2001, documents provided by Waitan Garden homeowners, nos. 64–65.

13. The justice bureau in the PRC administers lawyers, prisons, and legal aid centers.

14. Documents provided by Waitan Garden homeowners, no. 64.

15. Interview with Han Junru; documents provided by Waitan Garden homeowners, no. 106.

16. *Deng Xiaoping wenxuan,* 2:189.

17. "Gongqingtuan yinggai weiwunian pufa jiaoyu douzheng" (The Communist Youth League should struggle with the five-year enhancement of the public's awareness of the law), *China Youth Daily,* January 9, 1986.

18. Gong, ed., *Dangdai zhongguo de falü geming,* 287. See also Peerenboom, *China's Long March toward Rule of Law,* 55.

19. Local courts in China rely on the local governments to provide financial support. Local governments also control the Party membership of the judges and their promotion. This relationship between local administration and the courts originated in the former Soviet Union, and the CCP simply adopted it after it established the PRC. For the Soviet Union model, see Peter H. Solomon Jr., *Soviet Criminal Justice under Stalin* (Cambridge: Cambridge University Press, 1996), 98–99. For the relations between local governments and the courts, see He Weifang, *Yunsong zhengyide fangshi* (The way of transporting justice) (Shanghai: Shanghai sanlian shudian chubanshe, 2002), 181.

20. Documents provided by Waitan Garden homeowners, no. 106.

21. The Soviet Union was the first socialist country to implement a planned economy.

China adopted a planned economy in the early 1950s to expedite industrialization. For the Soviet planned economy, see Peter J. Boettke, *Socialism and the Market: The Socialist Calculation Debate Revisited* (London: Psychology Press, 2000), 15; and Hanbing Kong, "The Transplantation and Entrenchment of the Soviet Economic Model in China," in *China Learns from the Soviet Union, 1949–Present*, ed. Thomas P. Bernstein and Hua-yu Li (Lanham, MD: Rowman & Littlefield, 2010), 153–66, 164. For the Chinese planned economy, see Wenran Jiang, "Prosperity at the Expense of Equality: Migrant Workers Are Falling Behind in Urban China's Rise," in *Confronting Discrimination and Inequality in China: Chinese and Canadian Perspectives*, ed. Errol P. Mendes and Sakunthala Srighanthan (Ottawa: University of Ottawa Press, 2009), 16–29; and Sujian Guo, *Chinese Politics and Government: Power, Ideology, and Organization* (London: Routledge, 2009), 269.

22. "Zhiwaitan huayuan chaiqian gongzuozu de weiwenxin" (A letter of sympathy to the Waitan Garden demolition work team), documents provided by Waitan Garden homeowners, no. 66.

23. "Chengshi fangwu chaiqian guanli tiaoli" (The regulations regarding the management of urban housing demolition), http://www.gov.cn/gongbao/content/2001/content_60912.htm.

24. Interview with Han Junru; documents provided by Waitan Garden homeowners, no. 69.

25. In 2005, a petitioner from Shandong Province who was petitioning central governments against powerful local officials said that it took a great deal of courage to go to Beijing to complain and that most people would not do it. Indeed, most petitioners Fang has interviewed in Beijing have had to endure similar intense sufferings and hardships. Unfortunately, few petitions for the redress of grievances are granted. For the experiences of the petitioners in Beijing in the late Qing and the contemporary PRC, see Fang, *Chinese Complaint Systems,* chaps. 2, 6.

26. Interview with Han Junru; documents provided by Waitan Garden homeowners, no. 69.

27. Interview with Han Junru; documents provided by Waitan Garden homeowners, no. 78.

28. For general accounts of literary inquisition in Chinese history, see Wang Yelin, *Zhongguo wenziyu* (Literary inquisition in China) (Guangzhou: Huacheng chubanshe, 2007); and Yang Qiankun, *Zhongguo gudai wenziyu* (Literary inquisition in ancient China) (Shanxi: Shanxi renmin chubanshe, 1999). For the Ming and Qing dynasties, see Li Wenjie, "Bamingdai wenxue dairu diyude yinhun: Hongwu wenziyu" (The ghost that brings Ming literature into hell: The literary inquisition in the Hongwu reign), *Journal of Simao Teachers College* 26, no. 1 (February 2010): 68–71; Timothy Brook, *The Chinese State in Ming Society* (London: Routledge, 2006), 99–136; Jonathan Spence, *Treason by the Book* (Harmondsworth: Penguin Books, 2002); and Zhou Zongqi, *Qingdai wenziyu* (The literary inquisition in the Qing) (Beijing: Renmin wenxue chubanshe, 2010). For the Cultural Revolution, see Jonathan Spence, *Mao Zedong: A Life* (Harmondsworth: Penguin Books, 2006), chap. 11; Jiaqi Yan and Gao Gao, *Turbulent Decade: A History of the Cultural Revolution* (Honolulu: University of Hawaii Press, 1996), 37; and Fang, "Resilient or Decaying?"

29. Yuanyuan Shen, "Conceptions and Receptions of Legality: Understanding the Complexity of Law Reform in Modern China," in Turner, Feinerman, and Guy, eds., *The Limits of the Rule of Law in China*, 20–44, 22.

30. Randall Peerenboom, "Judicial Independence in China: Common Myths and Unfounded Assumptions," in *Judicial Independence in China: Lessons for Global Rule of Law Promotion*, ed. Randall Peerenboom (Cambridge: Cambridge University Press, 2010), 69–94, 80.

31. Mary E. Gallagher, "Use the Law as Your Weapon! Institutional Change and Legal Mobilization in China," in *Engaging the Law in China: State, Society, and Possibilities for Justice,* ed. Neil Jeffrey Diamant, Stanley B. Lubman, and Kevin J. O'Brien (Stanford, CA: Stanford University Press, 2005), 54–83, 75.

32. Documents provided by Waitan Garden homeowners, no. 79.

33. Interview with Yan Fengjun; interview with Han Junru.

34. "Wuhan zhawaitan, gangyezhu shibao jiayuan" (Wuhan destroys Waitan Garden, Hong Kong residents swear to protect their homes), *Dongfang ribao,* December 21, 2001.

35. Interview with Yan Fengjun; documents provided by Waitan Garden homeowners, no. 81.

36. Kevin O'Brien and Lianjiang Li, "Suing the Local State: Administrative Litigation in Rural China," in Diamant, Lubman, and O'Brien, eds., *Engaging the Law in China,* 31–53, 35.

37. The State Compensation Law was promulgated by the NPC in 1994 and became effective on January 1, 1995. It provides details on state compensation to any citizen whose rights or interests have been infringed by the state.

38. Zhang Lijun, "Zhengque chuli waitan shijian, zhengfu qiemo yicuozaicuo" (Correctly dealing with the Waitan incident, the government must not commit mistakes one after another), December 23, 2001, documents provided by Waitan Garden homeowners, nos. 82–83.

39. Documents provided by Waitan Garden homeowners, no. 90.

40. For the case of the virgin prostitute, see Qiang Fang, "The Case of the Virgin Prostitute: Chinese Media and Chinese Legal Reform," in *Stanford Journal of East Asian Affairs* 2, no 1 (Spring 2002): 26–40. See also Fang, "Resilient or Decaying?"

41. "Lüshi yijianshu."

42. Interview with Yan Fengjun.

43. Michael Dutton, *Policing Chinese Politics: A History* (Durham, NC: Duke University Press, 2005), 139.

44. Interview with Han Junru; documents provided by Waitan Garden homeowners, no. 87.

45. Documents provided by Waitan Garden homeowners, no. 88.

46. Documents provided by Waitan Garden homeowners, no. 89.

47. Documents provided by Waitan Garden homeowners, no. 91.

48. Xu Bikang, "Suzhuang" (Indictment), December 25, 2001, documents provided by Waitan Garden homeowners, no. 90.

49. Documents provided by Waitan Garden homeowners, no. 96.

50. Documents provided by Waitan Garden homeowners, no. 91.

51. Documents provided by Waitan Garden homeowners, no. 96.

52. PRC Justice Department, "Guanyu lushi tiaozheng gongzihe jibie wentide yijianha" (An opinion letter regarding adjusting lawyers' salaries and ranks), September 19, 1956, Shanghai Archives, no. A11-1-2-47.

53. "Shanghaishi lushi shoufei shixing banfa" (The provisional method of lawyers' charge of fee in Shanghai), April 2, 1956, Shanghai Archives, no. B2-1-38-16.

54. Gong, ed., *Dangdai zhongguo de falü geming,* 343–55.

55. For the case of Zhen Enchong, see Qin Shao, *Shanghai Gone: Domicide and Defiance in a Chinese Megacity* (Lanham, MD: Roman & Littlefield, 2013), 216; and Fang, *Chinese Complaint Systems,* chap. 6. For Gao Zhisheng, see Gao Zhisheng, *A China More Just: My Fight as a Rights Lawyer in the World's Largest Communist State* (Sydney: Broad Press, 2007). For Li Zhuang, see Norman P. Ho, "Organized Crime in China: The Chongqing Crackdown," in *Law and Policy for China's Market Socialism,* ed. John Garrick (London: Routledge, 2012), 202–14;

John Garnaut, *The Rise and Fall of the House of Bo: How a Murder Exposed the Cracks in China's Leadership* (Harmondsworth: Penguin Books, 2012); and Li Zhuang's blog, http://blog.sina .com.cn/s/blog_89aa0dcd0101dihf.html.

56. Documents provided by Waitan Garden homeowners, no. 94.

57. Interview with Han Junru.

58. Ibid.,; documents provided by Waitan Garden homeowners, no. 98.

59. Documents provided by Waitan Garden homeowners, no. 101.

60. Shen Jiaben, *Jiyi wencun* (Jiyi's remaining works), 2 vols. (Taiwan: Shangwu yinshuguan, 1976), 1:20; Keishu Saneto, *Zhongguoren liuxue ribenshi* (History of Chinese students in Japan) (Beijing: Sanlian shudian, 1983), 327.

61. William T. Rowe, *Saving the World: Chen Hongmou and Elite Consciousness in Eighteenth Century China* (Stanford, CA: Stanford University Press, 2002), 299.

62. Sun Yat-sen, *Sunzhongshan quanji*, 10:460. See also Fitzgerald, *Awakening China*, 44–45.

63. Qiang Fang, *Zhongguo shangfang zhidu shihua (1100 BCE–1949)* (A short history of Chinese petition) (Beijing: China Youth Press, 2013), chap. 9.

64. We have checked fifty years of major newspapers such as the *People's Daily* and the *China Youth Daily* as well as material in the Shanghai Archives but did not find any use of *little people* by commoners. During the Mao era, terms similar to *little people* were denounced as feudal and capitalist. As the commoners had become the masters of the PRC, they were discouraged from using those old terms.

65. Interview with Han Junru; documents provided by Waitan Garden homeowners, no. 104.

66. Documents provided by Waitan Garden homeowners, no. 109.

67. Interview with Yan Fengjun; interview with Han Junru; documents provided by Waitan Garden homeowners, no. 102.

68. For example, Wu Liang was an advanced (*xianjin*) CCP lawyer in his law firm, which was an award given by the Justice Department.

69. Documents provided by Waitan Garden homeowners, no. 109.

70. Documents provided by Waitan Garden homeowners, no. 112.

3. Wuhan's Showdown at the Supreme Court

1. Anne-Marie Brady, *Marketing Dictatorship: Propaganda and Thought Work in Contemporary China* (Lanham, MD: Roman & Littlefield), 113.

2. "Wuhan Waitan huayuan dapi yezhu konggao defang zhengfu chuer faner yiquan daifa" (Many homeowners of the Wuhan Waitan Garden are accusing the local government of inconsistency and using power to replace law), Xinhua News Agency (Hubei branch), January 5, 2002.

3. Xinhua established branches in major cities that could also serve as the eyes of the central government, monitoring local officials and affairs. For the monitoring role of the agency in Hong Kong, see Peter T. Y. Cheung, "Intergovernmental Relations between Mainland China and the Hong Kong SAR," in *Public Administration in Southeast Asia: Thailand, Philippines, Malaysia, Hong Kong, and Macao*, ed. Even M. Berman (Boca Raton, FL: CRC Press, 2010), 255–82, 259.

4. For decentralization in the reformed China, see Meisner, *Mao's China and After*, 451; Kenneth Lieberthal, *Governing China: From Revolution through Reform* (New York: W. W. Norton, 1995), 301; Everett Zhang, "Introduction: Governmentality in China," in *Governance of Life in Chinese Moral Experience: The Quest for an Adequate Life*, ed. Everett Zhang, Arthur

Kleinman, and Tu Weiming (London: Routledge, 2010), 1–30, 8; and Godwin C. Chu, "The Changing Concept of Zhong (Loyalty): Emerging New Chinese Political Culture," in *Chinese Political Culture, 1989–2000*, ed. Shiping Hua (Armonk, NY: M. E. Sharpe, 2001), 42–69.

5. Ching Kwan Lee, *Against the Law: Labor Protests in China's Rustbelt and Sunbelt* (Berkeley and Los Angeles: University of California Press, 2007), 10.

6. Li Hanxiong, "'Sange daibiao' sixiangde hexin shidaibiao guangda renmin qunzhongde zuigenben liyi" (The core of the "Three Represents" is to represent the most fundamental interests of the masses), *People's Daily*, January 6, 2002.

7. Fu Yuanyuan, "Zhengfu weifa xingzheng: Weixie yezhu jingguo" (The illicit administration of the government: A homeowner's experience of government threats), January 9, 2002, documents provided by Waitan Garden homeowners.

8. Xiao Wenjia, "Renquan hezai? Guofa hezai?" (Where are the human rights? Where are the state laws?), Xinhua News Agency, January 13, 2002, http://news.xinhuanet.com/english/china/2012 (link inactive or blocked).

9. The state of Arizona's latest immigration law orders immigrants to carry their alien registration documents at all times and requires the police to question people if there is any reason to suspect that they are in the United States illegally. Randal C. Archibold, "Arizona Enacts Stringent Law on Immigration," *New York Times*, April 23, 2010; "Arizona's Bad Immigration Law Takes Effect," *Washington Post*, September 20, 2012.

10. For the constitution, see n. 43, chapter 1, above.

11. Documents provided by Waitan Garden homeowners, 2013.

12. For the history of the Chinese petition, see Fang, *Chinese Complaint Systems*, and "Hot Potatoes."

13. Minzner, "Xinfang," 124. See also Fang, *Chinese Complaint Systems*.

14. Interview with the head of the Letters and Visits Office in Shanghai, November 10, 2003.

15. "Gei Zhu Rongji zonglide shangfangxin" (Letter [from an anonymous Waitan Garden homeowner] to Premier Zhu Rongji), January 1, 2002, documents provided by Waitan Garden homeowners, nos. 107–8.

16. Documents provided by Waitan Garden homeowners, no. 107.

17. "Gei Jiang Zemin zhuxi de sahngfangxin" (Petition to President Jiang Zemin [from Waitan Garden homeowners]), January 17, 2002, documents provided by Waitan Garden homeowners.

18. "Gei Yu Zhengsheng shujide sahngfangxin" (Petition to Party secretary Yu Zhengsheng [from Waitan Garden homeowners]), January 17, 2002, documents provided by Waitan Garden homeowners.

19. "Gei renmin ribaode sahngfangxin" (Petition to the *People's Daily* [from Waitan Garden homeowners]), January 27, 2002, documents provided by Waitan Garden homeowners.

20. Stephen K. Ma, "'Policing the Police': A Perennial Challenge for China's Anti-Corruption Agencies," in *Preventing Corruption in Asia: Instituting Design and Policy Capacity*, ed. Ting Gong and Stephen K. Ma (London: Routledge, 2012), 81–96, 82.

21. William B. Simons and Stephen White, eds., *The Party Statutes of the Communist World* (Leiden: Brill, 1984), 111.

22. "Gei zhongyang jilü jiancha weiyuanhuide sahngfangxin" (Petition to the Central Commission for Discipline Inspection [from Waitan Garden homeowners]), February 1, 2002, documents provided by Waitan Garden homeowners.

23. Ibid.

24. For a detailed study of the role played by the *China Youth Daily*, see Fang, "Chinese Media and the Rule of Law," and "Resilient or Decaying?"

25. For the abuse of power and law violations of the Central Commission for Discipline Inspection, see Ronald C. Keith, Zhiqiu Lin, and Shumei Hou, *China's Supreme Court* (London: Routledge, 2013), 193; and Lin Ping, "Yu Qiyi feizhengchang siwangan baolu zhonggong 'shuanggui' tizhide canren heweifa" (The abnormal death of Yu Qiyi exposes the brutality and law violations of the CCP's "dual designation"), Free Asia Radio, October 24, 2013.

26. Willy Wo-Lap Lam, a professor at the Chinese University of Hong Kong, said that the anticorruption case against Zhou Yongkang is a pretext and that the main issue is still factional struggle within the Party. See "China Investigates Ex-Security Chief Zhou Yongkang, *NYT* Says," *Bloomberg News,* December 16, 2013.

27. Guo, *Wogao Chengweigao.*

28. Ellen Philips, *Shocked, Appalled, and Dismayed: How to Write Letters of Complaint That Get Results* (New York: Vintage Books, 1997).

29. O'Brien and Li, *Rightful Resistance in Rural China.*

30. For the details of the theory of "natural resistance," see Qiang Fang, "Introduction," in *Chinese Complaint Systems: Natural Resistance* (U.K.: Routledge, 2013): 1-12.

31. "Xinfang tiaoli" (Regulations regarding letters and visits), *People's Daily,* November 1, 1995; "Xinfang tiaoli" (Regulations regarding letters and visits), *People's Daily,* May 1, 2005.

32. Interview with Yan Fengjun; Yan Fengjun, "Qianmin yezhu jiangjinjing qingyuan" (One thousand homeowners will petition Beijing), January 16, 2002, documents provided by Waitan Garden homeowners.

33. A personal account written by an anonymous homeowner petitioner, n.d., documents provided by Waitan Garden homeowners; interview with Yan Fengjun.

34. Interview with Yan Fengjun.

35. Interview with the head of the Letters and Visits Office in Weishi County, Henan Province, November 25, 2003. See also Fang *Chinese Complaint Systems.*

36. He Feng, untitled personal account (2013), copy in authors' possession.

37. Fang interviewed many individual petitioners in Beijing in 2003 and 2005, and most of them had the experience of being retrieved at least one time. One old man had been retrieved several times by the local police, who allegedly hired someone to monitor him every day. As soon as he left his home, the police would be informed. He would then be detained and beaten before being sent back home. See Fang, *Zhongguo shangfang zhidu shihua;* and interviews with the head of a demolition company in Wuhan.

38. "Waitan huayuan yezhu zhuanggao Wuhanshi zhengfu he Hanyangqu zhengfu" (Indictment of the Waitan Garden homeowners against the Wuhan and Hanyang governments), January 10, 2002, documents provided by Waitan Garden homeowners.

39. "Zhuijiu falü zeren, yaoqiu yifa chaiqian" (Tracing legal responsibility and demanding relocation in accordance with the law), ca. November 20–December 30, 2001, documents provided by Waitan Garden homeowners. See also interview with Yan Fengjun.

40. Interview with Han Junru.

41. Documents provided by Waitan Garden homeowners, no. 71.

42. "Hubeisheng yuanfushengzhang beikaichu dangji hegongzhi" (Former vice governor of Hubei Province was expelled from the Party and discharged from office), *Gansu Daily,* September 26, 2000.

43. Interview with Han Junru.

44. *Yangzi Daily,* June 14, 2002. See also documents provided by Waitan Garden homeowners, no. 13.

45. Interview with an anonymous Waitan Garden homeowner. The homeowners used personal connections to meet with Wu Yi.

46. Sima Qian, *Shiji* (History record), 294 vols. (Beijing: Zhonghua shujü, 1975), vol. 68. The heir apparent could not be mutilated, but he was forced to stay in his palace for eight years (until the death of his father, Duke Qiao), and his two instructors were punished instead.

4. Xuzhou

1. For the Xuzhou military campaign, see Hans van de Ven, *War and Nationalism in China, 1925–1945* (London: Routledge, 2003), 217–19.

2. Interview with Wang Peirong, November 16, 2003.

3. Jiang Ming'an, a law professor at Peking University, conducted a study in 2005 on the methods that Wang Peirong had used to protect his rights. See Jiang Ming'an, "Shanyong xianyou weiquan ziyuan hewanshan xianxing quanli baozhang zhidu: Wang Peirong weiquan jinglide qishi" (Properly using current rights defending resources and perfecting current rights protection systems: The inspiration of Wang Peirong's experience in safeguarding rights), *Beida gongfawang*, December 1, 2006. http://www.148cn.org/data/2006/1201/article_29813.htm.

4. Huang Keru, "Guai: Fenghua kejiao anju xiaoqu junan'an" (Strange: It is difficult to stay calm in Fenghuayuan), *Zhongguo shehuibao*, November 27, 2003.

5. Wen Jian, "Zhuanggao wujiguan guansi tuzhongzhi, daxue jiaoshou shiyao mingao-guan" (The lawsuits were terminated after suing five government organs, the professor vowed to lodge lawsuits of commoners against officials), *Nanfangwang*, November 4, 2003, http://www.southcn.com/news/community/fzzh/200311041083.htm (link inactive or blocked).

6. Zhi Jian, "Weitao shuofa, daxue jiaoshou mingaoguan" (For an explanation, a college professor lodged a commoners-against-officials lawsuit), *Law and Life*, November 2003, 7–9.

7. Huang, "Guai."

8. Interview with Wang Peirong; documents provided by Wang Peirong, 2003–2013, 1.28. See also He Lei, "Xiaoqu yideng shoufei meiyou yideng fuwu Xuzhou yezhu zhuanggao guojiaji dajiang" (First-class charge does not have first-class service, Xuzhou homeowners suing the national award), *China Youth Daily*, October 26, 2004.

9. With the national award, the property management would have been able to charge the homeowners a higher fee. See interview with Wang Peirong; and documents provided by Wang Peirong, 2.13.

10. Kate Zhou, *China's Long March to Freedom: Grassroots Modernization* (New Brunswick, NJ: Transaction Publishers, 2011), 114; Zhou, *China's Peaceful Rise in a Global Context*, 43.

11. Interview with Wang Peirong; documents provided by Wang Peirong, 2.3.

12. Documents provided by Wang Peirong, 2.5.

13. Documents provided by Wang Peirong, 1.33; *Pengcheng Evening News*, July 18, 2000.

14. Mao Zedong, "Guanyu zhengque chuli renmin neibu maodun" (Correctly dealing with people's internal contradictions), 1957, in Mao Zedong, *Maozedong wenji* (Collected works of Mao Zedong), ed. Zhonggong zhongyang wenxian yanjiushi (Archive Research Unit of the Central Chinese Communist Party) (Beijing: Renmin chubanshe, 2001), 7:205–6.

15. For a detailed history of the letters and visits offices, see Diao Jiecheng, *Renmin xinfang shilue* (A brief history of people's letters and visits) (Beijing: Beijing jingji xueyuan chubanshe, 1996); Fang, *Chinese Complaint Systems*.

16. Wen, "Zhuanggao wujiguan guansi tuzhongzhi, daxue jiaoshou shiyao mingaoguan."

17. Interview with Wang Peirong.

18. See Fang, *Chinese Complaint Systems*.

19. "Danyuan fangdaomen dianfei zashou" (How can the antitheft doors and electricity be charged), *Metropolitan Morning News*, January 14, 2002.

20. "Zaojian xinwen lanmu" (The news column of the morning), Xuzhou TV, January 17, 2002.

21. Documents provided by Wang Peirong, 2.37.

22. Documents provided by Wang Peirong, 2.7–9.

23. The PRC judicial system consists of four tiers. At the top is the Supreme Court. In each province, autonomous region, or city, there are local courts, the intermediate court, and the high court. The local courts deal with first-instance cases. For most civil cases, the intermediate court makes the final decision. For some criminal cases, the high court will have the final say. The Supreme Court will accept serious criminal cases, civil cases, and administrative litigations with national import. See http://www.china.com.cn/ch-sifa/sifa-2/sifa2-1.htm.

24. Wen, "Zhuanggao wujiguan guansi tuzhongzhi, daxue jiaoshou shiyao mingaoguan"; documents provided by Wang Peirong, 2.9.

25. For the relations among the courts, the police, and the political and legal commissions, see Qian Haoping, "Zhengfawei shujiyu gong'an juzhangde hehe fefen" (The union and breach between the heads of the political and legal commissions and the heads of the police bureau), *Southern Weekend*, November 18, 2011.

26. Wen, "Zhuanggao wujiguan guansi tuzhongzhi, daxue jiaoshou shiyao mingaoguan."

27. Documents provided by Wang Peirong, 1.20.

28. Interview with Wang Peirong; documents provided by Wang Peirong, 1.25–27.

29. He, *In the Name of Justice,* 167. For a similar argument, see He Weifang, "Fuzhan junren jinfayuan" (Military veterans enter the court), *Southern Weekend*, January 2, 1998.

30. For a detailed account of legal education in China, see Liang, *The Changing Chinese Legal System,* 53–64; Gong, ed., *Dangdai zhongguo de falü geming,* 355; and Xiaobing Li and Qiang Fang, "Introduction: Legal Reforms in Twentieth-Century China," in *Modern Chinese Legal Reform: New Perspectives,* ed. Xiaobing Li and Qiang Fang (Lexington: University Press of Kentucky, 2013), 1–26.

31. The police were attacked in 1968 and subsequently put under the control of the military control commissions (*juguanhui*). But they continued to function as usual throughout the Cultural Revolution. Interview with a former cadre of the Shanghai Military Control Commission, February 20, 2004. See also Yang Xiancheng, "Wengezhong zalan gongjianfa heqingli jieji duiwu" (Smashing the police, procuratorate, and court and purging class ranks), *Yanhuang chunqiu* 2 (2013): 55–58.

32. H. L. Fu, "Punishing for Profit: Profitability and Rehabilitation in a Laojiao Institution," in Diamant, Lubman, and O'Brien, eds., *Engaging the Law in China,* 213–30.

33. *Laojiao* was formally abolished in late 2003. For *laojiao* being first used in 1957, see Michael Dillon, *Contemporary China: An Introduction* (London: Routledge, 2008), 94. For the abolition of *laojiao*, see "Feichu laojiao zhidu, zhongguo fazhi gengjiankang" (Abolishing the *laojiao* system, Chinese legal system will be more healthy), *China Youth Daily,* December 29, 2013.

34. Documents provided by Wang Peirong, 1.39.

35. Wen, "Zhuanggao wujiguan guansi tuzhongzhi, daxue jiaoshou shiyao mingaoguan."

36. Xu Jinyi, "Jiaoshou hegangao shizhengfu" (How dare a professor sue the city government), *Jiangnan shibao*, August 13, 2003.

37. For the opinion of O'Brien and Li, see O'Brien and Li, "Suing the Local State."

38. Documents provided by Wang Peirong, 1.17.

39. Fang, *Chinese Complaint Systems,* chap. 6.

40. Miu Liyan, "Shimin zhuanggao shizhengfu, kaiting zhiqian dajiaofeng" (Urbanite accusing the city government, the conflicts before the coourt opening), *Yangzi wanbao*, August 5, 2003. See also documents provided by Wang Peirong, 1.25–26.

41. Documents provided by Wang Peirong, 1.26–27; Miu, "Shimin zhuanggao shizhengfu, kaiting zhiqian dajiaofeng."

42. Wen, "Zhuanggao wujiguan guansi tuzhongzhi, daxue jiaoshou shiyao mingaoguan."

43. Ibid.

44. Some scholars have recently argued that the CCP has seldom meddled in administrative litigations. But the threats made by the Xuzhou Police Bureau in court were undoubtedly represented intervention. In addition, the court refusals to accept the administrative litigations filed by the Waitan Garden representatives and Wang Peirong were also directly or indirectly the result of the application of government power. For recent scholars' opinions, see Peerenboom, "Judicial Independence in China," 80.

45. Xu Jinyi, "Jiaoshou gaoguan hequ hecong" (What will be the outcome of the professor's lawsuit against governments), Jiangnan shibao, August 25, 2003.

46. Wen, "Zhuanggao wujiguan guansi tuzhongzhi, daxue jiaoshou shiyao mingaoguan."

47. Minxin Pei, China's Trapped Transition: The Limits of Developmental Autocracy (Cambridge, MA: Harvard University Press, 2009), 70.

48. Dong, Dongbiwu faxue wenji, 254. See also Zhengyuan Fu, Autocratic Tradition and Chinese Politics (Cambridge: Cambridge University Press, 1993), 216.

49. Pei, China's Trapped Transition, 70.

50. Zhu Suli, "The Party and the Courts," in Peerenboom, ed., Judicial Independence in China, 52–68, 60.

51. Xu Jinyi, "Jiaoshou gaoguan hequ hecong."

52. Xu Jinyi, "Xuzhou jiaoshou zhuanggao shifu youzhuanji 'Fenghuayuan' fangdaomen jinri genghuan" (The turning point arrives for Xuzhou professor's lawsuit against the municipal government, Fenghuayuan's antitheft doors will be replaced today), Jiangnan shibao, November 7, 2003.

53. "Shuizaiwan chuer faner" (Who is playing with the inconsistency). Jiangnan shibao, October 24, 2003.

54. Documents provided by Wang Peirong, 1.35.

55. Wen, "Zhuanggao wujiguan guansi tuzhongzhi, daxue jiaoshou shiyao mingaoguan."

56. Xu, "Jiaoshou hegangao shizhengfu."

57. Yan and Gao, Turbulent Decade, 33.

58. Guo, Wogao Chengweigao.

59. On May 16, 1951, Mao sharply denounced the bureaucratism that had ignored people's complaints and difficulties. See Mao Zedong, "Bixu zhongshi renmin qunzhong laixin" (We must pay serious attention to the popular masses' letters), 1951, in Zhonggong zhongyang wenxian yanjiushi, ed., Mao Zedong wenji, 6:164–65. For bureaucratism, see also Andrew J. Nathan, Chinese Democracy (New York: Columbia University Press, 1985), 73; and Meisner, The Deng Xiaoping Era, 175.

60. Xu, "Xuzhou jiaoshou zhuanggao shifu youzhuanji 'fenghuayuan' fangdaomen jinri genghuan."

61. Documents provided by Wang Peirong, 1.35.

62. Xu Jinyi, "Fenghuayuan fangdaomen shijian zuohuajuhao" (The incident of the Fenghuayuan antitheft doors ended yesterday), Jiangnan shibao, February 1, 2004. See also documents provided by Wang Peirong, 1.2.

63. For the difficulty in enforcing court decisions, see O'Brien and Li, "Suing the Local State"; and Fang, Chinese Complaint Systems, chap. 6.

64. Xu Chengde and Wang Gang, "Xuzhou fansi fangdaomen fengbo" (Xuzhou rethinking the incident of the antitheft doors), Xinhua Daily, February 26, 2004. See also documents provided by Wang Peirong, 1.35.

65. He, "Xiaoqu yideng shoufei meiyou yideng fuwu Xuzhou yezhu zhuanggao guojiaji dajiang"; "Jianshebu quxiao Fenghuayuan xiaoqu guoyou chenghao" (The Ministry of Construction withdrew the national excellence title from Fenghuayuan), *China Youth Daily,* January 24, 2005; documents provided by Wang Peirong, 1.11, 29.

66. Documents provided by Wang Peirong, 2.30.

67. Documents provided by Wang Peirong, 1.15–16, 2.30–31.

68. Shen, "Conceptions and Receptions of Legality," 28–29; Ren, *Tradition of the Law and Law of the Tradition,* 56–57.

69. Documents provided by Wang Peirong, 2.40.

70. Documents provided by Wang Peirong, 2.43.

71. For example, in 2006, Wang accused Liu Yongxiu, the head of the Fenghuayuan Residential Committee (*juweihui*), of evading taxes and embezzling large sums belonging to the homeowners. From 2007 to 2012, he engaged in a legal battle against Li Qirong, the Xuzhou Party vice secretary, accusing him of having three mistresses and several illegitimate children (*sishengzinu*), seeking bribes from inferiors, and hiring gang members to take revenge on him. (Wang was kidnapped and robbed, and Li also tapped his phones and pressed the university to fire him.) However, the court refused to accept his suit. See documents provided by Wang Peirong regarding Liu Yongxiu and Li Qirong, 2003–2013.

72. In the case of Virgin Prostitutes that took place in 2001, Jiang Ming'an also offered legal help to Ma Dandan, the young victim. For details about the case, see Fang, "The Case of the Virgin Prostitute."

73. Jiang, "Shanyong xianyou weiquan ziyuan hewanshan xianxing quanli baozhang zhidu."

5. Professor Wang's Costly Battle against Local Power

1. Anne-Marie Brady, "The Beijing Olympics as a Campaign of Mass Distraction," in *China's Thought Management,* ed. Anne-Marie Brady (London: Routledge, 2011), 11–35, 25.

2. "Zhonghua remin gongheguo chengshi jumin weiyuanhui zuzhifa" (PRC organizational law of urban neighborhood committees), December 26, 1989, http://china.findlaw.cn/info/guojiafa/jiguanzuzhi/jicengzizhi/juminwyh/124891.html.

3. Xu Feng, "New Modes of Urban Governance: Building Community/*Shequ* in Post-Danwei China," in *The Chinese Party-State in the 21st Century: Adaptation and the Reinvention of Legitimacy,* ed. André Laliberté and Marc Lanteigne (London: Routledge, 2008), 22–38, 28. See also Lena Y. Zhang, *Communities, Crime and Social Capital in Contemporary China* (London: Routledge, 2013), 6.

4. Gu Zhijian, "Wang Peirong beipanxing liuxia jiaoxun henduo" (Wang's imprisonment leaves many lessons), *Lushi zhichuang,* January 15, 2013, http://blog.sina.com.cn/s/blog_413dc44b0101714y.html (link inactive or blocked); Qiang Jianghai and Zhong Hui, "Yeweihui quzhu juweihui" (Homeowners committee expelling neighborhood committee), *Jiating,* December 2006, 10–12.

5. Qiang and Zhong, "Yeweihui quzhu juweihui."

6. "Fangwu hezuo shiyong xieyishu" (A contract of collaborative use of building), documents provided by Wang Peirong (December 2005).

7. Documents provided by Wang Peirong (August 25, 2006).

8. Qiang and Zhong, "Yeweihui quzhu juweihui"; documents provided by Wang Peirong via email (August 25, 2006).

9. Ibid.

10. Qiang and Zhong, "Yeweihui quzhu juweihui."

11. Wang Peirong, "Yezhu weiyuanhui zhijuweihui degongkaixin" (The open letter of the homeowners committee to the neighborhood committee), August 25, 2006, documents provide by Wang Peirong.

12. "Jubao zhihou" (After exposing), *Nandu zhoukan*, November 14, 2010.

13. Documents provided by Wang Peirong (September 24, 2006).

14. Hospital Report and separate documents provided by Wang Pierong via email to Qiang Li (September 24, 2006).

15. For the bad reputation of the Xuzhou local police, see the previous chapter.

16. Qiang and Zhong, "Yeweihui quzhu juweihui."

17. "Jubao zhihou." This report was blocked by the newspaper owing to government pressure. Documents provided by Wang Peirong via email (July 22, 2010) (original report).

18. Wang Peirong, "Bamian Liu Yongxiu changyishu" (A proposal to impeach Liu Yongxiu), August 2006, documents provided by Wang Pierong via email.

19. "Zhonghua remin gongheguo chengshi jumin weiyuanhui zuzhifa."

20. Wei Hongqian, "Juweihui zhuren wu'fa' bamian" (Is there no law that can impeach the head of the neighborhood committee), *Jiancha ribao*, August 17, 2009.

21. For example, the *People's Daily* had published an editorial in April 1989 denouncing the student demonstrations as "turmoil," paving the way to the Tiananmen massacre in early June. See "Qizhi xianmingdi fandui dongluan" (Unswervingly opposing the turmoil), *People's Daily*, April 26, 1989.

22. Qiang and Zhong, "Yeweihui quzhu juweihui."

23. Qiang and Zhong, "Yeweihui quzhu juweihui."

24. Wei, "Juweihui zhuren wu'fa' bamian."

25. Ibid.

26. Documents provided by Wang Peirong via email (September 15, 2007).

27. Wei, "Juweihui zhuren wu'fa' bamian"; documents provided by Wang Peirong via email (September 15, 2007).

28. Wei, "Juweihui zhuren wu'fa' bamian."

29. See Brady, "The Beijing Olympics as a Campaign of Mass Distraction"; Xu, "New Modes of Urban Governance."

30. Wei, "Juweihui zhuren wu'fa' bamian."

31. People who had lived through the politically turbulent periods of the 1950s and the 1960s would remember the men-fight-men movements during which millions of people had been attacked and prosecuted. For the political campaigns of the 1950s and 1960s, see Bill Brugger, *China, Liberation and Transformation, 1942–1962* (Lanham, MD: Rowman & Littlefield, 1981), 156–64; Yan and Gao, *Turbulent Decade;* and Daiyun Yue, *To the Storm: The Odyssey of a Revolutionary Chinese Woman* (Berkeley and Los Angeles: University of California Press, 1987).

32. Yang Gongzhan, "Ziyi wangwei wufa wutian: Fenghuayuan juweihui huanjie xuanju biduan juyao" (Arbitrariness and lawlessness: Highlights of fraudulent activities in the election of the Fenghuayuan Neighborhood Committee), November 27, 2009, documents provided by Wang Pierong via email.

33. "Zhonghua remin gongheguo chengshi jumin weiyuanhui zuzhifa."

34. Yang Zhangong, 2009, documents provided by Wang Pierong via email.

35. As we have seen, the homeowners committee was not an official government committee. So, if as the local governments claimed they could give only guidance to the neighborhood committee, itself a self-managing organization, the subdistrict office clearly exceeded its authority by dismissing Wang's announcements.

36. Documents provided by Wang Peirong via email (November 27, 2009).

37. Documents provided by Wang Pierong via email.

38. Wei, "Juweihui zhuren wu'fa' bamian."

39. Owing to increased competition and the declining state subsidies, some public media, especially national ones such as the *Southern Weekend* and the *China Youth Daily,* are bold enough to criticize local governments. But they are very wary of chastising the state government and the Party. The *Southern Weekend* has suffered some purges in the past several years. The latest one was in early 2013 when many rebellious editors and journalists were purged after a New Year's letter championing the constitution. For the bold reporting of the *China Youth Daily,* see Fang, "Chinese Media and the Rule of Law." For the *Southern Weekend* incident, see Didi Tang, "Chinese Newspapers Row Sparks Journalist Strikes, Protests against Censorship of Southern Weekly," *Huffington Post,* January 7, 2013. (The *Huffington Post* link is no longer active, but an abstract of sorts can be found at http://newslanc.com/chinese-newspaper-row-sparks-journalist-strikes-protests-against-censorship-of-southern-weekly.)

40. For Zheng Enchong, see Shao, *Shanghai Gone.* For Xu Zhiyong, see Simon Denyer, "Chinese Activist Xu Zhiyong Sentenced to Four Years in Prison," *Washington Post,* January 25, 2014. For Chen Gaungcheng, see Evan Osnos, "NYU, China, and Chen Guangcheng," *New York Times,* June 17, 2013.

41. Documents provided by Wang Peirong via email (February 23, 2008).

42. "Doushi" (Fighter), *Jiaren* 3 (2009): 13–17.

43. Fenghuayuan Neighborhood Committee, "Wang Peirong jingji wenti diyi bufen" (The first part of Wang Peirong's economic problems), May 23, 2006, documents provided by Wang Peirong via email.

44. Meng Zhen, "Minshi qisuzhuang" (Indictment of civil cases), July 2, 2006, documents provided by Wang Peirong via email.

45. Documents provided by Wang Peirong via email (December 24, 2006).

46. Fenghuayuan Neighborhood Committee, "Wang Peirong deyeweihui jingji neimu" (The economic inside story of Wang's homeowners committee), August 2, 2007, documents provided by Wang Peirong via email.

47. Fenghuayuan Neighborhood Committee, "Qing Wang Peirong buyao fugai juweihui gongbude zhengju cailiao" (Wang Peirong please do not cover up the evidence exposed by the neighborhood committee), September 10, 2009, documents provided by Wang Peirong via email.

48. For Wang Peirong's accusations against Dong Feng, see "Daxue fujiaoshou chengjubao doushi" (College associate professor becomes Web site fighter), *Qilu Evening News,* October 2, 2008; and Zhang Guo, "Wangluo fanfu zuoyong zhengmian dayu fumian" (The function of Internet anticorruption is more positive than negative), *China Youth Daily,* September 1, 2008.

49. "Wang Peirong shiyeji" (The record of Wang Peirong's unemployment), *Shidai zhoukan,* February 11, 2010.

50. Ding Guofeng, "Kuangda fujiaoshou zhangtie 'xiaozibao' manma taren beisu feibang" (Associate professor of the Chinese University of Mining and Technology posted "small-character posters" abusing others is charged with slander), *Legal Daily,* October 30, 2012.

51. "Xuzhou Quanshanqu renmin fayuan xingshi panjueshu" (The criminal verdict of the Xuzhou Quanshan District People's Court), November 30, 2012, documents provided by Wang Peirong via email.

52. Ding, "Kuangda fujiaoshou zhangtie 'xiaozibao' manma taren beisu feibang."

53. "Xuzhou Quanshanqu renmin fayuan xingshi panjueshu." See also Ding Guofeng, "Fujiaoshou zhangtie 'daxiao zibao' feibang shuren huoxing" (Associate professor sentenced

for posting "big- and small-character posters" to slander several people), *Legal Daily,* December 5, 2013.

54. "Xuzhoushi zhongji renmin fayuan xingshi panjueshu" (The criminal verdict of the Xuzhou Quanshan District People's Court), December 30, 2012, documents provided by Wang Peirong via email.

55. Ding, "Kuangda fujiaoshou zhangtie 'xiaozibao' manma taren beisu feibang."

56. Gu, "Wang Peirong beipanxing liuxia jiaoxun henduo."

57. Documents provided by Wang Peirong via email (January 30, 2008).

58. Documents provided by Wang Peirong (October 28, 2014).

59. Documents provided by Wang Peirong (August 9, 2014).

60. Documents provided by Wang Peirong via email (August 30, 2012).

61. Qiao Long, "Xuzhou kuangda jiaoshou Wang Peirong beizhi feibang beipanxing yinianban" (Professor Wang Peirong at Chinese University of Mining and Technology was accused of slander and sentenced to eighteen months), Free Asia Radio Station, January 8, 2013.

61. Ibid.

62. *Shidai zhoukan,* February 11, 2010.

64. "Jubao zhihou."

6. Shanghai and Chongqing

1. Human Rights Watch report, January 31, 2008, https://www.hrw.org/legacy/englishwr2k8/docs/2008/01/31/china17604.htm.

2. He, *In the Name of Justice,* 138.

3. For the increasing legal consciousness of many Chinese, see Mary E. Gallagher, "Mobilizing the Law in China: 'Informed Disenchantment' and the Development of Legal Consciousness," *Law and Society Review* 40, no. 4 (December 2006): 783–816.

4. A Supreme Court report noted that the total number of cases accepted by the people's courts in 2013 was more than 14 million, an increase of 7.4 percent over the number accepted in 2012 and 32.8 percent over the number accepted in 2008. See *Legal Daily,* March 13, 2014.

5. Human Rights Watch report.

6. According to an official working at the Pudong District in Shanghai, Chen Liangyu, a key member of the Shanghai faction, disrespected Wen in a meeting by knocking his fists on the table. This probably also contributed to Chen's quick fall. Interview with a government official in Shanghai Pudong District, June 10, 2009.

7. Cheng Li, "Was the Shanghai Gang Shanghaied? The Fall of Chen Liangyu and the Survival of Jiang Zemin's Faction," *China Leadership Monitor,* no. 20 (2007): 11–19.

8. Zheng Enchong, "Zhou Zhengyi xianxiang" (The phenomenon of Zhou Zhengyi), in *Shen ting, shuiyinbao Zhou Zhengyi'an* (Who has exploded the case of Zhou Zhengyi) (Hong Kong: Kaifang chubanshe, 2007), 15–24.

9. Ji Shuoming, "Zhuanggao Zhou Zhengyide lushi Zheng Enchong zhangwo Chen Liangyu cailiao" (Zheng Enchong, the lawyer who has possessed materials against Chen Liangyu, has been prosecuted), *Asiaweek,* October 1, 2006.

10. Zheng, "Zhou Zhengyi xianxiang."

11. Jin Zhong, "Shen Ting meiyou shuowande gushi" (The words that Shen Ting has not finished), January 5, 2008, Boxun.com, http://www.boxun.com/news/gb/pubvp/2008/01/200801051820.shtml.

12. Interview with a judge working at the Second Shanghai Intermediate People's Court, November 3, 2003.

13. The Criminal Verdict of the Second Shanghai Intermediate People's Court, October 25, 2003, http://www.hxzy365.com/2012/0628/286852.html.

14. Zheng, "Zhou Zhengyi xianxiang."

15. "Liuwei qinli Zheng Enchongan xinwen jizhede shengming" (The statement of six journalists who have experienced the case of Zheng Enchong), Kaidi shequ, January 5, 2008, http://www.aboluowang.com/2008/0105/69885.html.

16. Ibid.

17. Zhang Sizhi, "Zheng Enchongan zhongshen caiding bianxi" (An analysis of the final verdict of the case of Zheng Enchong), Falujie, June 12, 2010, http://news.mylegist.com/1604/2010-06-12/26554.html.

18. Jin, "Shen Ting meiyou shuowande gushi"; Wu Xue'er and Li Zhen, "Zhou Zhengyi," Dajiyuan, December 17, 2007, http://www.epochtimes.com/b5/7/12/17/n1944521p.htm.

19. Jiang Meili, "Zhiquanguo lushijiede gongkaixin" (A public letter to all Chinese lawyers), November 1, 2003, Boxun.com, http://www.peacehall.com/news/gb/china/2003/11/200311011304.shtml.

20. Cheng Li, "Cooling Shanghai Fever: Macroeconomic Control and Its Geopolitical Implications," China Leadership Monitor, no. 12 (2004): 1–12, http://www.hoover.org/sites/default/files/uploads/documents/clm12_lc.pdf.

21. Zheng Yongnian, The Chinese Communist Party as Organizational Emperor: Culture, Reproduction, and Transformation (London: Routledge, 2009), 88–89.

22. "Political Crisis in Beijing," Straits Times (Singapore), July 10, 2004.

23. Li, "Cooling Shanghai Fever."

24. Cheng Li, China's Leaders: The New Generation (Lanham, MD: Rowman & Littlefield, 2001), fig. 1.1, p. 11, and table 3.3, p. 58.

25. Cheng Li, "China's Inner-Party Democracy: Toward a System of 'One Party, Two Factions'?" China Brief 6, no. 24 (December 2006), https://jamestown.org/program/chinas-inner-party-democracy-toward-a-system-of-one-party-two-factions-2. See also Cheng Li, "Emerging Partisanship within the Chinese Communist Party," Orbis, Summer 2005, 387–400.

26. "Zao Jiang Zemin Zeng Qinghong paoqi, Chen Liangyu yuzhong pokou dama buzhangyi" (Abandoned by Jiang Zemin and Zeng Qinghong, Chen Liang lashed out them as betrayal), BackChina.com, September 8, 2007, http://www.backchina.com/forum.php?mod=viewthread&tid=558984&extra=page%3D1&mobile=2.

27. See "Chen Liangyu's Six Crimes" (Chen Liangyu liuzongzui), in Nanfang dushibao, July 27, 2007.

28. See, e.g., Jeremy Page, "Chongqing Mayor Reveals Role in Drama outside U.S. Consulate," Wall Street Journal, March 6, 2012.

29. Ian Johnson, "On Social Media, Chinese Ponder Crime Fighter's Fate," New York Times, February 8, 2012.

30. For time lines of the Bo Xilai scandal, see "Bo Xilai Scandal: How News Breaks in China," n.d., Committee to Protect Journals, http://cpj.org/reports/2013/03/challenged-china-media-censorship-timeline-bo-xilai.php; and "Bo Xilai Scandal: Timeline," November 11, 2013, BBC News, http://www.bbc.co.uk/news/world-asia-china-17673505.

31. "Bo Xilai Scandal: Timeline."

32. "Profile: Bo Xilai," September 22, 2013, BBC News, http://www.bbc.co.uk/news/world-asia-china-19709555.

33. Evan Osnos, "China's Crisis," New Yorker, April 30, 2012.

34. Jeremy Page, "Bo Xilai Found Guilty, Sentenced to Life in Prison," Wall Street Journal, September 22, 2013.

35. Such estimates are calculated by different groups, such as Tsinghua University. The current number, many believe, can only be higher. See Higers, "The Unraveling of Bo Xilai: China Loses a Popular Star," *Harper's Magazine,* March 2003, 41.

36. Ibid.

37. "The Inside Stories of Bo-Wang's Billion Dollars: The Heartache of the Court," March 20, 2013, http://boxun.com/news/gb/china/2013/03/201303200445.shtml#.UV5ih8rna0M.

38. Criminal Procedure Law of the PRC, promulgated 1979, rev. 1996 and 2012, http://www.gov.cn/flfg/2012–03/17/content_2094354.htm.

39. For example, to deter potential dissent, in the Tang dynasty Empress Wu Zetian hired two officers to torture people; in the late Ming dynasty, when the Donglin faction opposed the eunuchs, some officials had been brutally tortured before their execution; in the late Qing, officials at the local level tortured Yang Naiwu and Xiaobaicai and forced them to accept the charge of committing adultery and murdering Xiaobaicai's husband. For Empress Wu, see Sima, *Zizhi tongjian,* 207:6523. See also John Dardess, *Blood and History in China: The Donglin Faction and Its Repression, 1620–1627* (Honolulu: University of Hawaii Press, 1992); William P. Alford, "Of Arsenic and Old Laws: Looking Anew at Criminal Justice in Late Imperial China," *California Law Review* 72, no. 6 (December 1984): 1180–1256; and Wang Celai, *Yangnaiwu yu Xiaobaicai an* (The case of Yang Naiwu and Xiao Baicai) (Beijing: Zhongguo jiancha chubanshe, 2002), 150, 164.

40. Gao Hua, *Hongtaiyang shiruhe shengqide* (How did the Red Sun rise) (Hong Kong: Hong Kong Chinese University Press, 2000), 40–44.

41. In 1998, Du Peiwu, a former policeman, "confessed" under harsh police torture that he had killed his wife. It was not until the real murderer was caught two years later that Du's life was spared. See Guo Guosong and Zeng Min, "Siqiu yishu" (The will of a prisoner on death row), *Southern Weekend,* August 23, 2000. For the case of Ma Dandan, see Fang, "The Case of the Virgin Prostitute."

42. Sharon Lafraniere and Jonathan Ansfield, "Crime Crackdown Adds to Scandal Surrounding Former Chinese Official," *New York Times,* March 26, 2012.

43. Wang Haitao, "Bo Xilai kuxing shengguo zhazidong" (Bo Xilai's torture worse than Zhazidong), Kaifangwang, April 5, 2012, http://www.open.com.hk/content.php?id=725#.VUgRi2a4Nmt.

44. LaFraniere and Ansfield, "Crime Crackdown Adds to Scandal Surrounding Former Chinese Official."

45. Shen Xinwang, "Li Zhuangan quancheng neimu pilu: Wang Lijuncheng yaonaqi shayi jingbai" (Exposure of the entire internal story of the Li Zhuang case: Wang Lijun claims to punish him as an example), *Zhongguo xinwen zhoukan,* December 21, 2012.

46. Xu Qianchuan, "Wang Lijun zhuzhengxia Chongqing dahei yi'an beijiekai" (Remaining cases revealed of Chongqing's Smashing the Black under Wang Lijun), *Caijin Magazine,* November 4, 2013; "Chongqing dahei xingxun yi'an" (A remaining torture case of Chongqing's Smashing the Black), *Nanfang ribaowang,* November 4, 2013.

47. Liao Xin, "Chongqing lawjingcha beizhi cengshe Wen Qiang'an" (Old Chongqing policeman was regarded as being involved in the case of Wen Qiang), *Nanfang dushibao,* December 13, 2012.

48. "Yiwei laozhengfa shujide kusu" (The crying complaint of an old cadre of political and legal committee), April 13, 2013, http://blog.sina.com.cn/s/blog_89aa0dcd01019sli.html.

49. "Chongqing dahei meiyou xingxun bigong" (Chongqing has not used torture in Smashing the Black), *Shenzhen Evening News,* March 11, 2012.

50. Liu Qingsong, "Yituoshi laojiao'an dangshizhede koushu" (The dictation of the person

sentenced to labor camp in the case of a lump of waste), *Oral China,* May 19, 2014, http://liuqingsong.blog.ifeng.com/article/32950615.html.

51. Ibid.

52. Ruijinxian renmin fayuan (Ruijin County Court), ed. *Zhonghua suweiai gongheguo shenpan ziliao xuanbian* (Selected judging materials of the Chinese Soviet Republic) (Beijing: Renmin fayuan chubanshe, 1991), 245–51.

53. "Shanghaishi renmin fating fangeming panjueshu" (Verdicts against counterrevolutionaries of the Shanghai People's Court), October 1950–March 1951, Shanghai Archives, B1-2-30; "Gonganbu guanyu gongbu guanzhi fangeming fenzi zanxing banfade tongzhi" (A circular of the Ministry of Public Security regarding publicizing an interim solution of forced education of counterrevolutionaries), 1952, Shanghai Archives, no. B1-1-1227.

54. Harry Wu, *Laogai: The Chinese Gulag* (Boulder, CO: Westview Press, 1992).

55. Fan Zhongxin, "Fazhi zhuiqiuyu Chongqing moshide jiaoxun" (The pursuit of the rule of law and the lesson of the Chongqing paradium), speech at Southwest University of Politics and Law, June 23, 2012, http://blog.sina.com.cn/s/blog_89aa0dcd010131d8.html (link blocked).

56. The police account was first posted by Chen Youxi, a lawyer, on social media on June 25, 2012. According to Chen, a Shanghai lawyer named Yang Haipeng received the original account from a middle-ranking policeman in Chongqing. Chen has confirmed the authenticity of the account and modified the title to *The Days in Chongqing: The Solo Narration of a Policeman.* The Voice of Germany publicized the account on the same day. See *Jianzheng Wanglijun* (Witnessing Wang Lijun), June 25, 2012, *Jianzheng Wanglijun* (Witnessing Wang Lijun), June 25, 2012, https://docs.google.com/document/d/1zpAvcgSy6gO8RG8bJXi2DBMucVkYYOlW RaJ0uB1Z5Q8/edit.

57. Shen, "Li Zhuangan quancheng neimu pilu."

58. Criminal Procedure Law of the PRC.

59. Shen, "Li Zhuangan quancheng neimu pilu."

60. "Interview between Lawyer Wang Wanqiong and Gong Gangmo," Li Zhuang's blog, August 27, 2012, http://blog.sina.com.cn/s/blog_89aa0dcd01019hwz.html; Xu Dan, "Gong Gangmo yao Li Zhuang, jianhuile yitiaoming" (Gong Gangmo bites Li Zhuang and saves his life), Li Zhuang's blog, April 15, 2013, http://blog.sina.com.cn/s/blog_89aa0dcd01019usk.html.

61. The characters Jiang Jie and Xu Yunfeng are two brave Communists in the novel *Hongyan* (Red Rock) who were brutally tortured and executed by the Nationalist Party before the establishment of the PRC. Kong Pu, "Gong Ganghua: Dubuqi Li Zhuang, women dingbuzhule" (Gong Ganghua: Sorry to Li Zhuang, we could no longer stand), *Xinjingbao* (New Beijing newspaper), December 30, 2012.

62. "Guanyu Li Zhuang, wugaota, woyuanyi chengdan falu zeren" (Regarding Li Zhuang, I want to admit the legal responsibility for falsely accusing him), *Legal Daily,* March 25, 2013.

63. Shen, "Li Zhuangan quancheng neimu pilu."

64. "Li Zhuang' an ershen panjue quanwen" (Complete verdict of the Li Zhuang case), Chongqing First Intermediate People's Court, March 8, 2010. http://182.48.103.149/upload/201003085841013.pdf. See also Ni Zhigang, "Li Zhuang jiangshu qiannian xierenzui-shu cangtoushi shijian shimo" (Li Zhuang talks about the complete incident of his confession and covert poem in 2010), *Xiaoxiang chenbao,* November 28, 2012; He Weifang, "Li Zhuang beipanxing, juguo danyou" (The whole nation worries about the punishment of Li Zhuang), He Weifang's blog, January 17, 2010, http://blog.sina.com.cn/s/blog_488663200100h2g0.html; and Shen, "Li Zhuangan quancheng neimu pilu."

65. Shen, "Li Zhuangan quancheng neimu pilu."

66. Higers, "Unraveling of Bo Xilai," 41.

67. Peter Hessler, "Return to River Town," *National Geographic,* March 2013, http://ngm .nationalgeographic.com/2013/03/fuling-china/hessler-text.

68. Bao Tong, "Buzai changhong dahei haishi jianchi changhong dahei? shibada youliangzhong xuanze" (To Continue the 'Singing the Red' and 'Smashing the Black' or Not: The Two Choices of the Party's Eighteenth National Congress), RFA.org, August 29, 2012, http://www .rfa.org/mandarin/pinglun/baotong/bt-08292012092352.html.

69. Quoted by Higers, "Unraveling of Bo Xilai," 41. Wen's speech and the Party Central Committee's decision can be accessed on a variety of Web sites. A general translation runs as follows: "As Comrade Bo Xilai is suspected of being involved in serious discipline violations, the Central Committee of the CCP has decided to suspend his membership in the CCP Central Committee Political Bureau and the CCP Central Committee, in line with the CCP Constitution and the rules on investigation of CCP discipline inspection departments." To find more on the New Left defense of Bo Xilai, see Wuyou zhixiang (Utopia), http://www.wyzxsx.com (linked inactive or blocked).

70. "Bogu Kailai zuizheng quezao yingzhuijiu guyi sharenzui" (There is sufficient evidence to try Bogu Kailai for intentional murder), Xinhua News Agency, August 10, 2012.

71. There are different versions of this encounter between Bo and Wang. Some insist that Wang intended to use the recording to blackmail Bo and Gu. But no convincing evidence has yet emerged.

72. Pin Ho and Wenguang Huang, *A Death in the Lucky Holiday Hotel: Murder, Money, and an Epic Power Struggle in China* (New York: Public Affairs, 2013).

73. Ibid.

74. Gillian Wong, "Gu Kailai Trial: Chinese Court Hands Suspended Death Sentence to Wife of Politician Bo Xilai," *Huffington Post,* August 9, 2012.

75. Li Bin and Yang Weihan, "Zaifalude tianpingshang: Wang Lijun anjian tingshen jianqing shimo" (On the scale of law: A complete story of the Wang Lijun case and the court hearing), Xinhua News Agency, September 19, 2012, http://news.xinhuanet.com/legal/2012-09/19/c_113136404.htm.

76. See Xinhua News Agency, April 10, 2012, http://cpc.people.com.cn/GB/64093/64387 /17621277.html.

77. "Xinshi panjueshu" (Criminal verdict), Shandong Jinan Intermediate People's Court, September 22, 2013, http://news.xinhuanet.com/legal/2013-09/22/c_117450554_2.htm.

78. "Jianchi fazhi fanfu, jianshe lianjie zhengzhi" (Persisting in opposing corruption by the law and constructing clean politics), *People's Daily,* September 23, 2012.

79. See esp. Paul Armstrong, "Police Chief at Heart of Bo Xilai Scandal Jailed for 15 Years," September 24, 2012, http://www.cnn.com/2012/09/23/world/asia/china-wang-lijun-verdict.

80. See "Bo Xilai Scandal: Timeline."

81. "Bo Xilai tingshang paoxiao bugong" (Bo Xilai shouted in the court about the unfairness of the trial), October 26, 2013, http://news.creaders.net/china/2013/10/26/1309697.html.

82. See Editorial, *People's Daily,* September 23, 2012; editorial, *People's Daily,* July 23, 2013; editorial, *People's Daily,* August 27, 2013.

83. Yu Churu, *Bo Xilai hanyuan* (Bo Xilai claims grievance) (Hong Kong: Ha'ye chubanshe, 2013), 241.

Conclusion

1. Jia Yue, "Xi Jinping de fazhiguan" (Xi Jinping's comprehension of the rule of law), People.com.cn, October 21, 2014, http://politics.people.com.cn/GB/n/2014/1021/c1001-25878990.html.

2. Jiang, Zeming. "Gaojü Dengxiaoping lilunweida qizhi, bayouzhongguo tese shehui zhuyi shiye quanmian tuixiang ershiyi shiji" (Carrying high the flag of the Deng Xiaoping theory and pushing Chinese special socialism into the twenty-first century), *People's Daily,* September 22, 1997.

3. Yang Jiadai, "Beida jiaoshou Zhang Qianfan chengfan xianzheng benzhishang jiushi fanrenlei" (Beijing University professor Zhang Qianfan argues that anticonstitutionalism is akin to antihuman), Free Asia Radio, January 5, 2015.

4. "Haobu dongyao jianchi dangdui zhengfa gongzuode lingdao."

5. Elizabeth Economy, "China's Imperial President: Xi Jinping Tightens His Grip," *Foreign Affairs,* November/December 2014, http://www.foreignaffairs.com/articles/142201/elizabeth-c-economy/chinas-imperial-president.

6. Tyler Roney, "Lawyer, Activists Condemn Xu Zhiyong's Trial," *Diplomat,* January 23, 2014, http://thediplomat.com/2014/01/lawyers-activists-condemn-xu-zhiyongs-trial.

7. Many Chinese and English media sources have reported on this. See, e.g., Andrew Jacobs and Chris Buckley, "China Targeting Rights Lawyers in a Crackdown," *New York Times,* July 22, 2015; and Jennifer Duggan, "China Targets Lawyers in New Human Rights Crackdown," *Guardian,* July 13, 2015. For the major Chinese media, see Zhu Yongxiao, "Zhongguo baiyu weiquan lushi beibu fengbao" (The storm of arresting more than one hundred rights lawyers in China), *Asian Week,* July 26, 2015. See also *Singtao Daily,* July 26, 2015.

8. See Murong Xuecun, "Xi's Selective Punishment," *New York Times,* January 16, 2015; and "Zuishuai xiaozhang Zhou Wenbin shoushen" (Most smart president is being tried), *Legal Daily,* January 22, 2015.

9. *Using law to govern (yifa zhiguo)* or *fazhi* is often translated as *rule of law* to distinguish it from *fazhi* or *rule by law.* For Zhang's argument, see Zhang Chunxian, "Quanmian tuijin yifa zhijiang" (Pushing forward the use of law to govern Xinjian), *People's Daily,* January 7, 2015. For the debate on the rule of law vs. rule by law, see Dean Spader, "Rule of Law v. Rule of Man: The Search for the Golden Zigzag between Conflicting Fundamental Values," *Journal of Criminal Justice* 12, no. 4 (1984): 379–94; Liang Zhiping, "Explicating 'Law': A Comparative Perspective of Chinese and Western Legal Culture," *Journal of Chinese Law* 3 (1989): 55–91, 81; and Shen, "Conceptions and Receptions of Legality."

10. He, *Yunsong zhengyide fangshi,* 177–83. See also He, *In the Name of Justice,* 68, 82, 121.

Selected Bibliography

Primary Sources

Miscellaneous Documents

Documents provided by Waitan Garden homeowners. 2011–2013. Copies in authors' possession.
Documents provided by Wang Peirong. 2003–2013. Copies in authors' possession.
He Feng. Untitled personal account. 2013. Copy in authors' possession.

Interviews

Interview with a former cadre of the Shanghai Military Control Commission. February 20, 2004.
Interview with a government official in Shanghai Pudong District. June 10, 2009.
Interview with a judge working at the Second Shanghai Intermediate People's Court. November 3, 2003.
Interviews with anonymous Waitan Garden homeowners, 2010–2013.
Interviews with Han Junru. June 19, 2013.
Interview with Jin Baoqiang. June 18, 2013.
Interview with the head of a demolition company in Wuhan. City, June 18, 2013.
Interview with the head of the Letters and Visits Office in Shanghai. November 10, 2003.
Interview with the head of the Letters and Visits Office in Weishi County, Henan Province. November 25, 2003.
Interview with Tang Hanqing. Wuhan, Hubei Province, June 20, 2013.
Interview with Wang Peirong. Xuzhou, Jiangsu Province, November 16, 2003.
Interview with Yan Fengjun. Wuhan, Hubei Province, June 20, 2013.

Other Material

"Changjiang 'Waitan huayuan'shi ruhe jianshede" (How the Yangze River 'Waitan Garden' was constructed). 2010–2013. Material provided by the homeowner representatives of Waitan Garden.
Fenghuayuan Neighborhood Committee. "Wang Peirong jingji wenti diyi bufen" (The first part of Wang Peirong's economic problems). May 23, 2006. Copy in authors' possession.
———. "Wang Peirong deyeweihui jingji neimu" (The economic inside story of Wang's homeowners committee). August 2, 2007. Copy in authors' possession.
———. "Qing Wang Peirong buyao fugai juweihui gongbude zhengju cailiao" (Wang

Peirong please do not cover up the evidence exposed by the neighborhood committee). September 10, 2009. Copy in authors' possession.

"Gei Jiang Zemin zhuxi de sahngfangxin" (Petition to President Jiang Zemin [from Waitan Garden homeowners]). January 17, 2002. Copy in authors' possession.

"Gei renmin ribaode sahngfangxin" (Petition to the *People's Daily* [from Waitan Garden homeowners]). January 27, 2002. Copy in authors' possession.

"Gei Yu Zhengsheng shujide sahngfangxin" (Petition to Party secretary Yu Zhengsheng [from Waitan Garden homeowners]). January 17, 2002. Copy in authors' possession.

"Gei zhongyang jilu jiancha weiyuanhuide sahngfangxin" (Petition to the Central Commission for Discipline Inspection [from Waitan Garden homeowners]). February 1, 2002. Copy in authors' possession.

"Gei Zhu Rongji zonglide shangfangxin" (Letter [from an anonymous Waitan Garden homeowner] to Premier Zhu Rongji). January 1, 2002. Copy in authors' possession.

"Gonganbu guanyu gongbu guanzhi fangeming fenzi zanxing banfade tongzhi" (A circular of the Ministry of Public Security regarding publicizing an interim solution of forced education of counterrevolutionaries). 1952. Shanghai Archives, no. B1-1-1227.

PRC Justice Department. "Guanyu lushi tiaozheng gongzihe jibie wentide yijianha" (An opinion letter regarding adjusting lawyers' salaries and ranks). September 19, 1956. Shanghai Archives, no. A11-1-2-47.

"Shanghaishi lushi shoufei shixing banfa" (The provisional method of lawyers' charge of fee in Shanghai). April 2, 1956. Shanghai Archives, no. B2-1-38-16.

"Shanghaishi renmin fating fangeming panjueshu" (Verdicts against counterrevolutionaries of the Shanghai People's Court). October 1950–March 1951. Shanghai Archives, no. B1-2-30.

"Shanghaishi renmin fayuan chuxing biaozhun" (The Shanghai People's Court's guidelines for coping with cases). December 1949. Shanghai Archives, B1-2-308.

"Waitan huayuan goufanghu banqian anzhi shishi yijian" (Implementing opinions of the relocation and settlement of the Waitan Garden buyers). December 13, 2001. Copy in authors' possession.

"Waitan huayuan jiben qingkuang" (Basic information about Waitan Garden). November 22, 2001. Copy in authors' possession.

"Waitan huayuan wenti qingzhengfu sansier houxing" (The government needs to fully reconsider the issue of Waitan Garden before taking action). December 1, 2001. Documents provided by Waitan Garden homeowners.

"Waitan huayuan yezhu zhuanggao Wuhanshi zhengfu he Hanyangqu zhengfu" (Indictment of the Waitan Garden homeowners against the Wuhan and Hanyang governments). January 10, 2002. Copy in authors' possession.

Wang Peirong. "Bamian Liu Yongxiu changyishu" (A proposal to impeach Liu Yongxiu). August 2006. Copy in authors' possession.

———. "Yezhu weiyuanhui zhijuweihui degongkaixin" (The open letter of the homeowners committee to the neighborhood committee). August 25, 2006. Copy in authors' possession.

"Wuhan Waitan huayuan shenghui beiwanglu" (A life-and-ruin memorandum of the Wuhan Waitan Garden). December 13, 2001. Documents provided by Waitan Garden homeowners.

Yan, Fengjun. "Qianmin yezhu jiangjinjing qingyuan" (One thousand homeowners will petition Beijing). January 16, 2002. Copy in authors' possession.

"Yezhu husheng" (The voices of homeowners). November 25, 2001. Copy in authors' possession.

Zhang, Lijun. "Zhengque chuli waitan shijian, zhengfu qiemo yicuozaicuo" (Correctly dealing with the Waitan incident, the government must not commit mistakes one after another). December 23, 2001. Copy in authors' possession.

"Zhiwaitan huayuan chaiqian gongzuozu de weiwenxin" (A letter of sympathy to the Waitan Garden demolition work team). 2011–2013. Copy in authors' possession.

"Zhongyang renmin zhengfu zuigao fayuan laixin" (Letter from the Supreme Court of the Central People's Government). April 20, 1950. Shanghai Archives, B1-2-308-20.

"Zhuijiu falü zeren, yaoqiu yifa chaiqian" (Tracing legal responsibility and demanding relocation in accordance with the law). ca. November 20–December 30, 2001. Copy in authors' possession.

Secondary Sources

Alford, William P. "Of Arsenic and Old Laws: Looking Anew at Criminal Justice in Late Imperial China." *California Law Review* 72, no. 6 (December 1984): 1180–1256.

Archibold, Randal C. "Arizona Enacts Stringent Law on Immigration." *New York Times,* April 23, 2010.

"Arizona's Bad Immigration Law Takes Effect." *Washington Post,* September 20, 2012.

Armstrong, Paul. "Police Chief at Heart of Bo Xilai Scandal Jailed for 15 Years." September 24, 2012. http://www.cnn.com/2012/09/23/world/asia/china-wang-lijun-verdict.

Bai Xuemei. "Zhongguo chengshi zhuanxing dequshi, yingxiang yuzhengce zhixiang" (The trend, influence, and policy direction of China's urban transformation). In *Haiwai xuezhe shiye zhongde zhongguo chengshihua wenti* (The problems of Chinese urbanization from the perspectives of overseas scholars), ed. Tang Lei and Lu Zhe, 3–21. Beijing: Zhongguo shehui kexue chubanshe, 2013.

Bao Tong. "Buzai changhong dahei haishi jianchi changhong dahei? shibada youliangzhong xuanze" (To Continue the 'Singing the Red' and 'Smashing the Black' or Not: The Two Choices of the Party's Eighteenth National Congress). RFA.org, August 29, 2012. http://www.rfa.org/mandarin/pinglun/baotong/bt-08292012092352.html.

Bi Yuan. *Xu zizhi tongjian* (The continued comprehensive mirror for aid in government). Beijing: Zhonghua shujü, 1965.

"Bixu chedi gaige sifa gongzuo" (Must completely reform judicial work). *People's Daily*, August 17, 1952.

Boettke, Peter J. *Socialism and the Market: The Socialist Calculation Debate Revisited.* London: Psychology Press, 2000.

"Bogu Kailai zuizheng quezao yingzhuijiu guyi sharenzui" (There is sufficient evidence to try Bogu Kailai for intentional murder). Xinhua News Agency, August 10, 2012.

"Bo Xilai Scandal: How News Breaks in China." n.d. Committee to Protect Journals. http://cpj.org/reports/2013/03/challenged-china-media-censorship-timeline-bo-xilai.php.

"Bo Xilai Scandal: Timeline." November 11, 2013. BBC News. http://www.bbc.co.uk/news/world-asia-china-17673505.

"Bo Xilai tingshang paoxiao bugong" (Bo Xilai shouted in the court about the unfairness of the trial). October 26, 2013. http://news.creaders.net/china/2013/10/26/1309697.html.

Brady, Anne-Marie. *Marketing Dictatorship: Propaganda and Thought Work in Contemporary China.* Lanham, MD: Roman & Littlefield, 2009.

———. "The Beijing Olympics as a Campaign of Mass Distraction." In *China's Thought Management,* ed. Anne-Marie Brady, 11–35. London: Routledge, 2011.

Bray, David. *Social Space and Governance in Urban China: The Danwei System from Origins to Reform.* Stanford, CA: Stanford University Press, 2005.

Brook, Timothy. *The Chinese State in Ming Society.* London: Routledge, 2006.

Brugger, Bill. *China, Liberation and Transformation, 1942–1962.* Lanham, MD: Rowman & Littlefield, 1981.

Carlyle, R. W., and A. J. Carlyle. *A History of Medieval Political Theory in the West.* Vol. 6. New York: Barnes & Noble, 1936.

Cass, Ronald A. *The Rule of Law in America.* Baltimore: Johns Hopkins University Press, 2003.

"'Changjiang qingzhang zhalou' jinchen daxiang" (The cleanup and demolition of the buildings began this morning). *Xinmin wanbao,* January 25, 2001.

Chen Linghai. "Zhongguo gudai xiezhi shenpande guannian gouzao" (The conceptual construction of Xiezhi divine judgments in ancient China). *Xueshu yuekan* 4 (2013): 148–61.

Cheng, Sinkwan. Introduction to *Law, Justice, and Power: Between Reason and Will,* ed. Sinkwan Cheng, 1–21. Stanford, CA: Stanford University Press, 2004.

"Chengshi fangwu chaiqian guanli tiaoli" (The regulations regarding the management of urban housing demolition). http://www.gov.cn/gongbao/content/2001/content_60912.htm.

Cheung, Peter T. Y. "Intergovernmental Relations between Mainland China and the Hong Kong SAR." In *Public Administration in Southeast Asia: Thailand, Philippines, Malaysia, Hong Kong, and Macao,* ed. Even M. Berman, 255–82. Boca Raton, FL: CRC Press, 2010.

Chin, Josh. "'Rule of Law' or 'Rule by Law' in China: A Preposition Makes All the Difference." *Wall Street Journal,* October 20, 2014.

"China Investigates Ex-Security Chief Zhou Yongkang, *NYT* Says." *Bloomberg News,* December 16, 2013.

"Chongqing dahei meiyou xingxun bigong" (Chongqing has not used torture in Smashing the Black). *Shenzhen Evening News,* March 11, 2012.

"Chongqing dahei xingxun yi'an" (A remaining torture case of Chongqing's Smashing the Black). *Nanfang ribaowang,* November 4, 2013.

Chu, Godwin C. *The Great Wall in Ruins: Communication and Culture Change in China.* Albany: State University of New York Press, 1993.

———. "The Changing Concept of Zhong (Loyalty): Emerging New Chinese Political Culture." In *Chinese Political Culture, 1989–2000,* ed. Shiping Hua, 42–69. New York: M. E. Sharpe. 2001.

Conner, Alison W. "True Confession: Chinese Confessions Then and Now." In *The Limits of the Rule of Law in China,* ed. Karen G. Turner, James V. Feinerman, and R. Kent Guy, 132–62. Seattle: University of Washington Press, 2000.

The Constitution of the People's Republic of China. December 4, 1982. http://english. people.com.cn/constitution/constitution.html.

Criminal Procedure Law of the PRC. Promulgated 1979, rev. 1996 and 2012. http:// www.gov.cn/flfg/2012–03/17/content_2094354.htm.

The Criminal Verdict of the Second Shanghai Intermediate People's Court. October 25, 2003. http://www.hxzy365.com/2012/0628/286852.html.

"Danyuan fangdaomen dianfei zashou" (How can the antitheft doors and electricity be charged). *Metropolitan Morning News,* January 14, 2002.

Dardess, John. *Blood and History in China: The Donglin Faction and Its Repression, 1620–1627.* Honolulu: University of Hawaii Press, 1992.

"Daxue fujiaoshou chengjubao doushi" (College associate professor becomes Web site fighter). *Qilu Evening News,* October 2, 2008.

Deng Xiaoping wenxuan (The selected works of Deng Xiaoping). 3 vols. Beijing: Renmin chubanshe, 1938–1992.

Denyer, Simon. "Chinese Activist Xu Zhiyong Sentenced to Four Years in Prison." *Washington Post,* January 25, 2014.

Diao Jiecheng. *Renmin xinfang shilue* (A brief history of people's letters and visits). Beijing: Beijing jingji xueyuan chubanshe, 1996.

Dickson, Bruce J. "Cooptation and Corporatism in China: The Logic of Party Adaptation." *Political Science Quarterly* 115, no. 4 (Winter 2000–2001): 517–43.

———. *Wealth into Power: The Communist Party's Embrace of China's Private Sector.* Cambridge: Cambridge University Press, 2008.

———. "Updating the China Model." *Washington Quarterly* 34, no. 4 (Fall 2011): 39–58.

Dillon, Michael. *Contemporary China: An Introduction.* London: Routledge, 2008.

Ding Guofeng. "Kuangda fujiaoshou zhangtie 'xiaozibao' manma taren beisu feibang" (Associate professor of the Chinese University of Mining and Technology posted 'small-character posters' abusing others is charged with slander). *Legal Daily,* October 30, 2012.

———. "Fujiaoshou zhangtie 'daxiao zibao' feibang shuren huoxing" (Associate professor sentenced for posting "big- and small-character posters" to slander several people). *Legal Daily,* December 5, 2013.

Ding Xianjun and Yu Zuofeng, eds. *Wu Tingfang ji* (The collected works of Wu Tingfang). Beijing: Zhonghua shujü, 1993.

Dong Biwu. *Dongbiwu faxue wenji* (Selected legal works of Dong Biwu). Beijing: Falü chubanshe, 2001.

"Doushi" (Fighter). *Jiaren* 3 (2009): 13–17.

Duggan, Jennifer. "China Targets Lawyers in New Human Rights Crackdown." *Guardian,* July 13, 2015.

Dutton, Michael. *Policing Chinese Politics: A History.* Durham, NC: Duke University Press, 2005.

Eastman, Lloyd. *The Abortive Revolution: China under Nationalist Rule, 1927–1937.* Stanford, CA: Stanford University Press, 1974.

Economy, Elizabeth. "China's Imperial President: Xi Jinping Tightens His Grip." *Foreign Affairs,* November/December 2014. http://www.foreignaffairs.com/articles/142201/elizabeth-c-economy/chinas-imperial-president.

Editorial. *People's Daily,* September 23, 2012.

Editorial. *People's Daily,* July 23, 2013.

Editorial. *People's Daily,* August 27, 2013.

"Falü de shengli" (The triumph of the law). *China Youth Daily,* November 13, 1985.

Fan Zhongxin. 2012. "Fazhi zhuiqiuyu Chongqing moshide jiaoxun" (The pursuit of the rule of law and the lesson of the Chongqing paradium). Speech at Southwest University of Politics and Law, June 23. http://blog.sina.com.cn/s/blog_89aa0dcd010131d8.html (link blocked).

Fang, Qiang. "The Case of the Virgin Prostitute: Chinese Media and Chinese Legal Reform." *Stanford Journal of East Asian Affairs* 2, no. 1 (2002): 26–40.

———. "The Spirit of the Rule of Law in China." *Education about Asia* 13, no. 1 (Spring 2008): 36–41.

———. "Hot Potatoes: Chinese Complaint Systems from Early Times to the Late Qing (1898)." *Journal of Asian Studies* 64, no. 4 (November 2009): 1105–35.

———. "Lawlessness in the Cultural Revolution? The Case of a Historical Counterrevolutionary in 1969." *American Review of Chinese Studies* 12, no. 1 (2011): 33–52.

———. *Chinese Complaint Systems: Natural Resistance.* London: Routledge, 2013.

———. "Chinese Media and the Rule of Law: The Case of the *China Youth Daily.*" In *Modern Chinese Legal Reform: New Perspectives,* ed. Xiaobing Li and Qiang Fang, 27–58. Lexington: University Press of Kentucky, 2013.

———. "Legal Reform under Jiang Zemin." In *Evolution of Power: China's Struggle, Survival, and Success,* ed. Xiaobing Li and Xiansheng Tian, 227–50. Lanham, MD: Lexington Books, 2013.

———. *Zhongguo shangfang zhidu shihua (1100 BCE–1949)* (A short history of Chinese petition). Beijing: China Youth Press, 2013.

———. "Resilient or Decaying? The Case of China's Administrative Litigation." *Modern Chinese Studies* 2 (2014): 93–118.

Fang, Qiang, and Roger V. Des Forges. "Were Chinese Rulers above the Law? Toward a Theory of the Rule of Law in China from Early Times to 1949 CE." *Stanford Journal of International Law* 44, no. 1 (Fall 2007): 101–46.

"Fanghong hedaoli debieshu" (The villas built on the riverbed of flood control). In *Xinwen beihou* (Behind the news), 140–42. Beijing: Renmin wenxue chubanshe, 2005. http://read.jd.com/392/17168.html.

"Fangwu hezuo shiyong xieyishu" (A contract of collaborative use of building). December 2005. Copy provided by Wang Peirong.

"Feichu laojiao zhidu, zhongguo fazhi gengjiankang" (Abolishing the *laojiao* system, Chinese legal system will be more healthy). *China Youth Daily*, December 29, 2013.

Fitzgerald, John. *Awakening China: Politics, Culture, and Class in the Nationalist Revolution*. Stanford, CA: Stanford University Press, 1996.

Folsom, Ralph H., John H. Minan, and Lee Ann Otto. *Law and Politics in the People's Republic of China in a Nutshell*. St. Paul, MN: West Group, 1992.

Fu, H. L. "Punishing for Profit: Profitability and Rehabilitation in a Laojiao Institution." In *Engaging the Law in China: State, Society, and Possibilities for Justice*, ed. Neil Jeffrey Diamant, Stanley B. Lubman, and Kevin J. O'Brien, 213–30. Stanford, CA: Stanford University Press, 2005.

Fu Yuanyuan. "Zhengfu weifa xingzheng: Weixie yezhu jingguo" (The illicit administration of the government: A homeowner's experience of government threats). January 9, 2002. Copy in authors' possession.

Fu, Zhengyuan. *Autocratic Tradition and Chinese Politics*. Cambridge: Cambridge University Press, 1993.

Gallagher, Mary E. "Use the Law as Your Weapon! Institutional Change and Legal Mobilization in China." In *Engaging the Law in China: State, Society, and Possibilities for Justice*, ed. Neil Jeffrey Diamant, Stanley B. Lubman, and Kevin J. O'Brien, 54–83. Stanford, CA: Stanford University Press, 2005.

———. "Mobilizing the Law in China: 'Informed Disenchantment' and the Development of Legal Consciousness." *Law and Society Review* 40, no. 4 (2006): 783–816.

Gao Hua. *Hongtaiyang shiruhe shengqide* (How did the Red Sun rise). Hong Kong: Hong Kong Chinese University Press, 2000.

Gao, Zhisheng. *A China More Just: My Fight as a Rights Lawyer in the World's Largest Communist State*. Sydney: Broad Press, 2007.

"Gaoguan lushi wunai piaobo" (The lawyer who accuses officials has to wander aimlessly). *Southern Weekend*, February 7, 2002.

Garnaut, John. *The Rise and Fall of the House of Bo: How a Murder Exposed the Cracks in China's Leadership*. Harmondsworth: Penguin Books, 2012.

Glosser, Susan L. *Chinese Visions of Family and State, 1915–1953*. Berkeley and Los Angeles: University of California Press, 2003.

Gong Pixiang, ed. *Dangdai zhongguo de falü geming* (The legal revolution of modern China). Beijing: Falu chubanshe, 1999.

"Gongqingtuan yinggai weiwunian pufa jiaoyu douzheng" (The Communist Youth League should struggle with the five-year enhancement of the public's awareness of the law). *China Youth Daily*, January 9, 1986.

"Guanyu zhenya fanggeming huodongde zhishi" (Directives regarding suppressing counterrevolutionary activities). October 10, 1950. http://cpc.people.com.cn/GB/64162/64165/70486/70496/4844076.html.

Gu Zhijian. "Wang Peirong beipanxing liuxia jiaoxun henduo" (Wang's imprisonment leaves many lessons). *Lushi zhichuang,* January 15, 2013. http://blog.sina.com.cn/s/blog_413dc44b0101714y.html (link inactive or blocked).

"Guanyu Li Zhuang, wugaota, woyuanyi chengdan falu zeren" (Regarding Li Zhuang, I want to admit the legal responsibility for falsely accusing him). *Legal Daily,* March 25, 2013.

Guo Guangyun. *Wogao Chengweigao: Yige gognmin yu yige shengwei shuji de zhangzheng* (I accuse Cheng Weugao: A war between a citizen and a provincial party secretary). Beijing: Dongfang chubansh, 2004.

Guo Guosong, and Zeng Min. "Siqiu yishu" (The will of a prisoner on death row). *Southern Weekend,* August 23, 2000.

Han Feizi. With annotations by Chen Bingcai. Beijing: Zhonghua shujü, 2007.

"Haobu dongyao jianchi dangdui zhengfa gongzuode lingdao" (Unequivocally safeguard the Party's leadership of politics and law). *People's Daily,* January 9, 2014.

Harrison, Brigid, and Thomas Dye. *Power and Society: An Introduction to the Social Sciences.* Boston: Cengage Learning, 2013.

He Lei. "Xiaoqu yideng shoufei meiyou yideng fuwu Xuzhou yezhu zhuanggao guojiaji dajiang" (First-class charge does not have first-class service, Xuzhou homeowners suing the national award). *China Youth Daily,* October 26, 2004.

He Renmin. "Wuhanren danzizhuang, zhuzhai jianzai changjiangshang" (Wuhan residents are bold and build residence on the Yangze River). *China Economic Times,* December 23, 2000.

He Weifang. "Fuzhan junren jinfayuan" (Military veterans enter the court). *Southern Weekend,* January 2, 1998.

———. *Yunsong zhengyide fangshi* (The way of transporting justice). Shanghai: Shanghai sanlian shudian chubanshe, 2002.

———. "Li Zhuang beipanxing, juguo danyou" (The whole nation worries about the punishment of Li Zhuang). He Weifang's blog, January 17, 2010. http://blog.sina.com.cn/s/blog_488663200100h2g0.html.

———. *In the Name of Justice: Striving for the Rule of Law in China.* Washington, DC: Brookings Institution Press, 2012.

"Hedaoli jianqi shangpinlou" (Commercial buildings were constructed on the riverbed). *Jiaodian fangtan* (Focal interview), November 19, 2001. http://www.cctv.com.cn/news/china/20011119/425.html.

Hessler, Peter. "Return to River Town." *National Geographic,* March 2013, http://ngm.nationalgeographic.com/2013/03/fuling-china/hessler-text.

Ho, Norman P. "Organized Crime in China: The Chongqing Crackdown." In *Law and Policy for China's Market Socialism,* ed. John Garrick, 202–14. London: Routledge, 2012.

Ho, Pin, and Wenguang Huang. *A Death in the Lucky Holiday Hotel: Murder, Money, and an Epic Power Struggle in China.* New York: Public Affairs, 2013.

Huang Guangming and Chen Hai. "Yige 'guaitai'de shengyusi" (The birth and death of a "freak"). *Southern Weekend,* January 24, 2002.

Huang Keru. "Guai: Fenghua kejiao anju xiaoqu junan'an" (Strange: It is difficult to stay calm in Fenghuayuan). *Zhongguo shehuibao,* November 27, 2003.

Huang, Philip. *Code, Custom, and Legal Practice in China.* Stanford, CA: Stanford University Press, 2001.

Huang Weiming. *Dangdai zhongguo sixing panjue de biyaoxing* (The value of the death sentence reprieve in contemporary China). Beijing: Kexue chubanshe, 2007.

Huang, Yanzhong. *Governing Health in Contemporary China.* London: Routledge, 2013.

"Hubeisheng yuanfushengzhang beikaichu dangji hegongzhi" (Former vice governor of Hubei Province was expelled from the Party and discharged from office). *Gansu Daily,* September 26, 2000.

Hulsewé, A. F. P. "Ch'in and Han Law." In *The Cambridge History of China: The Ch'in and Han Empires, 221 B.C.–220 A.D.,* ed. Denis Twitchett and Michael Loewe, 524–29. Cambridge: Cambridge University Press, 1986.

Human Rights Watch report. January 31, 2008. https://www.hrw.org/legacy/english-wr2k8/docs/2008/01/31/china17604.htm.

"The Inside Stories of Bo-Wang's Billion Dollars: The Heartache of the Court." March 20, 2013. http://boxun.com/news/gb/china/2013/03/201303200445.shtml#.UV5ih8rna0M.

"Interview between Lawyer Wang Wanqiong and Gong Gangmo." Li Zhuang's blog, August 27, 2012. http://blog.sina.com.cn/s/blog_89aa0dcd01019hwz.html.

Jacobs, Andrew, and Chris Buckley. "China Targeting Rights Lawyers in a Crackdown." *New York Times,* July 22, 2015.

Jacques, Martin. *When China Rules the World: The End of the Western World and the Birth of a New Global Order.* New York: Penguin Books, 2012.

Ji Shuoming. "Zhuanggao zhou zhengyide lushi Zheng Enchong zhangwo Chen Liangyu cailiao" (Zheng Enchong, the lawyer who has possessed materials against Chen Liangyu, has been prosecuted). *Asiaweek,* October 1, 2006.

"Jianchi fazhi fanfu, jianshe lianjie zhengzhi" (Persisting in opposing corruption by the law and constructing clean politics). *People's Daily,* September 23, 2012.

Jiang Meili. "Zhiquanguo lushijiede gongkaixin" (A public letter to all Chinese lawyers). November 1, 2003. Boxun.com, http://www.peacehall.com/news/gb/china/2003/11/200311011304.shtml.

Jiang Ming'an. "Shanyong xianyou weiquan ziyuan hewanshan xianxing quanli baozhang zhidu: Wang Peirong weiquan jinglide qishi" (Properly using current rights defending resources and perfecting current rights protection systems: The inspiration of Wang Peirong's experience in safeguarding rights). *Beida gongfawang,* December 1, 2006. http://www.148cn.org/data/2006/1201/article_29813.htm.

Jia Yue, "Xi Jinping de fazhiguan" (Xi Jinping's comprehension of the rule of law). People.com.cn, October 21, 2014. http://politics.people.com.cn/GB/n/2014/1021/c1001-25878990.html.

Jiang, Wenran. "Prosperity at the Expense of Equality: Migrant Workers Are Falling Behind in Urban China's Rise." In *Confronting Discrimination and Inequality in China: Chinese and Canadian Perspectives*, ed. Errol P. Mendes and Sakunthala Srighanthan, 16–29. Ottawa: University of Ottawa Press, 2009.

Jiang Zemin. *Jiang Zemin wenxuan* (Selected works of Jiang Zemin). Beijing: Renmin chubanshe, 2006.

Jiang Zeming. "Gaojü Dengxiaoping lilunweida qizhi, bayouzhongguo tese shehui zhuyi shiye quanmian tuixiang ershiyi shiji" (Carrying high the flag of the Deng Xiaoping theory and pushing Chinese special socialism into the twenty-first century). *People's Daily*, September 22, 1997.

"Jianshebu quxiao Fenghuayuan xiaoqu guoyou chenghao" (The Ministry of Construction withdrew the national excellence title from Fenghuayuan). *China Youth Daily*, January 24, 2005.

Jianzheng Wanglijun (Witnessing Wang Lijun). June 25, 2012. https://docs.google.com/document/d/1zpAvcgSy6gO8RG8bJXi2DBMucVkYYOlWRaJ0uB1Z5Q8/edit.

Jin, Qiu. *The Culture of Power: The Lin Biao Incident in the Cultural Revolution*. Stanford, CA: Stanford University Press, 1999.

Jin Zhong. "Shen Ting meiyou shuowande gushi" (The words that Shen Ting has not finished). Boxun.com, January 5, 2008. http://www.boxun.com/news/gb/pubvp/2008/01/200801051820.shtml.

Jingji banxiaoshi (Economic half hour). CCTV, November 21, 2008.

Johnson, Ian. "On Social Media, Chinese Ponder Crime Fighter's Fate." *New York Times*, February 8, 2012.

Jones, William C. "The Constitution of the People's Republic of China." In *Law in the People's Republic of China: Commentary, Readings, and Materials*, ed. Ralph H. Folsom and John H. Minan, 39–49. Leiden: Martinus Nijhoff, 1989.

"Jubao zhihou" (After exposing). *Nandu zhoukan*, November 14, 2010.

Ke, Guo. "Newspapers: Changing Roles." In *New Media for a New China*, ed. James F. Scotton and William A. Hachten, 43–60. Hoboken, NJ: Wiley-Blackwell, 2010.

Guo, Sujian. *Chinese Politics and Government: Power, Ideology, and Organization*. London: Routledge, 2009.

Keishu Saneto. *Zhongguoren liuxue ribenshi* (History of Chinese students in Japan). Beijing: shenghuo dushu xinzhi sanlian shudian, 1983.

Keith, Ronald C., Zhiqiu Lin, and Shumei Hou. *China's Supreme Court*. London: Routledge, 2013.

Kong, Hanbing. "The Transplantation and Entrenchment of the Soviet Economic Model in China." In *China Learns from the Soviet Union, 1949–Present*, ed. Thomas P. Bernstein and Hua-yu Li, 153–66. Lanham, MD: Rowman & Littlefield, 2010.

Kong Pu. "Gong Ganghua: Dubuqi Li Zhuang, women dingbuzhule" (Gong Ganghua: Sorry to Li Zhuang, We Could No Longer Stand). *Xinjingbao* (New Beijing newspaper), December 30, 2012.

Koskenniemi, Martti. "Legal Universalism: Between Morality and Power in a World of States." In *Law, Justice, and Power: Between Reason and Will,* ed. Sinkwan Cheng, 46–69. Stanford, CA: Stanford University Press, 2004.

Ku, Hok Bun. *Moral Politics in a South Chinese Village: Responsibility, Reciprocity, and Resistance.* Lanham, MD: Rowman & Littlefield, 2003.

Lafraniere, Sharon. "People's Congress Gets to Work in China." *New York Times,* March 4, 2010.

Lafraniere, Sharon, and Jonathan Ansfield. "Crime Crackdown Adds to Scandal Surrounding Former Chinese Official." *New York Times,* March 26, 2012.

Lam, Willy Wo-lap. "Zhao Ziyang's Contributions to Reform in Historical Perspective." In *Zhao Ziyang and China's Political Future,* ed. Guoguang Wu and Helen Lansdowne, 151–63. London: Routledge, 2008.

Lee, Ching Kwan. *Against the Law: Labor Protests in China's Rustbelt and Sunbelt.* Berkeley and Los Angeles: University of California Press, 2007.

Lenin, Vladimir. *The State and Revolution: The Vulgarisation of Marxism by the Opportunists.* 1917. http://www.marxists.org/archive/lenin/works/1917/staterev/ch06.htm.

Li Bin and Yang Weihan. "Zaifalude tianpingshang: Wang Lijun anjian tingshen jianqing shimo" (On the scale of law: A complete story of the Wang Lijun case and the court hearing), Xinhua News Net, September 19, 2012, http://news.xinhuanet.com/legal/2012-09/19/c_113136404.htm.

Li, Cheng. *China's Leaders: The New Generation.* Lanham, MD: Rowman & Littlefield, 2001.

———. "Cooling Shanghai Fever: Macroeconomic Control and Its Geopolitical Implications." *China Leadership Monitor,* no. 12 (2004): 1–12. http://www.hoover.org/sites/default/files/uploads/documents/clm12_lc.pdf.

———. "Emerging Partisanship within the Chinese Communist Party." *Orbis,* Summer 2005, 387–400.

———. "China's Inner-Party Democracy: Toward a System of 'One Party, Two Factions'?" *China Brief* 6, no. 24 (December 2006): 8–11.

———. "Was the Shanghai Gang Shanghaied? The Fall of Chen Liangyu and the Survival of Jiang Zemin's Faction." *China Leadership Monitor,* no. 20 (2007): 11–19.

Li Hanxiong. "'Sange daibiao' sixiangde hexin shidaibiao guangda renmin qunzhongde zuigenben liyi" (The core of the 'Three Represents' is to represent the most fundamental interests of the masses). *People's Daily,* January 6, 2002.

Li, Huaiyin. *Village China under Socialism and Reform: A Micro-History, 1948–2008.* Stanford, CA: Stanford University Press, 2009.

Li Jun and Joseph Y. S. Cheng. "Cadre Performance Appraisal and Fabrication of Economic Achievement in Chinese Officialdom." In *China: A New Stage of Development for an Emerging Superpower,* ed. Joseph Y. S. Cheng, 117–48. Hong Kong: City University of Hong Kong Press, 2012.

Li, Lianjiang, Mingxin Liu, and Kevin O'Brien. "Petitioning Beijing: The High Tide of 2003–2006." *China Quarterly* 210 (June 2012): 313–34.

Li Peilin. *Dangdai zhongguo chengshihua jiqi yingxiang* (Urbanization in modern China and its effects). Beijing: Shehui kexue wenxian chubanshe, 2013.

Li Rui. *Lirui lunshuo wenxuan* (Arguments of Li Rui). Beijing: Zhongguo shehui kexue chubanshe, 1998.

Li Wenjie. "Bamingdai wenxue dairu diyude yinhun: Hongwu wenziyu" (The ghost that brings Ming literature into hell: The literary inquisition in the Hongwu reign). *Journal of Simao Teachers College* 26, no. 1 (February 2010): 68–71.

Li, Xiaobing, and Qiang Fang. "Introduction: Legal Reforms in Twentieth-Century China." In *Modern Chinese Legal Reform: New Perspectives,* ed. Xiaobing Li and Qiang Fang, 1–26. Lexington: University Press of Kentucky, 2013.

"Li Zhuang' an ershen panjue quanwen" (Complete verdict of the Li Zhuang case). Chongqing First Intermediate People's Court, March 8, 2010. http://182.48.103.149/upload/201003085841013.pdf.

Li Zhuang's blog. http://blog.sina.com.cn/s/blog_89aa0dcd0101dihf.html.

Liang, Bin. *The Changing Chinese Legal System, 1978–Present: Centralization of Power and Rationalization of the Legal System.* London: Routledge, 2008.

Liang, Zhiping. "Explicating 'Law': A Comparative Perspective of Chinese and Western Legal Culture." *Journal of Chinese Law* 3 (1989): 55–91.

Liao Xin. "Chongqing lawjingcha beizhi cengshe Wen Qiang'an" (Old Chongqing policeman was regarded as being involved in the case of Wen Qiang). *Nanfang dushibao,* December 13, 2012.

"Liaoning zhuanhe minzhong zhengfu menqian xiagui" (People from Liaoning Zhuanghe knelt down in front of the government gate). *Nanfang dushibao,* April 13, 2010.

Lieberthal, Kenneth. *Governing China: From Revolution through Reform.* New York: W. W. Norton, 1995.

Lin Qian. *Chuantong zhongguode quanyufa* (The power and law of traditional China). Beijing: Falu chubanshe, 2013.

Lin Ji. *Juzhengzhuan* (A biography of Ju Zheng). Hubei: Hubei renmin chubanshe, 1993.

Lin Ping. "Yu Qiyi feizhengchang siwangan baolu zhonggong 'shuanggui' tizhide canren heweifa" (The abnormal death of Yu Qiyi exposes the brutality and law violations of the CCP's "dual designation"). Free Asia Radio, October 24, 2013.

Ling Bo. "Huajie dongqian maodun yicheng dangwu zhiji" (The top issue is to dissolve the contradiction of urban disposal). *Shanghai xinfang* 10–12 (2003): 11.

Liu Chonglai, Xu Shirui, and Zheng Jiafu, eds. *Mingshilu leizuan: Sifa jianchajuan* (Classified edition of the veritable record of the Ming: Volume of judiciary and inspection). Wuhan: Wuhan chubanshe, 1994.

Liu Qingsong. "Yituoshi laojiao'an dangshizhede koushu" (The dictation of the person sentenced to labor camp in the case of a lump of waste). *Oral China,* May 19, 2014. http://liuqingsong.blog.ifeng.com/article/32950615.html.

Liu Zehua, Wang Maohe, and Wang Lanzhong. *Zhuanzhi quanli yuzhongguo shehui* (Authoritarian power and Chinese society). Tianjin: Tianjin guji chubanshe, 2005.

"Liuwei qinli Zheng Enchongan xinwen jizhede shengming" (The statement of six journalists who have experienced the case of Zheng Enchong). Kaidi shequ, January 5, 2008. http://www.aboluowang.com/2008/0105/69885.html.

Locke, John. *Two Treatises of Government.* London: Whitmore & Fenn, 1821.

Lu Shilun. *Lienin falu sixiangshi* (The history of Lenin's thought). Beijing: Falu chubanshe, 2000.

Lundmark, Thomas. *Power and Rights in US Constitutional Law.* Oxford: Oxford University Press, 2008.

"Lüshi yijianshu" (The lawyers' opinions). December 7, 2001. Copy in author's possession. This document is also sometimes referred to as "Lüshi shitiao" (The lawyers' ten points).

Ma, Stephen K. "'Policing the Police': A Perennial Challenge for China's Anti-Corruption Agencies." In *Preventing Corruption in Asia: Instituting Design and Policy Capacity,* ed. Ting Gong and Stephen K. Ma, 81–96. London: Routledge, 2012.

MacCormack, Geoffrey. *The Spirit of Traditional Chinese Law.* Athens: University of Georgia Press, 1996.

MacFarquhar, Roderick, and Michael Schoenhals. *Mao's Last Revolution.* Cambridge, MA: Harvard University Press, 2006.

Mao Zedong. "Zhongguo shehui gejieji defenxi" (An analysis of China's social classes). December 1925. In *Maozedong xuanji* (Selected works of Mao Zedong), vol. 1. http://www.qstheory.cn/zl/llzz/mzdxjd1j/200906/t20090630_4006.htm.

———. "Lun fandui riben diguozhuyi decelue" (The tactics against the Japanese imperialists). December 27, 1935. In *Maozedong xuanji* (Selected works of Mao Zedong), vol. 1. http://www.qstheory.cn/zl/llzz/mzdxjd1j/200906/t20090630_4031.htm.

———. "Bixu zhongshi renmin qunzhong laixin" (We must pay serious attention to the popular masses' letters). 1951. In *Mao Zedong wenji* (Collected works of Mao Zedong), ed. Zhonggong zhongyang wenxian yanjiushi (Archive Research Unit of the Central Chinese Communist Party), 6:164–65. Beijing: Renmin chubanshe, 2001.

———. "Guanyu zhengque chuli renmin neibu maodun" (Correctly dealing with people's internal contradictions). 1957. In *Mao Zedong wenji* (Collected works of Mao Zedong), ed. Zhonggong zhongyang wenxian yanjiushi (Archive Research Unit of the Central Chinese Communist Party), 7:205–6. Beijing: Renmin chubanshe, 2001.

Marx, Karl. *The Civil War in France.* Gloucester: Dodo Press, 2009.

Meisner, Maurice. *The Deng Xiaoping Era: An Inquiry into the Fate of Chinese Socialism, 1978–1994.* New York: Hill & Wang, 1996.

———. *Mao's China and After: A History of the People's Republic.* New York: Free Press, 1999.

Meng Zhen. "Minshi qisuzhuang" (Indictment of civil cases). July 2, 2006. Copy in authors' possession.

"Mingaoguan shinian pandian" (A ten-year study of people accusing officials). *China Youth Daily,* April 16, 1999.

Minzner, Carl. "Xinfang: An Alternative to the Formal Chinese Legal System." *Stanford Journal of International Law* 42, no. 1 (2006): 103–79.

Miu Liyan. "Shimin zhuanggao shizhengfu, kaiting zhiqian dajiaofeng" (Urbanite accusing the city government, the conflicts before the court opening). *Yangzi wanbao,* August 5, 2003.

Montesquieu. *The Spirit of Laws*. New York: Colonial Press, 1900.

Murong Xuecun. "Xi's Selective Punishment." *New York Times,* January 16, 2015.

Nathan, Andrew J. *Chinese Democracy*. New York: Columbia University Press, 1985.

———. "China's Changing of the Guard: Authoritarian Resilience." *Journal of Democracy* 14, no. 1 (January 2003): 6–18.

Ni Zhigang. "Li Zhuang jiangshu qiannian xierenzuishu cangtoushi shijian shimo" (Li Zhuang talks about the complete incident of his confession and covert poem in 2010). *Xiaoxiang chenbao,* November 28, 2012.

O'Brien, Kevin J. "Rightful Resistance." *World Politics* 49, no. 1 (October 1996): 31–55.

O'Brien, Kevin J., and Lianjiang Li. "The Politics of Lodging Complaints in Rural China." *China Quarterly,* no. 143 (September 1995): 756–83.

———. "Suing the Local State: Administrative Litigation in Rural China." In *Engaging the Law in China: State, Society, and Possibilities for Justice,* ed. Neil Jeffrey Diamant, Stanley B. Lubman, and Kevin J. O'Brien, 31–53. Stanford, CA: Stanford University Press, 2005.

———. *Rightful Resistance in Rural China*. Cambridge: Cambridge University Press, 2006.

Osnos, Evan. "China's Crisis." *New Yorker,* April 30, 2012.

———. "NYU, China, and Chen Guangcheng." *New York Times,* June 17, 2013.

Page, Jeremy. "Chongqing Mayor Reveals Role in Drama outside U.S. Consulate." *Wall Street Journal,* March 6, 2012.

———. "Bo Xilai Found Guilty, Sentenced to Life in Prison." *Wall Street Journal,* September 22, 2013.

Peerenboom, Randall. *China's Long March toward Rule of Law*. Cambridge: Cambridge University Press, 2002.

———. "Law and Development of Constitutional Democracy: Is China a Problem Case?" *Annals of the American Academy of Political and Social Science* 603 (January 2006): 192–99.

———. "Judicial Independence in China: Common Myths and Unfounded Assumptions." In *Judicial Independence in China: Lessons for Global Rule of Law Promotion,* ed. Randall Peerenboom, 69–94. Cambridge: Cambridge University Press, 2010.

Pei, Minxin. *China's Trapped Transition: The Limits of Developmental Autocracy*. Cambridge, MA: Harvard University Press, 2009.

———. "Is CCP Rule Fragile or Resilient?" *Journal of Democracy* 23, no. 1 (January 2012): 27–42.

Philips, Ellen. *Shocked, Appalled, and Dismayed: How to Write Letters of Complaint That Get Results*. New York: Vintage Books, 1997.

"Political Crisis in Beijing." *Straits Times* (Singapore), July 10, 2004.

Potter, Pitman. *The Chinese Legal System: Globalization and Local Legal Culture*. London: Routledge, 2001.

"Profile: Bo Xilai." September 22, 2013. BBC News. http://www.bbc.co.uk/news/world-asia-china-19709555.

Qian Haoping. "Zhengfawei shujiyu gong'an juzhangde hehe fefen" (The union and breach between the heads of the political and legal commissions and the heads of the police bureau). *Southern Weekend,* November 18, 2011.

Qiang Jianghai and Zhong Hui. "Yeweihui quzhu juweihui" (Homeowners committee expelling neighborhood committee). *Jiating,* December 2006, 10–12.

Qiao Long. "Xuzhou kuangda jiaoshou Wang Peirong beizhi feibang beipanxing yinianban" (Professor Wang Peirong at Chinese University of Mining and Technology was accused of slander and sentenced to eighteen months). Free Asia Radio Station, January 8, 2013.

Qiu Dengchang. "Wosheng xinfang gongzuo mianlin de xinxingshi" (The new complaint situation in our province). *Xuexi luntan* 2 (2000): 39–40.

"Qizhi xianmingdi fandui dongluan" (Unswervingly opposing the turmoil). *People's Daily,* April 26, 1989.

Ren, Xin. *Tradition of the Law and Law of the Tradition: Law, State, and Social Control in China.* Westport, CT: Greenwood Publishing, 1997.

Roberts, Dexter. "Almost Half of China's Rich Want to Emigrate." *Bloomberg Business News,* September 15, 2014.

Roney, Tyler. "Lawyers, Activists Condemn Xu Zhiyong's Trial." *The Diplomat,* January 23, 2014. http://thediplomat.com/2014/01/lawyers-activists-condemn-xuzhiyongs-trial.

Rowe, William T. *Hankow: Conflict and Community in a Chinese City, 1796–1895.* Stanford, CA: Stanford University Press, 1989.

———. *Saving the World: Chen Hongmou and Elite Consciousness in Eighteenth Century China.* Stanford, CA: Stanford University Press, 2002.

Ruijinxian renmin fayuan (Ruijin County Court), ed. *Zhonghua suweiai gongheguo shenpan ziliao xuanbian* (Selected judging materials of the Chinese Soviet Republic). Beijing: Renmin fayuan chubanshe, 1991.

Scotton, James F. "The Impact of New Media." In *New Media for a New China,* ed. James F. Scotton and William A. Hachten, 28–42. Hoboken, NJ: Wiley-Blackwell, 2010.

Shambaugh, David. "The Illusion of Chinese Power." *National Interest,* June 25, 2014. www.nationalinterest.org/feature/the-illusion-chinese-power-10739.

———. "The Coming Chinese Crackup." *Wall Street Journal,* March 6, 2015.

Shangshu (The ancient book). Edited by Liang Hong. Hunan: Shidai wenyi chubanshe, 2003.

Shao, Qin. *Shanghai Gone: Domicide and Defiance in a Chinese Megacity.* Lanham, MD: Rowman & Littlefield, 2013.

Shen Jiaben. *Jiyi wencun* (Jiyi's remaining works). Taiwan: Shangwu yinshuguan, 1976.

Shen Xinwang. "Li Zhuangan quancheng neimu pilu: Wang Lijuncheng yaonaqi shayi jingbai" (Exposure of the entire internal story of the Li Zhuang case: Wang Lijun claims that he is being punished as an example), *Zhongguo xinwen zhoukan,* December 21, 2012.

Shen, Yuanyuan. 2000. "Conceptions and Receptions of Legality: Understanding the Complexity of Law Reform in Modern China." In *The Limits of the Rule of Law in*

China, ed. Karen G. Turner, James V. Feinerman, and R. Kent Guy, 20–44. Seattle: University of Washington Press, 2000.

"Shuizaiwan chuer faner" (Who is playing with the inconsistency). *Jiangnan shibao,* October 24, 2003.

Sima Guang. *Zizhi tongjian* (Comprehensive mirror for aid in government). 294 vols. Beijing: Zhonghua shujü, 1956.

Sima Qian. *Shiji* (History record). 294 vols. Beijing: Zhonghua shujü, 1975.

Simons, William B., and Stephen White, eds. *The Party Statutes of the Communist World.* Leiden: Brill, 1984.

Solinger, Dorothy J. *Contesting Citizenship in Urban China: Peasant Migrants, the State, and the Logic of the Market.* Berkeley and Los Angeles: University of California Press, 1999.

Solomon, Peter H., Jr. *Soviet Criminal Justice under Stalin.* Cambridge: Cambridge University Press, 1996.

Solomon, Richard H. *Mao's Revolution and the Chinese Political Culture.* Berkeley and Los Angeles: University of California Press, 1971.

Spader, Dean. 1984. "Rule of Law v. Rule of Man: The Search for the Golden Zigzag between Conflicting Fundamental Values." *Journal of Criminal Justice* 12, no. 4 (1984): 379–94.

Spence, Jonathan. *Treason by the Book.* Harmondsworth: Penguin Books, 2002.

———. *Mao Zedong: A Life.* Harmondsworth: Penguin Books, 2006.

Su, Yang. "Mass Killings in the CR: A Study of Three Provinces." In *The Chinese Cultural Revolution as History,* ed. Joseph W. Esherick, Paul G. Pickowicz, and Andrew G. Walder, 96–123. Stanford, CA: Stanford University Press, 2006.

Sun Yat-sen. *Sunzhongshan quanji* (The complete works of Sun Yat-sen). 11 vols. Beijing: Renmin chubanshe, 1981.

———. *Sunzhongshan xuanji* (The selected works of Sun Yat-sen). Beijing: Renmin chubanshe, 1981.

Tang, Didi. "Chinese Newspapers Row Sparks Journalist Strikes, Protests against Censorship of *Southern Weekly.*" *Huffington Post,* January 7, 2013. The *Huffington Post* link is no longer active, but an abstract of sorts can be found at http://news-lanc.com/chinese-newspaper-row-sparks-journalist-strikes-protests-against-censorship-of-southern-weekly.

Tanner, Harold M. *Strike Hard: Anti-Crime Campaigns and Chinese Criminal Justice, 1979–1985.* Ithaca, NY: Cornell University Press, 1999.

Tarrow, Sidney. "Prologue: The New Contentious Politics in China: Poor and Blank or Rich and Complex?" In *Popular Protest in China,* ed. Kevin O'Brien, 1–10. Cambridge, MA: Harvard University Press, 2009.

Tsai, Kellee S. "Adaptive Informal Institutions and Endogenous Institutional Change in China." *World Politics* 59 (October 2006): 116–41, 118.

———. *Capitalism without Democracy: The Private Sector in Contemporary China.* Ithaca, NY: Cornell University Press, 2007.

Tuo Tuo, Yuan. *Song shi* (History of the Song dynasty). Beijing: Zhong Hua Shu Jü, 1977.

Turner, Karen. "Rule of Law Ideals in Early China?" *Columbia Journal of Chinese Law* 6, no.1 (Spring 1992): 1–35.

Unger, Jonathan. *The Transformation of Rural China.* Armonk, NY: M. E. Sharpe, 2002.

———. "The Cultural Revolution at the Grass Roots." *China Journal* 57 (January 2007): 109–37.

van de Ven, Hans. *War and Nationalism in China, 1925–1945.* London: Routledge, 2003.

Wakeman, Frederic, Jr. *Policing Shanghai, 1927–1937.* Berkeley and Los Angeles: University of California Press, 1995.

———. *Spymaster Dai Li and the Chinese Secret Service.* Berkeley and Los Angeles: University of California Press, 2003.

Wang Celai. "Yangnaiwu yu xiaobaicai an" (The case of Yang Naiwu and Xiao Baicai). Beijing: Zhongguo jiancha chubanshe, 2002.

Wang Haitao. "Bo Xilai kuxing shengguo zhazidong" (Bo Xilai's torture worse than Zhazidong). Kaifangwang, April 5, 2012. http://www.open.com.hk/content.php?id=725#.VUgRi2a4Nmt.

Wang, Hui. *China's New Order: Society, Politics, and Economy in Transition.* Cambridge, MA: Harvard University Press, 2003.

"Wang Peirong shiyeji" (The record of Wang Peirong's unemployment). *Shidai zhoukan,* February 11, 2010.

Wang Sixin and Chen Xie. "Wuhan waitan huayuan buneng 'yizha bailiao'" (Wuhan Waitan Garden should not end with an explosion). *Workers' Daily,* January 29, 2001.

Wang Yelin. *Zhongguo wenziyu* (Literary inquisition in China). Guangzhou: Huacheng chubanshe, 2007.

Wei Hongqian. "Juweihui zhuren wu'fa' bamian" (Is there no law that can impeach the head of the neighborhood committee). *Jiancha ribao,* August 17, 2009.

Wen Jian. "Zhuanggao wujiguan guansi tuzhongzhi, daxue jiaoshou shiyao mingaoguan" (The lawsuits were terminated after suing five government organs, the professor vowed to lodge lawsuits of commoners against officials). *Nanfangwang,* November 4, 2003. http://www.southcn.com/news/community/fzzh/200311041083.htm (link inactive or blocked).

Wong, Gillian. "Gu Kailai Trial: Chinese Court Hands Suspended Death Sentence to Wife of Politician Bo Xilai." *Huffington Post,* August 9, 2012.

Woo, Margaret Y. K. "Law and Discretion in Contemporary Chinese Courts." In *The Limits of the Rule of Law in China,* ed. Karen G. Turner, James V. Feinerman, and R. Kent Guy, 163–95. Seattle: University of Washington Press, 2000.

Wu Gou. "Yiwei gongzhengde faguan weishenme shudao weigong" (Why has one just judge been attacked). *Nanfang dushibao,* March 17, 2013.

Wu, Harry. *Laogai: The Chinese Gulag.* Boulder, CO: Westview Press, 1992.

Wu Xue'er and Li Zhen. "Zhou Zhengyi." *Dajiyuan,* December 17, 2007. http://www.epochtimes.com/b5/7/12/17/n1944521p.htm.

"Wuhan Waitan huayuan dapi yezhu konggao defang zhengfu chuer faner yiquan daifa" (Many homeowners of the Wuhan Waitan Garden are accusing the local government of inconsistency and using power to replace law). Xinhua News Agency (Hubei branch), January 5, 2002.

"Wuhan Waitan huayuan ganga qibao" (The embarrassing demolition of the Wuhan Waitan Garden). *Jinghua Times,* January 26, 2001.

"Wuhan zhalou: Weihu falu zunyan" (Blowing up building: Safeguarding the dignity of the law). Xinhua News Agency, January 25, 2002.

"Wuhan zhawaitan, gangyezhu shibao jiayuan" (Wuhan destroys Waitan Garden, Hong Kong residents swear to protect their homes). *Dongfang ribao,* December 21, 2001.

Wuyou zhixiang (Utopia). http://www.wyzxsx.com (link inactive or blocked). The New Left Web site.

"Xi Jinping qiangdiao yifa zhiguo yifazhizheng yifaxingzheng gongtong tuijin" (Xi Jinping stresses ruling, administering, and governing in accordance with the law and moving forward together). Xinhua News Agency, February 24, 2013.

Xianxing faling quanshu (A complete book on the contemporary law). 14 vols. Beijing: Zhonghua shujü, 1922.

Xiao Wenjia. "Renquan hezai? Guofa hezai?" (Where are the human rights? Where are the state laws?). Xinhua News Agency, January 13, 2002. http://news.xinhuanet.com/english/china/2012 (link inactive or blocked).

"Xinfang tiaoli" (Regulations regarding letters and visits). *People's Daily,* November 1, 1995.

"Xinfang tiaoli" (Regulations regarding letters and visits). *People's Daily,* May 1, 2005.

"Xinshi panjueshu" (Criminal verdict). Shandong Jinan Intermediate People's Court, September 22, 2013. http://news.xinhuanet.com/legal/2013-09/22/c_117450554_2.htm.

Xu Bikang. "Suzhuang" (Indictment). December 25, 2001. Copy in authors' possession.

Xu Chengde and Wang Gang. "Xuzhou fansi fangdaomen fengbo" (Xuzhou rethinking the incident of the antitheft doors). *Xinhua Daily,* February 26, 2004.

Xu Dan. "Gong Gangmo yao Li Zhuang, jianhuile yitiaoming" (Gong Gangmo bites Li Zhuang and saves his life). Li Zhuang's blog, April 15, 2013. http://blog.sina.com.cn/s/blog_89aa0dcd01019usk.html.

Xu Feng. "New Modes of Urban Governance: Building Community/*Shequ* in Post-Danwei China." In *The Chinese Party-State in the 21st Century:* **Adaptation and the Reinvention of Legitimacy,** ed. André Laliberté and Marc Lanteigne, 22–38. London: Routledge, 2008.

Xu Jinyi. "Jiaoshou gaoguan hequ hecong" (What will be the outcome of the professor's lawsuit against governments). *Jiangnan shibao,* August 25, 2003.

———. "Jiaoshou hegangao shizhengfu" (How dare a professor sue the city government). *Jiangnan shibao,* August 13, 2003.

———. "Xuzhou jiaoshou zhuanggao shifu youzhuanji 'Fenghuayuan' fangdaomen jinri genghuan" (The turning point arrives for Xuzhou professor's lawsuit against the municipal government, Fenghuayuan's antitheft doors will be replaced today). *Jiangnan shibao,* November 7, 2003.

———. "Fenghuayuan fangdaomen shijian zuohuajuhao" (The incident of the Fenghuayuan antitheft doors ended yesterday). *Jiangnan shibao,* February 1, 2004.

Xu Qianchuan. "Wang Lijun zhuzhengxia Chongqing dahei yi'an beijiekai" (Remaining cases revealed of Chongqing's Smashing the Black under Wang Lijun). *Caijin Magazine,* November 4, 2013.

Xu, Xiaoqun. *Trial of Modernity: Judicial Reform in Early Twentieth-Century China, 1901–1937.* Stanford, CA: Stanford University Press, 2008.

"Xuzhou Quanshanqu renmin fayuan xingshi panjueshu" (The criminal verdict of the Xuzhou Quanshan District People's Court). November 30, 2012. Copy in authors' possession.

"Xuzhoushi zhongji renmin fayuan xingshi panjueshu" (The criminal verdict of the Xuzhou Quanshan District People's Court). December 30, 2012. Copy in authors' possession.

Yan, Jiaqi, and Gao Gao. *Turbulent Decade: A History of the Cultural Revolution.* Honolulu: University of Hawaii Press, 1996.

Yan, Sophia. "Rich Chinese Overwhelmed U.S. Visa Program." *CNN Money,* March 25, 2014. http://money.cnn.com/2014/03/25/news/economy/china-us-immigrant-visa.

Yang Gongzhan. "Ziyi wangwei wufa wutian: Fenghuayuan juweihui huanjie xuanju biduan juyao" (Arbitrariness and lawlessness: Highlights of fraudulent activities in the election of the Fenghuayuan Neighborhood Committee). November 27, 2009. Copy in authors' possession.

Yang Hegao. *Songyuan mingqing falu sixiang yanjiu* (The legal thought of the Song, Yuan, Ming, and Qing dynasties). Beijing: Beijing University Press, 2001.

Yang Jiadai. "Beida jiaoshou Zhang Qianfan chengfan xianzheng benzhishang jiushi fanrenlei" (Beijing University professor Zhang Qianfan argues that anticonstitutionalism is akin to antihuman). Free Asia Radio, January 5, 2015.

Yang Jianjun. "Haofaguan deliangzhong xingxiang" (The two images of good judges). *Faxue luntan* 5 (2012): 28–36.

Yang Qiankun. *Zhongguo gudai wenziyu* (Literary inquisition in ancient China). Shanxi: Shanxi renmin chubanshe, 1999.

Yang, Su. "Mass Killings in the CR: A Study of Three Provinces." In *The Chinese Cultural Revolution as History,* ed. Joseph W. Esherick, Paul G. Pickowicz, and Andrew G. Walder, 96–123. Stanford, CA: Stanford University Press, 2006.

Yang Weihan. "Xi Jinping chuxi zhongyang zhengfa gongzuo huiyi" (Xi Jinping attended the central work meeting of the politics and law). Xinhua News Agency, January 8, 2014.

Yang Xiancheng. "Wengezhong zalan gongjianfa heqingli jieji duiwu" (Smashing the police, procuratorate, and court and purging class ranks). *Yanhuang chunqiu* 2 (2013): 55–58.

Yang Zhaolong. "Falujie dedang yufeidang zhijian" (The legal realm between Party and non-Party). *Wenhuibao,* May 8, 1957.

Ye Xiaoxin, ed. *Zhongguo fazhishi* (A history of the Chinese legal system). Shanghai: Fudan daxue chubanshe, 2002.

Yeh Wen-hsin. "Republican Origins of the *Danwei:* The Case of Shanghai's Bank of China." In Xiaobo Lü and Elizabeth J. Perry, *Danwei: The Changing Chinese Workplace in Historical and Comparative Perspective,* 60–90. Armonk, NY: M. E. Sharpe, 1997.

"Yiwei laozhengfa shujide kusu" (The crying complaint of an old cadre of political and legal committee). April 13, 2013. http://blog.sina.com.cn/s/blog_89aa0dcd01019sli.html.

Yu Churu. *Bo Xilai hanyuan* (Bo Xilai claims grievance). Hong Kong: Ha'ye chubanshe, 2013.

Yu, Keping. *Globalization and Changes in China's Governance.* Leiden: Brill, 2008.

Yue, Daiyun. *To the Storm: The Odyssey of a Revolutionary Chinese Woman.* Berkeley and Los Angeles: University of California Press, 1987.

"Zaojian xinwen lanmu" (The news column of the morning). Xuzhou TV, January 17, 2002.

"Zao Jiang Zemin Zeng Qinghong paoqi, Chen Liangyu yuzhong pokou dama buzhangyi" (Abandoned by Jiang Zemin and Zeng Qinghong, Chen Liang lashed out them as betrayal), BackChina.com, September 8, 2007, http://www.backchina.com/forum.php?mod=viewthread&tid=558984&extra=page%3D1&mobile=2.

Zeng Xianyi. *Zhongguo fazhishi* (The legal history of China). Beijing: Beijing University Press, 2000.

"Zhachu 'weifalou,' Wuhan shimin jiaohao" (Wuhan residents applaud the blowup of the "illegal building"). Xinhua News Agency, January 25, 2002.

Zhang Sheng, "Minchu daliyuan shenpan duli de zhidu yu shijian" (The independent system and practice of supreme court jurisdiction in the early Republic), *Zhongguo zhengfa daxue xuebao* (Journal of China University of Political Science and Law) 04 (2002): 146<n>52.

Zhang Chunxian. "Quanmian tuijin yifa zhijiang" (Pushing forward the use of law to govern Xinjian). *People's Daily,* January 7, 2015.

Zhang, Everett. 2010. "Introduction: Governmentality in China." *Governance of Life in Chinese Moral Experience: The Quest for an Adequate Life,* ed. Everett Zhang, Arthur Kleinman and Tu Weiming, 1–30. London: Routledge, 2010.

Zhang, Everett, Arthur Kleinman, and Tu Weiming, eds. *Governance of Life in Chinese Moral Experience: The Quest for an Adequate Life.* London: Routledge, 2010.

Zhang Guo. "Wangluo fanfu zuoyong zhengmian dayu fumian" (The function of Internet anticorruption is more positive than negative). *China Youth Daily,* September 1, 2008.

Zhang Jinfan. *Qingchao fazhishi* (The history of the Qing legal system). Beijing: Zhonghua shujü, 1998.

Zhang, Lena Y. *Communities, Crime and Social Capital in Contemporary China.* London: Routledge, 2013.

Zhang Sizhi. "Zheng Enchongan zhongshen caiding bianxi" (An analysis of the final verdict of the case of Zheng Enchong). *Falujie,* June 12, 2010. http://news.mylegist.com/1604/2010-06-12/26554.html.

Zhao Chen, Yang Yuanbiao, and Shen Zhiming, eds. *Zhongguo liufa quanshu* (Complete book of China's six laws). Shanghai: Shijie shujü, 1939.

Zhao Ling. "Chaiqian shinian beixiju" (Ten years of tragedies and comedies of urban disposal). *Southern Weekend,* September 4, 2003.

Zhao, Yuezhi. "The State, the Market, and Media Control in China." In *Who Owns the Media? Global Trends and Local Resistance,* ed. Pradip N. Thomas and Zaharrom Nain, 179–212. London: Zed Books, 2005.

Zheng Enchong. "Zhou Zhengyi xianxiang" (The phenomenon of Zhou Zhengyi). In *Shen ting, shuiyinbao Zhou Zhengyi'an* (Who has exploded the case of Zhou Zhengyi), 15–24. Hong Kong: Kaifang chubanshe, 2007.

"Zhengfa bumen xuyao chedi zhengdun" (The police and the judiciary need thorough revamps). *People's Daily,* December 20, 1957.

Zhengfu gongbao (Government gazette). 206 vols. Taiwan: Wenhai chubanshe, 1971.

Zheng, Yongnian. *The Chinese Communist Party as Organizational Emperor: Culture, Reproduction, and Transformation.* London: Routledge, 2009.

Zhi Jian. "Weitao shuofa, daxue jiaoshou mingaoguan" (For an explanation, a college professor lodged a commoners-against-officials lawsuit). *Law and Life,* November 2003, 7–9.

Zhong Shu. "Dangde daobazi: tongxiang minzhong yuqiege zijiu" (The Party's knife hilt: Stabbing the people and cutting and saving itself). *Cheng ming,* February 2014, 42–44.

"Zhonggong dangbao jiguan daobai lunzao tafa" (The argument of knife hilt by Party media is attacked). January 9, 2014. http://china.dwnews.com/news/2014-01-09/59367324-all.html#.

Zhongguo falü nianjian, 1987–1997 (The encyclopedia of Chinese law, 1987–1997). Beijing: Zhongguo falü nianjianshe, 1998).

Zhongguo falü nianjian, 1989 (The encyclopedia of Chinese law, 1989) (Beijing: Zhongguo falü nianjianshe, 1988): 1082.

Zhongguo falü nianjian, 1999. Beijing: Zhongguo falü nianjianshe, 1998.

Zhongguo falü nianjian, 2000. Beijing: Zhongguo falü nianjianshe, 1998.

Zhongguo falü nianjian, 2001. Beijing: Zhongguo falü nianjianshe, 2000.

Zhongguo falü nianjian, 2002. Beijing: Zhongguo falü nianjianshe, 2001.

Zhongguo falü nianjian, 2003. Beijing: Zhongguo falü nianjianshe, 2002.

Zhongguo falü nianjian, 2004. Beijing: Zhongguo falü nianjianshe, 2003.

"Zhonghua remin gongheguo chengshi jumin weiyuanhui zuzhifa" (PRC organizational law of urban neighborhood committees). December 26, 1989. http://china.findlaw.cn/info/guojiafa/jiguanzuzhi/jicengzizhi/juminwyh/124891.html.

"Zhonghua renmin gongheguo xingzheng susongfa" (The administrative litigation law of the People's Republic of China). April 4, 1989. http://www.law-lib.com/LAW/law_view.asp?id=5641.

"Zhongyang guanyu feichu GMD liufa quanshu hequeding jiefangqu sifa yuanze dezhishi" (The central directive regarding abolishing the GMD's six laws and determining the judicial principles of the liberated regions). February 22, 1949. http://cpc.people.com.cn/GB/64184/64186/66650/4491574.html.

Zhou Hulin. "Zengyang ladong qunzhong jifangde zhidong lianhuan" (How to pull the braking hoop of the mass collective complaints). *Minqing yuxinfang* 2 (2000): 21–27.

Zhou, Jinghao. *China's Peaceful Rise in a Global Context: A Domestic Aspect of China's Road Map to Democratization.* Lanham, MD: Lexington Books, 2010.

Zhou, Kate. 2010. *China's Long March to Freedom: Grassroots Modernization.* New Brunswick, NJ: Transaction Publishers, 2011.

Zhou Zongqi. *Qingdai wenziyu* (The literary inquisition in the Qing). Beijing: Renmin wenxue chubanshe, 2010.

Zhu Suli. "The Party and the Courts." In *Judicial Independence in China: Lessons for Global Rule of Law Promotion,* ed. Randall Peerenboom, 52–68. Cambridge: Cambridge University Press, 2010.

Zhu Xi. *Sishu zhangju jizhu* (Annotation of the Four Books). Liaoning: Liaoning jiaoyu chubanshe, 1998.

Zhu Yongxiao. "Zhongguo baiyu weiquan lushi beibu fengbao" (The storm of arresting more than one hundred rights lawyers in China). *Asian Week,* July 26, 2015.

"Zuishuai xiaozhang Zhou Wenbin shoushen" (Most smart president is being tried). *Legal Daily,* January 22, 2015.

Index

ASIA IN THE NEW MILLENNIUM

SERIES EDITOR: Shiping Hua, University of Louisville

Asia in the New Millennium is a series of books offering new interpretations of an important geopolitical region. The series examines the challenges and opportunities of Asia from the perspectives of politics, economics, and cultural-historical traditions, highlighting the impact of Asian developments on the world. Of particular interest are books on the history and prospect of the democratization process in Asia. The series also includes policy-oriented works that can be used as teaching materials at the undergraduate and graduate levels. Innovative manuscript proposals at any stage are welcome.

ADVISORY BOARD

William Callahan, University of Manchester, Southeast Asia, Thailand
Lowell Dittmer, University of California at Berkeley, East Asia and South Asia
Robert Hathaway, Woodrow Wilson International Center for Scholars, South Asia, India, Pakistan
Mike Mochizuki, George Washington University, East Asia, Japan and Korea
Peter Moody, University of Notre Dame, China and Japan
Brantly Womack, University of Virginia, China and Vietnam
Charles Ziegler, University of Louisville, Central Asia and Russia Far East

BOOKS IN THE SERIES

The Future of China-Russia Relations
Edited by James Bellacqua

North Korea and the World: Human Rights, Arms Control, and Strategies for Negotiation
Walter C. Clemens Jr.

Contemporary Chinese Political Thought: Debates and Perspectives
Edited by Fred Dallmayr and Zhao Tingyang

China Looks at the West: Identity, Global Ambitions, and the Future of Sino-American Relations
Christopher A. Ford

The Mind of Empire: China's History and Modern Foreign Relations
Christopher A. Ford

State Violence in East Asia
Edited by N. Ganesan and Sung Chull Kim

www.ingramcontent.com/pod-product-compliance
Lightning Source LLC
Chambersburg PA
CBHW031546260326
41914CB00002B/287